Healing with the

Medicine

of the

Prophet ﷺ

By: Imam Ibn Al-Qayyim Al-Jauziyah

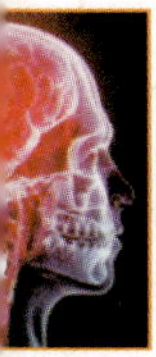

Revised. Edition: July 2010

Supervised by:

Abdul Malik Mujahid

HEAD OFFICE

P.O. Box: 22743, Riyadh 11416 K.S.A.Tel: 00966-1-4033962/4043432 Fax: 4021659
E-mail: darussalam@awalnet.net.sa, riyadh@dar-us-salam.com Website:www.darussalamksa.com

K.S.A. Darussalam Showrooms:

Riyadh

Olaya branch: Tel 00966-1-4614483 Fax: 4644945
Malaz branch: Tel 00966-1-4735220 Fax: 4735221
Suwaydi branch: Tel: 00966 1 4286641
Suwailam branch: Tel & Fax-1-2860422

- **Jeddah**
  Tel: 00966-2-6879254 Fax: 6336270
- **Madinah**
  Tel: 00966-04-8234446, 8230038
  Fax: 04-8151121
- **Al-Khobar**
  Tel: 00966-3-8692900 Fax: 8691551
- **Khamis Mushayt**
  Tel & Fax: 00966-072207055
- **Yanbu Al-Bahr** Tel: 0500887341 Fax: 04-3908027
- **Al-Buraida** Tel: 0503417156 Fax: 06-3696124

U.A.E

- **Darussalam, Sharjah U.A.E**
  Tel: 00971-6-5632623 Fax: 5632624
  Sharjah@dar-us-salam.com.

PAKISTAN

- **Darussalam,** 36 B Lower Mall, Lahore
  Tel: 0092-42-724 0024 Fax: 7354072
- **Rahman Market, Ghazni Street,** Urdu Bazar Lahore
  Tel: 0092-42-7120054 Fax: 7320703
- **Karachi,** Tel: 0092-21-4393936 Fax: 4393937
- **Islamabad,** Tel: 0092-51-2500237 Fax: 512281513

U.S.A

- **Darussalam, Houston**
  P.O Box: 79194 Tx 77279
  Tel: 001-713-722 0419 Fax: 001-713-722 0431
  E-mail: houston @dar-us-salam.com
- **Darussalam, New York** 486 Atlantic Ave, Brooklyn
  New York-11217, Tel: 001-718-625 5925
  Fax: 718-625 1511
  E-mail: darussalamny@hotmail.com

U.K

- **Darussalam International Publications Ltd.**
  Leyton Business Centre
  Unit-17, Etloe Road, Leyton, London, E10 7BT
  Tel: 0044 20 8539 4885 Fax:0044 20 8539 4889
  Website: www.darussalam.com
  Email: info@darussalam.com
- **Darussalam International Publications Limited**
  Regents Park Mosque, 146 Park Road
  London NW8 7RG Tel: 0044- 207 725 2246
  Fax: 0044 20 8539 4889

AUSTRALIA

- **Darussalam**: 153, Haldon St, Lakemba (Sydney)
  NSW 2195, Australia
  Tel: 0061-2-97407188 Fax: 0061-2-97407199
  Mobile: 0061-414580813 Res: 0061-2-97580190
  Email: abumuaaz@hotamail.com
- **The Islamic Bookstore**
  Ground Floor-165 Haldon Street
  Lakemba, NSW 2195, Australia
  Tel: 0061-2-97584040 Fax: 0061-2-97584030
  Email: info@islamicbookstore.com.au
  Web Site: www.islamicbookstore.com.au

CANADA

- **Nasiruddin Al-Khattab**
  2-3415 Dixie Rd, Unit # 505
  Mississauga
  Ontario L4Y 4J6, Canada
  Tel: 001-416-418 6619
- **Islamic Book Service**
  2200 South Sheridan way Mississauga, On
  L5J 2M4
  Tel: 001-905-403-8406 Ext. 218 Fax: 905-8409

FRANCE

- **Editions & Librairie Essalam**
  135, Bd de Ménilmontant- 75011 Paris
  Tél: 0033-01- 43 38 19 56/ 44 83
  Fax: 0033-01- 43 57 44 31
  E-mail: essalam@essalam com.

MALAYSIA

- **Darussalam**
  Int'l Publishing & Distribution SDN BHD
  D-2-12, Setiawangsa 11, Taman Setiawangsa
  54200 Kuala Lumpur
  Tel: 03-42528200 Fax: 03-42529200
  Email: darussalam@streamyx.com
  Website: www.darussalam.com.my

SRI LANKA

- Darul Kitab 6, Nimal Road, Colombo-4
  Tel: 0094 115 358712 Fax: 115-358713

INDIA

- **Islamic Books International**
  54, Tandel Street (North)
  Dongri, Mumbai 4000 09, INDIA
  Tel: 0091-22-2373 4180
  E-mail: ibi@irf.net

SOUTH AFRICA

- **Islamic Da'wah Movement (IDM)**
  48009 Qualbert 4078 Durban, South Africa
  Tel: 0027-31-304-6883 Fax: 0027-31-305-1292
  E-mail: idm@ion.co.za

الطب النبوي

HEALING WITH THE MEDICINE OF THE PROPHET ﷺ

By: Imam Ibn Al-Qayyim Al-Jauziyah

Translated by: JALAL ABUAL RUB
Edited by: ABDUL RAHMAN ABDULLAH
Formerly RAYMOND J. MANDEROLA
Fordham University, U.S.A.

DARUSSALAM
GLOBAL LEADER IN ISLAMIC BOOKS
Riyadh • Jeddah • Al-Khobar • Sharjah
Lahore • London • Houston • New York

بسم الله الرحمن الرحيم

In the Name of Allah,
the Most Gracious, the Most Merciful.

King Fahd National Library Cataloging-in-Publication Data

Ibn Qayyim Al-Jauziyah, Muhammad ibn Aby Bakr 751 H.
Healing with the medicine of the Prophet. / Muhammad ibn Aby Bakr 751 H. Ibn Qayyim Al- Jawziyyah ; Jalal Abualrab - Riyadh

428 p ; 21x14cm

ISBN.: -603-500-126-3

1- Islam and medicine 2- Islamic medicine

I-Jalal Abualrub(co.author) II-Title

214.61 dc 1431/6840

L.D.no.1431/6840

ISBN: -603-500-126-3

CONTENTS

PART IV. ALPHABETICALLISTING

Publisherís Note

All praise is for Allah The Almighty, Lord of the Universe. We praise Him, and seek His help, and His forgiveness, and we seek His protection from the accursed Satan. Whomever Allah The Almighty guides will never be misguided, and whom He allows to be misguided will never be guided. I bear witness that there is no deity worthy of worship except Allah, who is One alone and has no partners. I bear witness that Muhammad is His Servant and Messenger. May the blessings of Allah be upon him and his family and his Companions and the righteous who follow them until the Day of Judgment.

Throughout the history of humankind, man has been searching for cures for his many ailments. We are privileged to present this book, *At-Tibb an-Nabawee* (*Healing with the Medicine of the Prophet*), written by Shaykh-ul-Islam Ibn Al-Qayyim Al-Jawziyyah (may Allah have mercy upon him) to the readers in order to provide them with information, knowledge and wisdom in dealing with the numerous ailments that afflict us. No doubt, many of our modern ailments are brought about by a libertine lifestyle, coupled with a lack of faith and weakness of belief in our Creator. Allah The Almighty has clearly indicated to mankind that:

"Indeed in the Messenger of Allah (Muhammad) you have a good example to follow for him who hopes for Allah and the Last Day and remembers Allah much". (Qur'an, 33:21)

Prophet Muhammad ﷺ was sent as a guide, and mercy for all of humankind, and as such was given wisdom by Allah The Almighty that is beneficial to humanity. Allah The Almighty says:

``O Mankind! There has come to you a good advice from your Lord, and a healing for that which is in your breasts, a guidance and mercy for the believers." (Qur'an, 10:57).

The medicine of the Prophet ﷺ is not restricted to spiritual healing alone. In fact, it balances the healing of the soul and the physical body in order to prepare man for a better life in the Hereafter.

We at Darussalam thank Allah The Almighty for the opportunity he has granted us to publish this authentic book based on the Qur'an and *Sunnah* (tradition) of Prophet Muhammad ﷺ, who was a physician of the soul and the body. We also would like to thank brother Aqeel Walker for his tireless work in revising and editing the final draft of this project. We ask Allah The Almighty to accept this work, forgive us for our mistakes and to make this book a valuable asset for the believers of truth.

Abdul Malik Mujahid
General Manager
October 1999

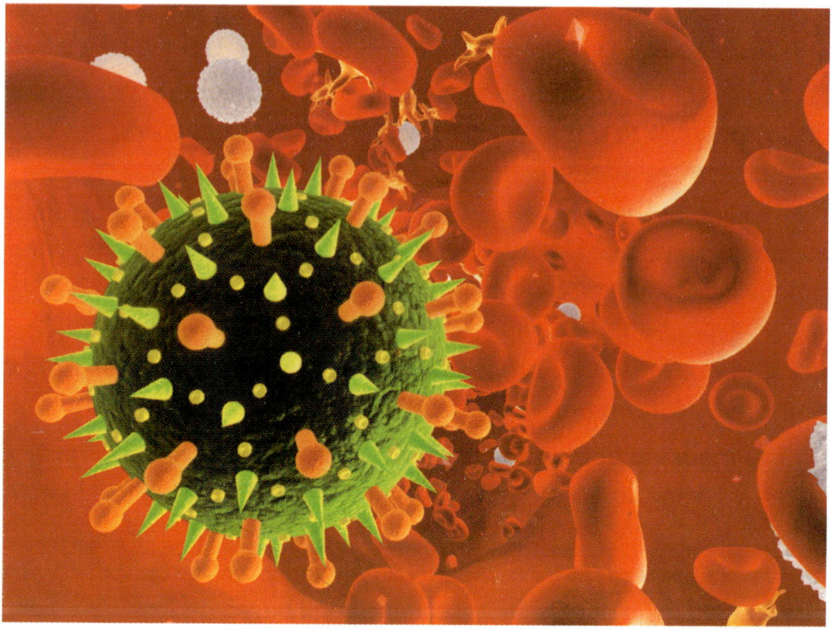

1

Part 1

KINDS OF DISEASES

KINDS OF DISEASES

There are two types of diseases that afflict the heart: one is doubt and error, and the second is lust and desire, and both are mentioned in the Qur'an.

Allah The Almighty says about the disease of doubt:

﴿ فِي قُلُوبِهِم مَّرَضٌ فَزَادَهُمُ ٱللَّهُ مَرَضًا ﴾

"In their hearts is a disease (of doubt and hypocrisy) and Allah has increased their disease." (Qur'an, 2:10)

﴿ وَلِيَقُولَ ٱلَّذِينَ فِي قُلُوبِهِم مَّرَضٌ وَٱلْكَٰفِرُونَ مَاذَآ أَرَادَ ٱللَّهُ بِهَٰذَا مَثَلًا ﴾

"... and that those in whose hearts is a disease (of hypocrisy) and the disbelievers may say: 'What does Allah intend by this (curious) example?'" (Qur'an,74:31)

Allah The Almighty says concerning those who refuse to make the Qur'an and *Sunnah* the basis of their judgments:

﴿ وَإِذَا دُعُوٓا۟ إِلَى ٱللَّهِ وَرَسُولِهِۦ لِيَحْكُمَ بَيْنَهُمْ إِذَا فَرِيقٌ مِّنْهُم مُّعْرِضُونَ ﴿٤٨﴾ وَإِن يَكُن لَّهُمُ ٱلْحَقُّ يَأْتُوٓا۟ إِلَيْهِ مُذْعِنِينَ ﴿٤٩﴾ أَفِى قُلُوبِهِم مَّرَضٌ أَمِ ٱرْتَابُوٓا۟ أَمْ يَخَافُونَ أَن يَحِيفَ ٱللَّهُ عَلَيْهِمْ وَرَسُولُهُۥ ۚ بَلْ أُو۟لَٰٓئِكَ هُمُ ٱلظَّٰلِمُونَ ﴿٥٠﴾ ﴾

"And when they are called to Allah (i.e., His Words, the

Qur'an) and His Messenger ﷺ, to judge between them, lo! a party of them refuses (to come) and turns away. But if the truth is on their side, they come to him willingly with submission. Is there a disease in their hearts? Or do they doubt or fear lest Allah and His Messenger ﷺ should wrong them in judgment. Nay, it is they themselves who are the Zalimun (polytheists, hypocrites and wrongdoers) ." (Qur'an, 24:48-50)

This is the disease of doubt and error.

Allah The Almighty says about desire and lust [which results in major sins like adultery and fornication]:

﴿ يَٰنِسَآءَ ٱلنَّبِيِّ لَسۡتُنَّ كَأَحَدٖ مِّنَ ٱلنِّسَآءِ إِنِ ٱتَّقَيۡتُنَّۚ فَلَا تَخۡضَعۡنَ بِٱلۡقَوۡلِ فَيَطۡمَعَ ٱلَّذِي فِي قَلۡبِهِۦ مَرَضٞ ﴾

``O wives of the Prophet! You are not like any other women. If you keep your duty (to Allah), then be not soft in speech, lest he in whose heart is a disease (of hypocrisy, or evil desire for adultery) should be moved with desire..."(Qur'an,33:32)

Physical diseases that attack the body

Allah The Almighty says:

﴿ لَّيۡسَ عَلَى ٱلۡأَعۡمَىٰ حَرَجٞ وَلَا عَلَى ٱلۡأَعۡرَجِ حَرَجٞ وَلَا عَلَى ٱلۡمَرِيضِ حَرَجٞ ﴾

``There is no restriction on the blind, nor any restriction on the lame, nor any restriction on the sick..." (Qur'an, 24:61)

These Verses refer to ailments that might afflict a person while performing the *Hajj* (pilgrimage), while fasting or making ablution. They contain a tremendous hidden wisdom, indicating the greatness and divine wisdom of the Qur'an and its sufficiency for those who have sound understanding and comprehension.

The science of medicine consists of three basic rules: preserving good health, avoiding what might cause harm (i.e., establishing immunity) and ridding the body of harmful substances. Allah The Almighty has mentioned these three basic principles in connection with *Hajj*, fasting, and ablution, as mentioned above:

﴿فَمَن كَانَ مِنكُم مَّرِيضًا أَوْ عَلَىٰ سَفَرٍ فَعِدَّةٌ مِّنْ أَيَّامٍ أُخَرَ﴾

``But if any of you is ill or on a journey, the same number (should be made up) from other days." (Qur'an, 2:184)

Allah The Almighty has allowed the sick person to break his fast because of illness. He has also permitted the traveler to break the fast in order to protect and preserve one's health and strength while traveling. Traveling involves physical effort and hardship that requires nourishment to sustain the body's energy. This is why the traveler has been given an exemption from fasting so that his body can receive the required nourishment.

Allah The Almighty says:

﴿فَمَن كَانَ مِنكُم مَّرِيضًا أَوْ بِهِۦٓ أَذًى مِّن رَّأْسِهِۦ فَفِدْيَةٌ مِّن صِيَامٍ أَوْ صَدَقَةٍ أَوْ نُسُكٍ﴾

``And whosoever of you is ill or has an ailment in his scalp (necessitating shaving), he must pay a Fidyah (ransom) of either observing Saum (fasts) (three days) or giving Sadaqah (charity - feeding six poor persons) or offering sacrifice (one sheep)." (Qur'an, 2:196)

Allah The Almighty has allowed the sick and those suffering from lice or ailments of the scalp to shave their head, which is normally prohibited, while in the state of *Ihram* (sacral state). Shaving the head and exposing the scalp in these cases removes the harmful substances and thus allows the sick person to get rid of whatever is causing his illness and to recover from the condition that is aggravated because of hair growing on the scalp. This is an example of ridding the body of harmful substances, which has a higher priority (thus the exemption) than the general rule of not shaving of the head while in the state of *Ihram*.

There are ten elements that might cause harm to the body when they accumulate in the body (become congested), unless the body eliminates them:

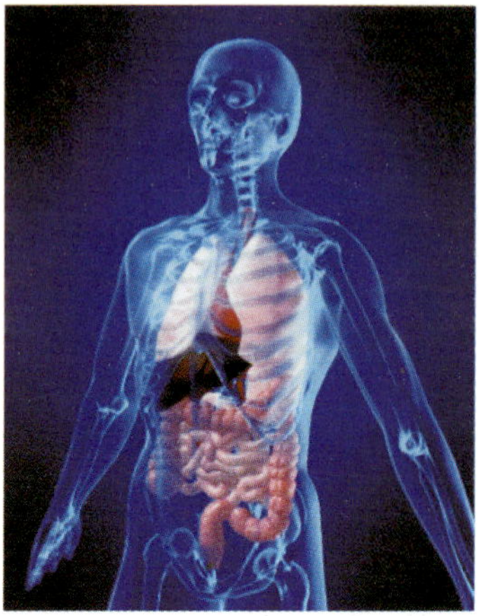

1. Blood (when it is contaminated)
2. Sperm (when it is excessive)
3. Urine
4. Excrement
5. Air
6. Vomit
7. The urge to sneeze
8. Sleep
9. Hunger
10. Thirst.

When any of these ten elements are not properly dealt with or satisfied, (as in the case of sleep), they will cause a particular type of illness. When Allah The Almighty permitted shaving the head to remove harmful substances on the scalp, His statement inspired His slaves to use the same practice in removing harmful substances caused by other ailments.

With regard to observing a certain precautionary measure (i.e, diet, or any other type of abstention), Allah The Almighty says:

﴿وَإِن كُنتُم مَّرْضَىٰٓ أَوْ عَلَىٰ سَفَرٍ أَوْ جَآءَ أَحَدٌ مِّنكُم مِّنَ ٱلْغَآئِطِ أَوْ لَٰمَسْتُمُ ٱلنِّسَآءَ فَلَمْ تَجِدُوا۟ مَآءً فَتَيَمَّمُوا۟ صَعِيدًا طَيِّبًا﴾

``And if you are ill, or on a journey, or one of you comes after answering the call of nature, or you have been in contact with women (by sexual relations) and you find no water, perform Tayammum with clean earth." (Qur'an, 4:43)

Allah The Almighty has allowed the sick person to use clean earth instead of water to perform his ablution for prayer; this spares his body from the repercussions of using water in a state of illness. This

Verse sets the precedent for every type of precautionary or preventive measure (diet etc.) that protects the body from harmful substances that one consumes or the body produces.

In this way, we see that Allah The Almighty has emphasized the three basic rules of the science of medicine that we mentioned above.

We will now give several instances and examples that prove that Prophetic medicine is superior and more comprehensive than any other system of medicine.

Proper remedies for ailments of the heart (referring to spiritual or emotional ailments) are provided only at the hands of Prophets عليهم السلام and Messengers of Allah. The heart is cured when it acquires knowledge of its Lord and Creator and by learning His Names, Attributes, Actions and Commandments. The heart also becomes healthy when it prefers obtaining the pleasure of Allah The Almighty instead of pursuing its own desires, and prefers what He likes, all the while avoiding His prohibitions and what might lead to His displeasure. There is no life, health, or wellbeing for the heart except by this method, which can be provided only by following the methodology of the Messengers.

It is wrong to think that one can ever attain wellbeing of the heart through any other way than through the guidance of the Messengers of Allah. Errors occur as a result of confusing the heart's true wellbeing with satisfying and strengthening its lower animal lusts and desires. By doing this, the heart is distanced from acquiring its true wellbeing and strength. In fact, its very existence is endangered in this way. Those who do not distinguish between these two paths should grieve for the life and wellbeing of their heart, or in fact, the lack thereof. Let such people also grieve because of being deprived of the light of true guidance and because they are completely submerged in an ocean of darkness.

Remedies for physical illnesses are divided into two categories

One type of remedy depends upon instinct, which is something that is possessed by all species and living creatures. There is no need for the doctor to cure this type of illness, which entails responding to hunger, thirst, cold and fatigue.

The second type of remedy requires deep thought and analysis and entails subduing and resisting the ailment, and moderating the patient's condition (temperament), which can result from fever, heat, coldness, dryness, or a combination of these symptoms. These ailments may have two causes: a physical cause, or an ailment that arises due to changes that affect the mood and the temper (of the body). The difference between the two types of causes is that the ailments of the temperament occur after the physical causes are eliminated. Their effects remain and alter the temperament. The ailments that are caused by physical elements are accompanied by their specific causes. In these cases of physical disease we should look at the cause first, the ailment second and the cure third.

Deep thought and careful analysis are also required with regard to repelling and removing the ailments that affect the various organs and cause alterations in them -- whether in the shape, cavity, blood vessels, texture (roughness), palpability (touch), number, bones, and so forth. When these organs, which collectively constitute the body, are working properly, they are described as being connected. Otherwise, they are described as having lost their proper connectivity.

These ailments that affect and alter the condition of the organs are included in the general ailments that affect the body.

As we have stated, these same ailments negatively affect the mood and temperament. The changes that accompany such ailments are of eight types: four simple and four compound types. The simple types include coldness, hotness, wetness and dryness. The compound types include being hot and wet, hot and dry, cold and wet or cold and dry.

The causes of these ailments are either physical or due to changes in the mood or temperament as we have previously stated.

There are three states that the body can exist in: normal, abnormal and a state in the middle (between normal and abnormal). When the state of the body is normal, the body is healthy. The abnormal state occurs when the body is ill, while the third state is in between the two, as one extreme does not become the opposite extreme except after passing through a middle stage.

There are internal reasons for the abnormal state that the body passes through, such as an imbalance in the humors that constitute the body, like coldness, hotness, wetness and dryness. There are external reasons for the abnormal state, such as pathogens which find the body susceptible and affect it.

The potential harm inflicted on the body could result from a bad temperament that is not moderated, an ailment that afflicts an organ, or a general weakness in the overall power of the body, or even due to weakness of the soul which sustains such power. The ailment can be caused by an increase in the substances or elements that should not be increased, or a decrease in what should not be decreased. A break in an essential connection [between organs] could also be the cause of an ailment, or the formation of a connection between organs which should not be connected. The ailment could also occur due to an extension of those body parts that should not be extended, or an alteration and change in the shape or position of some of the organs.

A doctor is able to distinguish between what might harm the body when connected and what should be connected. The doctor also distinguishes between what might cause harm if increased and what might cause harm if decreased. The doctor helps bring about good health or what preserves good health, and helps fend off the ailment with its antidote (opposite) or by using a corrective diet. You will see that all these guidelines are met by the guidance and advice of the Prophet ﷺ, by the will, power and support of Allah The Almighty.

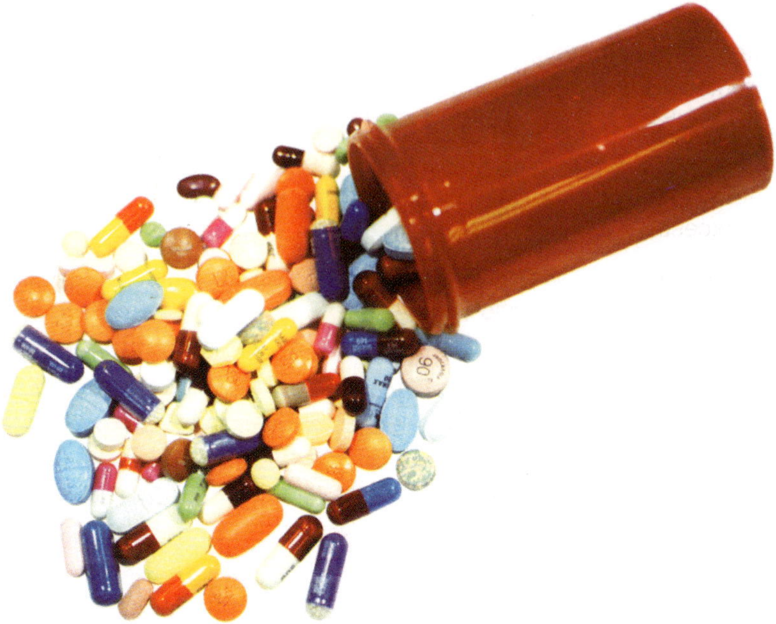

The Prophet ﷺ used medicine himself and prescribed medicine for his family and Companions

Yet, the type of medicines that the Prophet ﷺ and his Companions used to take was nothing like the chemical mixtures that are called *Aqrabathayn* (pharmacopeia). Rather, the majority of their medicine consisted of only one ingredient. Sometimes, they would take another substance to assist the medicine or make it taste better. This was, and still is, the case with most of the medicine used by many cultures such as Arabs, Turks, Indians and nomads. The Romans and the Greeks, on the other hand, use a mixture of substances or remedies in their medicine.

Medical experts agree that whenever an illness could be fought with nourishment and diet, then medicine should be avoided. They also agree that whenever it is possible to use only one substance or ingredient as a remedy, a compound remedy should not be used. They are also of the opinion that the body will be harmed if doctors overprescribe medicine. This is because the remedy might not find an illness to cure, or might find an illness that it cannot cure, or might be suitable for the illness, but an excess dose may be given, thereby compromising health.

The most experienced doctors use medications that contain one ingredient. The medication should be similar or related to regular foods that the patient is used to eating. Cultures that consume one or only a few types of food in their regular diet, generally suffer from few illnesses, and they should not use compound medicines. Those who live in cities and whose diets are complex, need medicines that are a mixture of several substances or ingredients, as these are the types of medicines that are most suited to their illnesses. The ailments of the people who live in the deserts are usually simple and thus simple medications are suitable for them. These principles entail basic facts that are known in the medical profession.

Prophetic medicine has a divine element to it. This element makes comparing Prophetic medicine to the medicines offered by regular doctors similar to comparing the medicine offered by doctors to folk medicine. The best medical authorities agree to this fact, since the science that they excel in is a result of comparisons, experimentation, inspiration, visions and hypothesis. Some of them state that their knowledge is acquired through the animal kingdom, for example, they observe cats swallowing a venomous creature and then observe it lick the oil in the lamp, thus neutralizing the effect of the venom. They also observe a snake that has an ailment in its eyes. The snake then wipes its eyes on fennel leaves and cures its condition. They also observe some birds that sip seawater when constipated. There are many similar examples that doctors mention concerning their observations of nature.

This type of knowledge cannot be compared to revelation from Allah The Almighty to His Messenger ﷺ and which informs him of what is good for him and what is not. Comparing scientific knowledge to revelation is like comparing the rest of the sciences to the knowledge that the Prophet ﷺ has been sent with. In fact, the Prophets provide us with a kind of medicine that the doctors can barely understand or reach by their experimentation, hypothesis and theories.

The Prophets deliver remedies that cure the heart from whatever afflicts it. These Prophetic remedies strengthen the heart and increase the reliance and dependence on Allah The Almighty. They also also aid in seeking refuge, being humble and showing meekness before Him, begging Him, giving charity and supplicating to Him. It includes repenting to Allah The Almighty, seeking His forgiveness, practicing kindness towards His creation and aiding those in desperate need and those who have suffered a calamity. These cures have been tried by various nations who have found them to carry the cure that doctors can never prescribe on their own, whether by experimentation or scientific observations.

We have tried the Prophetic cures and found that they are more powerful than any type of regular medicine. The hearts that are connected with the Lord of the Worlds - the Creator of the illness and its cure and He Who governs the affairs of everything and everyone -require special types of remedies that are nothing like those required for the hearts that are far away from their Lord. Besides, whenever the soul and the heart become stronger (spiritually), they will cooperate to defeat the illness.

How can anyone deny that the most effective cure for the ailment that afflicts the heart and soul occurs by feeling delight and joy when drawing closer to the Lord, loving Him, remembering Him, being totally dedicated and attentive to Him, depending on Him and seeking His help? Only the most ignorant people would deny these facts, especially those who have the dullest intellect, the worst comprehension and who are the farthest from Allah The Almighty and from knowing the true reality of humankind.

Soon after, Allah willing, we will mention the reason why reciting

Surah Al-Fatihah (the first chapter in the Qur'an) removed the effects of a poisonous sting, enabling the poisoned person to stand up as if he never suffered any pain. We will mention the two types of Prophetic medicine in as much detail as possible, according to the limited strength, knowledge and resources available to us. We rely only on Allah The Almighty for every type of good and righteous matter, while seeking His Bounty, for He is the Cherished Who grants favors without limit.

Every sickness has a cure

Muslim (may Allah have mercy upon him) narrated in his *Sahih* that the Prophet ﷺ said:

« لِكُلِّ دَاءٍ دَوَاءٌ؛ فَإِذَا أُصِيبَ دَوَاءُ الدَّاءِ: بَرَأَ بِإِذْنِ اللهِ عَزَّ وَجَلَّ » (مسلم: ٢٢٠٤)

``Every illness has a cure, and when the proper cure is applied to the disease, it ends it, Allah willing."

It is also narrated in the *Sahihayn* that the Messenger of Allah ﷺ said:

« مَا أَنْزَلَ اللهُ مِنْ دَاءٍ، إِلَّا أَنزَلَ لَهُ شِفَاءً » (البخاري: ٥٦٧٨)

``Allah has not sent down a disease except that He has also sent down its cure."

Further, Imam Ahmad (may Allah have mercy upon him) narrated that Usamah bin Shuraik (may Allah be pleased with him) said,

«كنتُ عند النبي صلى الله عليه وسلم، وجاءت الأعرابُ، فقالوا: يا رسول الله؛ أَنَتَدَاوَى؟ فقال: نعم يا عباد الله؛ تَدَاوَوْا: فإن الله عز وجل لَمْ يضَعْ داءً إلا وَضعَ له شِفاءً؛ غيرَ داءٍ واحدٍ. قالوا: ما هو؟ قال: الهَرَم». (أبو داود: ٣٨٥٥ وصححه الألباني)

``I was with the Prophet ﷺ when the Bedouins came to him and said, 'O Messenger of Allah, should we seek medicine?' He said: 'Yes, O slaves of Allah, seek medicine, for Allah has not created a disease except that he has also created its cure, except for one illness.' They said, `And what is that?' He said: `Old age."

In addition, it is related in the *Musnad* (by Imam Ahmad, may Allah have mercy upon him) that the Prophet ﷺ said:

« إنَّ الله عزَّ وجل لم يُنزل داءً، إلا أنزل له شفاءً: عَلِمَه مَنْ عَلِمَه، وَجَهِلَهُ مَنْ جَهِلَهُ»

(أحمد : ٤/ ٢٧٨ وقال في التحقيق حديث صحيح)

``Allah has not sent down a disease except that He also sent down its cure; whoever knows it (the cure), knows it, and whoever is unaware of it (the cure), he is unaware of it (the medicine), while those who are ignorant of it are unaware of it. " [An-Nasai', Ibn Majah, Al-Hakim and Ibn Hibban].

It is narrated in the *Musnad* (by Imam Ahmad, may Allah have mercy upon him) and the *Sunan* (of At-Tirmidhi and Ibn Majah) that Abu Khuzamah (may Allah be pleased with him) said,

«قلتُ يا رسول الله؛ أرأيتَ رُقًى نَسترْقِيهَا، ودواءً نَتداوَى به، وتُقَاةً نَتَّقِيهَا؛

هل تَرُدُّ من قَدَرِالله شيئًا؟ فقال: هي من قدرِ الله» (الترمذي : ٢٠٦٥ وضعفه الألباني)

``I said, 'O Messenger of Allah , about the Ruqyah (healing with supplications and the Qur'an) that we use, the medicine we take and the prevention we seek, does all this change Allah's appointed destiny?' He said: 'They are a part of Allah's appointed destiny."

These *Ahadith* (narrations) indicate that there are causes for whatever occurs in this world and also for the removal of these causes. The Prophet's statement that there is a cure for every disease might include both the curable and the humanly incurable diseases, for Allah The Almighty may have hidden these types of cures from mankind and blocked their path to acquiring them. And Allah knows best.

The Prophet ﷺ said that the disease ends when the proper cure is applied to it, indicating that there is an opposite for every created thing, and thus there is an antidote for every disease. The Messenger of Allah ﷺ has stated that when the two opponents meet - meaning, the proper remedy and the disease - recovery from the illness occurs. When the medicine is given in a dosage higher than what is needed, or when it is not the required medicine, it might lead the body to another type of disease. When the dosage is lesser than what is needed, it will not be sufficient to cure the disease. When the sick person and the disease are not treated with the suitable medicine, cure and recovery does not occur. Also, when the time is not suitable for the cure, or when the body is unsuitable for the prescribed medicine or unable to benefit from it, the cure will not be effective. When all circumstances are favorable, the cure will surely be effective. This is the best explanation available for these *Ahadith* .

On the other hand, these *Ahadith* might be specific, in that Allah The Almighty has not created a disease that can be humanly cured but has sent down a cure for it. This is similar to what Allah The Almighty says:

﴿ تُدَمِّرُ كُلَّ شَيْءٍ بِأَمْرِ رَبِّهَا ﴾

``Destroying everything by the Command of its Lord!" (Qur'an, 46:25)

This Verse means that everything prone to be destroyed was destroyed by the wind. In this case, the *Ahadith* do not include incurable diseases.

Those who observe various substances and their opposites in this world, and analyze the pacifying effect, opposing nature and resistance in relation to each other, would appreciate the perfect power, eternal wisdom and perfect creation of Allah The Almighty and His Oneness in the Lordship and in His Actions. Everything else except Allah The Almighty has an opponent or an antidote, but Allah Alone is Self Sufficient and Irresistible, while everything and everyone stands in need of Him.

The authentic *Ahadith* command Muslims to seek and take the appropriate medicine, while indicating that this action does not contradict dependence on Allah Alone for everything, just as satisfying one's hunger, thirst or protecting oneself from the heat or cold does not contradict the dependence on Allah The Almighty. On the contrary, the belief in *Tawhid* (Oneness of Allah) can only be complete by pacifying and responding to the various harmful elements in the manner and method that Allah The Almighty has commanded and that which will help in such cases.

Besides, refraining from using these cures or antidotes is, in fact, contradictory to total dependence on Allah The Almighty, along with contradicting the commandments and the Wisdom (of Allah The Almighty). Not using these cures will also weaken our *Tawakkul* (reliance and dependence on Allah) even though the person might think that he is strengthening his reliance and dependence by not seeking a cure. Abandoning the cure is in fact contradictory to true reliance and dependence, in that, reliance and dependence in essence includes the heart of the slave relying on Allah The Almighty in acquiring what benefits him in his life and his religious affairs, while fending off what harms his life and religion. The correct method of reliance and dependence includes seeking these benefits for the slave; otherwise one will not be implementing the commandments and the wisdom [that the Prophet ﷺ was sent with]. The slave should not call his weakness and helplessness dependence on Allah The Almighty, nor consider his true reliance and dependence as an inability.

These *Ahadith* also contradict those who do not seek medicine, saying, *``If the cure has been written or is destined to occur, then the medicine will be of no use. If the cure is not destined, then the medicine will not be useful."*

One might say in a similar manner, *``The disease has occurred by the will of Allah, and no one and nothing can resist His will."*

The last statement is similar to the question that the Bedouins asked the Messenger of Allah ﷺ. As for his close companions, who had more knowledge of Allah The Almighty, His Wisdom and His Attributes, they did not think the way the Bedouins did.

The Prophet ﷺ gave the Bedouins an answer that comforted their heart, saying that *Ruqyah* (healing with supplications and the Qur'an), medicines and preventative measures, are all part of the destiny appointed by Allah The Almighty. Therefore, there is no escape from His destiny, except by taking refuge in His destiny. Taking medicine is a part of the destiny of Allah The Almighty and it also repels a part of His destiny. In short, there is no way that the creation can escape the destiny of Allah The Almighty, no matter what they do. This is similar to putting an end to one's hunger, thirst, warm or cold conditions with what satisfies or pacifies them. It is also similar to repelling the enemy, which is a part of destiny of Allah The Almighty, with *Jihad* (struggle), which is also the commandment of Allah The Almighty and His appointed Destiny. Thus, the cause, its removal and those who remove it are all a part of the destiny appointed by Allah The Almighty.

Another way of answering those who ask similar questions (concerning taking medicine) is that this logic requires them to refrain from seeking their benefit or fending off harm altogether. Following their logic, if the benefit or harm was destined to occur, then it would surely occur, and if it were not destined, then it would never occur! This method, if implemented, would bring utter destruction to life, religion and the entire world. Besides, this rhetoric only comes from those who arrogantly deny the truth and reject it, and this is why they mention destiny concerning this subject in order to refute the truth when it is presented to them. This is the exact case with the polytheists, who said:

﴿ لَوْ شَآءَ ٱللَّهُ مَآ أَشْرَكْنَا وَلَآ ءَابَآؤُنَا ﴾

``If Allah had willed, we would not have taken partners (in worship) with Him, nor would our fathers..." (Qur'an, 6:148)

﴿ لَوْ شَآءَ ٱللَّهُ مَا عَبَدْنَا مِن دُونِهِۦ مِن شَىْءٍ نَّحْنُ وَلَآ ءَابَآؤُنَا ﴾

``If Allah had so willed, neither we nor our fathers would have worshipped aught but Him." (Qur'an, 16:35)

The polytheists issued these statements to refute the proof against them when Allah The Almighty sent the Messengers to them.

Those who utter these questions concerning destiny, medicine and true reliance and dependence should know that there is an argument that they did not mention. Allah The Almighty has decided that certain matters will occur when some specific causes occur. Thus, if the cause is implemented or brought about, what was destined will also occur.

If one asks, *``If I am destined to bring about the cause, I will bring it about. Otherwise, I will not be able to bring it into existence."* We answer this claim by saying, *``Would you accept such reasoning from your servant, children or subordinate workers if they refuse to do what you have ordered them to do or commit an act that you have forbidden for them? If you accept such reasoning, then you have no right to blame those who disobey you, steal your property, question your honor, or transgress against your rights. If you chastize such persons for these acts, then how can you use the same logic to deny the rights of Allah The Almighty and His injunctions to you?"*

Jewish tradition states that Ibrahim عليه السلام once asked Allah The Almighty, *``O my Lord! Where does disease come from?"* He said, *``From Me."* Ibrahim عليه السلام said, *``Where does the cure come from?"* He said, *``From Me."* Ibrahim عليه السلام said, *``What is the role of the doctor then?"* He said, *``A man by whose hands I send and cause the cure."*

The Prophet's statement that there is a cure for every illness should strengthen the resolve of the sick person and the doctor, encouraging them to seek medicine. When the sick person feels that there is a cure for his illness, his heart will be full of hope, rather than despair, and thus the doors of positive anticipation will be wide open before him. When the resolve of the ailing person is strengthened, the various powers that exist within the person, the instinctive energy [or heat as Ibn Al-Qayyim, may Allah have mercy upon him, puts it], the soul and the psyche, will also be strengthened. These powers will in turn strengthen that part of the body affected and the disease will be more easily dissipated and defeated.

Moreover, when the doctor knows that there is a cure for an illness, he actively and energetically pursues that cure.

The diseases that afflict the body are similar to diseases that attack the heart. Just as Allah The Almighty has sent down a cure for every disease that strikes the heart, He has sent down a cure for every disease that attacks the body. If the person acquires knowledge of this cure and applies it in the proper manner, his heart will regain its health by the leave of Allah The Almighty.

The Prophetís guidance concerning food and drink

This includes observing a particular diet, refraining from excessive eating and the general guidelines that should be observed regarding eating and drinking.

Al-Musnad (by Imam Ahmad, may Allah have mercy upon him) narrates that the Prophet ﷺ said:

«ما مَلأَ آدَمِيّ وِعاءً شرًّا مِنْ بطْنٍ، بِحَسْبِ ابنِ آدمَ لُقَيْماتٌ يُقِمْنَ صُلبَه فإن كان لابدّ فَاعلاً: فثُلُثٌ لطعامِهِ، وثلثٌ لشرابه، وثلثٌ لنَفَسِه» (الترمذي : ٢٣٨٠ وصححه الألباني)

``The son of Adam never fills a vessel worse than his stomach. The son of Adam only needs a few bites that would sustain him, but if he insists, one third should be reserved for his food, another third for his drink and the last third for his breathing."

Physical ailments

Physical ailments attack and harm the body and alter its normal functions, because of the accumulation of certain substances in excess. This constitutes the cause of a majority of diseases and occurs because of overeating or consuming more than what the body needs, or by consuming that which brings about little benefit or is not digested easily, or due to large meals comprising a variety of food. When the son of Adam habitually fills his stomach with these types of foods, he will end up with various types of illnesses, some of which take a long time to cure. On the other hand, when one consumes moderate amounts of food and eats sensibly, the body will get the maximum benefit from this diet, as opposed to when one overeats.

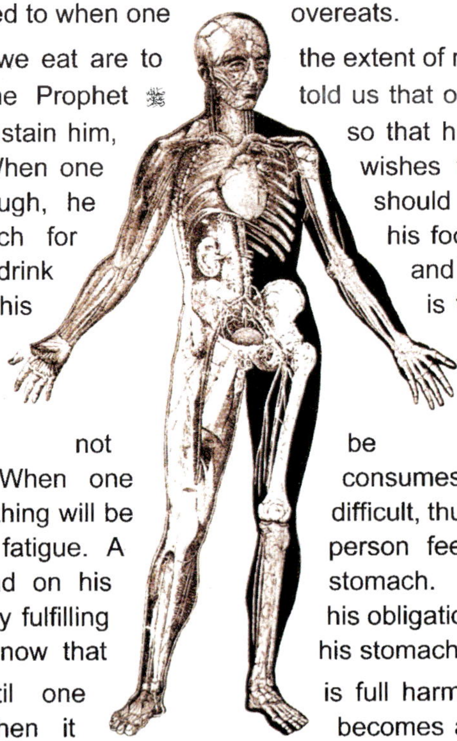

The foods we eat are to the extent of necessity, satiety or excess. The Prophet ﷺ told us that one only needs a few bites to sustain him, so that his strength does not fail him. When one wishes to exceed what is barely enough, he should reserve a third of his stomach for his food, another third for water or drink and the last third for breathing. This is the best method of eating, both for the body and the heart. When the stomach is full of food, there will not be enough space for drinking. When one consumes a drink on a full stomach, breathing will be difficult, thus bringing about laziness and fatigue. A person feels heavy, as if carrying a load on his stomach. Consequently, one will be lazy fulfilling his obligations and will seek other desires now that his stomach is full!

Eating until one is full harms the body and the heart, when it becomes a habit. There is no harm if one occasionally eats his fill. For example, Abu Hurairah رضي الله عنه once drank some milk in the presence of the Prophet ﷺ until he said, *"By He Who has sent you with the Truth! I do not have space for it."* The Companions at times used to eat their fill in the presence of the Prophet ﷺ. Eating until satiety as a matter of habit weakens the strength and the body, even as one becomes fatter. The body will be strong when it gets the nourishment it needs and can utilize, not from the quantity of food one eats.(1)

The human body consists of three basic elements: water, solids and air (whereas the fourth basic element is fire, according to the Greeks). This is why the Prophet ﷺ gave each of these elements its due share in the body [the stomach being part of the body -- Editor). If someone asks about the share of fire in the body, we say that doctors confirm that heat is utilized in reactions that occur in the body.

Others disagree with this opinion and state that there is no fiery part in the body. They reached these conclusions based on the following assumptions:

First: The fiery part could either descend from the air and be mixed with the watery and solid parts (of the human body)

Second: It could exist within the watery and solid matter.

The first assumption is not plausible, because fire naturally ascends and does not descend, otherwise it would depart from its center and descend to the earth. If in fact fire descends, it would have to pass through spheres of bitter cold that exist on earth and it would still have to remain intact. However, what we observe in this world is that a great fire can be extinguished with a [proportionately] little amount of water. Thus, if the fire were to descend from its center, it would certainly be

(1) Editor's note: The science at the time of the author 691 - 751 *Hijriah* (1364 - 1423) Gregorian approx.) Understood creation consisting of four basic elements: water, earth, fire and air. There was a dispute between the scientists of this time concerning whether the element of fire was part of the human body or not. From the prescription of the Prophet ﷺ concerning the proper proportions of food and drink our author seems to have brought this *Hidith* as evidence that fire was not part of the human body. The rest of the chapter is a divergence on this subject in support of his theory and not part of the Prophetic medicine.

extinguished due to the bitterly cold spheres it would pass through.

The second assumption is that fire is formed inside the solid and watery bodies. This is even less plausible, because the body that has turned to fire must have been watery, earthly, or composed of air beforehand, along with being surrounded by such elements. In this case, the element that is surrounded and interconnected with the watery or solid elements would not turn to fire on its own, because it is not composed of fire in essence. Besides, the elements that surround it are cold. How can the solid and watery body turn to fire under these conditions?

Some might suggest that parts of these elements are composed of fire and thus, they turn parts of the body to fire upon mixing with it.

We answer by stating that the refutation of this theory is explained in the refutation we offered regarding the first theory.

Some people might say that when they pour water on slaked lime, it causes fire to emerge from it. They might also say that sunrays start a fire when they pass through a crystal and that when they strike a stone on an iron rod, burst of fire occur. All the conditions that release fire occur when such substances are mixed, they might say, adding that this conclusion refutes what we stated in the beginning.

Those who reject this opinion say that they do not deny that violent impacts could sometimes start a fire, as when one strikes a stone with iron, or when the sun heats an object such as a crystal, causing bursts of fire to emerge. Yet, they refute the opinion that this might occur inside the bodies of animals and plants. The bodies of the animals and plants are not capable of producing fire upon violent impacts, because they are neither smooth nor polished enough to act like a crystal. In fact, sunrays fall on the outer bodies of the animals and plants, and do not cause them to burst into flames. So, how can sunrays that might or might not reach their interior start a fire inside their bodies?

Further, doctors agree that the longer a drink is kept [for aging], and the older it gets, the hotter it is. It is not possible that this inner warmth in the drink is caused by fire, otherwise the fiery part would be extinguished by the much larger watery part and would not remain intact for a long time.

Third: If the animals and the plants have elements of fire within them, then the fiery parts would be overwhelmed and dissipated by the watery parts. Some elements are superior to others in nature, and thus the weaker element succumbs to the stronger element. If such fiery parts exist in the body, they would certainly be turned into watery parts, which is the opposite of and superior to fire.

Fourth: Allah The Almighty mention the creation of mankind in His Book in many places. In certain instances Allah The Almighty informs us that He has created mankind from water. At other places He states that he created them from soil, a mixture of both and from clay that the sun and wind strike until it becomes just like a clay pot. All of these statements are true and describe the stages that humankind pass through. Allah The Almighty never states that He has created mankind from fire, as in the case with the creation of Satan, who is from the *Jinn*.

Imam Muslim (may Allah have mercy upon him) narrated that the Prophet ﷺ said:

« خُلِقَتِ الملائكةُ من نورٍ، وخُلِقَ الجَانُّ من مارجٍ من نارٍ، وخُلقَ آدمُ مما وُصفَ لكم »

(مسلم: ٢٩٩٦)

"The angels were created from light, while Satan was created from the smokeless flame of fire. As for Adam, he was created from what has been told to you."

This statement is clear in its indication that Adam (peace be upon him) was created from what Allah The Almighty has stated in His Book about this subject. Allah The Almighty did not state that He created Adam (peace be upon him) from fire or that fire exists within him.

Fifth: The best evidence they rely on, to prove that there are fiery parts in the body, is the warmth in the bodies of animals which they claim proves that the bodies are partly made of fire. We say that there is no proof in this observation, because there are several other causes for inner heat. For instance, fire produces heat, and so does movement, reflection of sunrays, the heat of the air and closeness to a source of fire, as the fire transmits the heat through the air. There are several causes behind the inner heat, but not necessarily fire.

The followers of the fire theory say that fire is necessary for sand and water to be mixed and blended. Otherwise, they would not blend or produce a compound. They also say that if the seed is buried in the mud so that the air and the sun cannot penetrate the mud to reach the seed, it would get spoiled. Therefore, they conclude that the seed should have an inner part that leads it to maturity, and later on to spoil,- that is, the fire. Otherwise, they say that the seed would only mature and then spoil due to an outside effect or else it would be in a frozen and immobile state. They say that when the outside effect ends, the body will not be heated unless there is an inner fiery part in it that matures it, such as the case with some foods and medicines that are warm by nature.

They also say that if the body did not consist of a fiery part that produces heat, the body would be cold. If the nature of the body is susceptible to coldness and the surrounding environment does not have the opposite effect, the body will reach the coldest degree it can possibly attain. In this state, the body will not feel the coldness because it will have reached a degree of such coldness that it would be frozen.

Therefore, the degree of coldness outside and within the body would be the same and thus the body would not feel the cold nor would it feel any pain because of the extreme cold. The same argument can be said when the body is in a lower temperature than the cold substance itself. Thus, if the body did not have any fiery part, it would not normally feel the cold nor be affected by it.

They also say that, ``*Your proofs only serve to refute the opinion that the fiery parts remain as fire within the bodies. We do not support this statement. Rather, we say that fire changes when it is mixed with the body.*"

Those who oppose this idea reply, ``*Why not say that the heat of the sun blends the earth, water and air? Then, when the resulting mixture reaches maturity, it is ready to take new shapes -- whether these shapes are plants, animals or minerals -- with heat as the medium. Why not say that the inner heat and warmth that exist in the body are the result of certain qualities and powers that Allah The Almighty brings into existence upon blending the mixture, not that they actually contain fiery parts? You have no way of denying this possibility, as some of the best medical authorities agree.*"

The fact that the body feels the cold only indicates that there is an inner heat in body. Who denies this fact anyway? But, what is the evidence that this heat is only produced by fire? Yes, the fire radiates heats, but not every type of heat is the result of fire. Rather, the correct statement in this regard is that some types of heat are produced by fire.

The statement that the fire's essence changes when it mixes with the body is not supported by the opinions of the best doctors, or by fact. Also, some of the foremost supporters of those who say that the body is part fire, (i.e., Ibn Sina, the misguided philosopher) has admitted in his book *Ash-Shifaa* (The Cure) that the four essential elements (water, fire, earth and air) retain their essential qualities when blended in a compound.

The Prophet ﷺ used three types of remedies for various ailments: natural, divine and a combination of both natural and divine

We will mention the three types of remedies that the Prophet ﷺ prescribed and used, starting with the natural medicines, then the divine remedies and lastly those composed of the two types.

The Prophet ﷺ was sent as a guide and a caller to Allah The Almighty and to His Paradise. He acquainted the people with Allah The Almighty and also informed them of what pleases Him and commanded them to implement these actions, and informed them of what angers Him and ordered them to avoid these actions. He told them stories of the Prophets and Messengers عليهم السلام and what occurred between them and their nations. He also acquainted the people with the creation of the world, its beginning, Resurrection and the reasons why souls will either receive misery or happiness.

As for the remedies of the bodies, this is a part of the *Sunnah* (tradition) of the Prophet ﷺ that completes it and makes it whole. The remedies of the body should be used when needed. Other than that, it is better to spend the time and energy curing the ills of the heart and soul, preserving their health, and preventing any harm from touching them. This is the ultimate goal that the Prophet's mission seeks to achieve. It is a fact that curing the ills of the body without curing the heart does not work or benefit anyone. However, curing the heart while the body is ill does not cause extensive harm since soon after, this harm will be removed and will be replaced with the ultimate, eternal benefit. All success comes from Allah The Almighty.

2

Part II

Using Natural Medicines

Curing fever

It has been narrated in the *Sahihayn* that the Prophet ﷺ said:

« إِنَّما الحُمَّى – أو شدَّةُ الحمَّى – مِن فَيحِ جَهنمَ؛ فَأَبْرِدُوهَا بِالماءِ » (البخاري : ٣٦٢٣)

``Verily fever - or severe fever - is a breath of the Hellfire, so cool it using water."

This *Hadith* has caused confusion for many ignorant doctors as they thought it contradicts the common method of treating fever. We will explain this *Hadith* in detail, Allah willing.

When the Prophet ﷺ issues a statement, it is either general for all people or for specific people and conditions. The majority of the statements of the Prophet ﷺ are of the first type. As for the second type, it is similar to the Prophet's statement:

« لا تستَقْبِلُوا القبلةَ بغائطٍ ولا بولٍ، ولا تَستدبِرُوها؛ ولكن شرِّقوا أو غَرِّبُوا »
(البخاري : ١٤٤)

``Do not face the Qiblah (direction of prayer) with urine or feces, nor leave it directly behind you. Rather, face either the East or the West."

This statement (facing the East or the West) is not for those who reside in the East, the West or Iraq, but for those residing in Madinah and Ash-Sham (Syria). It is the same case with the Prophet's statement:

« ما بينَ المشرقِ والمغربِ قِبلَةٌ » (الترمذي وصححه الألباني : ٣٤٤)

``What is between the East and the West is a Qiblah."

Keeping in mind this fact, we realize that what the Prophet ﷺ said regarding fever is particularly for the people of Hijaz (Western Arabia), for the people in this area are susceptible to a type of fever that results from sunstroke. This type of fever requires treatment by cold water, either by drinking it or taking a bath. Fever causes the body temperature to rise, which emanates from the heart and spreads throughout the entire body via the blood vessels and the soul, and disrupts the proper functioning of the body.

The body benefits from the fever more than it benefits from taking medicine. This is because the fever heats up and matures harmful substances [in the body], which it could not have done without the fever. Besides, the fever causes various blockages to open especially those that medicines cannot reach.

As for simple and chronic conjunctivitis, fever helps cure most of its types quickly and helps against facial paralysis, hemiplegia (paralysis affecting only one side of the body), spasms and many other ailments that result from [the accumulation of] thick substances or excesses.

Some of the best doctors feel relieved when fever breaks out in an ailing person, just as the sick person rejoices upon recovering from illness. This is because fever is more efficient than medication in some cases, since it matures the spoiled and septic substances that harm the body. When such substances reach maturity, the medicine reaches it when the substances are ready to be discarded out of the body, bringing this process to a successful conclusion. Thus, the fever becomes a part of the cure.

Based on these facts, it appears that the *Hadith* is talking about the accidental type of fevers that are relieved by being submerged into cold water or by drinking cold water. In this case, the sick person does not need any other medicine, because this type of fever is composed of heat that is connected to the soul. When a cold substance is introduced, the heat produced by the fever will be eliminated without having to get rid of any mixtures of substances or to wait for these substances to mature.

Galinus (Galen), one of the renowned doctors [in ancient times], admitted that cold water helps relieve this type of fever. He stated in the tenth article in his book, *'Healing Methods'*, *``If a young, healthy man, who does not suffer from an internal tumor takes a bath in the heat of* *the day or swims in it, he will gain a benefit."* He also stated that he used to prescribe this remedy on a regular basis.

Ar-Razi also said in his book, *'Al-Kabir'*,`

`If the strength is normal, but the fever is very intense and the maturity (of the harmful substances) is apparent, while [the patient is] suffering from any internal tumors or any type of ruptures, then drinking cold water becomes beneficial. If the ailing person is fat, the weather is hot and the person is used to taking cold showers, let him do just that."

In the Prophet's statement: *``Fever is a breath of the fire of Hell (Jahannam)."* There are two possible meanings.

First: The fever is a breath that is released from Hell so that the slaves become aware of it and thus learn a lesson from this fact. Therefore, Allah The Almighty has created reasons and causes for the fever to appear and break out. Similarly, comfort, joy, enjoyment and elation are a part of Paradise's joys that Allah The Almighty has allowed to appear in this world as an example and a lesson, and He has allowed such feelings to be connected to reasons and causes behind their appearance.

Second: The *Hadith* equates fever and the heat of day, to the intense heat of Hellfire, so that our hearts can imagine the intense torment of the Fire and the heat that emits from it.

The Prophet's statement: *"Cool it off with water"* might entail all types of water, and this is the correct opinion. Another opinion states that the water here means Zamzam water. Supporters of this opinion use as evidence what Al-Bukhari (may Allah have mercy upon him) narrated in his *Sahih* that Abu Jamrah, Nasr bin `Imran Adh-Dhuba'i (may Allah have mercy upon him) said, *``I used to be in the presence of Ibn `Abbas, ﵄, in Makkah until one day, I was struck by fever. He said, `Cool it off with Zamzam water, for the Messenger of Allah ﷺ said:*

« الحمَّى مِن فَيْحِ جهنمَ »

``Fever is a breath of Hellfire."

Therefore, cool it with water, or said with Zamzam water.'"

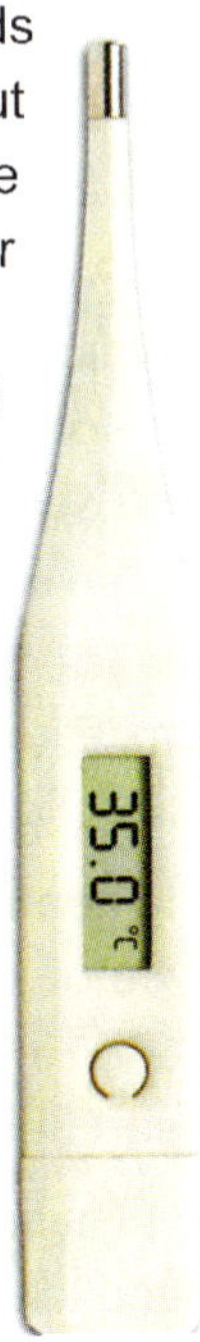

The narrator of the *Hadith* was in doubt as to the exact words of the Prophet ﷺ. Otherwise, it would be established without doubt that the Prophet ﷺ meant Zamzam water for the people of Makkah, because it is available. All others can use whatever water is available to them.

There is a difference of opinion concerning if the Prophet ﷺ intended by this *Hadith* to encourage giving away some water as a charity, or to actually use it. The correct opinion is that the *Hadith* means using it. I believe that those who thought the *Hadith* means giving away some water as a charity did not understand the purpose behind using cold water for fever. Yet, there is a good explanation for the Prophet's statement, for the reward [of a deed] is of a type comparable to the deed. Since thirsty people drink cold water to quench their thirst, Allah The Almighty dissipates fever with cold water, as well. Yet, this is an implication of the *Hadith*, as for the ruling contained in it, it simply means to use the water (not give it away in charity).

Abu Nu'aym (may Allah have mercy upon him) said, Anas رَضِيَ الله عَنْهُ narrated that the Prophet ﷺ said:

« إِذَا حُمَّ أَحَدُكم: فَلْيُرَشَّ عليه الماءُ البارِدُ ثلاثَ ليالٍ مِن السَّحَرِ »

(الحاكم : (٤/ ٤٠٣) وقال الذهبي على شرط مسلم وأقره في تحقيق الزاد وانظر الترمذي : ٢٠٨٤)

``If any of you comes down with fever, let him sprinkle cold water on himself for three consecutive nights before daybreak."

Ibn Majah (may Allah have mercy upon him) narrated that Abu Hurairah رَضِيَ الله عَنْهُ related from the Prophet ﷺ that he said:

« الحُمَّى مِن كِيرِ جهنمَ؛ فَنَحُّوهَا عَنْكُم بالماءِ البارِدِ » (ابن ماجه وصححه الألباني : ٣٤٧٥)

``Fever is a bellow of the heat of Hell, so remove it from you with cold water."

It is also narrated in the *Sunan* that Abu Hurairah رَضِيَ الله عَنْهُ said, *``Fever was mentioned in the presence of the Messenger of Allah ﷺ and a man cursed it. The Messenger of Allah ﷺ said:*

« لا تَسُبَّهَا؛ فإنها تَنْفِي الذنُوبَ كما تَنفِي النارُ خَبَثَ الحَدِيدِ » (ابن ماجه وصححه الألباني : ٣٤٦٩)

`Do not curse it, for it removes the sins, just as fire removes the impurity of the iron." [Also refer to Sahih Muslim].

Fever is usually treated by consuming beneficial foods and medicines and is followed by a diet that avoids improper food. The sick person's body will be cleansed from all impurities and septic elements and substances, having a purifying effect that is similar to fire when it removes the impurity of iron.

The physical benefits of fever are already known to medical practitioners.

As for cleansing the heart from its ills and impurities, only doctors of the heart [*This does not refer to cardiologists-Editor*] have access to this type of knowledge. Such experts will find that whatever the Prophet ﷺ stated in this regard is the plain truth. However, when the diseases of the heart become chronic, hope diminishes that they will ever be cured!

Thus, fever helps the body and the heart. Therefore, cursing such a beneficial matter would be an act of injustice and transgression.

Abu Hurairah رَضِيَ الله عَنْهُ said, *"No ailment that I might suffer from is dearer to me than fever, because it enters every organ of my body, and Allah gives each organ its due share of the reward."*

Therefore, using cold water to relieve fever during summer and in hot areas is beneficial, because the water will be furthest from the rays of the sun just before daybreak (at its coolest). Moreover, just before daybreak the body is at its strongest, for the ailing person will have taken his due share of sleep and relaxation and air pollution is the least at the time. The strength of the body will be added to the strength of the medicine - water in this case -- and they will both relieve the fever that is not a result of malignant tumors or septic substances or conditions. Allah The Almighty will then extinguish the heat of the fever by His will.

The Prophetís guidance on curing diarrhea

It is narrated in the *Sahihayn* that Abu Sa`id Al-Khudri رَضِيَ الله عَنْهُ said,

«أن رجلاً أتى النبيَّ صلى الله عليه وسلم، فقال: إِنَّ أخي يَشْتكِي بَطنَهُ، وفي رواية: استطلقَ بَطنُهُ، فقال: اسقِهِ عسَلاً. فذهب ثم رجعَ، فقالَ: قد سَقيتُهُ فلم يُغنِ عنه شيئًا. وفي لفظ: فلم يزده إلا استِطْلاقًا»مَرَّتَيْنِ أَوْ ثَلاَثً، كُلَّ ذَلِكَ يَقُولُ لَهُ: « اسقِهِ عسلاً»فَقَالَ لَهُ فِي الثَّالِثَةِ أَوِ الرَّابِعَةِ «صَدَقَ اللهُ وكَذَبَ بطنُ أخيكَ »

(البخاري : ٥٦٨٤ ومسلم :٢٢١٧)

``A man came to the Prophet ﷺ and said, `My brother is complaining about his stomach (or he is complaining from diarrhea).' The Prophet ﷺ said: `Give him some honey.' The man went and came back later, saying, 'I have given him some honey, but it did not help,' or he said, `It made his diarrhea worse.' He repeated this twice or three times, all the while the Prophet ﷺ continued saying to him: `Give him some honey.' On the third or fourth time, the Prophet ﷺ said: `Allah has said the truth while your brother's stomach has lied.'"

Honey has tremendous medicinal value, because it washes away the harmful substances that may have collected in the veins and the intestines. Honey also dissolves excess moisture, and is beneficial as a drink and as an ointment. It is of great value for the

elderly, and those suffering from phlegm and cold moods or conditions like chills. Honey is nutritious, softens the bowel movement and is a good preserving agent. Honey also reduces the bitter taste of other medicines, cleanses the liver and the chest, acts as a diuretic (aids in producing urine), and dissolves the phlegm that is accompanied by coughing.

When honey is consumed hot and mixed with rose oil, it cures animal bites and counteracts the effects of opium. Taking honey mixed with water helps against the bite of a rabid dog and the effects of eating poisonous mushrooms. If fresh meat is kept in honey, it preserves its freshness for three months. Likewise, if gourds, cucumbers and eggplants are kept in honey, they too will be preserved. Honey also keeps some types of fruit fresh for six months. It can even preserve cadavers (dead bodies), thus deserving to be called "The true preserver."

If honey is applied to someone infected with lice, it kills both the lice and the eggs. Honey also adds softness and beauty to the hair and encourages hair growth. When honey is applied to the eye as *Kuhl,* it strengthens weak eyesight. Honey also whitens the teeth, preserves their health and the health of the gums, dilates the opening of the veins and promotes the flow of menstruation. Licking honey on an empty stomach helps the body excrete mucus and phlegm. It cleanses the stomach

and rids it of harmful substances or mixtures, heats the stomach mildly and opens up the pores. Honey has similar effects on the kidney, the prostate and the liver. Furthermore, honey is the least harmful sweet substance for treating congestion of the liver and kidneys.

In addition to all the benefits mentioned here, honey does not have any side effects, or harm except for those suffering from disorders of the bile, and who are advised to take it with vinegar to neutralize its harm.

Honey is also a food, a drink, a sweet, a remedy, a type of refreshment and an ointment, along with its numerous medicinal values. Therefore, there is no other substance that is more beneficial than honey, or even one that rivals its value. This is why the people of old relied on honey, for most of the books of old do not mention sugar, which has been discovered only in modern times.

The Prophet ﷺ used to drink some honey mixed with water on an empty stomach. There is a wonderful secret behind this practice regarding preserving the health. Only those who enjoy sound comprehension will be able to recognize such a secret. We will mention this subject again when we explain the Prophet's guidance regarding persevering good health.

A *Hadith* [narrated by Ibn Majah and others] stated that the Prophet ﷺ said:

« عَلَيْكُم بِالشِّفَاءَيْنِ: الْعَسَلِ والقرآن »

(ابن ماجه : ٣٤٥٢ وصححه الألباني موقوفاً على ابن سعود، وانظر تحقيق الزاد ٤ / ٣٤)

``Make use of the two cures: honey and the Qur'an."

This *Hadith* joins the material and the divine cures, the medicine of the body and the soul, the earthly medicine and the heavenly cure.

Understanding these facts, let us go back to the man to whom the Prophet ﷺ had prescribed honey to cure his diarrhea, which was caused by overeating. The Prophet ﷺ prescribed honey for him to prevent his stomach and intestines from accumulating harmful substances or toxins that prevents the food in the stomach from being digested, because honey has a cleansing effect. The harmful, viscid substances were adhering to the stomach walls, which is similar to the material of a towel, polluting both the stomach and the food. Honey removes these substances that engulf the stomach, and it is the best cure for this condition. Honey is a potent cleanser and is effective in treating cases of diarrhea, especially when it is mixed with warm water.

The Prophet ﷺ repeated his command to the man to give some honey to his sick brother for a good reason. The prescribed medicine should be in sufficient doses; otherwise the ailment will not be fully cured. When the prescribed medicine is in a larger than necessary dose, it will weaken the body and cause side effects. When the Prophet ﷺ first ordered the man to give his brother honey, he did not give him a sufficient amount to cure his condition. When the man said that his brother was not cured, the Prophet ﷺ knew that the dose was not sufficient, so he told the man several times to give his brother more honey, so that the dose would reach a sufficient amount. When the sick person has several doses of honey in a sufficient amount to fight the disease, the cure occurs by the permission of Allah The Almighty.

Giving the correct dose of the proper medicine is a major part of the science of medicine.

When the Prophet ﷺ said to the man:

« صدَقَ اللهُ و كذَبَ بطنُ أخيكَ »

``Allah has said the truth and your brother's stomach has lied."

This indicates the certain efficacy of honey as a cure. It also indicates that the illness remained, not because the prescribed medicine was not effective, but because the stomach had a large amount of spoiled substances in it. Therefore, the Prophet ﷺ ordered the man to take more medicine because his stomach contained excessive amounts of spoiled substances.

Prophetic medicine is not similar to that offered by doctors and physicians. Prophetic medicine is indeed the most effective treatment and cure provided by the revelation and the guidance of the Prophet ﷺ coupled with a sound and perfect mind. In comparison, the majority of remedies prescribed by someone other than a prophet are built on hypothesis, observation and experimentation.

It is a fact that many people do not benefit from Prophetic medicine, because it will help only those who acknowledge and have faith in it. Thus, they believe that it will help them and they then submit to it. If the Qur'an, which is a cure for whatever the heart conceals, is not acknowledged and accepted with faith, it will not provide a cure for the heart. In fact, the Qur'an will only add more evil and disease to the hearts of the hypocrites.

Prophetic medicine is only suitable for good and pure people, just as the Qur'an is only suitable for righteous souls and sensitive hearts. Therefore, when the people ignore Prophetic medicine, it is like ignoring the help and guidance of the Qur'an, which is the most effective medicine. Again, when the medicine (the Qur'an and the Prophetic medicine) do not work, it is due to the negativity in the body and soul that are not suitable for accepting the medicine - not because the medicine does not work. All success comes from Allah The Almighty.

ëWherein is healing for mení

There is a difference of opinion concerning the words of Allah The Almighty:

﴿يَخْرُجُ مِنْ بُطُونِهَا شَرَابٌ مُّخْتَلِفٌ أَلْوَانُهُۥ فِيهِ شِفَآءٌ لِّلنَّاسِ﴾

``There comes forth from their bellies, a drink of varying color wherein is healing for men." (Qur'an, 16:69)

The disagreement revolves around the words *{``wherein is healing for men"}:* do they refer to the drink or the Qur'an? There are two opinions on this matter, the closest to the truth is what Ibn Mas'ood, Ibn `Abbas, Al-Hasan, Qatadah رَضِيَ الله عَنْهُم and the majority of the scholars stated, that these words refer to the drink. The *Ayah* (Verse) is talking about the drink and not the Qur'an. Adding to this fact, the Prophet ﷺ said in the previous *Hadith*: ``*Allah has said the truth,*" as it is clear in determining that the verse is referring to the drink. And Allah knows best.

The Prophet ﷺcommanded Muslims not to enter a plague-infested area

In the *Sahihayn* it is narrated that Sa`d bin Abi Waqqas رَضِيَ الله عَنْهُ asked Usamah bin Zayd رَضِيَ الله عَنْهُما about what he heard the Prophet say concerning the plague.

Usamah رَضِيَ الله عَنْهُ said that the Messenger of Allah ﷺ said:

((الطاعُونُ رِجْزٌ أُرْسِلَ عَلَى طائفةٍ من بني إسرائيلَ - وعلى مَن كانَ قَبْلَكم، فَإذا سَمِعتم به بأرض: فلا تدخُلُوا عليه، وإذا وَقعَ بأرض - وأنتم بها - فلاَ تَخرُجُوا مِنها فِرَارًا مِنْهُ)) (البخاري : 3743)

``*The plague is a punishment that was sent down on some of the Children of Israel and on those who were before your time. So if you hear that it has struck a land do not enter that land, and if it breaks out in a land that you are residing in, do not go out of that area escaping from it.*"

Furthermore, in the *Sahihayn* it is narrated that the Messenger of Allah ﷺ said:

« الطاعونُ شهادةٌ لكلِّ مسلِمٍ» (البخاري : ٢٨٣٠)

``*The plague is a martyrdom for every Muslim.*"

Linguistically, *Ta`oon*, the plague, is a type of disease. In medical terms, the plague causes the appearance of fatal, vicious tumors that are the result of a very strong and painful infection, quickly turning the infected area into black, green or brown color. Soon afterwards, ulcers start to appear around the infected area. The plague usually strikes three areas: under the arms, behind the ear and the tip of the nose, and/or, the soft (flaccid) tissues of the body. `A'ishah رضي الله عنها narrated that she asked the Prophet ﷺ about the plague, and he said:

((غُدَّةٌ كَغُدَّةِ البَعِيرِ يَخْرُجُ فِي المَرَاقِّ والإِبْطِ)) (أحمد ٦/ ١٤٥ وسنده حسن كما في تحقيق الزاد ٤/ ٣٨)

"A gland that is similar to the camel's gland and which appears in the tender parts of the abdomen and under the arms."

Doctors say that when a septic infection occurs in the soft flesh, such as under the arms or behind the ears, it is called the plague. The plague is caused by spoiled, septic blood [infected by a pathogen that carries the disease from infected rodents]. The infected blood affects the part of the body that it reaches, sometimes causing the formation of pus or leading to hemorrhage. In this case, the affected organ sends the infected blood to the heart, thus causing symptoms like vomiting, unconsciousness and rapid heartbeat. Although the plague describes every infection that sends septic blood to the heart, becoming fatal sometimes, it particularly describes the infection that attacks the soft tissues of the body.

Since the infected blood is septic, the various organs reject the blood, except those that have become weak. The worst types of the plague are those that strike behind ears and under the arms, because they are closer to the essential organs of the body. There is little chance to be cured from the black plague, while the red plague and the yellow plagues are less dangerous. Since the disease breaks out in polluted areas, it is called a plague, although this word describes every epidemic, as we have stated, and as Al-Khalil has concurred.

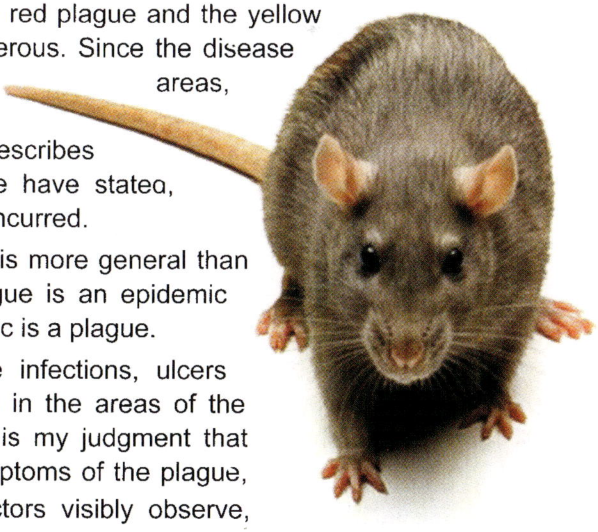

The word epidemic is more general than the plague. Every plague is an epidemic while not every epidemic is a plague.

The plagues cause infections, ulcers and malignant growths in the areas of the body we described. It is my judgment that these are only the symptoms of the plague, since this is what doctors visibly observe, thus prompting the doctors to call them symptoms of the plague.

There are three meanings for the word 'plague'.

First: The symptoms of the disease that the doctors observe and record.

Second: Death that occurs to those inflicted by the plague, as the Prophet ﷺ said:

« الطَّاعونُ شَهادةٌ لكلِّ مُسلِمٍ » (البخاري : ٣٤٧٣)

``The plague is a martyrdom for every Muslim."

Third: The reason behind the outbreak of the plague, which is mentioned in the *Hadith*,

« إنهُ بَقِيَّةُ رِجزٍ أُرسِلَ عَلَى بَنِي إسرائيلَ »

(مسلم وعنده: آية الرِّجْز ٢٢١٨٧، أما قوله هنا: بقية عَذاب فهي من واية شعبة عند البيهقي (٣/ ٣٧٦)في الكبرى)

``The plague is the remnant of a punishment that was sent upon the Children of Israel."

The plague was also described in another *Hadith*:

« إنَّهُ وَخْزُ الجنِّ » (أحمد : ٤/ ٣٩٥ على اختلاف بعض رجال في السند وصححه في تحقيق الزاد ٤/ ٣٩)

``It is a result of the Jinn's touch."

Further, the Prophet ﷺ said that the plague is:

« أنهُ دَعوةُ نبيٍّ » (لم نعثر عليه)

``A Prophet's supplication."

Doctors cannot refute the reasons we have mentioned explaining why the outbreak of plague occurs, although they feel that there is no physical proof that supports them. The Messengers informed us of matters of the Unseen, while the doctors' expertise deals with the physical symptoms of the plague. However, the symptoms of the plague that doctors are familiar with do not provide them with any material evidence that the plague does not engage the soul in some manner, for there is a tremendous connection between the soul and what the body suffers due to disease and ultimately death. Only the most ignorant people will deny the effects of the soul on the body and on human nature as a whole. Allah The Almighty gives the soul certain powers over the body of the sons of Adam at such times when an epidemic breaks out or when the air is contaminated.

The soul has certain effects on the body when it experiences the ailments that are caused by septic substances, especially when the blood, semen or black bile is irritated. Evil forces take control of the body when it experiences such emotions and ailments, unless the person repels it with an even stronger power, such as remembering Allah The Almighty, supplicating to Him, invoking and pleading to Him, giving in charity and reciting the Qur'an. In this case, angels will descend and will defeat and neutralize the evil effects of the devilish souls (evil forces).

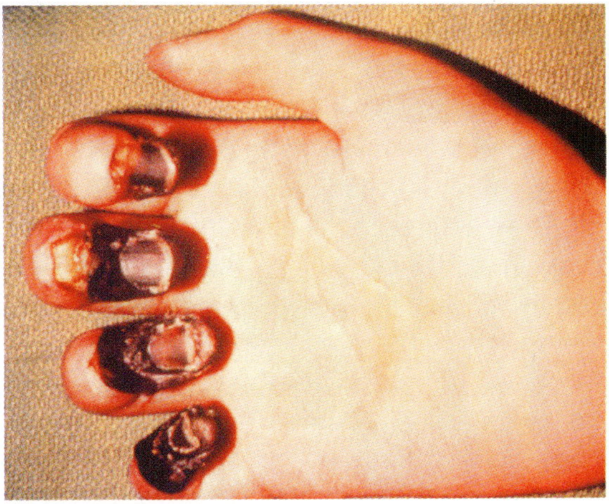

We have successfully tried this method innumerable time (so much so that only Allah The Almighty is Able to count them), and we have witnessed the wonderful effects of such positive forces (good souls) in strengthening one's resolve and ridding a person of harmful elements [in the body] in the early stages. This method almost never fails, by the will of Allah The Almighty.

When one feels that evil is close to him, he should turn to good deeds as we have explained, so that they deter and fend off the evil forces (souls). This is the best medicine in such cases for those whom Allah The Almighty leads to success. However, when Allah The Almighty decides that His appointed destiny takes over, He draws the slave's heart away from knowing and intending to perform these good deeds. In this case, the slave does not decide or intend to perform these good deeds, so that what Allah The Almighty has decided takes over.

Allah willing, we will elaborate further on this subject when we discuss the divine remedies of healing with *Ruqyah* (literally: incantations) with the help of the Qur'an, the Prophet's supplications, the various types of *Du'a* (supplications and prayers), specific forms of remembering Allah The Almighty and performing righteous deeds. We will also reiterate and affirm that comparing Prophetic medicine to regular medicine is just like comparing folk medicine to that provided by doctors, as some of the best doctors have conceded. We will also elaborate on the fact that bodies are more affected by the soul and that Islamic supplications are better and more powerful than the most powerful medicines; that they can even neutralize the effect of deadly poisons.

We must re-emphasize the fact that unhealthy air plays a major role in causing the plague. Air becomes unhealthy when it becomes contaminated because of disease-causing agents (pathogens) or pollutants, no matter what time of year, although it usually happens in the latter part of the summer and in the autumn. This is because during these times of the year (and when the air is most polluted), acute bilious excretions that accumulate during the summer will not have maturated by the end of the season. In autumn, the air is usually cold and thus the immature excretions that accumulated in the summer will heat up and start getting spoiled and decayed, thus causing putrid illnesses. This is especially the case when the body is susceptible to such ailments, being inactive and having excessive septic materials, both of which rarely spare the body from ailments.

We should state that the best season of the year is spring especially with respect to the air. Hippocrates said, *``Autumn carries the worst types of ailments and deadly sicknesses. Spring, on the other hand, is the best season and has the least occurrences of death."* Pharmacists and those who prepare dead bodies for burial usually borrow money during spring and summer, rather than autumn. This is because, to them, autumn is their spring so that they are eager for its advent and feel happy when it starts (due to the increased number of deaths in the autumn).

It was reported in a *Hadith*:

« إذا طَلع النَّجْمُ: ارْتَفَعَت العَاهَةُ عن كلِّ بلَدٍ »

(أحمد ٢/ ٣٤١ وهو حسن كما في تحقيق المسند، ويؤيده أثر البخاري ٢١٩٣)

``When the Najm (literally: star) appears, every epidemic is removed from every land."

The *Najm* is said to mean the star, or the plants that appear in spring.

﴿ وَٱلنَّجْمُ وَٱلشَّجَرُ يَسْجُدَانِ ﴾

``And the herbs (or stars) and the trees both prostrate themselves (to Allah)." (Qur'an, 55:6)

This means during spring, because it is the season when the trees are at their prime and thus the epidemics are removed.

As for the *Najm* (the North Star in this case), ailments intensify when it rises and then sets just about dawn. At-Tamimi (may Allah have mercy upon him) said in his book, *'The Secret of the Existence'*, *``The worst two times of the year and the most harmful for the body are: when the North Star sets just before dawn, and when it appears from the east before the sun rises on the world. This is the time when spring is about to end. Yet, the harm that occurs when it appears is less than the harm caused by its setting."*

Further, Abu Muhammad bin Qutaibah, (may Allah have mercy upon him) said,

`Whenever the Pleiades (in astronomy, the star cluster was named by the ancient Greeks after the ``Seven Sisters" of mythology, the Arabs called it Al-Thurayya) rises or sets, it brings about an epidemic for people and camels. Yet, its setting is worse than when it is rising."

There is a third opinion regarding the meaning of the *Hadith*, that is, the star means the Pleiades and the epidemic is that which attacks the plants and fruits during winter and in the beginning of spring. When the star rises, the plants will be safe from such epidemics during that time. This is why the Prophet ﷺ disallowed selling or buying fruit before it is apparent that they are ripe and good.

The Prophet ﷺ commanded Muslims not to enter a plague-infested area and to remain in the infected area

Once there breaks out the plague where one happens to reside.

This is the best type of prevention, for when one enters a plague-infested area, he exposes himself to the risk of infection and harm. Exposing oneself to such danger defies the dictates of the religion and a sound mind. Staying away from plague-infested areas is a type of prevention that Allah The Almighty has directed and guided people to. In this case, one observes a form of prophylaxis by avoiding contaminated areas and air.

As for the Prophet's prohibiting the Muslims from escaping from the epidemic infested area, it has two possible meanings.

1. Encouraging the heart to depend and rely on Allah The Almighty while observing patience and being content with what Allah The Almighty has decided.

2. The best medical authorities say that in order to avoid becoming sick during an epidemic, one needs to help the body get rid of harmful fluids and moisture, follow a diet and preserve the body's dryness in general. They warn against strenuous sports activities and taking [frequent] baths. The human body usually contains harmful substances that are latent and which sometimes become activated by sports and [frequently] taking baths. They might then mix with the beneficial substances in the body and cause several ailments. Therefore, when the plague strikes a land, the best thing one can do is to remain in that land, so that the harmful substances in the body are not aroused or irritated. Leaving the plague-infested area requires some sort of activity and physical effort, both of which are very harmful in this case.

These are the statements of the best medical authorities of the past and present times, that help in shedding light on the veracity of the Prophet's commands, that assure the wellbeing of the heart and body.

If someone asks, *"When the Prophet ﷺ said: 'Do not abandon it and take flight,' this refutes the meaning that has been stated. Leaving the infested land for another purpose than escaping, such as traveling, is exempt from the prohibition."*

We answer this question by stating that no person, whether a doctor or otherwise, says that all types of movements are prohibited when plague strikes a land, for the people cannot act as if they are fixed objects. Rather, engaging in excessive physical movement and activities that are not necessary is discouraged during the outbreak of an epidemic. There is no reason behind abandoning the plague-infested land, other than escaping from the plague, whereas being at rest and staying calm are better for the people's hearts and bodies in this situation. Moreover, staying inactive satisfies the required condition of dependence and reliance on Allah The Almighty and submitting to His decisions.

As for those who need to move about, such as hired hands, craftsmen and travelers, they are not required to remain completely inactive, but to refrain from any unnecessary movements such as traveling to escape the plague.

There is a great wisdom behind commanding the people to remain in the plague-infested area, which can be understood as follows:

1. Avoiding harm and the paths that might lead to harm.
2. Preserving one's health, which is the medium that people rely on to acquire the necessities of life and to fulfill the requirements of the Hereafter.
3. Preventing people from falling sick due to breathing polluted and contaminated air.
4. Avoiding close contact with those afflicted by the plague, to

avoid catching the infection themselves.

5. Preserving the body and soul from infection and superstition, which only harms those who believe in it.(1)

In short, the prohibition on entering plague-infested areas is a preventive measure and a type of prophylactic method that leads a person away from the paths of harm. The prohibition on leaving the area where the plague has struck entails submitting to the will and decision of Allah The Almighty. The first order teaches and trains, while the second order entails submission and referring all matters to the will of Allah The Almighty.

It is narrated that `Umar رَضِـيَ الله عَنْهُ was on his way to Ash-Sham when he reached the area of Sargh where he met Abu Ubaydah bin Al-Jarrah رَضِـيَ الله عَنْهُ with some people. They told `Umar رَضِـيَ الله عَنْهُ that there was an outbreak of the plague in Ash-Sham and they disputed among each other about what to do. So `Umar رَضِـيَ الله عَنْهُ said to Ibn `Abbas رَضِـيَ الله عَنْهُما , *`Summon the early Emigrants.'*

Ibn `Abbas رَضِـيَ الله عَنْهُما said,

'I summoned them and they also disputed, as some of them said (to 'Umar) that he had gone out for a certain purpose and they did not recommend going back until it is fulfilled. Other Emigrants said, `You have the best of the people in your company and the remainder of the Companions of the Messenger of Allah. Therefore, we do not recommend that you send them towards the epidemic.' `Umar رَضِـيَ الله عَنْهُ said, `Go away from here.' He then said, `Summon Al-Ansar (The Helpers) for me.'

I [Ibn `Abbas] summoned them and 'Umar رَضِـيَ الله عَنْهُ asked for their opinions. The Ansar disputed just as the Emigrants had disputed and

(1) **Editor's note:** The medical concept of quarantine was not yet established at the time of our author although this *Hadith* preceded the author by approximately 700 years. This *Hadith* established quarantine through faith before the knowledge required was available to medical scholars even seven centuries later.

behaved in the same manner. `Umar رَضِيَ اللهُ عَنْهُ said, `Go away from here.' `Umar then said, `Summon whoever is present from the leaders of Quraish from those who embraced Islam in the aftermath of the Fath (Conquest of Makkah).'

I [Ibn `Abbas] summoned them and no two men among them disputed, as they all said, `We recommend that you go back with the people and do not expose them to the epidemic.' `Umar رَضِيَ اللهُ عَنْهُ then ordered the people to leave, saying, `In the morning, I will be riding on my animal's back, and so should you too.'

Abu 'Ubaydah bin Al-Jarrah رَضِيَ اللهُ عَنْهُ said, 'O leader of the believers! Do you run away from Allah's appointed destiny?' 'Umar رَضِيَ اللهُ عَنْهُ said, 'I wish that somebody else had uttered these words, O Abu `Ubaydah! Yes, we run away from Allah's appointed destiny to Allah's appointed destiny. If you had a herd of camels that arrived at a valley that has two slopes, one fertile and the other barren and you let your camels graze on the fertile slope, you will do so by Allah's leave, will you not? And if you allow them to graze on the barren slope, you will do so by Allah's leave, will you not?'

Soon after, Abdur Rahman bin `Awf رَضِيَ اللهُ عَنْهُ came back from attending to some of his needs and said, 'I have some knowledge regarding this matter. I heard the Messenger of Allah ﷺ say:

« إِذَا كَانَ بِأَرْضٍ وَأَنْتُمْ بها: فَلَا تخرُجوا فِرارًا منه؛ وَإِذَا سَمِعْتُمْ بِهِ بأرضٍ: فلا تَقْدَموا عليه » (البخاري: ٥٧٢٩)

``If you hear about it (the plague) in a land that you are in, do not run away from it, and if you hear that it has broken out in a certain land, do not enter that land." [Al-Bukhari, Muslim, Abu Dawud, At-Tirmidhi, An-Nasai', Ibn Majah and Ahmad].

The Prophetís remedy for dropsy

In the *Sahihayn* it is narrated that Anas bin Malik رَضِيَ الله عَنْهُ said,

``Some people of (the tribes of) `Ukl and `Uraynah tribe came to Madinah and its climate did not suit them. So the Prophet ﷺ ordered them to go to the herd of camels reserved for charity, and to drink their milk and urine (as a medicine). So they went as directed. After they became healthy, they killed the shepherds of the Prophet's camels and drove away all the camels, thus becoming aggressors against Allah and His Messenger. The Prophet ﷺ sent (men) in their pursuit and they were captured. The Prophet ﷺ then ordered that their hands and feet to be cut off (and it was done), and their eyes were branded with heated pieces of iron. They were then kept in the sun until they died."

The proof that these people were complaining of dropsy, is from Imam Muslim (may Allah have mercy upon him) who narrated in his *Sahih* from the same *Hadith* above that the Bedouins said, *``We do not find Madinah suitable for us and our stomachs have swelled, our*

organs have become weak..." until the end of the *Hadith*.

Dropsy is a physical disease that occurs when a harmful cold substance penetrates the external organs of the body and other organs [other than those used in digestion], causing them to swell. There are three types of dropsy: that which occurs in body tissue (fleshy), which is the most serious of the three; that which occurs in a body cavity (ascites), and in an organ (drum).

The remedy for this disease includes mild laxatives and diuretic medicines that help rid the body of fluids. These diuretic qualities exist in the milk and urine of camels and that is why the Prophet ﷺ ordered them to drink them. Camel milk is a mild laxative, diuretic, cleanses and opens that which is closed, removes the obstructions and soothes the body. This is especially the case when the camels graze on beneficial herbs, such as wormwood, lavender, chamomile, daisy and lemongrass which help against dropsy.

Dropsy is usually symptomatic of an ailment in the liver, especially due to congestion in the liver. The milk of the Arabian camels helps in this case, because of its many benefits as mentioned and which help open the clogged passages and the obstructions. Ar-Razi said, *``The she-camel's milk soothes the liver and the effects of a*

spoiled constitution."

Al-Israili also said,``*The she-camel's milk is the softest, least concentrated and lightest milk. It is the best choice for moving the bowels, as a laxative and for opening the clogged passages and obstructions. What makes this evident is the fact that this type of milk is mildly salty, as a result of the animal's instinctively hot nature. Therefore, the she-camel's milk is the best remedy for the liver as it soothes it, opens its pores and veins and softens the hardness of fresh food. Fresh, warm camel's milk is beneficial against dropsy, especially when taken with fresh, warm camel urine, thus making the combination more salty and adding strength to its effectiveness in dissolving harmful fluids and as a laxative. If the [combination of milk and urine] did not purge the stomach, then one should take a stronger laxative.'*

The author of *'Al-Qanun'* (Canon) also commented, ``*Do not listen to those who claim that milk does not provide cure from dropsy. Rather, know that camel's milk is an effective cure, because it cleanses gently and easily, due to its other qualities. This type of milk is so beneficial that if a person substitutes water and food with camel's milk, he would be cured [from dropsy and other ailments]. Some people tried this remedy and were soon cured. We should state that the best camel urine is that of the camels of Bedouin people."*

The story mentioned in the last *Hadith* has several areas of interest, as follows:

The *Hadith* encourages the use of medicines and cures.

The *Hadith* also indicates the purity of the milk of the animals that Muslims are allowed to eat, for using what Allah The Almighty has prohibited in medicine is disallowed.

Further, the people mentioned in the *Hadith* were not commanded to rinse their mouths or their clothes for the prayer, although they were new Muslims [indicating that rinsing the mouth and the clothes in such cases is not necessary].

The Prophet ﷺ cannot delay the necessary details of a religious command when such elaboration is necessary.

This story also emphasizes the fact that the aggressor is punished by the same method by which he transgresses.

The people mentioned in the *Hadith* killed the shepherd and branded his eyes, as evident in another narration of this *Hadith* by Imam Muslim (may Allah have mercy upon him). The *Hadith* also mentioned that the entire group was killed for killing one person.

This story indicates that when the aggressor deserves to be punished for multiple crimes, one punishable according to the law of equality and the other for an act of aggression, then both laws are applied.

The Prophet ﷺ ordered that the hands and feet of the aggressors be cut off, as a punishment from Allah The Almighty for their audacious raid and aggression. They were also killed because they had killed the shepherd.

The *Hadith* also indicates that when armed aggressors steal money and commit murder, their hands and feet are cut off, and they are then executed. The *Hadith* also indicates that the punishment for multiple crimes is multiplied, because the people who were mentioned in the story reverted from Islam, killed a human being, disfigured the dead shepherd, stole other people's property and announced their armed aggression.

Also, the entire armed band mentioned in the story were executed, not only those who actually committed the murder, as the Prophet ﷺ did not consider this fact, nor did he ask about who actually committed the murder.

Furthermore, assassination warrants capital punishment and cannot be pardoned [by the relatives of the deceased] or compensated, according to the scholars of Madinah and the *Math-hab* (school of Islamic jurisprudence) of Imam Ahmad (may Allah have mercy upon him), which our *Shaykh* (Ibn Taymiyyah, may Allah have mercy upon him) has chosen.

The Prophetís guidance on treating wounds and cuts

In the *Sahihayn* it is narrated that Sahl bin Sa'd رَضِيَ الله عَنْهُ was asked about how the injuries of the Messenger of Allah ﷺ were treated in the Battle of Uhud. Sahl رَضِيَ الله عَنْهُ said,

"The Prophet's face was injured, his tooth was broken and the helmet he was wearing was smashed on his head. Fatimah رَضِيَ الله عَنْها, the daughter of the Messenger of Allah ﷺ, was washing the blood off while `Ali رَضِيَ الله عَنْهُ was pouring water on her hands with his shield. When Fatimah رَضِيَ الله عَنْها realized that the bleeding was not stopping, she took a burned mat (of palm leaves) and inserted the ash in the wound of Allah's Messenger ﷺ and the bleeding stopped."

The ashes of burnt palm leaves are very effective in stopping bleeding, because it is a strong drying agent and because it has the least burning effect (on the exposed skin). Other strong drying remedies have a burning effect on the skin and cause irritation of the skin and may intensify the bleeding. When the ashes of palm leaves are applied alone or mixed with vinegar to a bleeding nose, it will stop the bleeding. The author of *'Al-Qanun'* said, *"Al-Baradii (Papyrus) is effective in stopping bleeding and coating exposed flesh when it is placed on a wound. In ancient Egypt, paper was made of the Baradii, which has a cold, dry nature. Baradii ash is effective in treating oral fungus and infection, hemoptysis (spitting up blood) and also prevents malignant infections from spreading."*

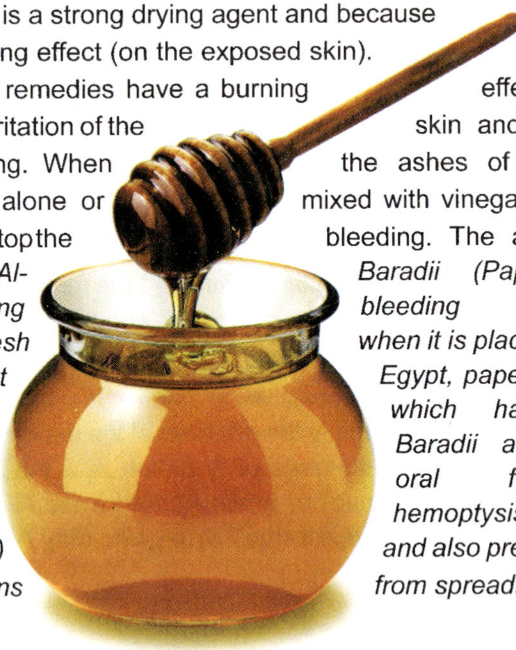

The Prophetís guidance on using honey, cupping and cauterizing as remedies

Al-Bukhari (may Allah have mercy upon him) narrated that the Prophet ﷺ said:

« الشِّفاء في ثَلاثٍ: شَرْبَةِ عَسَلٍ، وشَرْطةِ مِحْجَمٍ، وكَيَّةِ نارٍ. وأنا أنْهَى أُمَّتي عنِ الكَيِّ » (البخاري : ٥٦٨٠)

``There is cure in three substances, a drink of honey, a slash with a knife used for cupping and cauterizing by fire. I forbid my nation from cauterizing by fire."

Abu `Abdullah Al-Maziri (may Allah have mercy upon him) said,

"Conditions caused by the accumulation of certain substances in excess in the body (plethoric conditions) are either sanguineous (bloody), bilious, phlegmy, or melancholic. Curing sanguineous plethora entails extracting the blood. If plethora is from the other three types of substances, its cure is in softening the stool as warranted for each disease. The Prophet ﷺ has indicated that honey is used as a laxative and that cupping is used to extract [septic] blood. Some people said that when the slash by a cupping knife does not work, the last resort is branding by fire (cauterizing). The Prophet ﷺ mentioned branding by fire as a last resort when the body has a strong resistance against medicine, rendering it ineffective. The Prophet ﷺ then said: *"I forbid my Ummah (nation) from branding by fire (cauterizing),"* and in another narration: *"I do not like to be branded by fire."* Cauterizing by fire should be the last resort and only used in case of extreme necessity because of the intense pain it causes, which is unwarranted if it is used to remove a lesser pain."

Some doctors have said that diseases related to the temperament are either material or non-material. The material types are either cold, hot, wet or dry or a combination of these conditions. The four conditions, hotness and coldness are said to be 'effected', while the other two, wetness and dryness, are usually 'affected'. When one of the two effective temperaments is stronger than the other, it is usually accompanied by one of the affected temperaments.

Temperamental ailments are usually caused by whichever effective condition is dominant, hotness or coldness. The Prophet's statement directs us to the origin of ailments, whether hotness and coldness. If the ailment is hot, the cure entails extracting the blood by cupping or puncturing the veins, both of which help extract the septic matter, cooling the temperament. If the ailment is cold, we treat it with heat, such as by taking honey. If we need to extract the cold material that has caused the ailment, honey also helps in this case because it leads the various substances to maturity along with its other qualities of cleansing, softening, soothing and purging the affected organs. In this case, the septic material will be gently extracted while saving the body the annoyance of using strong laxatives.

Physical ailments are either acute (which do not need cauterization because they are quickly neutralized), or chronic ailments, for which cauterizing the proper organ is the best remedy after extracting the septic substances. Chronic diseases usually result from thick, cold septic substances residing in the affected organ, ailing it, spoiling its constitution and, thereby, inflaming the parts of the body that are directly connected to the affected organ. In such cases, cauterizing should be used to dissipate and extract the septic substances in the affected organ with fire.

The *Hadith* explains treatments for all types of physical ailments, just as we learned the method of treating all simple ailments (accompanied by fever) from the *Hadith*,

إِنَّ شِدَّةَ الْحُمَّى مِنْ فَيْحِ جَهَنَّمَ، فَأَبْرِدُوهَا بِالْمَاءِ (البخاري: ١٤٤)

"The heat of fever is from the breath of Hell Fire; cool it with water."

Cupping

As for cupping, Ibn Majah (may Allah have mercy upon him) narrated in his *Sunan* that the Messenger of Allah ﷺ said:

مَا مَرَرْتُ ليلةَ أُسرِيَ بِي بمَلأٍ، إلا قالوا: يا محمد مُر أمَّتَك بالحِجامة

(ابن ماجه: ٣٤٧٩ وصححه الألباني)

"During the night of Isra' (the overnight journey from Makkah to Jerusalem and then to the heavens), every company (of angels) that I passed by would say, 'O Muhammad! Order your nation to use cupping.'"

Also, in the *Sahihayn* it is narrated that the Prophet ﷺ once had his blood cupped (medically) and paid the person who applied the cupping.

Further, in the *Sahihayn* it is narrated,

Abu Taybah رَضِيَ الله عَنْهُ cupped Allah's Messenger ﷺ, who then ordered that Abu Taybah رَضِيَ الله عَنْهُ be paid one *Sa'* (a measure pertaining to food) of dates and ordered his masters to reduce his tax (as he was a slave and had to pay a tax to them). The Prophet ﷺ then said:

« خيرُ مَا تدَاوَيْتم بِه الحِجَامة » (البخاري: ٢١٠٢)

"Cupping is among your best remedies."

The benefits of cupping include cleansing the exterior parts of the body more than puncturing the veins. Venesection, or puncturing the veins, is better when used to extract blood from the internal parts of the body. Cupping entails removing blood from various areas of the skin.

The use of either cupping or puncturing the veins depends on the time of year, the location, the age and physical state of the ailing person. For instance, cupping is more beneficial than puncturing the veins in warm areas, warm weather and in hot tempered people, whose blood is near maturity (with respect to the septic substances in the blood). In this case, the septic, maturing blood will collect near the skin. Cupping extracts the septic blood more efficiently than puncturing the veins. This is why using cupping for children and those who cannot bear puncturing the veins, since it is better and more beneficial.

Doctors affirm that cupping is preferred in the middle of the month or soon after, especially in the last quarter in the month. In the beginning of the month, the blood will have already become irritated (thus carrying septic materials that need to be cupped). At the end of the month, the blood is considered to be idle, unlike the middle and last quarter of the month when the blood is agitated and sufficiently produced.

The author of *'Al-Qanun'* said, *"Cupping is not preferred at the beginning of the month, because the body's various humors will not be agitated then, nor is it preferred at the end of the month, because by then the humors would have decreased. Cupping is preferred in the middle of the month when the substances (of the constitution, or condition) accumulate and become agitated."*

It was reported that the Prophet ﷺ said:

« خيرُ مَا تدَاوَيْتم بِه الحِجَامة » (البخاري: ٥٦٩٦)

``Cupping and puncturing the veins are your best remedies."

This *Hadith* is directed at the people of Hijaz and warm areas in general, for their blood is delicate and circulates closer to the surface of the skin, while the pores on their skin are open wide and their strength weakens (i.e., during summer). Puncturing the veins is harmful for them. Puncturing of each of the veins usually has a special benefit. For instance, puncturing of the basilic vein (the large vein running on the inner side of the upper arm) is useful against the heat of the liver and spleen and various blood-related tumors in these two organs. It is also useful for tumors of the lungs (emphysema), arterial pulsation, pleurisy and all blood-related diseases of veins in the lower part of the knee to the hip.

Puncturing of the median vein helps against the various swellings that appear throughout the entire body, especially when the swelling is blood-related, and contains contaminated blood in general. In addition, puncturing of the vein in the arm helps against the ailments in the head and neck that result from excessive amounts of blood or from septic blood. Puncturing of the jugular vein helps against the ailments of the spleen, asthma, thoracic cavity and forehead pain.

Cupping the upper section of the back helps against the aches of the shoulder and the throat. Further, cupping the two jugular veins helps against the ailments of the head, face, teeth, ears, eyes, nose and throat, if these ailments are caused by excessive volume of blood, contaminated blood or both.

Anas رَضِيَ الله عَنْهُ said,

« كَانَ رَسُولُ الله صلى الله عليه وسلم يَحْتَجِمُ فِي الأَخْدَعَيْنِ والكَاهل »

(أحمد ٣/ ١٩٢ وإسناده صحيح كما في تحقيق المسند-أبو داود: ٣٨٦٠ وصححه الألباني)

*``The Messenger of Allah ﷺ used to apply cupping on the two jugular veins and the upper part of the back.`` [Abu Dawud, At-*Tirmidhi, *Ibn Majah, Ahmad and Al-Hakim].*

``The Messenger of Allah ﷺ used to apply cupping on three areas: his upper back area and the two jugular veins." [Al-Bukhari and Muslim].

It is also narrated in the *Sahih* that the Prophet ﷺ used cupping on his head when he was in a state of *Ihram* (sacral state for *Hajj* or *Umrah*) due to a headache.

In addition, Abu Dawud (may Allah have mercy upon him) narrated that Jabir رَضِيَ الله عَنْهُ said that the Prophet ﷺ used cupping on his hip because of the effects of an injury that he suffered from.

Doctors have conflicting opinions regarding cupping on the nape cavity.

Some doctors approve of this form of cupping, saying that it helps against exophthalmos (abnormal protrusion of the eyeballs), heaviness in the eyebrows and the eyelids and against infections of the eyelid.

A *Hadith* states:

«عَلَيْكُم بالحِجَامَة في جَوْزَةِ القَمَحْدُوَة، فإنَّهَا شِفاءٌ مِن اثْنَين وسَبْعِينَ داءً»

(مجمع الزوائد: ٥/ ٩٤ وقال: رواه الطبراني ورجاله ثقات)

``Use cupping on the nape cavity, for it cures seventy two kinds of ailments."

Further, it was narrated that when Ahmad bin Hanbal (may Allah have mercy upon him) needed cupping on the nape cavity, he did it on the two sides of the nape but not on the cavity itself.

The author of *'Al-Qanun'* also disliked cupping the cavity of the nape saying, *``It causes forgetfulness just as our Prophet Muhammad ﷺ has stated. This is because the back of the brain is the location of the area that controls memory and cupping it affects that power."*

Other people did not approve of his opinion, saying that the *Hadith* that he referred to is not authentic. They said that even if the *Hadith* is authentic, cupping weakens the brain if cupping is done without a physical condition or ailment that warrants it. When warranted, cupping the nape cavity is medically beneficial in countering the pressure of blood on the cavity. Authentic narrations have stated that the Prophet ﷺ used cupping in many areas on the back of his neck and in other areas of his body, as much as was required.

Cupping under the chin helps against toothache, face ailments and throat infections when used at the proper time

Cupping under the chin also cleanses and purifies the head and the jaws. Further, cupping on top of the foot substitutes for the puncturing of the saphenous vein, which is a vein on the heel. This kind of cupping also helps against the ulcers that occur on the thighs and legs, the interruption of monthly periods and skin irritation on the testicles.

Cupping on the lower part of the chest helps against spots, sores and fungal infections on the thigh. It also helps against gout, hemorrhoids, elephantiasis and itchiness on the back.

When is cupping preferred

Anas رَضِيَ الله عَنْهُ related from the Prophet ﷺ that he said:

«كَانَ رَسول الله صَلَّى الله عليه وسلم يَحْتَجِمُ في الأخدَعَين والكَاهل؛ وَكَانَ يَحتَجِم لِسَبعة عَشر، وَتسعَة عَشر، وَفي إحدى وَعِشرين» (الترمذي: ٢٠٥١ وصححه الألباني)

``The Messenger of Allah (ﷺ) used to be cupped on the jugular veins and the upper part of the back on the seventeenth, nineteenth or twenty-first (day of the month)." (At-Tirmidhi)

Anas رَضِيَ الله عَنْهُ related from the Prophet ﷺ that he said:

« مَن أراد الحجَامة فَلْيَتَحَرَّ سَبْعةَ عشرَ، أَو تسعةَ عَشرَ، أو إحدى وعِشْرين، لاَ يتبَيَّغْ بأَحَدِكم الدم، فيقتله» (ابن ماجه:٣٤٨٦ وصححه الألباني)

``Those who intend to have cupping let them do that on the seventeenth, nineteenth or twenty-first (of the month), to prevent the septic blood from causing death to one of you." (Ibn Majah)

Abu Dawud narrated that Abu Hurairah رَضِيَ الله عَنْهُ related from the Prophet ﷺ that he said:

« مَن احتجم لِسبْعَ عشرةَ، أو تسعَ عشرةَ، أو إحدى وعشرين كانت شِفاءً من كلِّ داءٍ» (أبو داؤد: ٣٨٦١ وصححه الألباني)

``Those who have cupping on the seventeenth, nineteenth or twenty-first will be cured from every disease."

``Every disease" mentioned in the *Hadith* means the blood-related diseases. [Both of the last two *Ahadith* are weak].

These *Ahadith* conform to the position taken by doctors that cupping is preferred in the latter half of the month and the third quarter, rather than the beginning or the end of the month. However, if cupping is necessary, it will be useful during any part of the month including the beginning and the end. It was reported that Imam Ahmad bin Hanbal (may Allah have mercy upon him), used to practice cupping during any part of the month when the contaminated blood became agitated.

The author of *'Al-Qanun'* said, *"Cupping is preferred during the day, the second or the third hour and after one takes a bath. When warranted, one should take a bath then rest for an hour or so and then use cupping."* Cupping is not preferred when the stomach is full, for it might cause various ailments, especially after taking a heavy meal.

It is said that cupping on an empty stomach is a cure, and when one's stomach is full is a disease, and when it is done on the seventeenth [of the month] it becomes a remedy. Choosing the best time for cupping preserves good health and helps prevent harm from occurring to the body. However, when the illness intensifies, cupping becomes warranted and is required whatever the circumstances, for the Prophet ﷺ said:

« لا يَتَبَيَّغْ بأحدِكم الدمُ، فيقتُلَهُ » (ابن ماجه :٣٤٨٦ وصححه الألباني)

``So that the septic blood does not cause death to one of you."

We have stated before that Imam Ahmad (may Allah have mercy upon him) used to use cupping during any time of the month if cupping was medically warranted.

Al-Khallal said that Imam Ahmad (may Allah have mercy upon him) was asked about the days when cupping is not preferred, and he said, `` *As for the best days of the week to undergo cupping: Wednesday and Saturday.*" Al-Khallal also narrated that Imam Ahmad (may Allah have mercy upon him) was once asked about the days when cupping is disliked and he answered, *``Saturday and Wednesday, and also Friday, as was reported."* [However, all the *Ahadith* that state the time when cupping is either preferred or disliked are weak, according to the scholars of *Hadith*].

The *Ahadith* we mentioned previously state that seeking the cure, including cupping, is preferred. Cupping is also done in the part of the body that most needs it. Those who have assumed *Ihram* are allowed o use cupping, even if it involves cutting some hair and they do not ave to pay a penalty. Further, it is allowed for those who are fasting to ıse cupping as Al-Bukhari, may Allah have mercy upon him, narrated hat the Messenger of Allah ﷺ used cupping while he was fasting.

There are several *Ahadith* that state that cupping breaks the fast. The only *Hadith* that appears to contradict this ruling is the *Hadith* that he Prophet ﷺ had cupping while fasting. In this case, for the *Hadith* to nean that cupping does not break the fast, it should satisfy one of the ollowing four conditions:

First: Fasting should have been made obligatory by the time the ncident in the *Hadith* [narrated by Al-Bukhari above] occurred.

Second: It should be proven that the Prophet ﷺ was not traveling when he had cupping].

Third: It should be proved that the Prophet ﷺ was not suffering from an illness that warranted cupping.

Fourth: It should be proved that this *Hadith* came after the Prophet ﷺ said: *"Those undergoing cupping and those who do it have both broken their fast."*

If these four conditions are satisfied, only then can we say that cupping does not break the fast relying on the *Hadith* [that the Prophet ﷺ had cupping when he was fasting]. Otherwise, the fast mentioned in the *Hadith* might have been a voluntary fast that one is allowed to break when cupping is warranted. Or it could have occurred during *Ramadhan* but while the Prophet ﷺ was traveling. Or, the *Hadith* could be talking about a compulsory fast during *Ramadhan* but that it was necessary to have cupping due to an illness. Or, cupping could have been done during *Ramadhan* and without a necessity that warrants it, but before the Prophet ﷺ issued his statement that cupping breaks the fast of those involved in it. There is no proof that any of the four conditions we mentioned above were satisfied, so how about all four of them? [That is why Ibn Al-Qayyim, may Allah have mercy upon him,

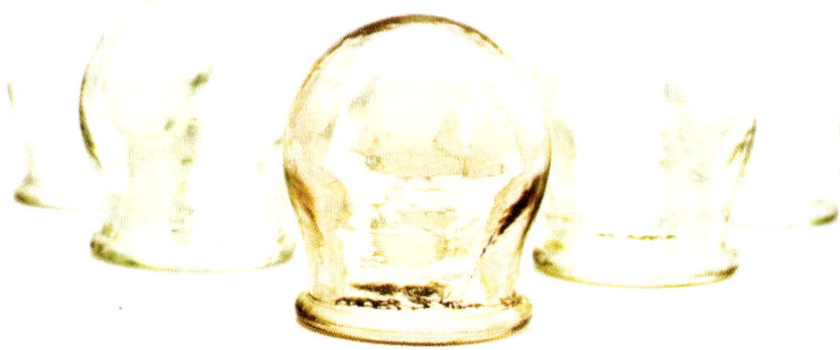

asserts that cupping breaks the fast of those who are doing it and those who are having it done].

The *Hadith* also proves that one is permitted to hire a doctor for a certain purpose and then pay him for his services without a service contract.

The *Hadith* [that the Prophet ﷺ paid the person who performed cupping for him] also indicates that some people are allowed to make cupping their profession. The Prophet ﷺ gave the man who performed cupping some money and that person spent that money on his necessities. Furthermore, cupping is similar to garlic and onion in that they are described as being impure. But we are still allowed to use them.

Finally, the *Hadith* proves that one is allowed to collect reasonable taxes from his slave and that the slave is allowed to use whatever is left after paying the tax. Otherwise, if the master is going to take all the money anyway, it will not be called a tax anymore! Therefore, whatever is left with the slave beyond the required tax is his property and he can do whatever he wishes with it.

The Prophetís guidance regarding cauterization and puncturing of the veins

Jabir bin `Abdullah رَضِيَ الله عَنْهُ narrated that the Prophet ﷺ once sent a doctor to Ubay bin Ka`b رَضِيَ الله عَنْهُ and that the doctor used puncturing on one of Ubay's veins and then cauterized the wound." (Al-Bukhari)

When Sa`d bin Mu`adh رَضِيَ الله عَنْهُ was injured in his medial arm vein, the Prophet ﷺ had it cauterized and then cauterized again when the wound became swollen. In another narration of this *Hadith*, the Prophet ﷺ cauterized Sa`d bin Mu'adh رَضِيَ الله عَنْهُ in his medial arm vein using the tip of an arrow. Afterwards, Sa`d bin Mu'adh رَضِيَ الله عَنْهُ, or someone else, cauterized the wound again.

Another narration states that one of the Ansar (Helpers) was injured in his medial arm vein and the Prophet ﷺ ordered that he be cauterized. [These *Ahadith* are narrated by Muslim, Abu Dawud, and others].

Abu `Ubayd رَضِيَ الله عَنْهُ also narrated that a man, who was prescribed cauterization, was brought to the Prophet ﷺ and the Prophet ﷺ ordered that he be cauterized. Then hot stones were applied on the wound to close it.

Jabir رَضِيَ الله عَنْهُ narrated that the Prophet ﷺ once cauterized him in his medial arm vein.

Al-Bukhari (may Allah have mercy upon him) narrated that Anas رَضِيَ الله عَنْهُ said that he was once cauterized because he was complaining from pleurisy while the Prophet ﷺ was still alive. At-Tirmidhi (may Allah have mercy upon him) also narrated that Anas رَضِيَ الله عَنْهُ said, ``*The Prophet ﷺ cauterized As`ad bin Zurarah when he came down with a septic finger."*

We have mentioned that the Prophet ﷺ said in the *Hadith* narrated by Al-Bukhari and Muslim:

«وَمَا أُحِبُّ أن أَكتوِيَ » (البخاري:٥٦٨٣)

``I do not like to be cauterized."

« وأنا أنْهَى أمّتي عن الكَيِّ » (البخاري:٥٦٨٠)

``I forbid cauterizing for my nation."

Further, it was narrated [by At-Tirmidhi, Abu Dawud and Ahmac that one of the Companions said that the Prophet ﷺ has disallowe cauterizing, *``But we were tested (i.e., with various ailments) and we di have cauterization, so we neither were successful nor did we acquir an advantage."*

Al-Khattabi (may Allah have mercy upon him) commented, *``Th Prophet ﷺ only cauterized Sa`d* رَضِيَ الله عَنْهُ *to stop the bleedinc because he feared that bleeding would not stop until Sa`d* ضِيَ الله عَنْهُ *died."* Cauterization is usually used in drastic cases, such as when hand or a leg is amputated. As for prohibiting cauterizing, it might b specifically directed at whoever is seeking a cure with it (not to close a open wound). In early times, the people used to superstitiously believ that whoever did not have cauterization would certainly die and thi is why the Prophet ﷺ disallowed it. It was also said that the Prophe ﷺ disallowed `Imran bin Husayn رَضِيَ الله عَنْهُ in particular from usin cauterization because he was suffering from a sore in a delicate place That is why the prohibition could be specific to cases where cauterizin is dangerous. And Allah knows best.

Further Ibn Qutaybah (may Allah have mercy upon him) said tha cauterizing is of two types. The first type entails a healthy person usin cauterization to fend off illness and it is this type that is referred to b the statement: *"Whoever reverts to cauterizing will not have practice Tawakkul (depending on Allah The Almighty),"* as such people see to fend off whatever is destined for them in the future. The secon type entails cauterizing infected wounds and amputated limbs, an cauterization is effective in these cases. As for the type of cauterizatio that might or might not work, it is apparently disliked.

There is a *Hadith* narrated in the *Sahihayn* [Al-Bukhari and Muslim about the seventy thousand Muslims who will enter Paradise withou reckoning, describing them as:

((الذينَ لاَ يَسْتَرْقُونَ، ولاَ يكتَوُونَ، ولا يتطيَّرُونَ؛ وعَلَى ربِّهم يتوكَّلُونَ))

(البخاري: ٥٧٠٥)

*``They are those who do not seek prayer formulas (Ruqyah literally incantations), nor cauterization, nor are they superstitious, and they depend on their Lord (for each and everything)." [Also narrated by At-*Tirmidhi*, An-Nasa'i and Ahmad].*

In short, the *Ahadith* that discussed the subject of cauterization fall under four categories: practicing it, disliking it, praising those who do not revert to it and disallowing it. There is no contradiction between these categories. When the Prophet ﷺ had someone cauterized, he indicated that practicing it is allowed. Further, the Prophet's disliking cauterization for his *Ummah* (nation) does not indicate that it is prohibited. In addition, the Prophet's praising those who avoid cauterization indicates that avoiding it is better. Finally, disallowing cauterization can either be explained that in general, cauterization is disliked, or that it is directed at those who revert to cauterizing to fend off a future illness. And Allah knows best.(1)

(1) Editor's note : *Ruqyah* (incantations / prayer formulas) and cauterization were practiced in pre-Islamic times based on superstitions, it was these practices that the Prophet stopped. The benefit in these practices was rehabilitated by Islam and they were practiced only when necessary in the correct way according to Islamic law, without superstition. *Ruqyah* , Islamic prayer formula, is recited for a certain number of times according to the specific *Ruqyah* or Islamic prayer formula. The one reciting the Islamic prayer formula will spit (without saliva) after each recitation on the target of the prayer formula. This is a standard Islamic practice to preserve spiritual and physical health.

There is another point that needs to be clarified and that concerns the word prayer. What we call prayer in English has two different words to describe it in Arabic. *Salat* , the formal prayer with specific movements and *Du`a*, the informal prayer in which one asks the Creator for what they want in their own words or according to formulas set by the Prophet or the *Qur'an*. One of the pillars of Islam is the five daily prayers. This is a formalized system of praying that has specific movements and times. In Arabic this is called *Salat* . The other form of prayer, when we ask Allah for anything, in our own words or in prayer formulas set by the Prophet or by the *Qur'n*, is called *Du`a* . This form of prayer is sometimes referred to as supplication in English, which is a very good word to describe this form of prayer. The only problem with translating *Du`a* as ``supplication" is that the word ``supplication" is very formal and rarely used in verbal communication. *Du`a* is used constantly throughout the day. Any English speaking person who is continuously calling on God, will describe what they are doing as praying, which is the simple common way to describe this act. When we call *Ruqyah* (literally incantations) Islamic prayer formulas, we are using the word prayer in its informal meaning *Du`a* and not the formal meaning *Salat* .

The Prophetís guidance on treating epilepsy and spiritual possession[1]

In the *Sahihayn* it is narrated that `Ata bin Raba`h (may Allah have mercy upon him) said,

``Ibn `Abbas رَضِيَ الله عَنْهما said to me, `Should I tell you about a woman from among the people of Paradise?' I said, `Yes.' He said, `The black woman, who came to the Prophet ﷺ and said, 'I suffer epileptic fits during which I inadvertently become exposed. So invoke Allah The Almighty on my behalf.'

He said:

(إنْ شِئْتِ صَبَرْتِ ولكِ الجُنَّةُ؛ وإن شئتِ دعوتُ اللهَ لكِ أن يعافِيَكِ) (البخاري: ٥٦٥٢)

`If you wish, be patient and you will acquire Paradise; and if you wish, I will supplicate to Allah to cure you.'

She said, `Rather, I will observe patience.' She then said, 'I keep taking off my clothes during these fits, so supplicate to Allah for me that I do not do so. The Prophet ﷺ supplicated (to Allah) on her behalf.'''

Epilepsy is of two kinds, one that results from negative forces and the second type is physical that results from bad mixtures (chemical and material imbalance). The doctors often talk about the second type and explain its causes and treatment.

As for the epilepsy that results from negative forces, the best doctors and the wisest medical practitioners among them affirm that it exists. They also confirm that this type of disease is treated by the support of righteous, exalted souls so that they neutralize the effect of the evil and render its efforts harmless.

When Hippocrates explained the cures for epilepsy he stated that,

(1) Editor's note : The name of epilepsy in Arabic is *Sar*, it is derived from the word *Sara'a* meaning to knock down, strike down, or bring to the ground. This is the classic symptom of epilepsy and thus in Arabic its name was derived from it. Possession by evil spirits or jinn, which requires exorcism for its cure, has the same classic symptom and was called by the same name. Epilepsy in Arabic therefore is described as being of two types, the classic physical epilepsy and spiritual possession.

``These cures are effective in treating the epilepsy that results from chemical and material causes. As for the epilepsy that results from negative forces, these remedies [that he explained and detailed] do not cure it."

As for the most ignorant and immoral doctors, and those who consider heresy a virtue, they deny the type [of epilepsy] that occurs by negative forces and deny that it has any effect on the body. They have only ignorance to support them, because the medical authorities cannot actually disprove the epilepsy that is caused by these negative forces.

Fact and experience assert and prove the existence of this type of epilepsy. That is why when the doctors explain the reason behind epilepsy as being natural or physical, their statement is true regarding some types of epilepsy but not all of them.(1)

The doctors of old used to call epilepsy, `The divine disease', stating that it is caused by negative forces. On the other hand, Galinus and other doctors misinterpreted the term divine ailment, saying, *``They called it divine because it attacks the head and thus causes harm to the apparent divine organ where the brain resides."* This explanation, however, resulted from their ignorance of the soul and its effects.

As for the heretical doctors, they only confirm the kind of epilepsy that results from physical causes. Whoever has a sound mind and good knowledge of the soul and its effect [on the body], will laugh at the ignorance shown by these doctors and at their weak minds.

Curing the type of epilepsy caused by negative forces has two components: One which involves the person afflicted with epilepsy, and another that involves those who treat them.

The part that the person afflicted with epilepsy plays in his treatment involves strengthening his heart and being sincere in repentance to the Creator from the negative forces and seeking sincere refuge with Him both by heart and tongue. This is a type of warfare that the person

(1) Editor's note : The author is referring to a type of spiritual possession.

afflicted with epilepsy engages in against evil. To defeat the enemy, warfare requires the warrior to acquire beneficial, suitable weapons and to have a strong arm. When one of these two elements does not exist, the effort will not be very effective. The situation becomes more difficult when the person is missing both essential requirements, in this case, the heart will be lacking *Tawhid* (Islamic Monotheism), *Tawakkul* (trusting in Allah The Almighty), *Taqwa* (righteousness), and *Tawajjuh* (awareness of the Presence of Allah The Almighty), and the person does not have sufficient material armament.

The second part of the treatment of epilepsy involves the person who is treating the ailment and who is also required to have the same essential weapons mentioned above. When these weapons are ready, one sometimes merely needs to say (to the evil spirit), *`Get out of him,'* or, *'In the Name of Allah,'* or, *`There is no power nor strength except with Allah.'*

The Prophet ﷺ used to say in such cases:

« اُخْرُجْ عَدُوَّ اللهِ؛ أَنَا رَسُولُ اللهِ »

(أحمد ٤/ ١٧١ وفيه انقطاع وفي الباب عنده عن ابن عباس فلعله يتقوى به ١/ ٢٥٤)

``O enemy of Allah, depart! I am the Messenger of Allah."

I once witnessed our Shaykh (Ibn Taymiyyah, the renowned Imam of Islam, may Allah have mercy upon him) send someone to speak to an evil spirit that had possessed a person, saying, *``The Shaykh says this to you: Get out of this body for you are not allowed therein!``* The person afflicted with epilepsy (possession) then woke up from his seizure. Sometimes, our Shaykh would even speak to the evil spirit directly, or would use physical punishment to repel the rebellious evil spirit. When the patient would wake up, he would not feel any pain, as we have ourselves witnessed on numerous occasions. The Shaykh would sometimes read the following *Ayah* (verse), in the ear of the person afflicted with epilepsy (possession):

﴿ أَفَحَسِبْتُمْ أَنَّمَا خَلَقْنَٰكُمْ عَبَثًا وَأَنَّكُمْ إِلَيْنَا لَا تُرْجَعُونَ ﴾

``Did not think that We had created you in play (without any purpose), and that you would not be brought back to Us?" (Qur'an, 23:115)

The Shaykh once told me that he read this *Ayah* (verse), in the ear of the person afflicted with epilepsy and that the evil spirit that possessed him answered by saying, *`Indeed!'* extending her voice (mocking the Qur'an). So the Shaykh, may Allah have mercy upon him, said,

``So I took a stick and beat the sick person on his neck with it until my hands became tired. Those present did not doubt that the patient would die from this severe beating.

While beating the patient, the she-devil said, *'I love this person.'* I said, *`But he does not love you.'* She said, *'I want to accompany him to perform Hajj.'* I told her, *`He does not want to go to Hajj with you.'* She said, *'I will leave him in your honor.'* I said, *`No, but as an obedience to Allah and His Messenger.'* She said, *`Then, I will leave him alone.'*

The patient then woke up and started looking around, saying, *`What brought me to the presence of the Shaykh?'* They asked him, *`What about the beating you took?'* He said, *`Why would the Shaykh beat me while I have not done anything wrong?'* He had no idea that he had been beaten.'"

Further, the Shaykh used to recite *Ayat Al-Kursi* [Qur'an, 2:255] and would order those who suffer from and those who cure epilepsy (possession) to recite it along with the last two chapters of the Qur'an [113 and 114].

In general, no one can deny the type of epilepsy that is caused by negative forces except those who have little knowledge and comprehension. We should also state that the majority of those afflicted by the touch of evil spirits are themselves in error due to weak faith and errant hearts and tongues that do not remember Allah The Almighty, they fail to seek refuge with Him and they fail to use Prophetic guidance, (supplications and remedies). The evil spirits find the people that are vulnerable and take advantage of them.

If the truth were laid bare, we would discover that the majority of humankind is under the influence of negative forces which guides the people according to their evil wishes. The people are unable to set themselves free from this control or even oppose it. Most people suffer from this common type of possession ([a kind of] epilepsy), from which the afflicted person cannot wake up. Unless the veil that obstructs their sight is removed, they will not realize that it is they who are actually afflicted by epilepsy. We seek Allah Alone for His help.

Curing (epilepsy) possession that results from the touch of evil requires the cooperation of a sound mind and sincere faith in what has been sent down to the Prophets عليهم السلام . Then one would act as if both Heaven and Hell are right in front of his eyes and heart. They would remember that the people of this earthly life suffer calamities and trials that come down on their homes just as the rain does, all the while being unaware of what is going on around them.

The epilepsy that evil causes is truly severe, but since it touches so many people and is so common, people are no longer surprised by it. Since they are so many afflicted by it, it is strange to see someone who is not touched by it.

When Allah The Almighty wills that a certain slave should acquire what is good for him, that slave will wake up from these fits of epilepsy and will realize that the offspring of this worldly life are suffering from [a kind of] epilepsy. He will discover that some of them have surrendered to insanity and that some of them might briefly recover from a bout, to fall back into another bout soon after. Some of them awaken from a bout and act like sane people, but when he falls into another bout, he acts confused. [This is the state of those who do not have the correct faith.]

Epilepsy that results from physical causes

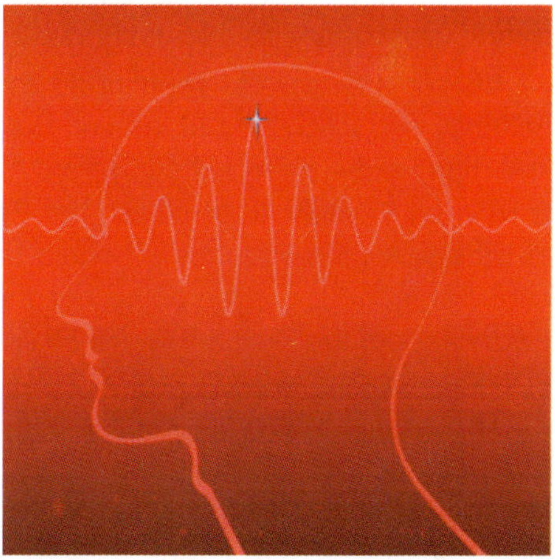

This type of epilepsy alters the constitution and is accompanied by spasms that prevent the limbs from functioning normally or perform normal movements. The epilepsy related to the physical body or constitution occurs due to the accumulation of thick, viscous substances near the brain that partially obstructs the cerebral cavities. In this case, the area of the brain responsible for the senses and the various movements is impeded, and accordingly, the organs (including limbs) of the body suffer from the same condition.

There are other causes for this type of epilepsy, such as the accumulation of thick flatulence that impedes the soul in some manner, or a viscous vapor accumulates in an organ of the body and ascends to the brain, or from an acute ailment. The brain suffers from spasms due to fighting the harmful substances that are affecting the brain, and accordingly, the various organs of the body suffer from spasms. The person will not be able to stand up straight for very long, he or she will fall down and foam accumulates in and around the mouth.

This type of epilepsy causes intense pain during seizures. It is also a chronic illness that is hard to cure and that remains for many years, especially if the person afflicted by it is more than twenty-five years old, who repeatedly falls into epileptic fits. Hippocrates said that epilepsy remains with such people until they die.

As for the woman mentioned in the *Hadith* who suffered from epilepsy and who used to take off her clothes because of epileptic fits, she might have been suffering from the physical type of epilepsy. That is why the Prophet ﷺ promised her Paradise if she observes patience, or otherwise, the Prophet ﷺ would have asked Allah The Almighty to cure her without guaranteeing her that she will be cured. She chose Paradise, but the Prophet ﷺ asked Allah The Almighty on her behalf to prevent her from becoming exposed during these fits.

The *Hadith* indicates that it is allowed for, Muslims to forgo the use of a remedy. Furthermore, the *Hadith* indicates that the cure of the soul is exclusively tied to invoking Allah The Almighty and turning to Him sincerely, and that this type of medicine has such profound effects on the human body that no regular medicine prepared by any doctor could ever compare to it. We have tried this medicine on numerous occasions [and witnessed its success].

The best medical authorities confirm the fact that the psyche has an effective role in curing disease. The medical profession suffers from some ignorant, heretic doctors who do not do service to their profession.

As we have stated, it appears that the woman mentioned in the *Hadith* suffered from the epilepsy that is caused by a physical condition (chemical imbalances). Yet, she might have been suffering from the type that is caused by evil negative forces. We stated that the Messenger of Allah ﷺ gave her the choice to observe patience and then acquire Paradise or that he would invoke Allah The Almighty to cure her. She chose the first option but asked to be relieved from discarding her clothes because of the epileptic fits.

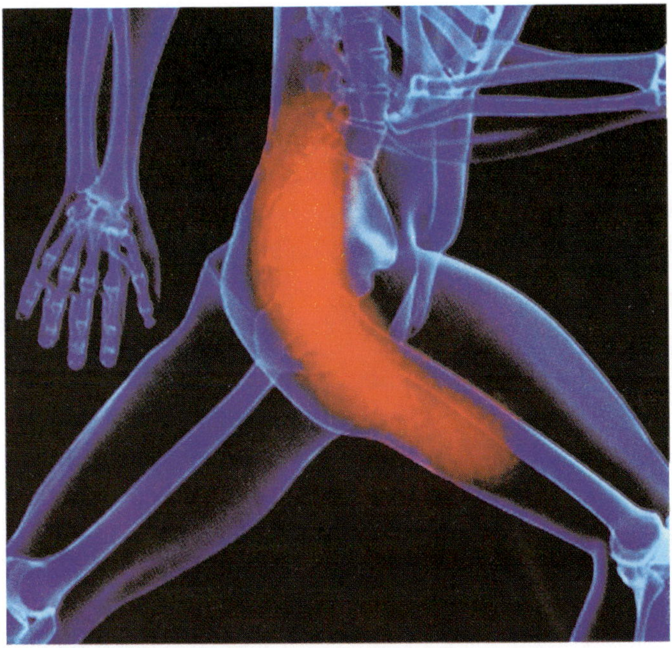

The Prophetís guidance on curing sciatica

Ibn Majah narrated in his *Sunan* (collection of Hadith) that Anas bin Malik رَضِيَ الله عَنْهُ said, *"I heard the Messenger of Allah ﷺ saying:*

« دواءُ عِرقِ النَّسَا: أَلْيَةُ شاةٍ أعْرابِيّةٍ تُذابُ، ثمَّ تُجَزَّأُ ثلاثةَ أجزاءٍ ثُمّ تُشرَبُ على الرِّيق: في كُلِّ يومٍ جزءٌ » (ابن ماجه وصححه الألباني: ٣٤٦٣)

``The cure for sciatica is [accomplished by] melting the fat from the tail of a nomad's ewe. Then, the fat is divided into three parts and one part per day is drunk on an empty stomach."

Sciatica is an ailment that starts from the hip joint, then descends to the thigh from the backside of the body. Sometimes, sciatica reaches the ankles and the longer the ailment remains, the lower it descends and the weaker the legs and thighs become.

There are two beneficial conclusions in the *Hadith* mentioned, from the medical and linguistic point of view:

Linguistically, the *Hadith* proves that we are allowed to call this ailment *`Irq* (nerve) *Nasa* (sciatic nerve), to the contrary of the opinion of some people. They said that the *Nasa* is the nerve itself and thus the two words together are redundant.

lavender

Answering this claim takes two forms. First, the word *`Irq* (nerve) is more general than the word *Nasa* (sciatic nerve). Hence the term *`Iraq An-Nasa* gives the general and the specific meanings desired.

Second, *Nasa* is an ailment that attacks the nerve and thus the word *Nasa* should be included in the name given to the ailment [as it specifies the area where the nerve is causing pain]. It was reported that the name *`Irq Nasa* is called as such because it makes the people forget (*Nasa*) any other pain. The sciatic nerve starts from the hips until the bottom of the foot from behind the ankles.

The Messenger of Allah ﷺ , as we have noticed in previous *Ahadith*, sometimes used two types of meanings in his expressions. One meaning may be general, for all conditions and people; while the other would be specific, its meaning and indications were specifically directed at some particular people or situation. The *Hadith* in this section is the specific type, it is directed at Arabs and the people of Hijaz in particular, including the Bedouins of those areas. The remedy mentioned in the *Hadith* is the best cure for the people of those areas as *`Irq An-Nasa* is caused by dryness or thick, septic accumulations. The best treatment for this ailment is using a laxative. The fat on the ewe's tail has two qualities: bringing the septic substances to maturity and softening (the stool in this case), both are required to cure*` Irq An-Nasa* .

Moreover, the nomad's ewe has several qualities, such as being small in size, producing lesser excrements and having a soft essence. The nomad's ewe also grazes on beneficial wild plants, such as wormwood and lavender cotton, and so forth. When the ewe feeds on these wild plants, they will mix with and soften the ewe's flesh, especially the fatty tail. Although the ewe's milk carries in it the effective ingredients of the wild plants, the tail has two qualities that the milk does not have, being a laxative and leading the septic substances to maturity [making them ready to be extracted from the body].

We mentioned before that the regular medicines and remedies of different nations and peoples are based on the type of diet that the people are used to. Indians and Bedouins have a simple diet, therefore the do not use complex medicines. As for the Romans and the Greek, they use compound medicines. They all agree, however, that the best treatment for an ailment is a specific diet. Otherwise, the doctors will first prescribe simple and then compound medications, when necessary.

If the diet is simple, simple medications are suitable for the simple ailments. The compound ailments, on the other hand, usually occur due to a complex diet and this is why compound medicines are suitable in those cases. And Allah knows best.

The Prophetís guidance on treating constipation

At-Tirmidhi and Ibn Majah (may Allah have mercy upon them) narrated that the Messenger of Allah ﷺ asked Asma' bint `Umais رَضِيَ الله عَنْها ,

« بماذا كنت تَسْتَمْشِينَ ؟ قالت: بالشُّبْرُم قال: حارٌّ جارٌّ. ثم قالت استَمْشيْتُ بالسَّنا. فقال: لو كان شيءٌ يشفِي من الموتِ لكان السَّنا »

(الترمذي:٢٠٨١ وضعفه الألباني لكن قله في «النسا» المتضد بغيره فهو صحيح لما سيأتي والنظر تحقيق أحمد ٦/ ٣٦٩ فيتقوى به آخر الحديث)

"How do you deal with constipation?" She said, ``By using Shubrum (Euphorbia piteous)." The Prophet ﷺ said: ``(It is) hot and too strong a laxative." She then said, ``I also use Senna," and the Prophet ﷺ replied: ``If there is a cure that prevents death, it would be Senna."

Further, Ibn Majah (may Allah have mercy upon him) narrated that `Abdullah ibn Umm Haram (may Allah be pleased with them both) said that he heard the Messenger of Allah ﷺ saying:

«عليكم بالسَّنا والسَّنُّوت فإن فيهما شِفاءً من كل داء إلاّ السَّامَ. قيل يا رسول الله وما السامُ؟ قال : المَوْتُ»

(ابن ماجه وصححه الألباني:٣٤٥٧)

``Use Senna and Sanoot (cumin), because they cure every disease, except Saam ." He was asked, ``What is Saam ?" He said: `Death'. "

The Prophet ﷺ asked the woman Companion about what she used to treat constipation, meaning what cure she used to help soften

SENNA FLWWER

cumin

the stool, so that the body is able to get rid of its harmful waste.

In another narration of the *Hadith*, the Prophet ﷺ asked Asma' رَضِيَ الله عَنْها about what she used to cure constipation, and she mentioned *Shubrum* (*Euphorbia piteous*), which is the bark of the root of the Euphorbia tree and which is dry and hot in the fourth degree. The best type of *Shubrum* is the one reddish in color, which is soft and feels like wrapped skin. *Shubrum* is among the medications that doctors do not advise people to use because it is a very strong laxative. In the *Hadith*, the Prophet ﷺ described *Shubrum* as being hot and a strong laxative.

Senna is a plant that grows in Al-Hijaz (Western Arabia) and the best kind of it grows in Makkah. Senna is hot and dry in the first degree and it is a good, mild medication that does not cause any side effects. Senna helps against ailments of the bile and black bile and strengthens the heart, which is another good quality that this medication contains.

Senna is useful against melancholic obsession and corporal incisions, relaxes the muscles and improves the hair. It also helps against lice, headache, mange, pustules, rashes and epilepsy. It is better to cook the *Senna* whole and drink three measures of its soup than cooking it crushed. It is also better to cook the *Senna* mixed with violet flowers and red raisins, after removing the seeds.

Ar-Razi said, *"Senna and fumitory help extract mature humors (bodily wastes) and help against leprosy and rashes, when one takes four to seven measures of each remedy."*

As for *Sanoot* (cumin), there is a difference of opinion concerning its

Euphorbia

nature. Umar bin Bakr As-Saksaki for instance, said that *Sanoot* is either honey or butter extract. Another opinion suggests that *Sanoot* is a seed that resembles the *Kammon* (cumin), as Ibn Al-`Arabi has asserted. The fourth and fifth opinions suggest that *Sanoot* is the Persian cumin or fennel, according to Abu Hanifah Ad-Daynoori. The sixth opinion suggests that it is the *Shibitt* (dill), and the seventh opinion suggests that it is the date, according to Abu Bakr bin As-Sunni.

The eighth opinion suggests that it is honey that is placed in butter-skin, according to Abdul-Latif Al-Baghdadi. Some doctors also stated that the last meaning is the most probable. In this case, the *Sanoot* is prepared by blending *Senna* powder with some honey mixed with *ghee*, as this is better than taking the *Senna* by itself. Then one licks the mixture that contains the *Senna*, as in this case the taste of *Senna* will be made milder because of the honey and butter, which will also assist the laxative power of the *Senna*. And Allah knows best.

The Prophetís guidance on treating skin rashes and scabies caused by mites

In the *Sahihayn* it is narrated that Anas رَضِيَ الله عَنْهُ said, *``The Messenger of Allah ﷺ allowed Abdur Rahman bin 'Awf and Az-Zubayr bin Al-'Awwam رَضِيَ الله عَنْهما to wear silk garments because of a skin rash they had."*

In another narration, *``Abdur Rahman bin `Awf and Az-Zubayr bin Al-`Awwam رَضِيَ الله عَنْهما complained to the Prophet ﷺ during a battle that they had mites, and he allowed them to wear silk garments which I saw them wearing."*

There are two areas of interest regarding this Hadith, one in the area of Fiqh (Islamic jurisprudence) and another medical.

In the area of *Fiqh* (Islamic jurisprudence), the *Sunnah* of the Messenger of Allah ﷺ is that wearing silken garments is allowed for women and disallowed for men, except when there is a legitimate need. For instance, [men are allowed to wear silken garments] in cold weather, when one has only a silken garment to wear and when complaining from mange, rashes, mites or lice, as evident by the last *Hadith* .

According to Imam Ahmad and Shafi`i (may Allah have mercy upon them), wearing silken garments is allowed [for men if a necessity warrants it]. The permission given to some Muslims [such as wearing

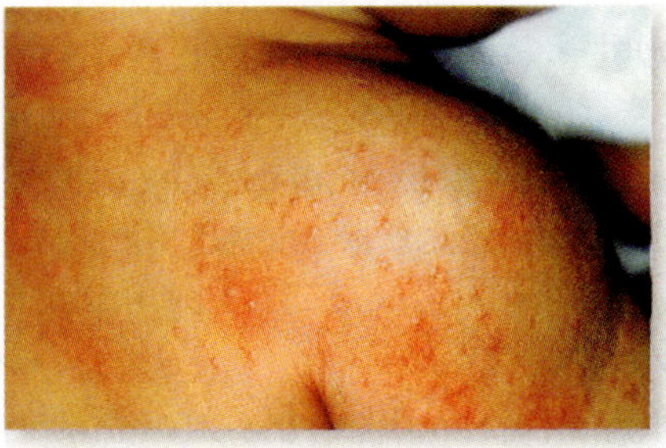

RASHES

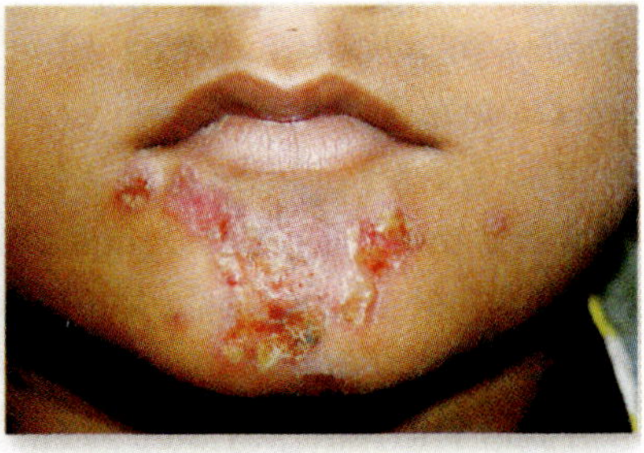

SCABIES

Silken garments are allowed for women and disallowed for men !

silken garments for men in this case] due to special circumstances applies to all those who face similar circumstances.

Several scholars said that the *Ahadith* that disallow silken garments for men apply in general. They said that the *Hadith* (narrated above) might entail a specific permission for only `Abdur-Rahman bin `Awf and Az-Zubayr رَضِيَ الله عَنْهما. They say that it is possible, though, that this permission applies to other Muslims. When there is a probability, adhering to the general text is warranted. This is why some of the narrators of this *Hadith* commented, *``I do not know if the permission applies to whoever comes after them (`Abdur-Rahman bin `Awf and Az-Zubayr)."*

The correct opinion is that the permission is general in its indication and that there is no evidence that it is specific or restricted. Similarly, the Prophet ﷺ once said to Abu Burdah رَضِيَ الله عَنْهُ : *``This permission applies to you and none else after you."*

Allah The Almighty said to His Prophet ﷺ regarding the woman who offered herself in marriage to the Prophet ﷺ :

﴿ خَالِصَةً لَّكَ مِن دُونِ ٱلْمُؤْمِنِينَ ﴾

``*A privilege for you only, not for the (rest of) the believers.*"(Qur'an, 33:50)

Since disallowing wearing silken garments for men is a precautionary measure, it is allowed in certain situations and for a benefit that warrants it. For instance, gazing at women is disallowed as a precautionary measure, but it is allowed when there is a real need. Such is the case with disallowing performing voluntary prayers at certain times [while the sun is rising or setting], to prevent even a hint of resemblance between Muslims and sun worshippers. Yet, in some cases, it is allowed for Muslims to offer voluntary prayers during these times for a real need and benefit. We have explained the cases when wearing silken garments is allowed in our book on this subject, At-Tabiri.

Medically, silk is produced by an animal and it is a remedy. Silk has many benefits, such as soothing and strengthening the heart and helping relieve several of its ailments. Silk also helps against black bile and whatever ailments it might cause. Further, silk strengthens the eyesight when used as eyeliner. Raw silk, which is used in preparing medications and remedies, is hot and dry in the first degree. When silk is used in clothes, it is mild and heats the body. Sometimes it could chill the body.

Ar-Razi said, ``*Silk is hotter than linen, colder than cotton and develops the flesh. Every type of thick cloth weakens the body and hardens the skin.*"

There are three types of clothes: one that brings warmth and also heats the body. Another type of clothes brings warmth but no heat to the body. The third type does not bring warmth or heat. There is no type [of cloth] that brings heat but not warmth to those wearing it. For instance, clothes made of wool and animal hair raise body temperature and bring warmth to the skin. On the other hand, silk, *Kittan* (linen) and cotton garments only bring warmth to the skin. *Kittan* clothes are cold and dry, wool clothes are hot and dry, while cotton garments are moderate. Silken garments are softer and less hot than wool. The author of *'Al-Minhaj'* stated that wearing silk, *``[...]Does not bring as much warmth as cotton, because it is milder."*

Every type of soft, polished cloth heats the body less and is less effective in helping the decomposition process. That is why it is better that this type of clothes is worn during summer and in hot areas.

Since silken garments are neither dry nor thick like the other types of clothes, they help as a treatment for skin rashes that result from dry, thick material. Hence, the Prophet ﷺ allowed Az-Zubair and 'Abdur-Rahman رَضِيَ الله عَنْهما to wear silken garments due to their skin rash. Also, silken garments are the least hospitable to mites or lice, for it is not the best environment where mites live and thrive.

The types of garments that neither elevate the body temperature nor bring warmth are made of iron, lead, wood, sand, and so forth.

If one asks, *``Since silk provides the best type of clothes and the ones considered most suitable for the body, why was it prohibited for men) by the Islamic legislation, which is the most honorable, perfect legislation and which allows the good and pure things and only disallows the impure things?"* We should mention that this is a question that the Muslims have differences of opinion with regard to its answer.

Those who deny that there is wisdom behind the Islamic legislation do not even need to answer this question.

As for those who affirm that there is a wisdom behind the Islamic legislation (who are the majority), say that Islam disallowed silken garments for men so that they observe patience and abandon wearing them for the sake of Allah The Almighty. In this case, they will be rewarded by Allah The Almighty, especially since there are other types of clothes to wear.

Some people say that silk was created for the benefit of women, as is the case with gold. Hence, silk is prohibited for men so that they do not imitate women. Some Muslims say that silk was prohibited because it leads to arrogance and pride. Others say that silk was disallowed because of its softness on the skin that leads to feminine behavior while weakening manhood and masculinity.

Hence, you rarely see a man wearing silken garments who is not affected by its softness by inadvertently imitating feminine behavior and softness, even if he was among the most masculine men. Wearing silken garments will certainly diminish the manly qualities and masculinity, although these qualities will not disappear altogether. As for those who do not comprehend these facts, let them submit to the wise decisions of Allah The Almighty. Finally, we should state that according to the correct opinion, young boys should not be allowed to wear silken garments, because they will acquire feminine behavior.

An-Nasa'i (may Allah have mercy upon him) narrated that the Prophet ﷺ said:

« إن اللهَ أحلّ لإناثِ أُمّتي الحريرَ والذّهبَ، وحَرَّمَه على ذُكُورِها »

(النسائي: ٥٢٦٥ وصححه الألباني)

``Allah has allowed silk and gold for the females of my Ummah (Muslim nation) and disallowed them for the males of my Ummah."

In another narration, the Prophet ﷺ said:

« حُرّم لِباسُ الحَريرِ والذَّهَبِ عَلى ذُكورِ أُمّتي، وأُحِلَّ لإناثِهِم »

(الترمذي وصححه الألباني: ١٧٢٠)

``Wearing silk and gold is disallowed for the males of my nation and allowed for the females."

Al-Bukhari (may Allah have mercy upon him) also narrated that the Messenger of Allah ﷺ disallowed wearing and sitting on silken garments and *Dibaj* (pure silken clothes), and then added: *``It is for them (whoever wears them among men) in this life and for you in the life Hereafter."*

The Prophetís guidance on treating pleurisy

Doctors divide pleurisy into two types: true and false. The first type is an infected growth that appears on the pleura that coats the lungs The second type causes a similar pain and attacks the pleura as a result of thick, congested flatulence between the peritoneum (smooth transparent membrane that lines the abdominal cavity and part of the pelvic region). The pain caused by the false pleurisy is acute while the true pleurisy causes stinging pain.

The author of *'Al-Qanun'* said, ``*Sometimes, the flank (of the body), the peritoneum, chest muscles and ribs and surrounding areas suffer from an extremely painful growth called pleurisy. Sometimes, there could be pain in these same areas of the body not as a result of growth, but as a result of accumulating harmful gases (flatulence), and thus, the people think that it is the first type when in fact it is not.*"

He also said,

``Know that every type of disease that attacks the side or the flank is called Thatul Janb (pleurisy), which is derived from the place where it appears (i.e., the Janb, the flank). That is why every type of pain on the side or flank is called Thatul Janb regardless of the cause of the ailment. This is the meaning of Hippocrates' statement that those suffering from Thatul-Janb will benefit from taking a bath. It is said that his statement includes those who suffer from pleurisy, as well as lung disease, (pulmonary) pains that result from a bad constitution, congested conditions without tumors or fever."

Some doctors said that in Greek, the term 'pleurisy' means the warm growth that appears on the side [of the body] and the tumors of all internal organs. The tumor of any organ is called pleurisy when it is a warm tumor only. Besides, there are five symptoms that accompany true pleurisy: fever, coughing, stinging pain, hard breathing (dyspnea) and pneumonia.

Sea-costus (Indian costus) is used to treat the false pleurisy. When the Indian costus is ground to fine powder, blended with hot oil and then used as an ointment on the affected area, or when the ailing person licks it, it is a good cure for that ailment. In this case, the costus decomposes the septic substances, strengthens the internal organs and opens the obstructions or clogs. Al-Masi'hi said, ``*Costus is hot and dry and constipates, strengthens the internal organs, dissipates the wind, opens the clogs, helps against pleurisy and dries out excess moistures. Costus is also good for the brain and might help against the true pleurisy, if a phlegmy substance has caused it, especially when the illness is weakening. And Allah knows best.*"

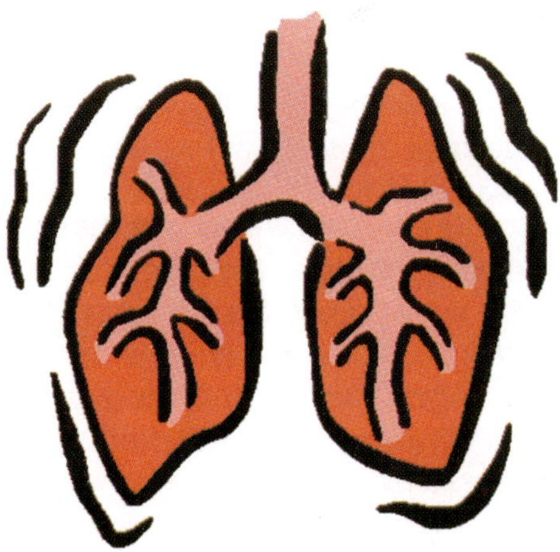

Thatul Janb is a dangerous disease. An authentic *Hadith* related by Umm Salamah رَضِـيَ الله عَنْهـا reads,

``The final ailment that the Messenger of Allah ﷺ suffered from started while he was in the house of Maymunah رَضِـيَ الله عَنْهـا *. Whenever the Prophet ﷺ felt the pain had eased, he would go out and lead the people in prayer. Whenever the pain intensified, he would say: `Order Abu Bakr* رَضِـيَ الله عَنْهُ *to lead the people in prayer.' The pain kept intensifying until the Prophet ﷺ lost consciousness.*

When the pain intensified, his wives, his uncle Al-`Abbas, Umm Al-Fadhl bint Al-Harith and Asma' bint `Umais رَضِـيَ الله عَنْهـم *discussed among each other about giving a medicine to the Prophet ﷺ , and they did just that while he was unconscious. When he woke up, he said: `Who did this to me? This is the work of some women who came from* *there,' pointing to the direction of Ethiopia with his hand. Umm Salamah and Asma' were the ones who had administered the medicine to the Prophet ﷺ [they were among those who had migrated to Ethiopia], and they said, 'O Messenger of Allah ﷺ ! We were afraid that you were suffering from Thatul Janb '*

He said: 'What medicine did you give me?' They said, `Some Indian costus, Wars and some drops of oil.' He said: `Allah would never inflict this type of disease on me.' He then said: 'I order you that every person present in this house take some of the same medicine, except for my uncle Al-`Abbas."

Further, in the *Sahihayn* (Al-Bukhari and Muslim) it is narrated that `Aishah رَضِيَ الله عَنْها said,

«لَدَدْنَا رسولَ الله صلى الله عليه وسلم؛ فأشار: أن لا تَلُدُّونِي. فقلنا: كراهِيةُ المريض للدَّواءِ. فلما أَفَاقَ قال: ألم أَنْهَكُمْ أن لا تَلُدّونِي؟ ! لا يبقى مِنكم أحد إلا لُدَّ، غيرُ عَمِّيَ العباسِ: فإنه لم يَشْهَدْكُم » (البخاري:٥٧١٢)

``We administered some medicine to the Messenger of Allah ﷺ although he indicated that he did not want to be given medicine. But we attributed his refusal to what the sick usually feel about taking medicine. When he woke up, he said: ``Did I not proscribe you from giving me this medicine? Therefore, everyone present should take some of that medicine, except for my uncle Al-`Abbas because he was not with you."

The last *Hadith* allows treating the aggressor in the same manner he treats others, as long as the action the aggressor committed is not prohibited by Allah The Almighty, and there are more than ten proofs to this ruling that we elaborated on in another book. This ruling also confirms the rulings of the four Rightly Guided Caliphs رَضِيَ الله عَنْهم and Imam Ahmad (may Allah have mercy upon him). This *Hadith* also indicates that reprisal for striking the face and hitting is of the same nature, as there are several *Hadith* on this subject that are unequivocal.

The Prophetís guidance on treating headaches and migraines

Headaches are defined as pain that appears in some part of the head or all of it, but when the headache afflicts one side of the head, it is called migraine. The type that attacks the entire head is sometimes called a helmet, for it resembles the helmet that covers the head. Furthermore, headaches sometimes afflict only the back or the front side of the head.

There are many types of headaches that result from various conditions. Headaches usually start when the head becomes hot due to the pressure of a septic vapor that accumulates near the head and which seeks a way out of the body, but fails. Then, the pressure of the vapor intensifies, just as a pot when it is heated but the steam is not able to escape from it. It is a fact that when moisture heats up, it seeks more space to expand. Similarly, the vapor accumulates near the head and then causes a headache in the entire head because it is unable to expand or escape from the body as it heats up. This condition causes a type of dizziness.

HENNA LEAVES

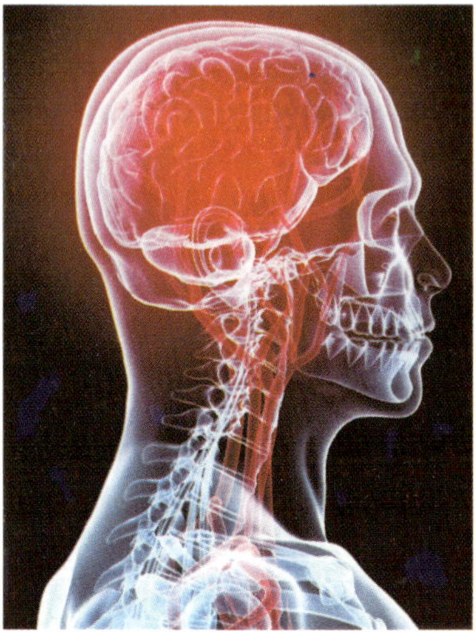

There are various specific causes for headaches:

When one of the four essential conditions (coldness, hotness, dryness and wetness) becomes predominant.

Ulcers of the stomach cause headaches, because the cephalic (relating to the head) nerves and the stomach are connected.

Thick flatulence might accumulate in the stomach then later ascend to the head and cause headaches.

Headaches are sometimes caused by a tumor in the gastric veins that cause pain in the head, because the stomach and the head are connected.

When the stomach is full of food it sometimes provokes headaches, as some of the food remains undigested.

Headaches sometimes occur after sexual intercourse because the body will then be weakened and thus exposed to the heat of the air.

Headaches sometimes occur after vomiting due to excessive dryness, or to accumulating gaseous materials (flatulence) that ascend to the head from the stomach.

Sometimes hot weather and air provoke headaches.

Headaches are sometimes caused by the cold weather and from the vapor that accumulates in the head and which is unable to decompose.

Not having enough sleep also causes headaches.

Headaches are sometimes caused due to the pressure exerted on the head, such as when one carries a heavy object on his head.

Excessive talking sometimes weakens the mind in a way that causes headaches.

Strenuous movements and sports activity can also provoke headaches.

Sadness, depression, obsession and evil thoughts also provoke headaches.

Excessive hunger provokes headaches, as in this case; the excess gaseous materials (flatulence) that accumulate in the stomach ascend to the brain and provoke headaches.

Those who suffer from a tumor in the cerebral lining sometimes feel as if hammers are constantly pounding on their heads.

Fever also provokes headaches because of the intense heat that the body suffers from them.

And Allah knows best.

Headaches result from changes in the system that affect the cerebral blood vessels.

The weaker side of the brain will accept septic material and the migraine headache will be accompanied by pulsation in the arteries. The pain can be relieved in this case when one ties a bandage so that the pulsing of the arteries is stopped and thus the pain is lessened.

Henna

Abu Na`im (may Allah have mercy upon him) said in his

book on Prophetic Medicine that migraine headaches used to afflict the Prophet ﷺ and that it would prevent him from going out of his house for one or two days at a time. Also, Abu Na`im related from Ibn `Abbas رَضِيَ الله عَنْهُما that he said, *``Once, the Messenger of Allah delivered a speech while a cloth was tied around his head."*

The *Sahih* states that the Prophet ﷺ said during the illness that preceded his death: *``O my head!"* He used to tie a piece of cloth around his head.

Tying a piece of cloth around the head helps soothe the pain of headaches and migraines.

Treating headaches varies according to their type and causes

Hence, headaches could be relieved by inducing vomiting, eating, being calm and staying inactive, using cold compresses, cooling the body, elevating the temperature, avoiding noise, etc.

Knowing these facts, we should mention that treating headaches with Henna is partial and that it cures only some types of headache. If the headache is caused by high fever and not a spoiled substance that requires extraction, Henna helps soothe the headache somewhat. Crushed Henna blended with vinegar and applied to the forehead will relieve the headache. Henna also soothes the nerves when used as a bandage. Finally, Henna is not only favorable to relieve headaches, but also for the various organs of the body and for the hot tumors and inflammations when used as a bandage.

Henna is cold in the first degree and dry in the second degree

The Henna tree has two special qualities: decomposing due to its warm watery essence, and constipating due to the cold earthly essence it contains.

Henna is useful in treating burns and soothes the nerves when used as a bandage, as we have stated. When chewed, Henna helps treat cankers and thrush that appear in the mouth. Henna also heals stomatitis (inflammation of the mucous membranes of the mouth) that appear in the child's mouth. Using Henna to bandage hot tumors also helps, as it has a similar effect on open sores as the dragon's blood tree has on them. When the Henna flower is blended with pure wax and rose oil, it helps against the aches of the side (*Thatul Janb*).

When the symptoms of smallpox start to break out on children and Henna is then applied on the bottom of their feet, the eyes will be immune from the sores that accompany smallpox. When the flower of the Henna is placed between wool clothes, it will perfume it and will prevent mold or mites. Furthermore, when the leaves of the Henna are submerged in fresh water, then squeezed and drunk for forty days, twenty measures each day along with ten measures of sugar while eating the meat of a young ewe, it prevents leprosy with its amazing qualities.

We were told that a man once complained from fissuring in his fingers and that he offered monetary rewards to whoever could cure him, but to no avail. Later on, a woman prescribed for him a drink of Henna for ten days but he could not stand the idea of drinking it. Later on, he soaked Henna leaves in water and drank the water and his fingers were healed and regained their beauty.

Henna is also used as an ointment for the fingers, as it polishes and strengthens them. Henna is also useful when blended with butter and then used as a bandage for the hot tumors that drain yellow residue. Henna also benefits against chronic mange, helps the hair grow, makes it stronger and strengthens the head. Finally, Henna helps against the blisters and the pustules that appear on the legs and feet and the rest of the body in general.

The Prophetís guidance concerning feeding the sick with what they like and not forcing them to eat or drink

At-Tirmidhi and Ibn Majah (may Allah have mercy upon them) narrated that the Prophet ﷺ said:

«لا تُكرِهُوا مَرْضاكم عَلَى الطّعام والشَّراب؛ فإن الله عز وجل يُطْعِمُهم ويَسقِيهم»

(الترمذي وصححه الألباني: ٢٠٤٠)

``Do not force your patients to consume food or drink, for Allah, the Exalted and Most High, feeds them and gives them drink."

Some doctors commented, *``How beneficial and true is this statement by the Prophet ﷺ that contains divine wisdom, especially for the doctors who treat patients! When the patient does not feel like eating or drinking, it is because the body is busy fighting the illness, or because the instinctive heat (or the appetite) becomes weaker. Either way, it is not allowed to give the patients food in this case."*

The feeling of hunger results from the body's appetite for food so that it refuels itself with the requisite energy replacing that which the body has spent. The various organs of the body will spend the available energy until it runs low on supply, the stomach will alert the person, who would then feel hungry. Food will then be distributed from the stomach to the rest of the organs of the body starting with the closest ones. When one is ill, the body will be busy maturing and getting rid of the alien, septic substances (toxins) and does not require food or drink.

When the sick person is forced to eat some food, the body's energy will be divided between digesting the food and concentrating on fending off the invading septic substances (pathogens) that caused the ailment. The patient will be harmed in this case, especially when one is suffering from acute ailments or lessening in the instinctive heat, as these conditions will only add strength to the ailment and bring about harm.

The patient should only eat what is required to sustain his strength and should avoid what can aggravate his condition. The patient should consume light food and juices like nenuphar (water lily), apples and tender rosewater drinks, etc. As for the types of foods the patient should consume, they should include aromatic chicken soup.

The patient should also refresh his body with good scents and listen to good news. The doctor is the servant of nature, not someone who hinders it or obstructs its path.

We should state that fresh, healthy blood provides nutrition to the body. We should also know that phlegm is a type of blood that has not properly matured. Therefore, when the patient's body has excess phlegm on an empty stomach, the body will lead the phlegmy blood to maturity and then turn it into fresh blood that will supply energy to the organs of the body. The nature of the human body is that of an engine and vehicle that Allah The Almighty has entrusted with preserving the body and its health and guarding it throughout its term.

Sometimes, compelling the patient to eat and drink becomes necessary when the ailments involve sanity.

The *Hadith* indicates that the patient could live without nourishment for longer than a healthy person could.

The Prophet's statement: *``For Allah provides food and drink for them,"* entails more far-reaching implications than the doctors think. Only those who are experienced in knowledge of the heart and soul and in their effects on the nature of the body and vice versa will be able to uncover the implications of the Prophet's statement.

It is a fact that when the heart is busy with such feelings as joy, sadness or fear, it will be busy attending to these feelings, thus ignoring the need to eat or drink. In this condition, one does not feel hunger or thirst or even the cold or the heat. Rather, the body in this case will be busy attending whatever troubles it and causes it pain. Every person experiences such moods, and thus would agree that when the heart is busy attending to a concern, it will not feel the need for food.

When the concern is a matter that brings joy, the feeling of elation will be a substitute for the food. Jubilation will fill the body and will energize it and the blood will be pumped to the various organs until it appears under the skin. In this case, the face will radiate with delight and life. Indeed, happy feelings relax the heart and fill the veins with blood. The organs do not require food in this case because they are busy dealing with what is even better for their nature than food. When human nature acquires what it likes, then it will disregard what is less favorable or important.

When the concern entails sadness, anguish or fear, the body will be busy attending to such concerns and will ignore seeking food in this case, because it is busy conducting its own war. When the body wins the war against such feelings, the feelings of joy will re-ignite the body's strength and will become a substitute for the regular energy through food and drink. When the war against these concerns is lost, the body will feel as low and weak as the size of defeat it suffered. If the war against such concerns is sometimes won and sometimes lost the body will feel energetic at times and weak at other times. Certainly, this type of war resembles the actual war between two enemies, where the upper hand belongs to the victorious, while defeat entails suffering casualties, dead, wounded or captured.

The sick person receives supplies from Allah The Almighty that provide nutrition for him, in addition to the nutrition that he receives through the blood which the doctors confirm. This divine help varies in amount according to the amount of submission and humility that one shows before his Lord and which will earn him closeness to Him. The closest the slave will be to his Lord is when his heart submits to Allah The Almighty and in return the mercy of Allah The Almighty will draw closer to the slave. When the slave is one of the loyal supporters of Allah The Almighty, his heart will receive sufficient support and aid that will nourish his body and strength more than the nourishment that his body receives through material nourishment. The stronger the slave's love, happiness, certainty, eagerness and contentment with Allah The Almighty becomes, the more divine strength he will feel. This cannot be described with words, nor can any doctor explain or attain knowledge of it on his own.

Those who do not have sound comprehension and thus are unable to understand the aforementioned facts, let them observe the miserable condition of whoever covets a part of the material existence -- whether a picture, a position, money or knowledge. Many people have discovered amazing facts concerning their own selves and other people by deep observation.

In the *Sahih* it has been stated that the Prophet ﷺ used to continue fasting for days at a time, yet he would prohibit his Companions from imitating him, saying:

« لستُ كَهَيْئَتِكُمْ؛ إِنِّي أَظَلُّ يُطعِمني ربي ويَسقِيني » (البخاري:١٩٦٤)

``I am not like any of you, my Lord provides me with food and drink."

The food and drink mentioned in the *Hadith* is not the type that people eat with the mouth. Otherwise, the Prophet ﷺ would not have continued the fast. Rather, the Prophet ﷺ said: *``My lord provides me with food and drink,"* thus drawing a difference between him and the Companions in that he is able to bear what they cannot bear. If the Prophet ﷺ were talking about the regular food and drink, he would not have said: *``I am not like any of you."* Those who understand regular food and drink from this *Hadith* do not have a significant supply from the true nutrition that the heart and soul require. Nor do they have knowledge of the effect of this divine nutrition on the strength and revival of the body, along with providing it with the true sustenance that is much more powerful and sustaining than material food.

The Prophetís guidance on treating tonsillitis and administering the medication orally

In the *Sahihayn* it is narrated that the Prophet ﷺ said:

« خيرُ مَا تَدَاوَيْتُم به الحِجَامةُ، والقُسْطُ البَحْرِيُّ ،وَلَا تُعذِّبُوا صِبْيانكُم بالغَمْزِ من العُذْرَةِ » (البخاري:٥٦٩٦)

``Cupping and marine costus are among your best remedies; and do not torture your children by pressing their uvula to cure tonsillitis."

Also in the *Sunan* and the *Musnad* (by Imam Ahmad, may Allah have mercy upon him) it is narrated that Jabir رَضِيَ الله عَنْهُ said, *``The Messenger of Allah came to `Aishah رَضِيَ الله عَنْها and saw a boy with a bleeding nose and said, `What is this?' They said, `He is suffering from tonsillitis, or a headache.'*

He said:

« وَيلَكُنَّ ! لا تَقْتُلْنَ أولادكُنَّ؛ أَيُّما امرأةٍ أصاب ولدَها عُذْرةٌ أو وَجَعٌ في رأْسِه: فَلْتَأْخُذْ قُسطًا هِنْدِيًّا، فلْتَحُكَّهُ بماءٍ ثم تُسْعِطْهُ إِيَّاهُ»

(الحاكم:٤/ ٢٠٥ وأحمد ٣/ ٣١٥ وسنده قوي كما في تحقيق المسند)

``Woe unto you! Do not kill your children! Let the mother whose child is suffering from tonsillitis or headache scrub Indian costus (aloes) with water and then administer it to the child through the nose.'

When `Aishah رَضِيَ الله عَنْها ordered that the prescription be followed, the boy was cured." [Ahmad, Al Hakim, Abu Ya'la and Al-Bazzar].

Abu `Ubaidah رَضِيَ الله عَنْهُ said, *``Tonsillitis is a blood-related throat irritation."* It was also said that in tonsillitis an ulcer [or enlarged growth] appears between the ear and the throat, that especially afflicts young children.

Administering scrubbed aloes through the nose helps against tonsillitis, which is essentially composed of blood related phlegm that accumulates in the bodies of young boys. Costus or Aloes tighten the uvula and pulls it up to its proper place. Aloes also help against other hot ailments. The author of *'Al-Qanoon'* stated that costus, Yemeni alum and marjoram seeds help against tonsillitis.

INDIAN COSTUS

The marine costus mentioned in the *Hadith* is the Indian aloes, particularly the one whitish in color, and it is sweet and has many benefits. In earlier times, people used to treat their children who suffered from tonsillitis by pressing the uvula and sometimes affixing an object to the uvula. The Prophet ﷺ disallowed this practice and guided the people to what is better, more beneficial and easier for the afflicted children.

Administering the medicine through the nose involves either simple or compound remedies that are ground and dried. Then, when warranted, the medication is administered through the nose of the afflicted person while he lies on his back and while his shoulders are elevated so that the head lies back. In this position, the medication would reach the head and extract the disease by sneezing.

The Prophet ﷺ praised using this method when there is a need that warrants it. Further, Abu Dawud (may Allah have mercy upon him) mentioned in his *Sunan* that the Prophet ﷺ used this method himself.

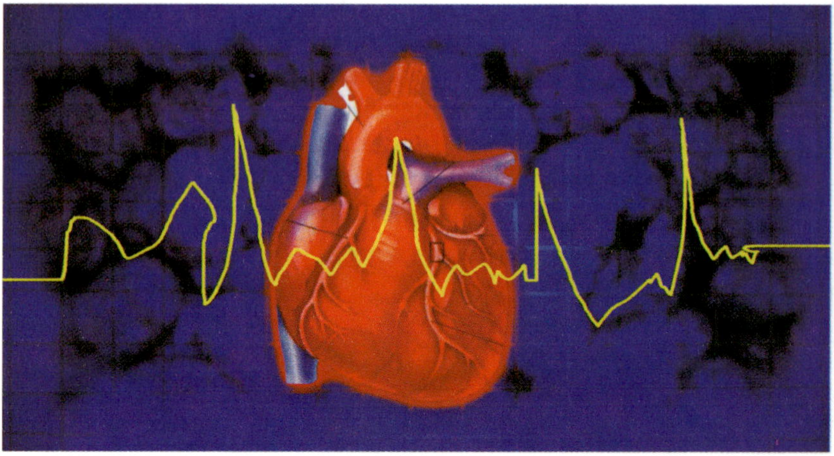

The Prophetís guidance on treating diseases of heart

Abu Dawud (may Allah have mercy upon him) narrated that Sa`d رَضِيَ الله عَنْهُ said, ``*Once, I became ill and the Messenger of Allah ﷺ came to visit me and placed his hand on the center of my chest, until I felt its coldness on my heart.* He then said:

«إنّكَ رجُلٌ مَفؤُودٌ؛ فأْتِ الحارثَ بْنَ كَلَدَةَ أَخا ثَقِيفٍ، فإِنَّهُ رجلٌ يتطبَّبُ؛ فَلْيَأْخُذْ سبعَ تَمَراتٍ من عجوَةِ المدينةِ. فَلْيَجَأْهُنَّ، ثم لِيَلُدَّكَ بهنَّ »

(أبو داود: ٣٨٧٥وضعفه الألباني وجوده في تحقيق الزاد ٤/ ٩٦)

``You are complaining from your heart. Go to Al-Harith bin Kaladah, from (the tribe of) Thaqhif, for he knows about medicine. Let him take seven dates from Madinah, grind them with their seeds and then give them to you."

Dates in general and dried dates in particular, especially from Madinah, possess tremendous qualities and are especially effective in treating heart ailments. Using seven dates is another quality that can only be known through the revelation.

In the *Sahihayn* it is narrated that Sa`d bin Abi Waqqas رَضِيَ الله عَنْهُ said, ``*The Messenger of Allah ﷺ said:*

« من تصبَّحَ بسَبْعِ تَمَراتٍ من تَمْر العَالِيَةِ، لم يضُرَّهُ ذلك اليومَ سُمٌّ ولا سِحْرٌ »

(مسلم:٢٠٤٨)

``Whoever eats seven dates from the area of Al-Aliah when he gets up in the morning then no poison or magic would harm him that day."

In another narration, the Prophet ﷺ said:

«مَن أكَلَ سبعَ تَمَراتٍ ممَّا بَيْنَ لاَ بَتيْهَا، حينَ يُصْبحُ، لم يُضَرُّه سُمٌّ حتى يُمسِيَ»(مسلم:٢٠٤٧)

``Whoever eats seven dates produced between the two areas in Madinah that are covered with burned black stones in the morning, will not be harmed by poison until he reaches the night."

Dates are warm in the second degree and dry in the first degree. Dates constitute a good type of nutrition, especially for those whose

regular diet contains dates, such as the people of Madinah. Dates are the best type of food for the residents of the hot and mildly warm countries, more so than for the residents of cold areas who have an elevated inner temperature, whereas those in warm areas have a colder inner temperature.

This is why the people in Hijaz, Yemen and Tai'f, and similar areas, eat hot foods such as dates and honey. They also use pepper and ginger in their food more than other areas; sometimes tenfold as much. Some of them even eat *Zanjabil* (ginger) just as other people eat sweets. They even carry these types of foods with them when traveling. As we have stated, these types of food are suitable for the residents of warm areas and do not harm them because of the lower inner temperature of their bodies. On a similar note, we should mention that well-water becomes colder during summer and warmer during winter. Further, the stomach digests thick (or complex) foods in winter more than during summer.

For the people of Madinah, dried dates are their staple diet like wheat is to other people. Also, dried dates from the area of Al-`Aliyah in Madinah are one of the best kinds of dates because they are firm, delicious and sweet.

Dates are a type of fruit that is also used for its nutritional and medicinal value, being favorable for most bodies and for their role in strengthening the natural heat. Also, dates do not produce harmful wastes or excrements like the other types of foods and fruits. Rather, dates preserve the bodily wastes from being spoiled and from rotting, especially for those used to eating dried dates.

The *Hadith* we mentioned about dried dates [in the beginning of the chapter] is specifically for the people of Madinah and surrounding areas. It is a fact that the medicinal value of the herbs and plants that grow in certain areas is closely related to the quality of the air and the type of soil in those areas. A certain medicinal herb might be useful in its natural habitat but not if it is grown elsewhere. The various lands differ in their nature and characteristics, just as people differ from each other. Sometimes, a certain type of plant might be a regular staple in the diet in a certain area, while it may be harmful or even poisonous in other areas. Sometimes, certain remedies that people use in a certain land might be a regular staple for other people in another area. Some types of medicine might provide a cure for some illnesses for some people, while curing other kinds of diseases for other people. Moreover, there might be a beneficial cure in some area that does not work in other areas.

Using seven dates has a spiritual and material significance. Allah The Almighty has created seven heavens, seven earths, seven days in the week and made the creation of mankind pass through seven stages. Allah The Almighty made the *Tawaf* seven circumambulations, and the *Sa'i* also seven circuits between Safa and Marwah. Also, the *Jamarat* (pillars) are stoned with seven pebbles each and the *Takbir* during the *`Eid* prayer is made seven times. In addition, the Prophet ﷺ said about young children:

«مُرُوهُم بالصَّلاة لسَبْع » (أبوداود وقال الألباني حسن صحيح:٤٩٥)

``Command him to pray upon reaching the age of seven."

When the child reaches the age of seven, he is given the choice [of staying, in the event of divorce] between his father and mother, according to some opinions. When the Prophet ﷺ was ill he ordered that water be poured on him from seven different water skins. Allah The Almighty has also sent the destructive wind on the people of `Ad for seven consecutive nights. The Messenger of Allah ﷺ also asked Allah The Almighty in supplication to test his people with a similar seven years of famine that the people of the Prophet Yusuf (Joseph) عليه السلام were tested with.

Furthermore, when Allah The Almighty gave the example of charity, He compared it to a grain (of corn); it grows seven ears, and each ear has a hundred grains. Also, the ears of corn that the king saw during the time of Prophet Yusuf (Joseph) عليه السلام were seven and the number of the years during which the king's people would farm the land was also seven. Also, charity is multiplied seven hundred times, to much more. Further, there are 70,000 members of the Muslim nation who will enter Paradise without questioning. The number seven has a special significance more than other numbers and only Allah The Almighty has full knowledge of the wisdom behind choosing this number above other numbers.

The *Hadith* mentioned that eating seven dates from a certain area in Madinah prevents poisoning and magic, indicating the special qualities of this type of date. Had it been Hippocrates or Galinus who issued this statement rather than the Prophet ﷺ, the doctors would quickly accept the statement without question, even though they would be issuing it based on guesswork and not on fact. The statements that come from the Prophet ﷺ, whose words are certainly true and divinely revealed, deserve to be believed in more and submitted to, without any hesitation or denial.

The dried dates mentioned in *Hadith* as being useful against certain poisons and only in some areas

Further, we should state here that it is a condition that the sick person should believe that the medicine will help him, so that his body accepts it and benefits from it. It is a fact that sometimes merely believing that the medicine will work helps cure some ailments, as many people have witnessed in this regard. When the heart accepts that a certain medicine carries the cure, the body will feel an elevation in its strength and in the instinctive heat that will help the body get rid of and extract harmful substances. On the other hand, sometimes an effective medicine fails to work because the patient does not believe that it will cure him, and consequently, his body neither accepts it, nor benefits from it.

Even the Qur'an, which is the best, most beneficial remedy ever, both in this life and in the Hereafter, and which is a cure for every disease, will not benefit the heart that does not believe in its value as a cure and a remedy. Rather, the Qur'an only increases the disease in such evil hearts.

There is no more effective cure for the diseases of the heart than the Qur'an, for it completely eradicates the ills of the heart, preserves its health and wellbeing and defends it against all that might bring harm to it. Yet, most of the hearts ignore the Qur'an and do not believe in it, and thus refrain from using it. Instead, such people refer to other types of medicine that were prepared by their like from among humankind, thus preventing their hearts from benefiting from the Qur'an. Consequently, the symptoms that attacked their hearts will persist and will expose their hearts to even more ailments. With the passage of time, both the doctors and the patients will get used to the medicines produced and prescribed by their like, leaders, or those whom they respect. In this case, disasters will accumulate and the diseases will become harder to cure. And the more they (those who ignore the Qur'an) use these medicines, the more strength they will add to the ailment!

The Prophetís guidance on neutralizing the harm of various foods and fruits

In the *Sahihayn* it is narrated that `Abdullah bin Ja`far رَضِيَ الله عَنْهُ said, ``*I saw the Messenger of Allah ﷺ eat ripe dates with cucumbers.*"

Ripe dates are hot in the second degree, increase sexual desire and add strength to the cold stomach. However, ripe dates rot quickly, induce thirst, harm the teeth, spoil the blood and cause headaches, various clogs and pain in the prostate. Cucumbers are cold and wet in the second degree and they prevent thirst, have a refreshing aroma and cool the stomach. When the seeds of the cucumbers are dried then crushed and are boiled with water, they produce a drink that will quench the thirst, help produce urine and soothe the pain in the prostate. When cucumber seeds are crushed and then sifted, they will whiten the teeth when brushed with it. Further, when cucumber plant leaves are crushed and blended with raisin jelly and used as a bandage, they will help against the bite of a hydrophobic dog.

CUCUMBERS PLANT

In general, dates are hot while cucumbers are cool, and each is suitable for the other and also neutralizes each other's harm. This is a type of balancing off the harm of one substance by combining it with its opposite or antidote, and these are the goals that preventive science seeks to achieve. In fact, these are the goals that the science of medicine as a whole seeks to achieve.

Combining the foods or medicines with their antidotes or opposites makes the product milder and rids it of any harmful side effects. Consequently, the body will preserve its health, strength and wellbeing.

`Aishah رَضِيَ الله عَنْها once said, ``*They tried to make me fatter using every type of food, but I did not get fatter. But when they fed me ripe dates and cucumbers, I became fatter.*"

In short, neutralizing the effect of the hot substance with the cold, the cold with the hot, the dry with the wet and the wet with the dry produces a milder substance that is considered among the best remedies and preventive measures. We mentioned before the Prophet's guidance concerning blending *Senna* and *Sanoot* (honey and butter) and stated that this method will make the *Senna* milder. May Allah bestow His peace and blessings on him, who was sent with all that brings life to the hearts and bodies and what brings about their benefit in this life and the Hereafter.

The Prophetís guidance on observing preventive measures as part of the cure

All types of cures and medicines entail the use of either a certain restricted diet or other preventive measures. When one feels ill, he needs to rid the body of harmful substances and bodily wastes. These three elements are what medicine is all about.

There are two types of preventive measures: one is an abstention from what might bring on an illness, and the second is an abstention from what might intensify the illness. The first type of preventive measure is for the healthy and the second type is for those with an illness. When the patient observes a certain preventive measure, the illness will not progress and thus the powers contained in the body will cooperate and collaborate towards ridding the body of the ailment.

The most basic element regarding prevention is what Allah The Almighty said:

﴿وَإِن كُنتُم مَّرْضَىٰٓ أَوْ عَلَىٰ سَفَرٍ أَوْ جَآءَ أَحَدٌ مِّنكُم مِّنَ ٱلْغَآئِطِ أَوْ لَٰمَسْتُمُ ٱلنِّسَآءَ فَلَمْ تَجِدُوا۟ مَآءً فَتَيَمَّمُوا۟ صَعِيدًا طَيِّبًا﴾

``And if you are ill, or on a journey, or one of you comes after answering the call of nature, or you have been in contact with women (by sexual relations) and you find no water, perform Tayammum with clean earth." (Qur'an , 4:43)

Allah The Almighty has excused the sick person from using water when there is a chance that it might harm him.

Ibn Majah (may Allah have mercy upon him) narrated that Umm Al-Munthir bint Qays رَضِيَ الله عَنْها said,

``The Messenger of Allah ﷺ came along with `Ali رَضِيَ الله عَنْهُ who was then recovering from an illness. At that time, we had some hanging clusters of dates. The Messenger of Allah ﷺ started eating from them

and then `Ali* رَضِيَ الله عَنْهُ *joined him. The Messenger of Allah* ﷺ *kept saying to `Ali رَضِيَ الله عَنْهُ *: 'You are still recovering', `until `Ali* رَضِيَ الله عَنْهُ *stopped eating.' I then made some barley and chard (similar to spinach) and brought it to them. The Prophet* ﷺ *said, to `Ali* رَضِيَ الله عَنْهُ*`:Eat from this food, it is more beneficial for you." In another narration, the Prophet* ﷺ *said: ``Eat from this food for it is more suitable in your condition."*

[Abu Dawud, Ahmad and Al-Hakim].

Ibn Majah (may Allah have mercy upon him) also narrated that Suhayb رَضِيَ الله عَنْهُ said, *``I came by the Messenger of Allah* ﷺ *and found that there were some dates and bread in front of him. The Prophet* ﷺ*said: 'Come closer and eat.' I picked up some dates and started eating from them. Then the Prophet* ﷺ *said: `Do you eat dates while you are suffering from conjunctivitis (an inflammation of the covering membrane of the eye)?' I said, 'O Messenger of Allah, I am chewing from the other side.' The Messenger of Allah* ﷺ *then smiled." '* [At-Tirmidhi and Al-Hakim].

In another *Hadith*, the Prophet ﷺ said:

« إنّ اللهَ إذا أحبَّ عبدًا: حَماَه من الدُّنيا . كما يَحْمي أحدُكم مريضَه عن الطَّعام والشَّرابِ» « إن الله يَحْمِي عبدَه المُؤْمن مِنَ الدنيا » (الترمذي وصححه الألباني:٢٠٣٦)

``When Allah loves a slave, He helps him observe abstinence from the life of this world, just as one of you puts his patient on a diet from food and drink. Allah puts His believing slave on a diet from the life of this world."

The famous statement: *``Diet is the best medicine; and the stomach is the home of diseases; give each person what he is used to [of food and medicine],"* is not a *Hadith*, according to the scholars of *Hadith*. Rather, it is the words of Al-Harith bin Kaladah, the renowned Arab doctor.

Al-Harith stated, *"Diet is the head of medicine."* In the opinion of doctors, a diet by healthy people is as harmful as unhealthy eating habits for patients. Consequently, the best type of diet is that observed by those recovering from an illness, because until then, their body organs would not have regained their normal strength and wellbeing. In this condition, the digestion process would not be at its normal efficiency while the various organs of the body would still be prone to sickness. At this time, unhealthy eating habits might cause the disease to come back stronger than it was before.

Know that the Prophet's disallowing `Ali رَضِي الله عَنْهُ from eating the hanging clusters of dates while still recuperating from an illness is one of the best preventive measures. Fruits are not beneficial for sick or recovering patients as they get digested quickly at a time when the body is still fighting the ailment and is not strong enough to deal with an excess amount of food. Ripe dates in particular are heavy on the stomach at a time when the body is still resisting the ailment and removing its effects. Whatever part of the ailment that remains would either dissipate or recur and intensify, depending on the condition of the body.

Therefore, when cooked barley and chard were brought to the Prophet ﷺ, he ordered `Ali رَضِي الله عَنْهُ to eat from it. Cooked barley and chard represent one of the best types of foods for the recovering patients and those with weak stomachs. It does not produce any harmful substances or bodily wastes. The water of cooked barley is cool and nourishing, along with its other qualities of soothing, relaxing the bowels and strengthening the body in general, especially when it is cooked with chard.

Zaid bin Aslam (may Allah have mercy upon him) once said, *"`Umar رَضِي الله عَنْهُ once made a patient observe such a strict diet that he used to suck on date stones."* In short, diet is one of the most beneficial preventive measures before and after the disease strikes, in which case diet will prevent the disease from spreading or progressing.

We should know that when healthy, recovering or sick people have a taste for a type of food or drink, it would not harm them if they consume small amounts of it. Rather, the food might even help and benefit the body, as the stomach will accept and easily digest the food, more so than when one takes a medicine that it detests. This is why the Prophet ﷺ

allowed Suhaib رَضِـيَ الله عَنْهُ to eat a few dates when he was suffering from conjunctivitis, since it was just a small amount and would not harm him.

It was reported that `Ali رَضِـيَ الله عَنْهُ said that he once came by the Prophet ﷺ, when he, (`Ali رَضِـيَ الله عَنْهُ), was complaining from conjunctivitis, and found the Prophet ﷺ eating dates. The Prophet ﷺ asked him, ``O `Ali, do you have a taste for dates?" He then threw a date and then another date to `Ali رَضِـيَ الله عَنْهُ, until he threw seven. The Prophet ﷺ then said: ``*That is enough, O Ali.*" [Abu Na`im in his book on Prophetic Medicine].

Ibn Majah (may Allah have mercy upon him) narrated that Ibn `Abbas رَضِـيَ الله عَنْهُما said:

« أَنَّ النبيَّ صلى الله عليه وسلم عادَ رجُلاً، فقال له: ما تشتَهِي ؟ فقال: أشتهِي خُبزَ بُرٍّ، وفي لفظٍ: أشتَهِي كَعْكًا، فقال النبيُّ صلى الله عليه وسلم: مَن كان عندَه خبزُ بُرٍّ، فليَبْعَثْ إلى أخيه. ثم قال: إذا اشتَهَى مريضُ أحدِكم شيئًا، فلْيُطْعِمْه»

(ابن ماجه وضعفه الألباني:١٤٣٩)

``Once, the Prophet ﷺ visited a sick person and asked him: ``What do you have a taste for?" The man said, ``I have a taste for wheat bread, or I have a taste for a cake." The Prophet ﷺ then said: ``Whoever has wheat bread, let him send some to his brother." He also said, ``When your ailing [patients] have a taste for something, give them some of it."

The last *Hadith* contains a secret, because when the sick person eats what he has a taste for while also hungry, it will be less harmful than what he does not have a taste for. If what he has a taste for is not beneficial in his condition, then his preference for it will prevent its harm. In addition, eating what one does not like will cause harm to the patient even if the substance is beneficial itself. In general, the type of food that is tasty and that the person likes will be accepted by the body and will be digested in the best way, especially when the appetite for it is strong.

The Prophetís guidance on treating conjunctivitis with rest and observing a special diet

We mentioned that the Prophet ﷺ indicated to Suhaib رَضِيَ الله عَنْهُ that he should abstain from eating dates when he was suffering from conjunctivitis, and did the same with `Ali رَضِيَ الله عَنْهُ when he was suffering from the same condition. Furthermore, Abu Na`im narrated in his book, *'Prophetic Medicine'*, *``Whenever any of the Prophet's wives would come down with conjunctivitis, he would not touch her until her eyes were cured."*

Conjunctivitis is an infection that attacks the conjunctiva, that is, the white part of the eye. The disease is caused by one of the four conditions [hotness, coldness, dryness and wetness], or by the accumulation of hot flatulence in the head and body, that later reaches the eye and cause conjunctivitis. When the eye is injured, the blood and the soul will rush to the aid of the affected eye, which then becomes swollen.

We should know that there are two types of moistures that ascend to the air. One is hot and dry and the other hot and wet. These moistures form the clouds that shade the sky from our eyes. Likewise, gaseous substances and moistures ascend from the stomach to the upper parts of the body and cause many ailments, such as conjunctivitis.

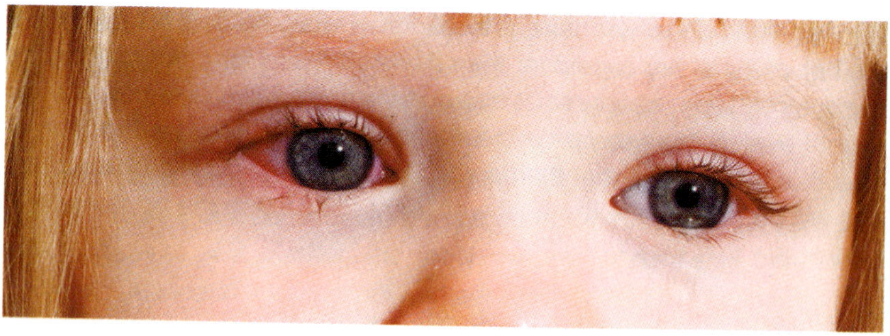

When the body's resistance is strong, it will push these gaseous substances to the nose and cause a congestion that usually accompanies colds. When these substances are pushed up through the uvula and the nostrils, they cause angina. When these moistures are pushed towards the side, they cause causes pleurisy, and when they reach the chest they causes pneumonia. When the moistures reach the heart they cause rapid pulse, and when they reach the eyes they cause conjunctivitis. When they reach the intestinal cavity, they cause diarrhea and when they reach the brain they cause forgetfulness. If the brain receives excessive amounts of these gaseous moistures, they might cause heavy sleeping. This is why sleep is wet while being awake is dry.

When the septic gases unsuccessfully seek to depart from the body through the head, they will cause headaches and less sleep. When these gases attack one side of the brain, they cause migraines. If these gases reach the cerebral barrier and cause its coldness, hotness or wetness, it will cause sneezing. If the gases cause the accumulation of phlegm in the cerebral barrier, so that its hot nature becomes weak, they may cause unconsciousness and a stroke.

If the gases excite the black bile, they will cause obsession, and if they reach the nerves, they will cause true epilepsy. When the cerebral nerves receive these gases they will suffer from facial paralysis. If these gases are caused by inflamed yellow bile that heats the brain, they will cause cerebral tumors, and when the chest receives a part of these gases, they will cause pleurisy.

In short, the condition of the head and body will be irritated because of conjunctivitis, and having sexual intercourse in this state will only aggravate the condition even more. Intercourse entails a movement that is shared by the entire body, the heart and the soul. As for the body, it heats up due to the intense movements during sexual intercourse, while the heart will seek to obtain the object of its lust and pleasures. The soul will follow the lead of the body and the heart, as the first part that is connected to the soul is the heart, which in turn affects the res of the body. As for the body, it sends the semen that is needed to bring the sexual intercourse to conclusion. Thus, sexual activity involves a movement by the entire body, the heart and the soul, and every move excites the various conditions and causes them to move to the weaker parts of the body, such as the eye when suffering from conjunctivitis.

We should state that the body benefits from conjunctivitis in that it helps the body extract harmful substances and cleanses the body and the head from septic elements. Conjunctivitis also compels the affected person to observe abstinence and avoid sadness, grief, strong movements and hard work. Further, one of our righteous predecessors said, *"Do not hate conjunctivitis, because it prevents blindness."*

In addition, conjunctivitis requires rest and avoiding touching the eye to prevent more harmful substances from accumulating in it. Some of the *Salaf* once said, *``The example of the Companions of Muhammad ﷺ is like the example of the eye: its cure is in avoiding touching it."'*

A *Hadith* (the authenticity of which we are not sure about) states that sprinkling cold water on the eye helps cure conjunctivitis. The remedy mentioned in the *Hadith* is beneficial for hot conjunctivitis, since water is cold and thus cools down the heat that accompanies conjunctivitis. This is why when the wife of `Abdullah bin Mas`ud رَضِيَ الله عَنْهُ complained about her eyes, he said to her, *``If you had done what the Prophet ﷺ used to do, it would have been better for you and would have brought fast healing to your eyes. Splash water on your eyes and then say: `Cure the ailment, O Lord of the people! Bring about the cure, for You Alone bring the cure and there is no cure except that which you bring about. Bring a type of healing that eradicates every ailment."*

We mentioned before that these types of remedies are suitable for certain areas and for some ailments that attack the eye. Do not understand the Prophet's statements that are specific to be general or vice versa. Otherwise, mistakes will certainly occur.

The Prophetís guidance on treating narcolepsy

Abu Ubaid رَضِيَ الله عَنْهُ said in his book on the unusual words used in some *Ahadith* that some people passed by a tree that they ate from and they were immobilized soon after, just as if a wind had swept through by them and frozen them. The Prophet ﷺ said:

« قَرِّسُو المَاءَ فِي الشِّنَانِ، وصُبّوا عليهِم فيما بين الأَذانَيْن » (ابن أبي شيبة مرسلا: ٢٣٧١٤)

``Cool some water in water skins and then pour the water on them between the two Adhans (the Fajr call to the prayer and the Iqamah)."

The Prophet ﷺ mentioned the water skins because they cool the water more than clay containers. He also called the *Iqamah* an *Adhan* in this *Hadith* .

Some doctors stated that the remedy that the Prophet ﷺ prescribed in the *Hadith* is the one of the most effective against narcolepsy if it occurs in the area of Hijaz, which is a hot dry land. The inhabitants of that area have a weak instinctive heat. Pouring cold water on the people afflicted by narcolepsy during the above mentioned time, which is the coolest time of the last part of the night, will cause the instinctive heat that is scattered throughout the body to be energized and accumulate in the inner parts of the body where the ailment resides. The powers of the body will then concentrate on expelling and resisting the ailment by the will of Allah The Almighty.

If it were Galinus or Hippocrates who had prescribed this remedy, the doctors would have been amazed by its perfect effectiveness!

The Prophetís guidance on food and drink contaminated by flies

In the *Sahihayn* [actually, only Al-Bukhari narrated it in his *Sahih*] it is narrated that the Messenger of Allah ﷺ said:

« إذا وقعَ الذُّبابُ في إناءِ أحدِكم: فامْقُلُوه، فإن في أحدِ جناحَيْه داءً، وفي الآخَر شِفاءً » (البخاري: ٢٣٢٠)

``If a housefly falls in the drink of anyone of you, he should dip it (in the drink), for one of its wings has a disease and the other has the cure for the disease."

Ibn Majah (may Allah have mercy upon him) also narrated that the Messenger of Allah said ﷺ:

«أحدُ جناحَي الذُّبابِ سُمٌّ، والآخَرُ شِفاءٌ. فإذا وَقَعَ في الطعام: فامْقُلُوه فِيه؛ فإنه يقدِّم السُّمَّ، ويؤخرُ الشِّفاءَ »(ابن ماجه وصححه الألباني: ٣٥٠٤)

``One of the fly's wings carries poison while the other carries a cure. When it falls in the food, dip it, for the sake of Allah, for verily He (Allah) makes the poison (take effect) first and He makes the cure come last."

This *Hadith* contains two areas of interest: *Fiqh* (Islamic jurisprudence) and medicinal. As for the *Fiqh* part, the *Hadith* states that when a fly falls in water or fluids, it does not make it impure, according to the majority of the scholars. None among the early generations contradicted this ruling.

The Prophet ﷺ ordered the fly that falls on the food be dipped in it, thus killing the fly, especially if the food is hot. If the fly's death inside the food would make the food impure, the

Prophet ﷺ would have ordered us to discard the food. On the contrary, the Prophet ﷺ sought to salvage the food.

Bees, hornets, spiders and all similar insects are treated in the same manner as houseflies, because the ruling that we derive from the Prophet's commandment in this *Hadith* is general. Since the reason why dead animals are impure is that their blood remains trapped in their bodies, therefore the insects, which do not have blood are pure. The first person to use the words *``What does not have a soul (meaning blood)?"* was Ibrahim An-Nakha'i (may Allah have mercy upon him) and then the scholars used these terms after him.

As for the medicinal value contained in the *Hadith*, Abu `Ubaidah رَضِيَ الله عَنْهُ said that the purpose behind dipping the fly [in the drink] is to extract the cure from [its other wing], just as the poison was extracted from the wing that fell on the food.

Houseflies carry poisonous materials as evidenced by the effect of their bite, such as rash and infection, and this poison is the fly's weapon of defense. When the fly falls into what harms it, it tries to defend itself with the available weapons. The Prophet ﷺ ordered that we neutralize the poisonous substances produced by the fly with the cure that Allah The Almighty has kept on its other wing. The fly should then be submerged in the water or the food so that the cure could neutralize the effect of the poison.

This is a remedy that the best medical minds would never be able to discover on their own, because it comes from Prophetic knowledge. The doctors who have good knowledge and comprehension submit to this Prophetic remedy and admit that he who was sent with it, is indeed the perfect human being who is supported by divine revelation that is beyond human power.

Several doctors have stated that when one anoints the inflammation caused by scorpion and hornet bites with the housefly, it reduces the severity o pain due to the cure that the fly carries in its wing. When the head of the housefly is amputated and the body is used to scrub the tumor that appears in the eyelid, it will cure it, Allah willing.

The Prophetís guidance on treating pimples

Ibn As-Sunni (may Allah have mercy upon him) said in his book tha one of the Prophet's wives said, ``*Once, the Messenger of Allah came by when I had a pimple on my finger. He said:*

« عندكِ ذَرِيرة ؟ قلتُ: نعم، قال: ضَعِيها عَلَيها. وقال:قُولي: اللّٰهم مُصَغِّرَ الكَبِير، ومكبِّرَ الصَّغِير؛ صغِّر مابي » (السني في عمل الليوم والليلة: ٦٣٥ وإسناده صحيح إلا كانت عمريم بنت إياس صحبة وقد توقف عليه في تحقيق المسند ٥/ ٣٧٠ وانظر الإخباربها لا يصح للباكستاني (ص ٢٢٣)

``Do you have Tharirah (Arum)?' I said, `Yes.' He said: "Place it on the pimple." He then said: `Say, O Allah who transforms the big to small and the small to big, make what I am suffering from small." [Al-Hakim also narrated the Hadith].

Arum

Tharirah (Arum) is an Indian remedy made of arum cane. Arum is hot and dry and helps against stomach and liver tumors and dropsy and also strengthens the heart.

In the *Sahihayn* it is narrated that `Aishah رَضِيَ الله عَنْها said, ``*I perfumed the Messenger of Allah ﷺ with my hand using Tharirah (Arum) during the Farewell Hajj during the state of Ihram and otherwise."*

The pimple is a growth that results from hot harmful, septic substances that push towards the skin to find a way out of the body The pimple needs to mature and to then be opened and extracted, such as by using the *Tharirah*, which helps extract the septic matter from the pimple, along with giving a good aroma. In addition, the *Tharirah* soothes the hotness of the pimple. This is why the author of the *'Al-Qanun'* said, ``*There is no better remedy for fire burns than the Tharirah , when it is blended with rose essence and vinegar."*

The Prophetís guidance in treating tumors and abscesses with surgery

Abu Hurairah رَضِيَ الله عَنْهُ narrated that the Prophet ﷺ ordered a doctor to incise an abscess on the abdomen of a man. He was asked, *`Does medicine help, O Messenger of Allah?'* He said:

«الَّذي أَنزل الداء: أنزلَ الشفاء، فيما شاء»

(كم نجده بهذه الزيادة ولعلها مدرجة لبيان المعني ورواية أبي هريرة رواه البزار وهي ضعيفة المجمع ٥/ ٩٩)

``He Who has sent down the disease has also sent down whatever He wills of the cure."

The tumor, which accompanies most ailments, is a growth in the organ due to the accumulation of unnatural, septic materials engineered by the four conditions: hotness, coldness, dryness and wetness, plus water and wind. When the tumor swells with septic material, it is called an abscess. Every hot tumor ends up decomposing, or becoming pus, or hardening. If the body is strong enough, it dissolves the tumor, and this is the best end of tumors. If the body is not strong, it turns the tumor into a white substance, pus, and opens an exit for the pus to go out of the body. If the body is weak, the tumor will be full of immature pus and the body will not be able to open an exit to discard the pus. In this case, it is possible the tumor will spoil the affected organ. The doctor's help is then sought to incise the tip of the tumor to extract the septic substance.

Puncturing or incising the tumor has two benefits: extracting the harmful substance and preventing more harmful substances from accumulating around the tumor making it even worse.

The *Hadith* stated that the Prophet ﷺ ordered a doctor to incise a tumor on a man's abdomen that was filled with putrid or rotten fluid.

The scholars have conflicting opinions regarding incising tumors, some of them did not allow it because it is dangerous in their opinion. Other doctors said that there is no cure for dropsy except incision. As we have stated, dropsy is of three types: drum dropsy, which causes the stomach to swell with accumulated gases, that if one pounds on the stomach it will produce a similar sound as the drum. There is the

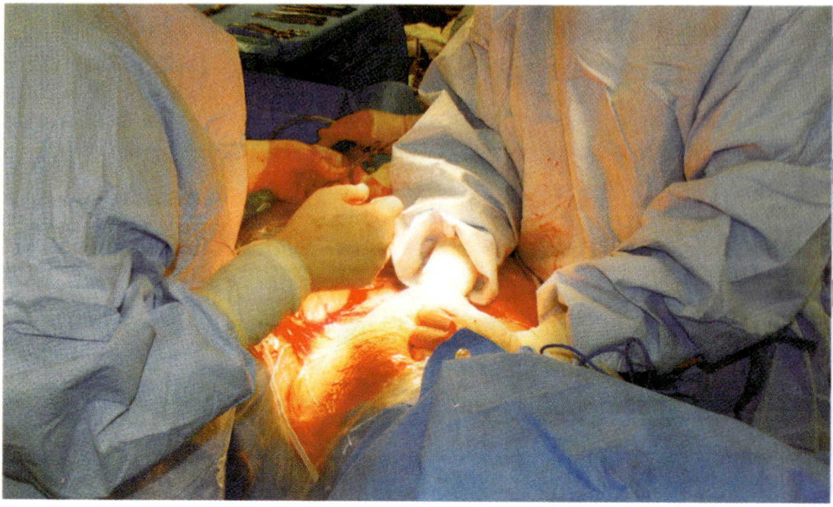

fleshy dropsy that causes the flesh to swell accompanied by phlegm that spreads throughout the body through the blood. This type is worse than the first one.

Third, there is the dropsy that causes the accumulation of toxic materials in the lower part of the stomach. When one moves in this case, his stomach will produce a sound similar to the shaking of a water skin. Most doctors consider this type of dropsy the worst, while others consider the fleshy dropsy the worst of the three types.

Curing the third type of dropsy requires extracting the accumulating water by incision, which is similar to extracting spoiled blood by puncturing the veins. Yet, this procedure is dangerous, although the *Hadith*, if proven authentic, allows using this method. Allah has the best knowledge.[1]

(1) Editor's note : By giving permission for this procedure the vision of modern surgery was opened even though after seven centuries these surgical operations were still doubted by many doctors. The field of surgery had not developed the proper techniques required to make this a universal standard procedure at the time of our author.

The Prophetís guidance on treating the sick by encouraging them and strengthening their resolve

Ibn Majah (may Allah have mercy upon him) narrated that Abu Sa'eed Al-Khudri رَضِيَ الله عَنْهُ said, The Messenger of Allah ﷺ said:

إذا دخَلْتم على المَرِيض: فَنفِّسوا له في الأجَلِ فإنَّ ذلك لا يَرُدُّ شيئاً، وهو يطيِّبُ نَفْسَ المريض» (الترمذي:٢٠٨٧ وقال الألباني ضعيف جدًا)

``When you visit a sick person, say good words to him, for the sake of Allah for although that does not prevent any harm, it still brings relief to the patient's heart." [At-Tirmidhi also narrated the Hadith].

This *Hadith* contains one of the most honorable remedies, that is, relieving the anxiety of the sick with some good words that will enhance his resolve and strength. In this case, the inner energy would be elevated and would help the body against the disease, which is the best the doctor could wish for.

Relieving the anxiety of the sick person and bringing relief to his heart has a surprisingly good effect in curing the body and lessening the effects of an ailment. It will also bring strength to the heart and the soul of the sick person, further encouraging the body to fight the disease. People have witnessed that the sick feel refreshed and energized in the company of those they like and respect when they visit them. This is one of the benefits gained from visiting the sick, which carries four types of benefits: for the sick person, the visitor, the sick person's family and the general public.

We mentioned before that the Prophet ﷺ used to ask the sick about their complaints and how they felt. He would also ask them about what they had a taste for and would place his hand on the forehead, or even on the chest, asking Allah The Almighty to bring about whatever benefits them in their condition. Sometimes, the Prophet ﷺ would perform ablution and then pour the water he used on the sick person. Sometimes, the Prophet ﷺ would say to the sick person:

« لا بَأْس؛ طَهورٌ إن شاءَ الله تعالى » (البخاري:٣٦١٦)

``It is alright. You will be purified (cured), Allah willing."

This, indeed, is the kindest way to treat the sick when visiting them.

The Prophetís guidance on treating various illnesses with food and medicine the body is used to

This is also one of the major pillars and the most beneficial parts of the science of medicine. When the doctor errs in prescribing the correct medicine, the patient will be harmed while the doctor is thinking that he is benefiting him. Only the most ignorant doctors will fail to recognize the importance of using the most favorable types of foods and medicines that are the most suitable for different patients. For instance, the Bedouins neither benefit from *Nenuphar* (water lily that is used as a drink) or rose-syrup, nor do these remedies have any effect on them, nor would the majority of the medicines used in villages and cities have much effect on them. This fact is known through experience and observation.

Those who read through this book will find that the Prophetic medicine and remedies are all suitable and favorable to the sick person and entail what the patient is accustomed to of food and medicine. We have stated that this is a pillar of the science of medicine, as the best medical authorities concur. For instance, the renowned Arab doctor, Al-Harith bin Kaladah, said, *``Diet is the best cure; and the stomach is the home of diseases; give each body what it is accustomed to (of food and medicine)."* In another statement, Al-Harith said, *`Azm is a cure,'* [meaning hunger]. In fact, going on a diet is a better cure for plethoric illnesses (having an excess of blood in the body and therefore looking reddish), except when there is a fear that the condition would flare up with septic accumulation and aggravate the illness.

Al-Harith stated that the stomach is the seat or home of diseases. The stomach is a curved organ that looks like a gourd and consists of three layers of delicate and neural components called fibers and surrounded by flesh. The fibers of one layer are arranged longitudinally, while the second layer's fibers are horizontal and the third slanting. The tip of the stomach has more nerves, while the bottom has more flesh and its interior is coated and fuzzy. The stomach is located in the middle of the abdomen, leaning more to the right side, created in this shape by the wisdom of the All-Wise Creator.

The stomach is indeed the residence of the ailments, it is the center of the digestion and maturing process of all food and drink. After that, the digested food descends to the liver and the intestines. Meanwhile, excess amounts of partially digested substances that the stomach was not able to completely digest remain -- either because the amount of nourishment was excessive, spoiled, or was not consumed in the proper order -- or all of these reasons. Some of this undigested food remains in the stomach and the body is not be able to completely discard them, and this is why the stomach is the residence of ailments. Al-Harith indicates the importance of eating less food and preventing the heart from fulfilling its desires.

As for one's being accustomed [to certain things and foods] it is a part of the human nature. Habit has such a great influence on the person and on his body, that if we conduct an experiment on several people who have the same characteristics, the result will vary considerably. For instance, three young, hot-tempered men, one of them is used to eating hot foods, the second is used to cold foods, while the third man is accustomed to mild foods. When the first person eats honey, it would not harm him, unlike the second person, while the third person would be slightly bothered. Habit, therefore, is an important basis on which preserving the health and healing ailments relies. That is why the Prophet ﷺ said that each person should be treated according to what he is accustomed to of medicine and food.

The Prophetís guidance on treating the sick with the simplest types of food

In the *Sahihayn* it is narrated that `Aishah رَضِيَ الله عَنْها said that when a relative of hers would die the women would gather on that occasion and then would depart except for her family members and close associates. She would then order that milk soup (*Talbinah*) be prepared. Then, *Tharid* would be made and she would pour the milk soup on it. `Aishah رَضِيَ الله عَنْها would then ask them to eat saying, *``I heard the Messenger of Allah ﷺ saying:*

«التلبينةُ مُجِمَّةٌ لفُؤَادِ المَريضِ، تَذهَبُ ببَعْضِ الحُزن» (البخاري:٥٤١٧)

``Milk soup (Talbinah) brings relief to the heart of the sick and takes away some of the anguish." '

Milk soup means the kind of soup that is similar to milk in consistency. This is a beneficial food suitable for the sick, especially when well cooked until it acquires a soft consistency. The milk-like soups are as beneficial as barley soup, or even better. Barely soup is made of whole barley grains, while the milk-like soup is made of ground barley flour with its bran.

We mentioned that observing the habits and customs of a certain sick person benefits them with a favorable cure and nourishment. The people in Madinah were accustomed to eating barley soup ground not whole, thus making it more nutritious and beneficial for them. The doctors in cities recommend the use of whole barley grains, because the soup in this case is lighter and easier for the ailing person to digest. The people who live in cities are used to comfort and an easy life and that is why ground barley grain is heavy on their stomachs.

Whole grain barley soup is digested quickly, provides good nutrition, and cleanses the stomach, especially when taken while it is still hot. In this case, its cleansing and digestive qualities are stronger and the soup will also develop its instinctive heat quicker and will soften the outer layers of the stomach.

The Prophet's statement that the milk-like soup takes away some of the sadness refers to the effect of sadness on the mood and in weakening the instinctive wellbeing o a person, which in turn affects the soul and the heart. Milk-like soup brings strength to one's inner energy and thus the body will be able to rid itself of the sadness and grief that has taken over it.

We could also say that some foods bring relief to the heart, such as the type of soup mentioned above, because they possess a special quality that affects people's mood and brings them relief and comfort. And Allah knows best.

We might also say that the sick person's strength becomes weaker because of his grief and sadness that translates to dryness in the body and the stomach due to the scarcity of food. The milk-like soup brings wetness and strength to the stomach, which will also bring relief to the heart. The sick person may complain from an accumulation of harmful flatulence or phlegm in his stomach. The milk-like soup will dissolve these harmful substances or dilute them, so that the pain and harm they cause are diminished, especially for those accustomed to eating barley bread, such as the people of Madinah. During that time, barley bread was the staple diet for the people of Madinah as wheat was scarce at that time.

The Prophetís guidance on treating poisoning

Abdul Razzaq رَضِيَ الله عَنْهُ narrated,

``A Jewish woman brought to the Prophet ﷺ a roasted sheep that she had poisoned, while he was in Khaybar. The Prophet ﷺ asked: `What is this?' She said, 'A gift,' being careful not to say that it was from charity so that he would not eat it. The Prophet ﷺ and his Companions ate from the sheep, then the Prophet ﷺ said: `Stop eating.' He said to the woman: `Did you poison this sheep?' She said, `Who told you that?' He said: `This bone,' meaning the ewe's leg that he had in his hand. She said, `Yes.' He said: `Why?' She said, 'I thought that if you are a liar, the people would be relieved from you. However, if you are a true Prophet , it would not harm you.' The Prophet ﷺ then used cupping thrice on the upper part of his back and commanded that his Companions do the same. Yet, several of them died.'''

In another narration narrated by Musa bin `Uqbah رَضِيَ الله عَنْهُ , *``The Messenger of Allah ﷺ used cupping on his back because of what he ate of the poisoned sheep. Abu Hind, a servant for Bani Bayadhah, used a knife to cup him. Three years later, when the Prophet ﷺ was suffering from the illness that he died from, he said:*

«مَازِلتُ أجِدُ فِي الأُكْلَةِ التي أَكَلْتُ مِن الشَّاةِ يَوْمَ خَيْبَر، حَتى كانَ هذا أَوَانَ انْقِطَاعِ الأَبْهَرِ مِنِّي » (البخاري: ٤٤٢٨)

``I still feel the effects of the poisoned sheep I ate from during the Day of Khaybar, until now, when it is the time the aorta is cut off (meaning when death is near)".

Therefore the Messenger of Allah ﷺ died as a martyr.

Poisons are treated by extracting the poison and by using the proper antidotes to neutralize their effect. Whoever does not have access to the medicine, or the antidote, should use complete disgorging, the best method of which is cupping especially in warm areas and during hot weather. The poison passes through the veins and the blood vessels to the heart and then to the rest of the body, bringing certain death. Since the blood is the medium that transports the poison to the heart and the organs, when the infected blood is extracted by cupping, the body will get rid of the poison. Also, when one resorts to complete disgorging, the poison does not cause any further harm, the body gets enough strength to fight it and then weakens or even completely dissipates the poison.

When the Prophet ﷺ used cupping, he did it in the upper part of the back, which is the most direct route to the heart, and so the poison was extracted with the blood, in this case only partially. A part of the poison remained in the Prophet's system, in order to fulfill what Allah The Almighty had decreed for His Prophet ﷺ so he would acquire every type of good and righteous reward there is.

When Allah The Almighty decided that it was time for His Prophet ﷺ to die as a martyr, the effect of the poison reappeared, so that Allah's decision was fulfilled. Therefore the meaning of the following *Ayah* (verse), becomes apparent where Allah The Almighty says,

﴿أَفَكُلَّمَا جَآءَكُمْ رَسُولٌۢ بِمَا لَا تَهْوَىٰٓ أَنفُسُكُمُ ٱسْتَكْبَرْتُمْ فَفَرِيقًا كَذَّبْتُمْ وَفَرِيقًا تَقْتُلُونَ﴾

"It is that whenever there came to you a Messenger with what you yourselves desired not, you grew arrogant? Some you disbelieved and some you killed." (Qur'an, 2:87)

This Verse uses the word 'disbelieve' in the past tense and the word 'kill' in the future tense, indicating an uncompleted action that would continue to occur [meaning the Jews would kill the Prophet]. And Allah knows best.

The Prophetís guidance on treating sorcery

Some people have erroneously denied that sorcery could affect the Prophet ﷺ, they believe that it is not befitting his elevated rank and status. Actually, being affected by sorcery illustrates the human side of the Prophet ﷺ, just as he suffered from various other illnesses, and sorcery is an ailment just like poison.

In the *Sahihayn* it is narrated that `Aishah رَضِيَ الله عَنْها said,

« سُحِرَ رَسولُ اللهِ صلى اللهُ عليه وسلم، حتى إِنْ كَان لَيُخَيَّلُ إليه أنه يأتي نساءَه، ولم يأتِهِنّ » (البخاري:٥٧٦٥)

``The Messenger of Allah ﷺ was affected by sorcery until he thought that he had slept with his wives, while in fact he did not."

This is the worst type of magic spell.

Qadi `Iyadh (may Allah have mercy upon him) said, *``Sorcery is just like any other ailment that the Prophet ﷺ suffered from, and this fact by no means affects his status as a Prophet. Further, the fact that the Prophet ﷺ imagined something which he did not do, does not detract from his truthfulness regarding religion, there is a consensus that he is immune from error in this regard. Sorcery is just like any other matter of this life, which has nothing to do with the reason why he was sent and preferred above humankind. The Prophet ﷺ was subject to come down with all types of ailments that would touch other people. Therefore, it is not surprising that he would imagine doing something which in fact he did not do, and that he was soon cured."*

The Prophet ﷺ used two methods to treat sorcery, first by finding the spell and neutralizing it. The Prophet ﷺ supplicated to his Lord and Allah The Almighty showed him that the evil spell was hidden in a well. The Prophet ﷺ removed the evil spell, which consisted of a comb, combed material (hair) and a dry male spathe. When he discarded these objects, he was immediately cured, as if he was restrained and then suddenly released. This is the best cure from sorcery and is similar to removing septic materials by complete disgorging.

The second type: Extracting harmful substances from the organ most touched by magic works. Evil spells aggravate nature, produce harmful substances and adversely affect the mood. Disgorging the alien substance that affects a certain organ as a result of evil spells becomes necessary.

The effect of the sorcery reached the Prophet's head and affected one of his senses, he imagined he did something while in fact he had not. The sorcerer, therefore, affects some of the natural powers of the body so that it does not function normally.

Sorcery is a combination of the powers of evil spirits and the adverse effects they have on the normal functions of the body. The worst type of magic is that which affects the senses of the affected organ. Drawing blood from the organ most affected by magic is the most beneficial cure, if used in the proper manner. Hippocrates said, *"Cupping (or disgorging) should be used on the part most affected using the most favorable means available."*

Some people also said that when the Messenger of Allah ﷺ suffered from this condition, he first thought that it was caused by spoiled blood that reached the brain and affected the senses. In such cases, cupping is the best medicine, and this is what the Prophet ﷺ did. Then, when Allah The Almighty revealed to him that it was the effect of magic that caused his condition, he asked Allah The Almighty to show him where the evil spell was hidden and then he retrieved and discarded it. When he did so, he was cured, as if released after being restrained. Further the magic spell only affected the Prophet's senses not his sanity or heart. This is why he did not believe what he imagined of sleeping with his wives because he knew that this sensation was not real.

Divine cures are the best remedies against sorcery. Since sorcery is the work of evil spirits, then its best cure is that which neutralizes it, such as certain prayers and recitations of the Qur'an. The more powerful the defending army, the more powerful the adversary it will be able to remove and neutralize. This case is similar to two opposing armies, each of which carries its weapons and armaments. The army that has more weaponry and supplies, is the army that will prevail in the war. When the heart is full of Allah's remembrance and invokes Him often for its needs, and when the heart is joined by the tongue and righteous deeds, these acts will be the best medicine there is against sorcery and magic spells.

The sorcerers and magicians admit that their magic is most effective against those who have weak hearts that are busy satisfying the desires and lusts of the life of this world. That is why magic usually affects women, children, nomads, ignorant people, those who have weak faith, lack trust in Allah (*Tawakkul*) and lack the fundamentals of Islamic Monotheism (*Tawhid*), and those who neither remember Allah The Almighty often nor use the various Prophetic supplications and Islamic prayer formulas (*Ruqyah*). In general, the effect of sorcery and magic is more powerful against weak hearts that lean towards the lower desires of this world.

When the heart leans towards this earthly life, sorcery and magic becomes most effective against it, because evil spirits only search for evil in the soul that is prone to submit to their power. Surely, evil in the heart deprives one of divine power that is necessary to provide it with sufficient weapons of defense against these evil spirits. That is why these evil spirits, which seek evil, find the hearts weakened by evil unarmed and prone to submit to evil and this is when sorcery and magic spells are most effective. And Allah knows best.

The Prophetís guidance on vomiting as a remedy

At-Tirmidhi (may Allah have mercy upon him) reported that a person narrated that Abu Ad-Dardaa رَضِيَ الله عَنْهُ said, ``*The Prophet once performed ablution after he vomited. I met Thawban* رَضِيَ الله عَنْهُ *in the mosque of Damascus and mentioned what Abu Ad-Dardaa* رَضِيَ الله عَنْهُ *narrated to him and he said, `True'. I poured water for him (the Prophet* ﷺ *then."* At-Tirmidhi then commented that this *Hadith* is the most authentic on this subject. [Also, Ahmad, Al-Hakim, Ibn Al-Jard, Ad-Daraqutni, Al-Bayhaqi and At-Tahawi].

Vomiting is one of the five methods used to disgorge septic substances from the body. They are diarrhea, vomiting, cupping, the passing of air or wind and sweating. The *Sunnah* (tradition) has mentioned these five types.

As for diarrhea, we mentioned the *Hadith* that states, ``*Diarrhea is the best of your remedies."* We also mentioned the *Hadith* about *Senna.*

We mentioned cupping when we narrated the *Ahadith* about this subject.

As for getting rid of septic gases and vapors we will elaborate on this subject later on in this book.

As for getting rid of septic substances by sweating, it does not usually involve puncturing of the veins. The body naturally rids itself of these substances through the skin when sweat leaves the body through the open pores.

Vomiting involves throwing up the harmful substances through the upper part of the stomach. An enema and medicines that instigate disgorging artificially through the lower parts of the stomach are of two types: naturally-occurring and artificially instigated. The naturally instigated vomit should not be prevented, except when it becomes excessive and

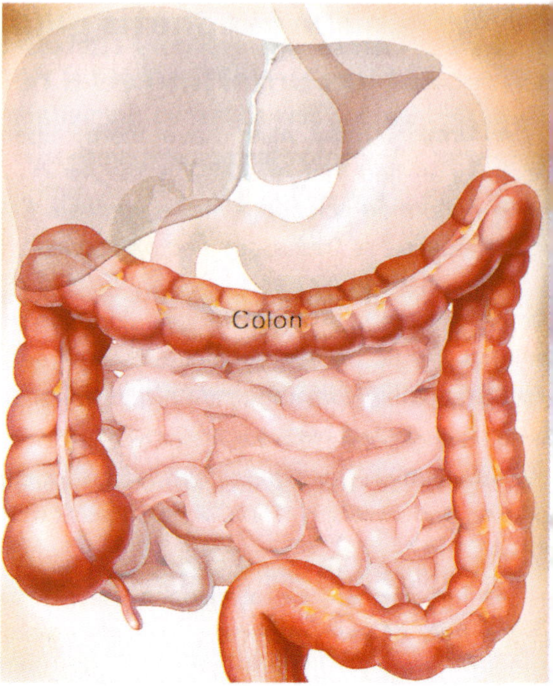

becomes unsafe. In this case one should take the medicines that stops vomiting. The second type of vomiting is used for medicinal purposes, at an appropriate time and under proper conditions.

There are ten causes for vomiting:

Excessive amounts of bile that float in the stomach and seek an exit out of the body.

Excessive amounts of phlegm in the stomach that also seek a way out of the body.

When the stomach is weak and unable to completely digest the food and the partially digested food seeks an exit out of the body.

When a harmful substance enters the stomach and causes a disruption in the digestion process.

When one eats excessive amounts of food or drink, more than the stomach can bear. In this case, the stomach will not be able to tolerate these excessive amounts of nourishment and will seek to throw them out.

When the food or drink consumed is not suitable for the stomach, which then throws them out.

When the stomach suffers from a condition that spoils the food and drink which then seeks an exit.

Nausea might also cause vomiting.

Depression, sadness and anguish cause disregard for the needs of the body and its necessities of food, including the need to mature and digest the food. Thus the stomach gets rid of this undigested food by vomiting.

Vomiting may occur under the pressure of various physiological conditions, because the body and the psyche both effect each other profoundly.

One might feel nauseous and then vomit upon seeing other people vomit.

Once, a doctor informed me that he had a nephew who was good at applying Kohl (antimony, a black powder used for the eyes) and when his nephew would apply Kohl to a person who was suffering from conjunctivitis, he himself would later catch conjunctivitis. When this was repeated several times, his nephew stopped this profession. I asked the doctor about the cause of his nephew's condition and he said that his nephew's body reacted to the condition of the men he was treating by catching the same ailment they suffered from. He also said that he knows of a man who saw a benign growth or an abscess on someone's body and that he started to scratch the same part on his body. Later on, he also had a growth in the same area.

I say that this proves that the psyche affects the body in such a way that when certain powers in the body are idle, it suddenly becomes active without a reason.[1]

---

(1) Editor's note : Time has proven the author's theory to be correct but the above examples to be suspect.

Vomiting is suitable as a remedy in hot weather and hot climates

In hot areas and hot weather, certain harmful substances are light and thus prone to float, and this is why vomiting becomes a proficient way to discard these mixtures. On the other hand, certain harmful substances in cold areas and in cold weather become thicker and are harder to extract from above. In this case, getting rid of these harmful mixtures is accomplished better by diarrhea.

The elimination of harmful mixtures is done by pulling them from the farthest exit or by extracting them from the nearest exit. For instance there are various mixtures of substances that are not stable and seek to either ascend or descend. If the mixture tends to ascend, then discarding it from below is better. If the mixture tends to descend, then pulling it from above is better. When the mixture becomes stable, then discarding it from the nearest exit is better.

When the mixture starts to harm the upper organs, it should be pulled down through the lower parts, and vice versa. When these mixtures become stable, they should be discarded from the nearest exit.

This is why the Prophet ﷺ had cupping sometimes in his arm vein, sometimes in his head and sometimes on the top of his foot, so that the spoiled blood was discarded from the nearest possible exit.

Vomiting cleanses the stomach from harmful substances

Vomiting strengthens the stomach, sharpens the sight, relieves headaches, ulcers, and infections in the kidneys and the prostate. Vomiting also relieves and soothes chronic illnesses, such as leprosy, dropsy, partial paralysis, or trembling.

A healthy person should induce vomiting once or twice a month each time vomiting two times, so that the second vomit rids the body of the substances that remain after the first one. Excessive vomiting harms the stomach and weakens its protective layers. It also harms the teeth, the sight and hearing along with causing headaches. Those suffering from swelling in the throat, weak chests, those who have small windpipes, or those who find it difficult to vomit intentionally or those prone to spitting up blood should not vomit intentionally.

Those who have the bad habit of filling their stomachs with food and then inducing vomiting will find that this method accelerates old age and leads to many harmful diseases, along with making vomiting habitual.

Inducing vomiting while suffering from dehydration, weak or defective intestines, senility, or general weakness in the body is dangerous for the health. The best time to induce vomit is during summer and spring, not winter or autumn. When vomiting intentionally, one should cover his eyes, wash the face with cold water when finished and should then drink apple juice with some mastic and rosewater if possible. Vomit should be expelled through the mouth or pulled from below in the form of diarrhea. Hippocrates said, ``*Vomit during the summer should be (naturally) expelled from above more than by using medicine, while in winter it should be pulled from below using medications.*"

The Prophetís guidance on seeking the best doctors

Imam Malik (may Allah have mercy upon him) narrated in his Muwatta that Zaid bin Aslam رَضِيَ الله عَنْهُ said:

أن رجلاً في زَمَن رسول الله صلى الله عليه وسلم أَصَابَهُ جُرحٌ، فَاحْتَقَن الدمُ. وإن الرجلَ دعا رجُلَيْن من بني أَنْمار، فنَظَرَ إليه. فزَعَمَا أنّ رسولَ الله صلى الله عليه وسلم، قال لهما: أيُّكما أطَبُّ؟ فقالا: أوَفي الطِّبِّ خيرٌ يا رسولَ الله؟ فقال: أنزَل الدواءَ الذي أنزل الدَّاءَ.

(الموطأ: ٢/ ٩٤٣ مرسلاً ولأصل الحديث شواهد صحيحة كما ستأتي)

``During the time of the Prophet ﷺ, a man was injured and the blood was congested in the wound. The man then called two doctors from Bani Anmar to examine him. The man then claimed that the Messenger of Allah ﷺ asked them: `Who is the best doctor among you?' They asked, `Is there preference in medicine, O Messenger of Allah?' He said: 'The One Who has sent down the disease also sent down the cure.'"

This *Hadith* indicates that Muslims should seek the best authority in each and every matter and field, because such expertise will ensure that the job is done with excellence. For instance, those inquiring about a matter of religion should seek the most knowledgeable scholar to answer their questions. Further, those who are unsure about the direction of the prayer should imitate the most knowledgeable person available. This is the way Allah The Almighty has created His slaves.

For instance, those traveling on land or sea should seek the best guides because their hearts will feel safer following their lead and in their presence. The religion, the mind and the way Allah The Almighty created mankind all emphasize this fact mentioned in the *Hadith*.

The Prophet's statement:

« أَنزَلَ الدَّواءَ الذي أنزَلَ الداءَ »

``He Who has sent down the disease also sent down the cure."

Like this has been mentioned in several other *Ahadith*. For example, Hilal bin Yusuf said,

«دخل رسول الله صلى الله عليه وسلم على مريضٍ يَعودُه، فقال: أرسِلُوا إلى طبيب، فقال قائلٌ: وأنتَ تقولُ ذلك يارسول الله؟! قال: نعم؛ إن الله عزوجل لم يُنزِلْ داء، إلاّ أنزَلَ له دواءً» (ابن ابي شيبه مرسلاً ٢٣٤٠٤ وأصله ثابت صحيح)

"The Messenger of Allah ﷺ once visited a sick man and said: `Send for a doctor.' A man said, `Do you say that, O Messenger of Allah?' He said: `Yes. Allah has not sent down a disease but also sent down a cure for it." (Ahmad)

In the *Sahihayn* it is also narrated that the Prophet ﷺ said:

« مَا أنزَلَ اللهُ مِن دَاءٍ، إلا أنزَلَ له شِفاءً » (البخاري:٥٦٧٨)

``Allah has not sent down a disease except that He sent down its cure."

There is a difference of opinion on the meaning of sending down the disease and the cure. Some people say that sending the cure down means the slaves become aware of it. This opinion is not valid, although Allah The Almighty has informed us about the fact that for every disease there is a cure, still the Prophet ﷺ said:

عَلِمَهُ مَن عَلِمَهُ، وَجَهِلَه مَن جَهله

``Those who know it are aware of it, and those who do not know it are ignorant of it."

Some people say that the Prophet's statement indicates that Allah The Almighty has created these cures on the earth, like another *Hadith*: *``Allah does not create a disease but creates its cure."* Although this opinion is better than the first one, it is still not valid because ``sending down" is more precise and specific than creating.

Another group says that the statement means that Allah The Almighty sends down the cure with the angels who are responsible for the affairs of mankind including the diseases and their cures. Indeed, the angels are responsible for the daily affairs of this world, especially the affairs of humankind from the time he or she is a fetus until they die. This opinion that the angels are sent down with the cure is more plausible.

Other people say that the majority of the medicine comes down with the rain, as the rain causes the growth of the vegetation and food, meaning the various sources for cure. Rain washes down various minerals from the mountaintops which are used in remedies and helps in the growth of various types of fruits and plants, and even spring water that are used in cures and remedies. This opinion is better than the previous three opinions, but Allah knows best.

This is the perfect wisdom of Allah The Almighty, that He tests His slaves with the disease and yet helps them find the cure. He also tests His slaves with sins, but helps them erase these sins by repenting to Him, by performing good deeds and by their enduring different calamities and disasters. Allah The Almighty also tests His slaves with evil, yet helps His slaves with angels. Allah The Almighty also tests His slaves with desires, but has allowed them to satisfy their desires by taking from the good, pure substances that are also desirable. Allah The Almighty has not tested His slaves with anything but provides them with what helps them sustain themselves against that trial and test. The difference between the slaves of Allah The Almighty in this state is in their knowing and acquiring such aids. Allah The Almighty is sought for help regarding each and every matter.

The Prophetís guidance on requiring compensation from those unqualified to practice medicine

Abu Dawud, An-Nasa'i and Ibn Majah (may Allah have mercy upon them) said that the Messenger of Allah ﷺ said:

« من تطبَّبَ – ولم يُعلَم منه الطِّبُّ قَبْلَ ذلك فهو ضَامن » (أبو داود : ٤٥٨٦ وحسنه الألباني)

``Those who practice Tibb, but are not knowledgeable in this profession are responsible for their actions." [Al-Hakim also narrated this Hadith].

There are three types of benefits in this *Hadith*: linguistic, religious and medical.

Linguistically, *Tibb* entails preparing a thing. It also entails excellence and thus denotes other than the profession of doctors. A person might be called *Tabib* (which usually means doctor) when they are proficient in anything. Also, a proficiency might be called *Tibb* sometimes even magic.

In the *Sahih* it is narrated that `Aishah رَضِـيَ الله عَنْها said, *``When the Jews worked magic on the Messenger of Allah ﷺ, two angels sat next to him one at his head and the other at his feet, one of them asked, `What is the matter with the man?' The other angel said, `He is Matbub (touched by magic).' The first angel asked, `Who did Tibb (sorcery) on him?' The second angel said, `Such and such Jewish fellow.' "*

Abu `Ubaid رَضِـيَ الله عَنْهُ said that those touched by magic are called *Matbub* , touched by magic. The medicine is also called *Tibb*.

Thus the word *Tabib* describes a knowledgeable person including doctors.

The religious benefit from this *Hadith* requires the ignorant doctor to pay for his mistakes, because he has practiced a profession although he was unqualified in it and then caused harm to the people, whom he has in fact cheated and deceived. Therefore, unqualified doctors are held responsible for any health risks they cause, according to the consensus of the scholars.

Al-Khattabi (may Allah have mercy upon him) said, *"There is no difference concerning the ruling that when one treats a sick person and causes him harm then he is financially responsible for his acts. Those who practice a profession that they are not proficient in are aggressors. Therefore, when their actions lead to harm, the aggressors ought to pay for their action, financially not physically since the sick person actually allows such ignorant people to treat him."*

There are five types of doctors:

First: A proficient doctor who gives the profession its due right and who acts responsibly. When such a person treats a sick person -- an act that is allowed both by the religion and the sick person -- and then commits a mistake, he is not liable for this mistake. For instance, when a doctor who is proficient in his job performs circumcision for a boy under favorable circumstances, but the organ suffers some type of damage, the doctor will not be liable for this mistake. Also, if a swelling is cupped by a proficient person in the proper time and manner, but a certain damage occurs, the doctor is not liable for that mistake.

Second: An ignorant doctor who treats a sick person and causes him harm. If the sick person had knowledge beforehand that this doctor is ignorant and yet allows him to treat him, then there is no compensation required in this case. This ruling does not contradict the *Hadith* we mentioned in the beginning of the chapter. The wording of the *Hadith* indicates that those who have to pay for their mistakes will have cheated the sick person and created the illusion that they were proficient doctors.

If the sick person thinks that a certain person is a proficient doctor and thus allows him to treat him, the ignorant doctor is required to compensate the sick person for whatever damage he might cause.

Also, when such a so-called doctor prescribes a medicine for the sick person who takes the medicine thinking that the doctor prescribed the medicine to him with knowledge, and if the medicine causes any harm, compensation would be required in this case. The *Hadith* is clear in its indication regarding this type.

Third: A proficient doctor who is given permission to treat a person but makes a mistake and causes harm to a healthy organ (meaning not the organ he was treating), then in this case compensation is required because it is an aggression by mistake. Does this person pay the compensation from his own money or from the Muslim treasury? There are two opinions on this subject: If the doctor is not Muslim, compensation is paid from his own money and if the doctor is Muslim there is a difference of opinion as we mentioned earlier.

Fourth: The proficient doctor who prescribes the wrong medicine for the sick person who dies as a consequence. There are two opinions on this subject: one of them requires the compensation from the Muslim treasury while the other requires it should be paid from the doctor's resources. Both of these opinions were attributed to Imam Ahmad (may Allah have mercy upon him).

Fifth: A proficient doctor who amputates an organ from an insane person or a child without permission, or who circumcises a boy without his parents' permission and the organ is harmed. Some scholars say that the doctor is required to pay compensation in this case because he was not given permission to operate. However, if the guardian or the parent allows the doctor to operate then the doctor is not required to pay for his mistake.

It is possible that the doctor who operates without permission may not have to pay compensation because he intended to do good and is therefore not liable for the damage he causes. The *Hadith* in the beginning of this chapter includes such medicinal professions as practitioners writing prescription remedies, applying Kohl, physicians, performing circumcision, cupping and incisions, fixing broken bones, cauterization and administering injections, veterinarians, and so forth. It is a recent practice to restrict the word doctor to mean a specific part of the profession.

The proficient doctor takes the following steps when treating any type of disease.

First diagnose the type of disease.

Search for the cause behind the disease.

Examine the sick person to decide if his body is able to fend off the disease or if it is weaker than the disease. If the patient is strong enough to resist the disease, the doctor should not prescribe medicine.

Examine the patient and his mood and condition.

Examine the changes in the state of the patient.

Examine the sick person's age,

Examine his habits and what he is accustomed to,

Remember seasonal effects.

Consider the sick person's place of origin.

Consider the atmospheric conditions at the time he caught the disease.

Search for the correct and suitable medicine.

Examine the effectiveness of the medicine and the correct dosage.

The doctor not only intends to cure the ailment, but also to prevent what is even more serious. For instance, if curing a certain disease leads the way to an even more serious disease, the doctor allows the current illness to remain and tries to make it milder. For instance, the orifice of the veins, which is treated by incision or cutting, might aggravate other acute ailments.

Choosing and prescribing the simplest medicine for treatment is warranted. For instance, the doctor does not prescribe medicine unless he investigates his options of food and diet. Also, the doctor should not prescribe multiple or complex medications until he investigates his options regarding simpler medications. It is a sign that the doctor is truly professional that he prescribes food when he can substitute it for medicine, and simple rather than complex medications.

The doctor examines if the illness is treatable or not. If the doctor finds out that he is unable to treat the disease, let him preserve his energy and reputation and avoid falling prey to his own greed so that he pretends to cure the incurable.

If the illness is curable, the doctor examines if it can be completely cured, or at least made milder. If the doctor discovers that he cannot cure the disease or decrease its intensity, he should examine the ways to stop it from being aggravated. In this case, medication should be administered for this purpose, to increase the strength of the body and stop the disease from increasing.

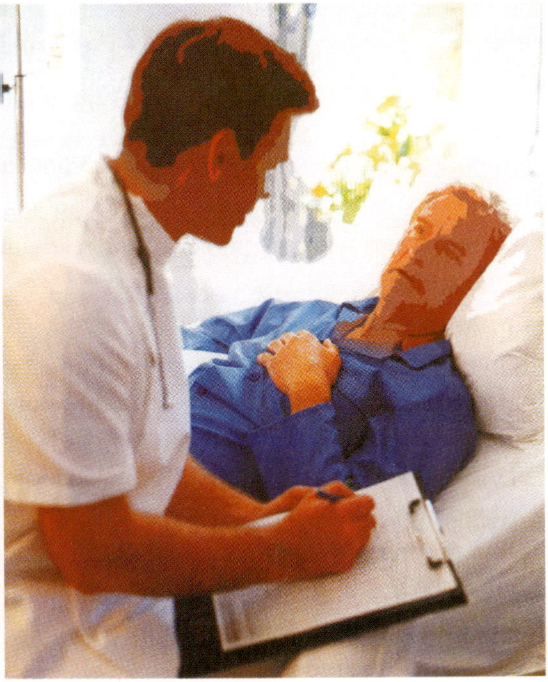

The doctor should not revert to excreting the septic substances before they become stable and mature.

The doctor should also be knowledgeable of the sicknesses of the heart and soul and the methods of treating such ailments. This, indeed, is a major aspect of medical science, for the effect of the heart's moods and feelings is apparent in the physical body. This is why we state that if a medical doctor is also proficient in the ills of the hearts, he will be the perfect doctor. On the other hand, the doctor who does not have knowledge of the ills of the heart while being knowledgeable in the ills of the body, he will be only half of a doctor.

He is not a doctor who does not examine the righteousness of the sick person's heart and encourage him to strengthen his soul and body by performing righteous, good deeds, such as charity and being interested in drawing closer to Allah The Almighty and acquiring the good of the Hereafter. Rather, he is a fake doctor.

In fact, the best cures are in performing righteous good deeds, charity, remembering Allah The Almighty, supplicating to Him, seeking His help, invoking Him and repenting to Him. Such good deeds have a truly profound effect in curing illnesses, more so than the usual medications, providing that the ailing person has faith in such divine remedies.

18. Being lenient and forbearing with the sick person, just as one is easygoing and lenient with a child.

19. The doctor should use the various types of medicinal and spiritual cures, along with using his imagination.

20. The doctor should make his treatment revolve around the six major principles, which are the cornerstone of his profession. First, the doctor should preserve the health. Second he should try and restore the lost health. Third, the doctor should cure the disease. Fourth, at least lessen the intensity of the disease. Fifth, the doctor should ignore the lesser evil and treat the bigger evil. Sixth, the doctor should ignore the lesser good to acquire the greater good. The science of medicine revolves around these six basic principles, and the doctor who does not rely on them is not a doctor. And Allah knows best.

The sick person passes through four stages:

The beginning.

The intense stage.

Receding

The end of the illness.

Since the sick person passes through four stages the doctor has to examine each of these stages carefully and treat them in the proper manner. For instance, if the doctor feels the body needs to remove and excrete harmful substances, if they are mature, he should do so. If this is not possible in the beginning of the ailment -- especially if the disease has already progressed, or because the body is weak, the weather is cold, or by mistake -- the doctor should not resort to excretion in these cases.

If the doctor ignores this warning, the body will be busy dealing with the medication and will not concentrate on resisting the disease. This is similar to requiring a soldier who is busy defending his post to do something else. Rather, the doctor's concern should be concentrated on preserving the strength of the body as much as possible at this stage.

When the disease has stopped progressing, the doctor should then use excretion and treating the causes of the disease. It is even better when the disease has started to subside and end. This case is similar to an enemy whose strength has started to depart and his ammunition nears its end, so capturing him in this case becomes easier. When the enemy starts to take flight, it is even easier to capture him. It is a fact that the strength of the enemy will be at a maximum in the beginning of his aggression. This is the exact case with medicine as regards the ailing body.

The skilled doctor uses the easiest treatment and cure first, then the more difficult or powerful medications. Therefore, the doctor moves from the less powerful to the more powerful, unless he fears that the strength of the body will be drained if he does not use the most powerful medicine first. Also, the skilled doctor does not keep using the same medications in a way that will allow the body to get used to the medicine and thus it loses its effectiveness.

We also mentioned that the doctor should first consider prescribing a diet before using medications. If the doctor is unsure about the nature of the disease, he should not prescribe medication before being sure of the correctness of his diagnosis. There is no harm if the doctor administers a medication that does not cause side effects or negative repercussions.

When several diseases attack the body, the doctor starts with the medicine that satisfies three conditions: First, treating the disease that might lead to curing the other diseases, such as when confronted with a swelling and an ulcer, he starts with the swelling.

Second, the doctor starts with the disease that has caused the other. For example, if the doctor is confronted with an embolism (the obstruction of an artery by an embolus, usually a piece of clotted blood which breaks away from one part of the circulatory system and travels to another) and septic-related fever, he starts with the cause of the first disease.

Third, when one of the two diseases is more serious than the other disease, then the doctor should start with the acute ailment. Yet, the doctor should also examine the progress of the other disease.

When a disease and a symptomatic ailment both attack the body simultaneously, the doctor starts with the disease, unless the symptomatic condition is stronger, such as in the case of painful constipation. The doctor first treats the pain then treats the embolism. If the doctor can substitute excretion or extraction (of the septic substances) with hunger, fasting, sleep, then he should do so.

The Prophetís guidance on preventing contagious diseases and enforcing quarantine

Muslim (may Allah have mercy upon him) narrated that Jabir bin `Abdullah رَضِيَ الله عَنْهُ said:

« إنه كان في وَفْد ثَقِيف رجلٌ مجذومٌ، فأرسل إليه النبي صلى الله عليه وسلم: ارجِعْ فقَدْ بايَعْناك». (مسلم: ٢٢٣١)

``Thaqif's delegation included a man with leprosy. The Prophet ﷺ sent to him: `Go back, for we have accepted your pledge of allegiance." [Ibn Majah, Ahmad, Ibn Khuzaymah and Ibn Jarir].

Al-Bukhari (may Allah have mercy upon him) narrated that the Prophet ﷺ said:

« لا تُدِيموا النَّظَرَ إلى المَجْذومِين ». (ابن ماجه وحححه الألباني : ٣٥٤٣)

``Do not keep looking at the person afflicted by leprosy." [Ahmad, At-Tayalisi, At-Tabarani and Al-Bayhaqi].

Further, in the *Sahihayn* it is narrated that the Prophet ﷺ said:

« لا يُورِدَنَّ مُمْرِضٌ على مُصِحٍّ». (البخاري:٥٧٧١)

``A healthy man should not be brought near a sick person." [Abu Dawud, Ahmad, Ibn Majah, Ahmad and Al-Bayhaqi]

Leprosy is an especially harmful disease that occurs due to the accumulation of black bile in the entire body, altering the condition or temperament and shape of the organs. In the final stages, leprosy might cause such bad corrosion that the affected limbs would start to fall off and disintegrate.

Leprosy is also called the disease of the lion, for three reasons. First, this disease usually attacks lions (or wild beasts). Second, because this disease causes the face to frown, like the lion's face. The third, leprosy is contagious and will devour its victim just as the lion devours its prey.

Leprosy is a contagious disease, and those who come near the person afflicted with leprosy will be bothered by the foul odor, just like those suffering from tuberculosis.

The Prophet ﷺ, who was full of mercy and pity for his nation, commanded them not to expose themselves to what might bring harm to their bodies and hearts. There is no doubt that certain bodies are disease prone and are easily affected by the surrounding environment, and as we have stated, leprosy is a contagious disease. Sometimes, someone's fear of the disease might actually help the disease attack the

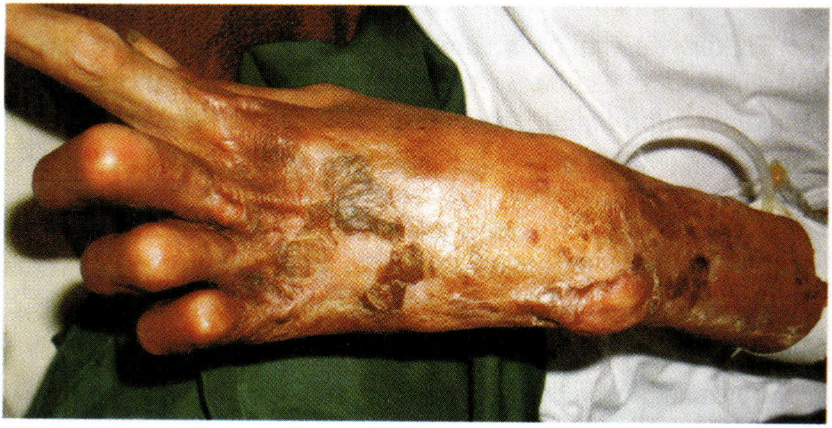

body, because fear prepares the organs of the body for the possibility of catching the disease. Sometimes, when one even smells the foul odor emitted by persons inflicted by certain diseases, they in turn catch the same disease, if their body is susceptible to catch the disease.

Some people stated that the *Ahadith* we mentioned in this chapter are overruled by some other *Ahadith* . They brought as evidence what the Prophet ﷺ said: "*There is no contagion nor evil omen.*" [Al-Bukhari, Muslim and Abu Dawud].[1]

We should state that there is no contradiction between the authentic *Ahadith*. When there is an appearance of contradiction, one of the *Ahadith*

(1) Editor's note : There is no contagion based on superstition, which was rampant in the pre-Islamic times.

might not be an authentic *Hadith*, sometimes, the narrators of *Ahadith* might have made mistakes, although they are truthful themselves. Or, one of the seemingly contradicted *Ahadith* might overrule the other.

Further, there are no two authentic *Ahadith* that are direct in meaning, yet which contradict each other in every respect. Allah The Almighty forbids that his truthful Messenger should ever contradict himself, and therefore, everything the Prophet ﷺ uttered is the ultimate truth, no doubt. Problems and errors sometime arise from the narrators of the *Hadith* , the shortcoming in comprehending the true meaning of some *Ahadith* or the inability to distinguish between authentic and forged *Ahadith*.

Ibn Qutaibah (may Allah have mercy upon him) said in his book, '*Ikhtilaf Al-Hadith*', while talking about the enemies of *Hadith*,

"They say, `These are Ahadith that contradict each other. You narrated that the Prophet ﷺ said: `There is neither contagion nor evil omen.' And that the Prophet ﷺ was told, `Wet mange attacks the camel's lip and then the camels catch leprosy,' and that he said: `What has transferred the ailment to the first camel?' You also narrated: `No healthy person should be brought near a sick person, and avoid the one with leprosy just as you avoid the lion.' You also reported that a man with leprosy came to give his allegiance to the Prophet ﷺ on Islam and that he said to him that his pledge is accepted, ordering him to return without meeting him. He also said: `Evil omen is in three things: the woman, the animal and the house,' and all these statements contradict each other."

Abu Muhammad (Ibn Qutaibah, may Allah have mercy upon him) then commented,

``We say that there is no contradiction, because each statement has its own meaning and timeframe. When the *Hadith* is used in its proper context, the appearance of contradiction will not be substantiated. There are two types of contagion: one of them is leprosy like contagion.

For instance, when the odor of the person afflicted with leprosy is felt by those who talk and sit near the patient for a long time, they might fall victim to the same disease. Such is the case with the wife of the person with leprosy who remains under the same roof with him and thus catches the disease. Also, the children of the person afflicted with leprosy might catch the disease later on in their life (hereditary).

Such is the case with those suffering from tuberculosis, hectic fever and mange. The doctors order that those suffering from tuberculosis and leprosy should be avoided, not because they fear that such cases are contagious but because the bad odor that emits from such people might affect the healthy persons when exposed to it for a long time. The doctors are the farthest people from believing in evil or good omens.

The same argument is true in the case with *Nuqbah,* which is a wet type of leprosy or mange that attacks camels. When the infected camel mixes or mingles with other healthy camels, the infection will be transferred through the water [open sores] or the mucus that the camel produces. This is the meaning that the Prophet ﷺ intended when he said: *'No sick person should be brought near a healthy person.'* He disliked that the sick people associate with healthy people, to prevent the healthy people from being exposed to any substances or rashes that the body of the sick person produces.

The second type of contagion, is the plague, for instance, that appears in a land and the person thus seeks to flee that land for fear of catching the disease. The Prophet ﷺ said: *'If it (the plague) appears in a land where you are residing, do not depart that land. If it appears in a land, do not enter it.'* The Prophet ﷺ ordered the people not to depart from the land afflicted by the plague, as they might think that by fleeing they would be avoiding Allah's appointed destiny. Also, the Prophet ﷺ ordered the people not to enter a land afflicted by the plague, for remaining in the healthy land brings calmness to the hearts and tranquility in livelihood. This type of contagion also includes the husband who suffers an affliction and attributes it to the bad omen of his wife or the house as is common. This is the type that the Prophet ﷺ meant when he said: *``There is neither contagion...' "*

Some other people said the Prophet ﷺ only recommended that leprosy patients be avoided and that it is still allowed to eat with them, as the Prophet ﷺ himself did.

Some other people said that these *Ahadith* contain specific commands for different types of people. For instance, some people have such a strong faith and reliance on Allah The Almighty that the strength of their faith saves them from contagious diseases, just as the natural powers that exist in the body sometimes fend off the harm of the disease. Some people, on the other hand, do not have a strong faith, so the Prophet ﷺ commanded them to be cautious.

The Prophet ﷺ implemented his own advice in both cases, so that the strong imitate his acts, depending on their trust in Allah The Almighty. On the other hand, the weak would imitate the Prophet ﷺ [when he avoided leprosy patients, for instance) to be cautious. Both ways are correct, but one is suitable for those who have strong faith while the other is suitable for those who have weak faith. Consequently, both groups of the believers will have their own method that is suitable for their own situation.

As another example, the Prophet ﷺ used cauterization by fire for medicinal purposes. Yet, he praised whoever refrains from using cauterization and mentioned avoiding it with the good deeds of shunning the bad omen and having total dependence on Allah The Almighty. There are many other examples on this subject. The Prophet's method [of admonishment] was always very gentle, and those who comprehend it in the correct manner will get rid of many suspicions that the authentic *Sunnah* contradicts itself.

Some other people stated that ordering people to run away from the one with leprosy prevents the transfer of the disease by mingling with the sick or by smelling their odor when such mingling and associations are extensive and prolonged. As for short visitations with such people for a good purpose, there is no harm in it and catching the disease will not be plausible during these brief contacts. The Prophet ﷺ prohibited prolonged exposure to sick people to preserve health and allowed brief contacts that would not cause harm. Therefore, where is the contradiction here?

Another group of people said it is plausible that the person who suffered from leprosy with whom the Prophet sat and ate was suffering from mild leprosy. There are several types of leprosy that vary in their seriousness and the degree of their contagion. In such cases, it is possible to mingle with some people suffering from mild leprosy that has not progressed and avoid catching the disease. When the illness is unable to progress in the sick person's body, it will be even less able to attack another person's body.

Another group of people said that the people before Islam believed that diseases themselves are contagious, without referring this matter to the power and will of Allah The Almighty in the beginning and the end. The Prophet ﷺ refuted their belief and ate with a person with leprosy to prove that Allah is the One Who causes the disease to come and Who brings about the cure. The Prophet ﷺ also prohibited the Muslims from mingling with the sick to teach them that sickness and diseases are created by Allah The Almighty to have a certain effect on people. The prohibition affirms these effects, while his action teaches us that such effects are totally controlled by Allah The Almighty, and that if He wills, these effects will not have any power. Also, if He wills, these effects will cause the harm that He has decided and willed.

Finally, some other people say that these *Ahadith* might be overruled by other *Ahadith*, and that in case we are unable to produce the latter *Hadith* that overrules the previous *Hadith*, we should refrain from discussing this matter further.[1]

(1) Editor's note : In pre-Islamic times called ``the days of ignorance" contagion was a - tributed to an evil wife, an evil location, etc.These practices were stopped by the Prophet as he stopped all such practices based on superstition and ignorance. His guidance on how to deal with lepers, those with tuberculosis, the plague and the general principals of not letting the healthy intermingle with the sick are all proofs of his Divine guidance.

The Prophetís guidance on prohibiting using what Allah The Almighty has forbidden for medicinal purposes

Abu Dawud (may Allah have mercy upon him) narrated that Abu Ad-Dardaa رَضِيَ اللهُ عَنْهُ said that the Messenger of Allah ﷺ said:

«إن اللهَ أنزل الداءَ والدَّواءَ، وجعل لكلِّ داءٍ دواءً فتداوَوْا لاتَتَدوَوْا بِالْمُحَرَّم»

(أبو دواد: ٣٨٧٤ وضعفه الألباني، وله شاهد عند مسمل كما سيأتي)

``Allah has sent down the disease and the cure and has created a cure for every disease. Seek the cure, but do not use what has been prohibited for medicinal purposes." [At-Tabarani].

Al-Bukhari also narrated that Ibn Mas'ood رَضِيَ الله عَنْهُ said,

«إن اللهَ لم يَجْعَلْ شِفاءَكم فيما حَرَّمَ عَلَيكم»

(البخاري، قبل: ٥٦١٤ تعليقاً وموقوفا على ابن مسعود، وسنده صحيح على شرط الشيخين)

``Verily Allah has not made your cure in that which has been forbidden for you".

Also in the Sunan [Abu Dawud and At-Tirmidhi] it is narrated that Abu Hurairah رَضِيَ الله عَنْهُ said,

``The Messenger of Allah ﷺ has disallowed using impure (prohibited) substances for medicinal purposes."

Imam Muslim (may Allah have mercy upon him) narrated that Tariq Ibn Suwayd Al-Ju'fi said that he asked the Prophet ﷺ about alcohol and that he has disallowed it or hated that he manufactures it. He said:

``I only make it for medicinal purposes."* The Prophet ﷺ said: *``It is not a cure. Rather, it is a disease."

Also in the *Sunan* it is narrated that the Prophet ﷺ was asked about *Al-Khamr* [alcohol] for medicinal purposes. The Prophet ﷺ said:

« إنَّ ذلِك ليس بِشِفَاءٍ، ولكِنَّه داءٌ » (ابن ماجه: ٣٥٠٠ وصححه الألباني)

``Verily that is not a cure, rather it is a disease." [Abu Dawud and At-Tirmidhi].

Also, Muslim narrated that Tariq bin Suwayd Al-Hadhrami said, ``I said, 'O Messenger of Allah! There are some vines in our land that we squeeze (for alcohol) and that we drink from.' He said: `Do not do it.' So I went back to him and said, `We use it for medicinal purposes.' He said:

« إنه ليس بدواءٍ، ولكنه داءٌ » (مسلم : ١٩٨٤)

*``It is not a cure. Rather, it is a disease.''' [Abu Dawud and At-*Tirmidhi*].*(1)

An-Nasa'i (may Allah have mercy upon him) narrated that a doctor mentioned using frogs to make medicine and the Prophet ﷺ prohibited killing the frog for that purpose. [Abu Dawud, Ahmad and Al-Hakim]

Using what Allah The Almighty has prohibited in medicines is an evil act according to the religion and the sound mind. As for the religion, we mentioned several *Ahadith* on this subject.

As for the mind, Allah The Almighty has prohibited whatever substances He has prohibited because they are impure. Further, Allah The Almighty has never disallowed a good, beneficial matter for the Muslims, as He has decided in the case of the Children of Israel:

﴿ فَبِظُلْمٍ مِّنَ ٱلَّذِينَ هَادُوا۟ حَرَّمْنَا عَلَيْهِمْ طَيِّبَٰتٍ أُحِلَّتْ لَهُمْ ﴾

``For the wrong-doing of the Jews, we made unlawful for them certain good foods which had been lawful for them".

Allah The Almighty has prohibited some matters and substances because of the harm that they carry and to save His slaves from such harm. It is not suitable that the slaves seek these harmful substances for medicinal purposes. Even if such substances appear to have an effect on the disease, they bring about a more serious illness in the heart because they are impure and unclean. In this case, the sick person who uses what Allah The Almighty has disallowed for medicinal purposes might be able to remove the physical illness but would cause himself a

(1) **Editor's note:** The Prophet ﷺ descibed alcoholism, as a disease, over one thousand four hundred year ago.

more serious disease in the heart.

Further, the Muslims are required to avoid what Allah The Almighty has disallowed, while using them in medicine means that one will not avoid them, as the religion requires. This is the opposite of what the prohibitions seek to achieve.

Also, what Allah The Almighty has prohibited is a disease as the

religion states by the tongue of the Messenger ﷺ. Therefore, Muslims are not allowed to use it as a medicine.

Furthermore, prohibited substances affect the heart and soul and make them impure, since the various substances that the body consumes affect the body. When a substance causes an evil outcome in the body, the nature of the body will acquire this evil temperament.

What about if the substance is impure and evil itself? In this case, when the substance is impure, the body becomes impure, as well. This is why Allah The Almighty has prohibited the impure types of foods, drinks and clothes because of the evil effects that such substances have on the body and soul.

Also, allowing the use of prohibited substances for medicinal purposes will later on encourage taking these substances to satisfy desire and the lust, especially when the heart likes such substances. This is especially the case when the heart thinks that such substances cure the illnesses of the body, thus making them even more desirable and likable. The religion, on the other hand, has closed the door to consuming or using prohibited substances. There is a contradiction if the religion closes the door to using prohibited substances on one hand and opens the door to using them in other instances on the other hand.

Also, prohibited substances that people might use in medicine carry more types of harm than the harm that they might remove. For instance, the mother of all evil substances, alcohol, which Allah The Almighty has not made a cure or a remedy, is very harmful to the brain, which controls the body, according to the doctors and many scholars of *Fiqh* (Islamic jurisprudence). Hippocrates, for example, said while discussing serious illnesses, ``*Alcohol has a serious harmful effect on the brain, because it reaches the brain quickly along with some other harmful substances*

that the body contains, thus causing harm to the brain." The author of *'Al-Kamil'* also said, *``Drinking [alcohol] brings harm to the brain and the nervous system.*

There are two other types of disallowed medicines: one that the heart does not like, such as snake meat and poisons. Such substances are heavy on the heart and the stomach [besides being dangerous] and are thus a disease not a cure. There are also some other medicines that are not disliked themselves, such as some drinks that pregnant women take. These substances carry more harm than benefit, and consequently, the mind and the religion corroborate on disliking them.

There is another wisdom behind disallowing the consumption of prohibited substances as medicine. One of the conditions for the efficacy of a medicine is one's belief that it will work and bring the cure by Allah's leave. Indeed, whatever is beneficial is also blessed, and the more benefit it carries, the more blessing it will bring about. What the people consider the most blessed is the substance that they think carries the most benefit.

The Muslim, on the other hand, believes that what Allah The Almighty has disallowed is not beneficial or blessed. Consequently, he will not have favourable thoughts about the disallowed substance and his system will not accept it. Rather, the stronger the slave's faith is, the more he hates the disallowed substances and believes that it is impure. In this case, if the slave takes such a substance it will indeed be a disease not a cure for him, unless he believes that it is pure and thus his dislike for it subsides. Therefore, the believer will not accept the disallowed substance and will consider it a disease, otherwise he will be contradicting the faith.

The Prophetís guidance on treating and removing lice from the head

In the *Sahihayn* it is narrated that Ka`b bin `Ujrah رَضِيَ الله عَنْهُ said, *``I was suffering from lice and I was carried to the Messenger of Allah = while lice were falling off on my face*, the Prophet ﷺ said:

ما كنتُ أُرى الجَهْدَ قد بَلَغ بكَ ما أَرَى فأمَرَه أن يَحلِقَ رأسه،وأن يُطْعِمَ فَرَقًا بَيْنَ ستةٍ، أو يُهدِيَ شاةً، أو يَصُومَ ثلاثةَ أيام (البخاري:١٨١٦)

``I did not realize that your trouble had reached the condition that I see (you in)"

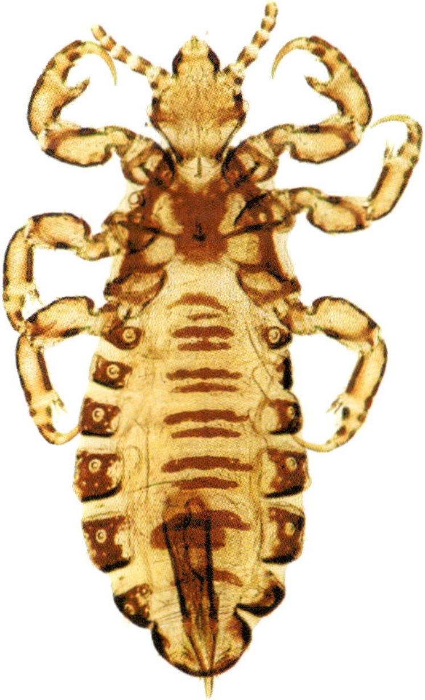

The Prophet ﷺ then ordered him to have his head shaved and either fast three days or feed six poor persons or slaughter one sheep as a sacrifice." [Also, narrated by Ahmad][(1)]

Lice appear on the head and body for two reasons: external and internal. The external cause occurs due to uncleanliness and impure substances that the skin might carry. The internal reason is caused by rotten substances (toxins) that the body expels through the skin that rot due to the wetness in the skin's pores. The lice appear then. (and feed on these rotted substances).

(1) Editor's note : The Prophet ﷺ described Alcoholism, as a disease, over one thousand four hundred years ago. * Editor's note : The Prophet ordered Ka'b to fast, feed poor persons, or slaughter a sheep as an expiation for shaving his head while in Ihram (ritual state of one performing *Hajj*). The fact that Ka'b was performing *Hajj* was not made clear by the author. Shaving the head in itself does not require such expiations outside of *Hajj*. AW.

Many times, lice appear after one suffers from various illnesses and diseases, because in this case cleanliness is ignored.

Also, children are the typical victims of lice because they usually play in and deal with wet things and because of their careless nature. This is why the Prophet ﷺ ordered that the heads of the sons of Ja'far رَضِيَ الله عَنْهُ be shaved, as shaving is one the best cures for lice because it exposes the skin to the sun and allows the harmful moisture on the skin to evaporate. Then, the head should be anointed with the remedies that prevent lice from reproducing and kill them.

Shaving is done for three reasons: As a legal ritual, as an act of innovation and polytheism, and as a cure. The first type is performed during *Hajj* and *Umrah*. The second type occurs for other than Allah The Almighty, such as when the students have their heads shaved for their masters sake saying, *'I shaved my head for such and such person's sake'*. This is similar to one's saying, *``I bowed down for such and such person."*

Shaving the head is an act of humility and worship, and this is why it is a ritual that completes the rites of *Hajj*. Imam Shafi' (may Allah have mercy upon him) even considers shaving the head a cornerstone of *Hajj* since it entails lowering the sides of the head in humility before the Lord and since it is also an honored act of worship. Furthermore, when the Arabs wanted to humiliate a captured warrior and then set him free, they would first shave his head.

Later on, the teachers of false guidance and evil who seek to acquire the rights of lordship for themselves and whose ministry concentrates on polytheism and innovations came along. Such evil teachers wanted their students to perform the acts of worship for their sake. Consequently, they encouraged their students to shave their heads for their sake, just as they lured them to prostrate before them, calling this act by other than its true name and claiming that it is not prostrating, but merely lowering the head before the teacher. By Allah! What is prostrating for the sake of Allah, if it is not lowering the head before Him? The evil teachers also lured their students to vow to them, repent to them and swear by their names! This is taking such teachers as gods beside Allah The Almighty.

Allah The Almighty said:

﴿ مَا كَانَ لِبَشَرٍ أَن يُؤْتِيَهُ اللَّهُ الْكِتَابَ وَالْحُكْمَ وَالنُّبُوَّةَ ثُمَّ يَقُولَ لِلنَّاسِ كُونُوا
عِبَادًا لِّي مِن دُونِ اللَّهِ وَلَٰكِن كُونُوا رَبَّانِيِّينَ بِمَا كُنتُمْ تُعَلِّمُونَ الْكِتَابَ وَبِمَا كُنتُمْ
تَدْرُسُونَ (٧٩) وَلَا يَأْمُرَكُمْ أَن تَتَّخِذُوا الْمَلَائِكَةَ وَالنَّبِيِّينَ أَرْبَابًا ۗ أَيَأْمُرُكُم بِالْكُفْرِ بَعْدَ إِذْ أَنتُم
مُّسْلِمُونَ (٨٠) ﴾

``It is not (possible) for any human being to whom Allah has given the Book and Al-Hukm (the knowledge and understanding of the laws of religion) and Prophethood to say to the people: ``Be my worshippers rather than Allah's." On the contrary (he would say): ``Be you Rabbaniyyin (learned men of religion who practise what they know and also preach others), because you are teaching the Book, and you are studying it. ``Nor would he order you to take angels and Prophets for lords (gods) Would he order you to disbelieve after you have submitted to Allah's Will?" (Qur'an, 3:79,80)

Prayer is the highest act of worship. Yet the teachers of false

guidance, the so-called scholars and tyrants have divided the acts of prayer between themselves. For instance, the teachers of false guidance chose the highest act in the prayer, prostrating, for themselves. Some so-called scholars have also allocated [the custom of] bowing down for themselves. When they meet each other, some of them bow down before the others just as one does while praying to Allah The Almighty! As for the tyrants, they acquired [the custom of] standing up for themselves! Free and slave men stand up before the tyrants while the tyrants are sitting down.

The Messenger of Allah ﷺ has prohibited these three acts for other than Allah The Almighty. Therefore, committing these prohibited acts is a clear violation of the Prophet's commands.

The Prophet ﷺ prohibited prostrating to other than Allah The Almighty. He said:

« لا يَنبغِي لأحدٍ أن يَسْجُدَ لأَحد » (الترمذي بنحوه: ١١٥٩ وقال الألباني: حسن صحيح)

``No one should prostrate to any other person."

He also criticized Mu'ath رَضِيَ الله عَنْهُ when he prostrated before him. Since prohibiting prostrating before the creation is clearly indicated in the Prophet's *Sunnah* , then those who allow such acts seek to dispute the rights of Allah and His Messenger ﷺ. Prostrating is one of the essential acts of worship. When the polytheist allows it to the creation, he will be allowing worshipping other than Allah The Almighty. The Prophet ﷺ was once asked, ``*When one sees his brother, should he bow down for him?" He said: `No.' He was asked, `Should he hug and kiss him?' He said: `No.' He was asked, `Should he shake his hand?' He said: `Yes.'*

Moreover, bowing down while greeting someone is a type of worship, just as Allah The Almighty says:

﴿ وَٱدْخُلُواْ ٱلْبَابَ سُجَّدًا ﴾

``*And enter the gate in prostration." (or bowing with humility)"*

(Qur'an, 2:58)

Besides, prostrating and entering through the door is not possible at the same time [the prostration mentioned in the Verse is bowing down]!

The Prophet ﷺ also prohibited standing up for someone just as the non-Muslims used to do. He even disallowed this act during prayer and commanded the Muslims to imitate the leader in the prayer, that if he sits down while praying due to an illness, they all sit behind him although they are healthy. Otherwise, they will be standing while the Imam is sitting down, although their standing is for Allah The Almighty. How about if standing was for other than Allah The Almighty?

The ignorant misguided people have associated others with Allah The Almighty in worship, thus prostrating before other than Allah The Almighty and bowing down for other than Him. They also stand up before the creation just as they do when they are praying. They also swear, vow, shave their heads, sacrifice, perform *Tawaf* (circumambulation of an object or person), love, fear, and obey other than Allah The Almighty, just as they do for Allah The Almightyand even more. They equate Allah, the Lord of the Worlds, Whom they worship, with the creation. These are the enemies of the messages of the Messengers of Allah, who equate Allah with the creation. They are the ones who will say in the Fire, while arguing with the false deities they were worshipping:

﴿ تَٱللَّهِ إِن كُنَّا لَفِى ضَلَـٰلٍ مُّبِينٍ ﴿٩٧﴾ إِذْ نُسَوِّيكُم بِرَبِّ ٱلْعَـٰلَمِينَ ﴾

``By Allah, we were truly, in a manifest error, When We hold you (false gods) as equals (in worship) with the Lord of the Al-`Alamin (mankind, Jinn and all that exists) (Qur'an, 26:97,98)

They are also the people, whom Allah The Almighty describes, when He says:

﴿ وَمِنَ ٱلنَّاسِ مَن يَتَّخِذُ مِن دُونِ ٱللَّهِ أَندَادًا يُحِبُّونَهُمْ كَحُبِّ ٱللَّهِ وَٱلَّذِينَ ءَامَنُوٓا۟ أَشَدُّ حُبًّا لِّلَّهِ ﴾

`And of mankind are some who take (for worship) others besides Allah as rivals (to Allah). They love them as they love Allah. But those who believe, love Allah more (then anything else)." (Qur'an, 2:165)

All these are among the acts of *Shirk* (polytheism, associating others with Allah The Almighty in worship) that He never forgives.

Part III

3

The Prophet's Guidance on using Divine *Ruqyah*

(Islamic Prayer) Formulas and Natural Medications

The Prophetís guidance on treating those touched by the evil eye

Imam Muslim [and Ahmad, Ibn Hibban, Al-Hakim and At-Tabarani] narrated that Ibn `Abbas رَضِيَ الله عَنْهما said, The Messenger of Allah ﷺ said:

«العَينُ حق؛ ولو كان شيءٌ سابَقَ القَدَرَ لسبقَتْه العَيْنُ» (مسلم: ٢١٨٨)

``The evil eye is true, and if there is anything that would precede Predestination, it would be the evil eye."

Also, Muslim narrated that Anas رَضِيَ الله عَنْهُ said:

«إِن النبي صلى الله عليه وسلم رَخَّص في الرُّقْية مِنَ الحُمَةِ والعَيْنِ والنَّمْلةِ»

(مسلم:٢١٩٦)

``The Prophet has allowed using Islamic prayer formulas(1) (Ruqyah, divine remedy) against fever, the evil eye and sores."

Also, in the *Sahihain* it is narrated that Abu Hurairah رَضِيَ الله عَنْه said that the Messenger of Allah ﷺ said, ``The evil eye is true." [Abu Dawud, Ibn Majah and Ahmad].

Abu Dawud reported that `Aishah رَضِيَ الله عَنْها said:

« كان يؤمَرُ العائنُ فيَتوضَّأ، ثم يغتسل منه المعِينُ »

(أبو داود: ٣٨٨٠ من قول عائشة رضي الله عنها، وهو صحيح الإسناد)

``The person who touched others with the evil eye was commanded to perform ablution and the person whom he touched by the evil eye would wash with that water." [Al- Bukhari, Muslim, An-Nasai', Ibn Majah, Abu Na`im and Al-Isma`ili] .

Further, `Aishah رَضِيَ الله عَنْها narrated, as the *Sahihain* reported:

« أمرني النبي صلى الله عليه وسلم، أو أمَرَ أن نَسْترْقِيَ من العينِ » (البخاري:٥٧٣٨)

``The Prophet commanded me, or commanded, that we should

(1) * Editor's note : *Ruqyah* in Arabic literally means incantation and they were used in pre-Islamic times for various purposes. After Islam the Prophet stopped their use and substituted prayers and supplications from the Qur'n and those that he used in praying to Allh.

use Islamic prayer formulas from the evil eye."

In addition, At-Tirmidhi narrated that Asma' bint Umays رَضِيَ الله عَنْها said, ``I said, O Messenger of Allah ! The children of Ja`far are usually touched by the evil eye. Should I perform an Islamic prayer formula for them?' He said:

« نعم، فلو كان شيءٌ يسبقُ القضاءَ، لسبقَتْه العينُ » (الترمذي:٢٠٥٩ وصححه الألباني)

``Yes. If there is anything that precedes Predestination, it would be the evil eye." [An-Nasai' and Ahmad].

Also, Imam Malik narrated that `Amir bin Rabi`ah once saw Sahl bin Hunaif take a bath and said, ``By Allah! I have never seen the skin of a virgin that is softer than what I have just seen." Sahl fell to the ground. The Prophet then came to `Amir while angry and said to him:

« عَلامَ يَقْتلُ أَحدُكم أخاه؟ أَلاَّ بَرَّكْتَ؛ اغْتَسِلْ لَه» (موطأ:٢/ ٩٣٩وابن ماجه وصححه الألباني٣٥٠٩)

``Why would one of you kill his own brother? Why have you not said Tabrik [Baraka Allah, (- بارك الله may Allah bless it)]? Take a bath for it."

`Amir then washed his face, hands, elbows, knees, feet and a part of his garment in a pot for what he had done and then poured the used water on Sahl. Soon after, Sahl started moving about with the people. [An-Nasai', Ibn Majah, Ahmad, Al-Hakim and Ibn Hibban].

Malik also narrated:

إن العَيْنَ حقٌّ؛ توضَّأْ لهُ »(موطأ:٢/ ٩٣٨)

``The evil eye is true, so perform ablution for it."

Another Hadith narrated by Abdul Razzaq reads:

« العَين حَقٌّ؛ ولو كان شيءٌ سابقَ القَدرَ: لَسَبقَتْه العين؛ فإذا اسْتُغْسِل أحدُكم فليغتسِلْ » (مسلم:٢١٨٨)

``The evil eye is true, and if there is anything that precedes Predestination, it would be the evil eye. When one is touched by the evil eye, he should take a bath for it."

At-Tirmidhi said:

``The person who touched others with the evil eye should be commanded to submerge his hand in a pot of water and then wash his mouth, then spit the water back into the pot. He should then wash his face in the pot, then submerges his left hand it and pour some water on the right knee above the pot, and then submerges his right hand and pour water on his left knee. He should then wash his garment inside the pot and the water should not be spilled on the ground. Rather, it should be poured on top of the person whom he touched by the evil eye from behind all at once."

There are two types of the evil eye, human and Jinn related. Umm Salamah رَضِيَ الله عَنْها said that the Prophet once saw a young girl, who had a certain expression on her face and said:

« اسْتَرْقُوا لها، فإنَّ بِها النَّظْرَةَ » (البخاري:٥٧٣٩)

``Seek an Islamic prayer formula for her because she is touched by the evil eye." [Al-Bukhari, Muslim, Al-`Hakim, Abu Na'im, Al-Isma`ili and At-Tabarani]

Abu Sa'id also narrated that:

« إنّ النبيَّ صلى الله عليه وسلم كَانَ يتعوَّذ من الجَانّ، ومن عَيْنِ الإنسَانِ »

(الترمذي وصححه الألباني:٢٠٥٨)

The Prophet used to seek refuge from the Jinn and the evil eye of mankind." [At-Tirmidhi and An-Nasai']

Some people who do not have sound comprehension or correct sight and hearing have rejected the fact that the evil eye causes harm, claiming that this is a superstitious, untrue belief. These people are indeed among the most ignorant people who have the least sound comprehension and the thickest minds. They are the farthest from acquiring knowledge of the soul and the heart and the effect of each on the natural world.

The best minds in every nation do not dispute the fact that the evil eye is true, although they differ on its causes and true effects. Some people say that when people who touch others by the evil eye feel evilness in their hearts, then their eyes transform the evil thoughts into harmful rays just like the type of snake that looks at its prey and causes it to perish.

Another group says that it is possible that invisible powers emit from the person who touches others with the evil eye and then enters the body of the person whom they touched and harms them.

However, other people say that Allah creates the harm on the person touched by the evil eye without any rays that emit from the eye of the

person who touched him. Yet, this is the method of those who deny the existence of the various spiritual powers that exist in this world. Allah has created special powers in some of the creation that have profound effects on other creations. For instance, the soul has such a profound effect on the body that no one can deny. Also, have you not noticed how the face of a shy person turns red if his sight falls on what is not suitable for him, and turns yellow when he looks at someone he fears? You can also witness the effect of the evil eye has on people and the weakness it causes in their bodies.

The evil eye is actually the effect exerted by the soul on the victim. Souls vary in their essence, powers, characteristics and qualities. Therefore, the soul of an envious person can harm a victim profoundly, and this is why Allah has commanded His Messenger to seek refuge with Him from the evil eye.

The harmful effect of an envious person on the envied person cannot be denied, except by those who are far away from reality. It is a fact that an evil envious soul touches the envied person in such an evil manner that it causes them harm. Similarly, the poisonous viper gets so enraged and evil when it meets the enemy that it has a special effect on the victim, sometimes leading to aborting the fetus or causing blindness. The Prophet described the short tailed viper and the striped viper as having the ability that they can affect sight and abort pregnancy. Some types of snakes have a negative effect on people by their mere sight, because of the viciousness of such creatures and the effect of this viciousness on people.

These effects that we mentioned are not restricted to physical contact, as some of those who have little knowledge in the natural world and the religion think. Rather, these effects could be caused by physical contact, sight, the soul directing its power to the victim, through imagination and evil omens, and so forth.

The envious person might be blind, yet when something is described to him or her, his envious soul affects the described object and harms it even though the blind person cannot see it. Allah said to His Prophet :

﴿وَإِن يَكَادُ ٱلَّذِينَ كَفَرُواْ لَيُزۡلِقُونَكَ بِأَبۡصَٰرِهِمۡ لَمَّا سَمِعُواْ ٱلذِّكۡرَ﴾

``And verily, those who disbelieve would almost make you slip with their eyes (through hatred) when they hear the Reminder (the Qur'n) ..." (68:51)

﴿قُلۡ أَعُوذُ بِرَبِّ ٱلۡفَلَقِ ١ مِن شَرِّ مَا خَلَقَ ٢ وَمِن شَرِّ غَاسِقٍ إِذَا وَقَبَ ٣
وَمِن شَرِّ ٱلنَّفَّٰثَٰتِ فِي ٱلۡعُقَدِ ٤ وَمِن شَرِّ حَاسِدٍ إِذَا حَسَدَ﴾

Say: ``I seek refuge with (Allah), the Lord of the daybreak, from the evil of what He has created, and from the evil of the *darkening (night) as it comes with its darkness; (or the moon as it sets or goes away), and from the evil of those who practise witchcraft when they blow in the knots, and from the evil of the envier when he envies." (113:1-5)*

Every person who touches others by the evil eye is an envious person, but not vise versa. Since envy includes the evil eye in its general meaning, seeking refuge from it includes seeking refuge from the evil eye also.

The evil eye includes throwing arrows of envy that depart the envious heart and soul in the direction of the envied person, sometimes falling on its target. If the envied person is unarmed and unprepared, the evil eye will cause him harm. If the envied person is prepared and armed, the arrows might turn back on the one who threw them. This is similar to what actually occurs when one shoots real arrows. The resemblance is that this occurs through the soul while the arrows are shot in the material world. The evil eye starts when the envious person likes something then follows it with his evil thoughts and desires and then the evil eye touches the envied object.

Sometimes a person might even touch his own self with the evil eye, which is one of the worst types of envy. Sometimes one might touch others with the evil eye just by his envious nature. Some of our scholars say that such envious people should be imprisoned and should be given what they need of sustenance until they die.

The Prophetic medicine for treating sorcery (the evil eye) was of several types

Abu Dawud narrated that Sahl ibn Hunaif ﷺ said:

«مرَرْنا بسَيْلٍ، فدخلتُ فاغتسلتُ فيه فخرجتُ مَحْمومًا. فَنُمِيَ ذلك إلى رَسولِ الله صلى الله عليه وسلم، فَقَالَ: مُرُوا أبا ثابت يَتعوَّذُ قَالَ: فَقُلتُ: يَا سيدِّي! وَالرُّقَى صَالِحَةٌ؟ فَقَالَ: لا رُقيةَ إِلا في نَفْسٍ أو حُمَةٍ أَوْ لَدْغةٍ» (أبو داود:٣٨٨٨ وضعفه الألباني)

``We came by a water fall and I went in it and took a bath, but when I finished I came down with a fever. When the Messenger of Allah was informed, he said, `Command Abu Ath-Thabit to seek refuge (with Allah for Sahl) with an Islamic prayer formula.' I said, 'O my master! Does an Islamic prayer formula bring about benefit?' He said, `There is no Islamic prayer formula except to fend off an evil eye and against fever and a (snake or a scorpion) bite."' [Also, Al-Hakim narrated this Hadith].

There are several types of Islamic prayer formulas, such as reciting the first chapter in the Qur'an, the Mu'awwithatan (chapters 113 and 114 of the Qur'an) and Ayat Al-Kursi (2:255).

Also, there are several types of Prophetic Islamic prayer formulas. For instance, one might recite:

« أعوذ بكَلِمات الله التَّامَّاتِ من شرِّ ماخَلَق » (مسلم : ٢٧٠٩)

``I seek refuge with Allah's Prefect Words from the evil of what He has created."

Also, one could recite:

«أعُوذ بكَلِمات الله التَّامَّةِ: من كُلِّ شيطانٍ وهَامَّةٍ، ومن كل عَينٍ لامَّةٍ » (البخاري:٣٣٧١)

``I seek refuge with Allah's Prefect Words from every devil and evil soul and from every evil eye."

Also, one might recite,

«أعوذ بِكَلِماتِ اللهِ التَّامَّاتِ الَّتِي لا يُجاوِزُهُنَّ بَرٌّ ولا فاجرٌ، من شر ما خلَق وذَرَأَ وبرَأ، ومن شرِّ ما ينزِل مِنَ السَّماء، ومِنْ شر ما يَعْرُجُ فيها، ومن شر ماذَرَأ في الأرضِ، ومن شر ما يَخْرُجُ مِنها، ومن شرّ فِتَنِ اللَّيلِ والنَّهارِ، ومن شر طَوارِقِ اللَّيل والنهار، إلا طارقًا يَطرُق بخَيرٍ يا رَحْمَنُ» (أحمد ٣/ ٤١٩ وحسنه الألباني في صحيح الترغيب ٢/ ٢٦٣)

``I seek refuge with Allah's Prefect Words, which no righteous or evil soul could ever encompass (or supercede), from the evil of what He has created, made and started; from the evil of whatever descends from the sky and whatever ascends to it; from the evil of what He has created on the earth and what comes out of it; from the evil of the trials of the night and the day; and from what comes by at night or during the day, except whoever comes with a righteous matter. O Merciful One!"

Also, this includes the supplication:

أعوذ بكَلِمات الله التامَّةِ من غَضَبه وعِقابه وَمِن شرّ عِبَاده ومِنْ هَمَزاتِ الشياطينِ وأنْ يَحضُرُونِ (الترمذي:٣٥٢٨ وحسنه الألباني)

``I seek refuge with Allah's Perfect Words from His anger and torment, from the evil of His slaves and from the whispers of the devils or that they might attend me."

Also, one might say the following supplication:

اللّهم إني أعوذ بوَجْهك الكريم وكَلِماتكَ التَّامَّات، من شَرّ ما أَنْتَ آخِذٌ بناصِيَتِهِ، اللّهُمَّ أنت تَكْشِفُ المأْثَمَ والمَغْرَمَ، اللّهُمَّ إنه لا يُهزم جُنْدُك، ولا يُخلَفُ وَعْدُك؛ سُبحانَك وبحَمْدِك» (النسائي في الكبرى وقال المعلق في تحقيقه: الحديث صحيح)

``O Allah! I seek refuge with Your Most Honorable Face and Your Prefect Words from the evil of every creation that is only in your grasp (or control). O Allah! You expel the sins and loss. O Allah! Your soldiers will never be defeated nor will Your Promise ever be broken. All praise and glorification is due to You."

Also, one might supplicate:

«أعوذ بوجهِ الله العظيم الَّذي لا شيءَ أعظَمُ منه، وبكَلِماته التَّامَّات الَّتي لا يجاوِزُهنّ برّ ولا فاجرٌ، وبأَسْماءِ الله الحُسْنَى - ما علمت منها وما لم أعلم - من شرِّ ما خلَقَ وذرأ وبرأ، ومن شرِّ كل ذِي شرٍّ لاَ أُطيق شرَّه، ومن شرِّ كل ذي شرٍّ أَنْت آخِذٌ بِنَاصِيَته؛ إن رَبِّي على صراطٍ مُسْتقيم» (لم نجده بهذا السياق كله وقد مضى جزء منه من رواية أحمد ٣/ ٤١٩ وابن أبي شيبة ٢٩٦١١ و٢٩٦١٢)

``I seek refuge with Allah's Most Exalted Face which is greater than everything else. And with His Perfect Words that no righteous or evil being could ever overcome; and with Allah's Most Prefect Names, those which I know and those which I have no knowledge of, from the evil of what He has created, shaped and made. From the evil of every creation that I cannot overcome and from the evil of every evil creation that only You control (or grasp its forelock). Certainly, my Lord is on a Straight Path."

Also, the Prophetic Islamic prayer formulas include:

« اللّهم أنت ربِّي لا إله إلاّ أنت، عَلَيك توكّلتُ، وأنت رَبُّ العَرْش العظيم؛ ما شاء الله كانَ، وما لَمْ يشَأْ لم يكُنْ؛ لا حول ولا قُوَّةَ إلا بالله؛ أعلم أنَّ الله على كُلِّ شيءٍ قديرٌ، وأنّ الله قد أحاط بِكُلِّ شيء علمًا، وأحصى كلَّ شَيْء عَدَدًا. اللّهم إني أعوذ بك من شرِّ نفسي وشِر الشيطان وشرْكِه، ومن شر كل دابَّةٍ أنت آخِذٌ بناصِيَتِها؛ إن ربي على صِراط مستقيم » (الطبراني في الدعا وهو ضعيف جدّاً، فيه أغلب بن تميم قال البخاري: منكرالحديث ولبعض أجزائه لها شواهد انظر الترمذي:٣٥٢٩، أبو داود ٥٠٧٥)

``O Allah! You Are my Lord, there is no deity worthy of worship except You. I depend on You (for every thing). You are the Lord of the Mighty Throne. What Allah wills, occurs, and what He does not will to happen, will never exist. There is no power or strength except with Allah. I know that Allah is Able to do everything, that His Knowledge has encompassed everything and that He has kept count of everything. O Allah! I seek refuge with You from the evil within myself, from the evil and the Shirk (polytheism) of Satan, and from the evil of every creation that only You grasp its forelock. Surely, my Lord is on the Straight Path."

Or, one might recite the following supplication,

« تَحَصَّنْتُ بالله الَّذي لا إله إلا هُو، إلهي وإله كل شيء، واعتصمتُ بربي وربِّ كل شيء، وتَوَكَّلْتُ على الحَيِّ الذي لا يمُوت، واستَدْفَعتُ الشَّرَّ بلاَ حولَ ولا قوةَ إلاَّ بالله؛ حسبيَ الله ونعمَ الوكيلُ، حسبيَ الرَّبُّ من العِباد، حسبيَ الخالقُ من المَخْلوق، حسبيَ الرازق من المرزوق، حسبيَ الذي هو حَسْبِيَ، حسبيَ الذي بيده ملكوتُ كل شيء، وهو يُجيرُ ولا يجارُ عليه؛ حسبي الذي وكَفَى، سمع الله لِمَنْ دَعا، وليس وراءَ الله مَرْمًي؛ حسبيَ الله لا إلهَ إلا هو، عليه توكَّلت، وهو رب العَرْش العظيم » (لم نعثر عليه، وكأنه تأليف بعض الصالحين)

``I seek refuge with Allah, other than Whom there is no god. He is my God and the God of everything. I seek refuge with my Lord and the Lord of everything. I depend on the Ever-Living Who never dies. I seek to fend off the evil with: no power or strength except from Allah.' Allah is enough of a supporter for me, and indeed, what an Excellent Helper. Allah is enough for me from the slaves. The Creator is enough for me from the creation. The Sustainer is enough for me from the sustained. Allah is indeed enough for me. He Who owns everything, Who grants refuge while no one can ever grant refuge against Him is indeed sufficient for me. Allah is sufficient for me. Allah's hearing who ever supplicates to Him is also sufficient for me. There is no goal to reach greater than Allah. Allah, other than Whom there is no god, is sufficient for me, I depend on Him (for each and everything), and He is the Lord of the Mighty Throne."

Those who try these different types of supplications and Islamic prayer formulas will surely understand their great value and benefit, and consequently, will recognize the great need for them. These supplications will shield one from the effects of the evil eye and will fend off its harm if the evil eye touched them, but according to the degree of Faith, strength of soul, degree of reliance (on Allah) and strength of heart of whoever recites them. These supplications are types of weapons, and their effectiveness depends on the skill of whoever uses them.

If the person fears that he might touch other people by the evil eye, let him fend off its harm by saying:

« اللَّهم بارك عَليهِ »

``O Allah! Bless him."

The Prophet ﷺ commanded `Amir bin Rabi`ah رضي الله عنه,

« ألاَّ برّكْتَ » (موطا: ٢/ ٩٣٩ وانظر ص ١٦٩)

``Why did you not say Tabrik [Baraka Allah, (may Allah bless it)] for him?"

Further, saying ``*Ma sha' Allah* (what Allah has willed), *La Quwwata ill Billah* (There is no power except from Allah)" also helps fend off the evil eye. Hisham bin `Urwah narrated that his father used to say, ``What Allah wills will certainly come to pass, there is no power except from Allah," upon seeing something that he likes and upon entering one of his gardens.

Also, Jibril once said an Islamic prayer formula for the Prophet ﷺ, which Muslim narrated in his *Sahih* :

« باسم الله أَرْقِيكَ، من كل شَيْءٍ يُؤذيك؛ من شرّ كل نَفْس أو عينِ حاسدٍ اللهُ يَشفِيك؛ بسم الله أرقِيكَ » (مسلم: ٢١٨٦)

``In the Name of Allah I say Islamic prayer formulas for your benefit, from every thing that might harm you and from the evil of every evil soul or envious person's eye. Allah will cure you, in the Name of Allah I say Islamic prayer formulas for your benefit." [At-Tirmidhi and An-Nasai']

Some of our rightly guided ancestors stated that there is no harm if some *Ayat* (Verse) from the Qur'an were written in ink and then washed with water and that the sick person drinks that water. Mujahid issued a statement to that effect, and so did Abu Qilabah. It was also reported that Ibn `Abbas once commanded that two verses from the Qur'an to be written for a woman who had hard pregnancies and that the Verses were then washed with water and she was to drink the water. Also, Ayub said, ``I saw Abu Qilabah write some Verses from the Qur'an, wash it with water and then give the water to a person who was suffering from some type of illness to drink it."

Also, the person who touches other people with the evil eye should be commanded to wash his limbs and the end of his garments, or his sexual organ according to one opinion, from the right side. He then pours the water on the head of the person whom he touched with the evil eye from behind him without notice. This is a type of cure that the doctors cannot produce with their medicine. Also, those who reject such type of Islamic prayer formulas would never benefit from it because they do not believe that the Islamic prayer formulas carry any benefit.

Since the doctors cannot explain many natural occurrences in the world, why would the hypocrites among them reject such powers and effects that the religion produces? Added to this is the fact that washing up with the water has a real benefit, experience testifies to its usefulness. Similarly, the anger will be washed away from the heart if one places his hand on the angry person's chest. This is similar to confronting a man who is carrying a lit torch that he wants to throw at you, but you keep pouring water on it while it is still in his hand until you extinguish it. This is why the Prophet ﷺ commanded the person who touches people by the evil eye to ask Allah to bless whatever he has envied, so that the evil thoughts that he feels go away and are replaced by the supplication, which is a type of good charity. The cure should be compatible to the disease so that it has an affect on it. It is possible that when one touches others by the evil eye that a certain power appears on the end of his garment, or his sexual organ as we stated, and that it is then transferred to the affected person or object. When it is washed by water, the evil power will be removed. Yet again, and as we have stated, this matter has a lot to do with evil spirits, which will be stopped from producing harm if washed by water. Also, it might be that washing

with water serves to cool the heart and thus cures the person who was about to touch others with the evil eye. Sometimes, when a poisonous insect bites someone and then the insect is killed, the bitten person feels a little relief afterwards. This might occur because the bitten person feels joy that the insect was killed and this feeling of elation helps to cure the poison faster. In short, when the person who touches others with the evil eye is washed, the evil that he thought of or felt will be washed away with the water.

If someone asks, ``If washing with the water helps the aggressor then what about the victim of the evil eye?''

We say that pouring the water on victims of the evil eye also helps cool the effect of the evil eye on the victim just as it extinguished the veiled thoughts from the aggressor's heart. Water, which is used to cool burning iron rods, is also often used as a medicine with which the doctors would concur. It is natural that the same water used to extinguish the evil eye is used to rid the victim of the evil eye of its effect.

Therefore, comparing the Prophetic medicine to regular medicine that doctors use is just like comparing the doctor's medicine to folk medicines. Rather, the comparison is even less appropriate, for the difference between the Prophets and the doctors is profoundly greater than the difference between the doctors and those who are not qualified

› practice medicine. You should have discovered by now the brotherly elation between religion and wisdom, and that they never contradict ach other. Allah guides whom He wills to the straight path and opens ie doors of success to those who knock on such doors. He Alone is the ource of all bounties and irrefutable proofs.

Fighting the evil eye is more likely to be successful if one conceals is blessings from the people.

For instance, Al-Baghawi narrated that once Uthman رَضِيَ اللهُ عَنْهُ aw a handsome boy and ommanded, ``Blacken his left chin so that the evil eye oes not touch him."

Al-Khattabi also narrated ı *Gharib Al-Hadith*, ``It was arrated that Uthman رَضِيَ اللهُ عَنْهُ once saw a handsome oy and that he said, `Hide is cleft chin with black olor.''' Uthman رَضِيَ اللهُ عَنْهُ vanted to hide the cleft chin f the handsome boy using lack color so that he was not ouched by the evil eye.

Another Islamic prayer ormula that helps ward off he evil eye was related by Abu `Abdullah Al-Tayya'hi who was once raveling for *Hajj* or *Jihad* using a good animal. There was a man in he caravan who would never look at something but would bring it to ts demise. Abu `Abdullah was then told, `Preserve your camel from his man's eye.' He said, `My camel cannot be touched by harm.' The erson who touched with the evil eye was informed of Abu `Abdullah's esponse and he waited for a chance when Abu `Abdullah was not resent and looked at the camel which soon fell on its feet! When Abu Abdullah came and was told that the person had touched it with the evil eye and that his camel was suffering, as was evident, he said, `Sho me the man.' When he came by him he said, `In the Name of Allah restraint that restrains, a hard rock and a blazing star: I ask that the ev eye returns to the person who started it and on the most dear people t him (meaning the envious person himself)"

Allah said:

﴿ فَٱرْجِعِ ٱلْبَصَرَ هَلْ تَرَىٰ مِن فُطُورٍ ﴿٣﴾ ثُمَّ ٱرْجِعِ ٱلْبَصَرَ كَرَّتَيْنِ يَنقَلِبْ إِلَيْكَ ٱلْبَصَرُ خَاسِئًا وَهُوَ حَسِيرٌ ﴾

Then look again: ``Can you see any rifts?" Then look agai and yet again, your sight will return to you in a state of humiliatio and worn out." (67:3,4)

Then, the person known for the evil eye lost his sight and the came was cured.[1]

---

(1) Editor's note : The problem of the manifestation of evil through human beings is sti a very perplexing problem. School boys who gun down their classmates for the most ir significant reasons, serial killers, child abusers, snuff movies (movies where they actuall kill a person on film), pornography, etc. are common examples that we all have learne to live with. As Muslims we know that there is a force of evil whose main purpose is t destroy the children of Adam (Human beings). We are also told that this force of evil ca whisper in the breasts of mankind. Without this knowledge we would have to assum that the source of all evil thoughts is the thinker. We, as Muslims, are told to seek refug in Allah from these thoughts and to reject them. Without this knowledge we would hav to reconcile our evil thoughts with our perceptions of our own character and how other perceive us. This conflict in our perceptions could produce a destructive form of confu sion. Without the Islamic knowledge available we would have to rationalize the evil, b hiding it, attributing it to another outside force, or assuming it is a part of ourselves (ou dark side). The final result of our investigation is that we find the only beneficiary of all c these activities is the force of evil itself. As any good investigator knows, the perpetrato of any crime is almost always the one who benefits the most. The perpetrator of the evil we mentioned above (serial killers, etc.) leave the human beings associated with it defec tive and psychologically deformed while the forces of evil are strengthened. Evil entice us to join it with the lure of material benefits, power, or the satisfying of desires, but i the end it only uses us to gain its goal of the destruction of human beings. Throughou the ages these forces of evil have committed themselves to use deception as their mos powerful technique, while we are debating their possible existence they are achievin their goals. They recruit those of mankind (with or without their awareness as suits th purpose of evil) who are useful to them and who can serve their purposes giving then limited knowledge and powers to serve them. The power of the evil eye is, as it is named based on evil. However evil will use the form most suited to its survival at any one give time without exposing itself as the source.

The Prophetís guidance on treating sickness in general with Islamic prayer formulas

Muslim narrated that Abu Sa'eed Al-Khudri رَضِيَ الله عَنْهُ said that Jibril عليه السلام came to the Prophet ﷺ and said to him:

« يا محمد، اشْتَكَيْتَ ؟ قال: نعم. فقال جبريل عليه السلام: باسم الله أَرقيكَ، من كل شَيْءٍ يُؤذيكَ، ومن شرّ كل نفْسٍ أو عينِ حاسدٍ الله يُشفيك؛ باسم الله أرقيكَ» (مسلم:٢١٨٦)

``O Muhammad, are you complaining from an illness?" He said, ``Yes." Jibril then said, ``In the Name of Allah I say Islamic prayer formulas for your benefit, from every thing that might harm you and from the evil of every evil soul or envious evil eye. Allah will cure you, in the Name of Allah I say Islamic prayer formulas for your benefit."

If someone asks, ``What do you say about the *Hadith* that Abu Dwud narrated:

« لا رُقْيَةَ إلاَّ من عَيْن أو حُمَة » (أبو داود:٣٨٨٤ وصححه الألباني وانظر مسلم: ٢١٩٦)

``There is no Islamic prayer formula except for an evil eye or fever."

To answer this question we say that the Hadith does not deny that the Islamic prayer formulas can be used in other instances. Rather, the *Hadith* only states that the Islamic prayer formulas work best for the evil eye and fever of all kinds. What further attests to this fact is that the *Hadith* itself narrated that Sahl ibn Hunaif asked the Prophet ﷺ when he was touched by the evil eye, ``Do the Islamic prayer formulas bring about benefit?" The Prophet ﷺ then answered:

«لا رُقْيَةَ إلا من نَفْس أو حمة » (أحمد ٣/ ٤٨٦ وقال في تحقيقه صحيح لغيره)

``There is no Islamic prayer formula (that works better) than in

the cases of evil eye and the fever."

Also, the various *Ahadith* in general allow Islamic prayer formulas. For instance, Muslim narrated that the Prophet ﷺ allowed using Islamic prayer formulas in the cases of the evil eye, fever and *Namlah* (ant's bite or sores).

The Prophet's guidance on treating one bitten (by an animal) by reciting Al-Fatihah

In the *Sahihain* [also At-Tirmidhi, Ibn Majah and Ahmad] it is narrated that Abu Sa'eed Al-Khudri ﷺ said, ``Some of the Companions of the Prophet ﷺ went on a journey till they reached some of the Arab tribes (at night). They asked the latter to treat them as their guests but they refused. The chief of that tribe was then bitten by a snake (or stung by a scorpion) and they tried their best to cure him but in vain. Some of them said (to the others), `Nothing has benefited him, will you go to the people who resided here at night, it may be that some of them might possess something (as treatment).' They went to the group of the Companions (of the Prophet) and said, `Our chief has been bitten by a snake (or stung by a scorpion) and we have tried everything but he has not benefited. Have you got anything

(useful)?' One of them replied, `Yes, by Allah! I can recite an Islamic prayer formula, but as you have refused to accept us as your guests, I will not recite the Islamic prayer formula for you unless you fix for us some wages for it.' They agreed to pay them a flock of sheep. One of them then recited (The chapter *Al-Fatihah* ): `All the praises are for the Lord of the Worlds' and puffed over the chief who became alright as if he was released from a chain, and got up and started walking, showing no signs of sickness. They paid them what they agreed to pay. Some of them (i.e., the Companions) then suggested to divide their earnings among themselves, but the one who performed the recitation said, `Do not divide them till we go to the Prophet and narrate the whole story to him, and wait for his order.' So, they went to Allah's Messenger and narrated the story. Allah's Messenger asked:

« وما يُدْريك أنها رُقْيةٌ » (البخاري:٢٢٧٦)

``How did you come to know that the chapter Al-Fatihah could be recited as an Islamic prayer formula?"

Then he added:

« قد أَصَبْتُم؛ اقْسِمُوا واضرِبُوا لي معكم سَهْمًا » (البخاري:٢٢٧٦)

``You have done the right thing. Divide (what you have earned) and assign a share for me as well."

It is a well-known fact that certain types of speech have a profound effect and benefit that experience testifies to. So how about the Words of the Lord of the Worlds that are as preferred to the creation's speech as Allah is preferred above His creation? Allah's Words contain the ultimate cure, the perfect immunity, correct guidance and an encompassing mercy, that if it was revealed to a mountain, it would turn to dust in appreciation of Allah's Glory. Allah said:

﴿ وَنُنَزِّلُ مِنَ ٱلْقُرْءَانِ مَا هُوَ شِفَآءٌ وَرَحْمَةٌ لِّلْمُؤْمِنِينَ ﴾

``And We send down of the Qur'an that which is a healing and a mercy to those who believe (in Islmic Monotheism and act on it)" (17:82)

﴿وَعَدَ اللَّهُ الَّذِينَ آمَنُوا وَعَمِلُوا الصَّالِحَاتِ مِنْهُم مَّغْفِرَةً وَأَجْرًا عَظِيمًا﴾

``Allah has promised those among them who believe (i.e., all those who follow Islmic Monotheism, the religion of Prophet Muhammad till the Day of Resurrection) and do righteous good deeds, forgiveness and a mighty reward (i.e., Paradise)." (48:29)

What could one think of the opening of the Qur'an (*Al-Fatihah*, the first chapter) that is not comparable to any Verse or chapter revealed in the Qur'an, the Torah, the Gospel or the Zabur (that was revealed to Prophet Dawud عليه السلام). *Al-Fatihah* contains the general meaning of all the Divine Books sent down by Allah. It contains Allah's Names and Attributes, such as Allah, the *Rabb* (Lord), *Ar-Rahman* (Most Merciful) and *Ar-Raheem* (Most Beneficent). It also affirms Resurrection, Allah's Oneness in Lordship. It also mentions the creation's dependence on Allah's help and guidance and that He Alone grants such bounties. It also contains the best and most beneficial supplication that the creation needs: being guided to the Straight Path that entails acquiring knowledge of His Names and Attributes, worshipping Him alone, obeying His Commands, refraining from His prohibitions and staying firm on this path until death. It also contains the kinds of creation that are divided into those who have acquired the bounty of knowing the Truth, and who prefer and implement its implications. On the other hand, there are those who have earned Allah's Anger by avoiding the truth after knowing it and there are those who are led astray from the True Path. These are the camps that the creation is divided into. Also, the *Al-Fatihah* affirms Predestination and the Commandments of the religion, Allah's Names and Attributes, Resurrection and Prophethood. It also purifies the heart and mentions Allah's Justice and Generosity. It also refutes all types of innovations and evil methods. We mentioned all these virtues for *Al-Fatihah* in our book that explains it, *Madariju As-Salikin*. Certainly, a chapter that contains all these virtues and benefits

deserves to be used as a cure for disease, as well as an antidote for poisonous stings.

Indeed, *Al-Fatihah* is the best cure because it contains sincere servitude to Allah, praising Him, relating all bounties to Him, seeking His help and support, and invoking Him for all types of advantages, such as the correct guidance that brings about benefit and fends off torment.

It was reported that the part in *Al-Fatihah* that contains the Islamic prayer formula is what Allah said:

﴿إِيَّاكَ نَعْبُدُ وَإِيَّاكَ نَسْتَعِينُ﴾

``You (Alone) we worship, and You (Alone) we ask for help (for everything)." (1:5)

Indeed, these are mighty powerful words that contain the strongest medicine contained in this chapter. These words entail sincere dependence and reliance on Allah, seeking refuge and help from Him and showing meekness and need of Him. Consequently, these words contain the best goals to seek, which is worshiping Allah Alone. Also they contain the best method to acquire these goals, that is, invoking

Allah for His support so that one achieves these goals.

While I was in Makkah, I once fell sick and had no access to a doctor or medicine. So I used to seek a cure in The *Al-Fatihah* by sipping a drink from the well of Zamzam that I recited the *Al-Fatihah* on. I found complete cure in this method and I used to rely on it whenever I felt pain. This cure always helped me.

There is a wonderful secret in using the *Al-Fatihah* as an Islamic prayer formula to treat poisons, and Allah has created a cure for every disease as we have stated. Venomous beasts have a special effect on their victims with their evil souls. Furthermore, the weapon that the venomous beasts use is the needle that they use to sting and inject the venom into their victims. Likewise, the person who is applying the Islamic prayer formula will have a positive effect on the person receiving the Islamic prayer formula, thus enhancing his chances of a speedy recovery by Allah's will. In this case, the victim will feel that his strength and resolve are enhanced with the Islamic prayer formula and the divine remedy, similar to the relation that exists between regular medicine and the sick person. Also, the wetness and the air contained in the spit of the person who recites the Islamic prayer formula, that contains the supplication and the remembrance of Allah, will all enhance the chances of recovery. Since the person who recites the Islamic prayer formula recites it with both his heart and mouth, then adding some of the air and moisture that exists inside his body through the spit will maximize the effectiveness, power and strength of the remedy. Certainly, this mixture of heart and soul used in the divine remedy works just as regular medicine works on the body.

The person who applies the Islamic prayer formula has an advantage over the evil forces (including poisonous snakes, etc.,) since he adds words of the Islamic prayer formula and spit to the strength of his inner self to remove the effects of the evil forces and the venom. Also, the more strength of heart the person has, the stronger the Islamic prayer formula he recites becomes. There is another secret behind using spit in the divine remedy, which is also used by the evil forces, just as Allah said,

﴿وَمِنْ شَرِّ النَّفَّاثَاتِ فِي الْعُقَدِ﴾

``And from the evil of those who practise witchcrafts when they blow in the knots." (113:4)

The body is greatly affected by what the heart feels and so blowing the air and spitting resembles a way to intensify the effect of what the heart feels and intends. Those who work sorcery tie some knots and blow onto them words of sorcery, which work on the victim although he or she might not be present. In this way, the evil force helps transferring the words of sorcery and their effect to the victim. When the force for good retaliates by using the Islamic prayer formula and then breathing unto the victim, the more powerful of the warring parties wins. War between good and evil forces resemble real war that occurs between people. The spiritual forces essentially use and enlist physical bodies in their wars against each other. Whoever is only concerned about the material world will not feel any of this raging war since he is attached to the environment that he believes in, that is, the material world, and he is far away from the world of spiritual forces and their effect on mankind.

In short, when the good spiritual force is strong enough and feels the effects and the meanings contained in the *Al-Fatihah*, along with the breathing that accompanies reciting it, the Islamic prayer formula will have the intended effect against the evil forces and will thus remove their harmful effect. Allah knows best.

The Prophetís guidance on treating scorpion stings

The chapter *Al-Ikhlas* contains the essentials of the Faith and the Creed, various aspects of *Tawhid*, and attesting to and affirming Allah's Oneness that entails denying all types and forms of *shirk* with Him. It also entails affirming that Allah is the Sustainer, along with asserting every type of perfection for Him. Consequently, the creation seeks Allah for each and every need. This chapter also denies that Allah has a parent, an offspring, or an equal, and this is why it equals one third of the Qur'an. Furthermore, Allah's Name " *As-Samad* (the Sustainer)' that the chapter contains includes each and every type of perfection. Also, the chapter denies that Allah has an equal, while Allah's Name *Al-Ahad* (the One) also denies the existence of a partner with Allah. These are the three essential cornerstones of *Tawhid* [Allah's Oneness in Lordship and worship and in His Names and Attributes].

linen seeds

The *Mu'awwidhatan* (chapters 113 and 114 of the Qur'an) also includes seeking refuge with Allah from every type of evil and harm. Seeking refuge from the evil that Allah has created includes every type of evil that such creations, whether physical or spiritual, can ever produce and cause. Seeking refuge from the night when its sign, (the moon), sets, entails seeking refuge from the evil souls that thrive during the night, as opposed to the light of the day. This is because when the darkness falls and the moon sets, the evil forces come out. Also, seeking refuge from those who tie knots and blow on them includes seeking refuge from the evil of sorcerers and their sorcery. Also, seeking refuge from envious people means seeking refuge from the evil forces that cause harm through the envious people's bodies and sight. The second chapter (114) of the *Mu'awwidhatan* entails seeking refuge from the evil of humans and Jinn. Consequently, the two *Mu'awwidhatn* entail seeking refuge from every type of evil. Therefore, they have a great benefit as a shield against evil before it occurs. This is why the Messenger of Allahﷺ advised `Uqbah bin `Amir to recite them after every prayer, as At-Tirmidhi has narrated. This advice from the Prophet contains a great secret and benefit that helps repulse all types of evil during the time between the prayers. The Prophet also described the *Mu' awwidhatan* when he said:

« ما تَعوَّذ المُتَعوِّذون بِمِثْلِهما » (أبو داود:١٤٦٣ وصححه الألباني)

``No one who seeks refuge can ever find a refuge like them."

It was also reported that when the Prophet ﷺ was the victim of sorcery the spell contained eleven knots tied each with a special incantation blown on it, and that whenever Jibril عليه السلام recited a Verse from the *Mu'awwidhatan*, a knot was untied, until all eleven knots were untied. Then, the Prophet ﷺ was cured, as if being released from a restraining chain.

As for using regular medicines to cure scorpion sting, salt has a great value in this regard. The author of *Al-Qanoon* said, ``Salt should be used in a bandage with linen seeds to cure the scorpion's sting." Salt helps dissolve the poison, which has a burning pain that needs to be cooled. The cool moisture contained in the linen seed cools the pain, while the salt helps extract and remove the poison. This is one of the best and easiest types of remedies for scorpion stings, which require cooling the pain and extracting the venom. Allah knows best.

Muslim narrated that Abu Hurairah رَضِيَ الله عَنْهُ said, ``A man came to the Prophet and said to him, 'O Messenger of Allah ! I have suffered greatly from a scorpion that stung me last night." The Prophet said:

«أما لو قلتَ حين أَمْسَيْتَ: أعوذُ بكلماتِ الله التَّامَّات مِن شرِّ ما خلَق؛ لم تَضُرَّك»

(مسلم:٢٧٠٩)

``Had you said these words when you went to sleep, 'I seek refuge with Allah's Perfect Words from the evil of what He has created,' it would not have harmed you." [Ahmad]

Know that the Divine cures help after one catches a disease and also help prevent it from happening. If any type of harm befalls one afterwards, it will not be severe. Natural medicines, on the other hand, only help after the disease attacks. Islamic prayer formulas and the various supplications either prevent the disease from happening or make it milder after it happens, depending on the strength of soul and heart of the sick person. Therefore, the Islamic prayer formulas and supplications are used as preventive measures and also as a cure.

As for prevention, in the *Sahihain* it is narrated that `Aishah ﷺ said:

« كان رسولُ الله صلى اللهُ عليه وسلم إذا أَوَى إلى فِراشِه: نَفَث في كفَّيه بقُلْ هو الله أحدٌ والمُعَوِّذتين، ثم يمسَحُ بهما وجهَه، وما بلغت يدُه من جَسَده » (البخاري:٥٠١٧)

``Whenever the Messenger of Allah would go to bed, he used to breathe into his hands with

Qul huwa Allahu Ahad (Al- Ikhlas) and the *Mu'awwidhatan*." He then would wipe his face and whatever he could reach of his body with his hands."

Also, in the *Sahihain* it is narrated that the Prophet ﷺ said:

« مَن قرأ الآيَتيْن من آخِر سورةِ البَقَرة، في ليلة، كفَتاه» (البخاري:٤٠٠٨)

"Whoever reads the last two Verses from Chapter Al-Baqarah (the second chapter in the Qur'an), at night, they will be enough for him."

Also, Muslim narrated that the Prophet said:

« من نَزَل منزِلاً، فقال: أَعُوذ بكلماتِ الله التَّامَّات مِن شرِّ ما خلَق؛ لم يضُرّه شيء حتى يرتَحِل من منزله ذلك» (مسلم: ٢٧٠٨)

"Whoever resided in a place and said, 'I seek refuge with Allah's Perfect Words from the evil of what He has created,' then nothing will harm him until he departs that place."

Abu Dawud also narrated that the Messenger of Allah used to say at night when he was traveling:

« يا أرضُ؛ ربِّي وربُّكِ اللهُ؛ أعوذ بالله من شرِّكِ وشرِّ ما فيكِ، وشرِّ ما يدُبُّ عليكِ؛ أعوذ بالله من أَسَد وأَسْوَدَ، ومن الحيَّة والعقْرب، ومن ساكن البَلَد، ومِنْ والدٍ وما وَلَدَ » (أحمد ٢/ ١٣٢ وأبو داود: ٢٦٠٣ وضعفه الألباني)

O land! My Lord and your Lord is Allah. I seek refuge with Allah from your evil, from the evil of whatever is in you and from the evil of whatever walks on your surface. I seek refuge with Allah from a lion, a despot (or jinn), a snake and a scorpion and from those who reside in this land, and from the begetter (son of Adam) and that which he begot (his progeny)."

As for the second benefit of *Ruqyah*, providing a cure, we mentioned healing the ill person by reciting the *Al-Fatihah* and also reciting the *Ruqyah* to cure scorpion stings.

The Prophetís guidance in treating the *Namlah* (Sore)

We mentioned the *Hadith* narrated by Anas رَضِيَ اللهُ عَنْهُ in *Sahih Muslim* that the Prophet of Allah allowed using the *Ruqyah* from every type of fever, evil eye and *Namlah*.

Also, Abu Dawood narrated that Ash-Shifaa bint Abdullah said, ``The Messenger of Allah came by while I was with Hafsah and said:

﴿ ألا تُعلّمين هذه رقية النملة كما علّمتيها الكتابة ﴾ (أبو داود:٣٨٨٧ وصححه الألباني)

``Why do you not teach her (Hafsah, his wife) the Ruqyah from Namlah as you taught her how to write." An-Namlah literally, the ant, is called as such because it is a type of swelling that appears on the sides of the body. The Namlah is a known disease and causes a type of sting in the sides that makes one think that an ant is crawling on his side and biting him. There are three types of this disease.

Al-Khallal narrated that Ash-Shifaa bint `Abdullah used to recite *Ruqyah* from the *Namlah* during the time before Islam. When she emigrated to the Prophet in Madinah, after she had given him her pledge of allegiance in Makkah, she said, ``O Messenger of Allah! I used to recite the *Ruqyah* from the *Namlah* during the time of *Jahiliyyah* (before Islam) and I want to read it to you." She recited it to him, ``In the Name of Allah! May the harm be extracted until it goes back to where it came from without harming anyone. O Allah! Remove the harm, O Lord of the people." She used to recite it on a clean branch of wood seven times, choose a clean place, rub the branch on a clean stone with sour wine vinegar and then anoint the affected area with it. The *Hadith* also asserts the fact that it is legislated to teach women to read and write.

The Prophetís guidance in treating the snakeís bite

We mentioned the *Hadith* in which the Prophet said,

« لا رُقيةَ إلا في عَيْنٍ أو حمةٍ » (مسلم:٢١٩٦)

``There is no Ruqyah more beneficial than one recited for the evil eye and fever."

Also, Ibn Majah said that 'Aishah رَضِيَ الله عَنْها narrated, ``The Messenger of Allah allowed using the *Ruqyah* for the scorpions and the snakes bite." Further, Ibn Shihab Az-Zuhri narrated, ``One of the Companions of the Messenger of Allah was stung by a snake. The Prophet said, `Is there a person who could recite *Ruqyah*?' They said, 'O Messenger of Allah! The children of Al-`Hazm used to recite a *Ruqyah* for snake's bite but abandoned the practice when you prohibited using *Ruqyah*.' He said, `Summon `Umarah bin `Hazm.' When they summoned him, he recited his *Ruqyah* to the Prophet ﷺ who said that there is no objection to it. Hence, the Prophet allowed him to use it, and `Umarah recited the *Ruqyah* on the victim.' " [Al-Bukhari, Muslim, An-Nasai' and Ahmad].

The Prophetís guidance in treating an ulcer and various wounds

In the *Two Sahihs* it is narrated that 'Aishah رَضِيَ الله عَنْها said:

«كان رسول الله صلى اللهُ عليه وسلم، إذا شتكَى الإِنسانُ أو كانت به قَرْحةٌ أو جُرْحٌ، قال بإصبعه هكذا - ووضَعَ سُفْيانُ سَبَّابَتَهُ بِالأَرْضِ ثم رَفَعَها- وقال: باسم الله تُرْبةُ أرْضِنَا، بِرِيقةِ بَعْضِنا؛ لِيُشْفَى بِهِ سَقِيمُنا، بإذنِ ربِّنا »(البخاري:٥٧٤٥)

``Whenever a person would complain from an ulcer (or a canker), or a wound, the Messenger of Allah would put his finger in the soil (on the ground after inserting it in his mouth, then raise it),

saying, 'In the Name of Allah: with the soil of our earth moistered with the saliva of some of us, let our sick be cured, with our Lord's permission.' "

SAND

This is an easy, beneficial cure for the various ulcers and fresh wounds, especially when there is no available medicine. The sand, which is cold and dry and is available on all parts of the world, dries out the moisture that accumulates around the ulcer or wound. This moisture prevents quick healing by natural means, especially in warm areas. Most ulcers and wounds are also accompanied by a hot fever, which, when added to the irritant of warm weather, would only intensify the pain of those who are especially sensitive to heat. Since pure sand is cold and dry, more cooling than even the most effective medications for this purpose, the coolness of the sand will effectively pacify the warmth caused by the wound, especially when the sand is washed and dried. Pure sand also helps dry out most harmful moistures and wetness, because it is a strong drying agent against the wetness that prevents quick healing, as we stated. Further, pure sand helps cool the hotness in the ailing organ, which will strengthen its power of resistance (immunity) and thus end the pain by Allah's Leave.

The *Hadith* indicates that one should place some saliva on his index finger then place it on pure sand, some of which will stick on to his finger. The finger should then be placed on the affected organ or the wound, and then one recites the supplication mentioned in the *Hadith*. This practice joins the blessings of mentioning Allah's Name, relating all matters to Him and trusting in Him, adding both the cure and the supplication that will make the remedy even more effective.

There are two opinions regarding the Prophet's statement, ``The sand of our land", if whether it entails the sand of the entire earth or just the sand of Madinah. There is no doubt that some types of sand are more effective remedies for various ailments than sand from other areas. Galinus said, ``In Alexandria, I saw many people who suffer from severe dropsy and an ailing spleen use the sand of Egypt as ointment on their legs, thighs, hands, backs and ribs, and they used to benefit from this remedy." He also said, ``Hence, this ointment (muddy sand) could help cure Putrid and limp tumors." He continued, ``I know of many people, whose bodies have swollen due to excessive bleeding, who benefited from remedy using mud. I also know of others who used it to cure terminal illnesses that attacked various organs, and the terminal ailments were eradicated." Another author said, ``Sand that is imported from the area of Kannus - known as the island of Mastic - is an effective cleanser and causes the flesh to grow in and around ulcers, thus effectively eradicating them."

Since various types of sand have a healing effect, what about the sand of the best and most blessed area on the face of the earth, especially when mixed with the Prophet's saliva? Added to these blessings is the supplication that the Prophet ﷺ recited and in which he mentioned the Lord's Name and related all matters to Him. We mentioned that the *Ruqyah* increases in effectiveness according to the strength of faith of the person who is reciting it and the response of the ill person to the *Ruqyah*. No sane, honorable Muslim doctor can deny this fact. However, if any of these qualities is absent, let such a person say whatever falsehood he wishes!

The Prophetís guidance on treating pain in general with Islamic prayer formulas

Muslim [Ibn Ma`jah, Ahmad and At-Tabarani ] narrated in his *Sahih* that `Uthman bin Abu Al-'Aas complained to the Prophet from a pain in his body that he suffered from ever since he became a Muslim. The Prophet said:

« ضَعْ يدكَ على الَّذي تَأَلَّمَ من جسدك، وقل: بِاسم الله ثلاثًا؛ وقل سَبْعَ مراتٍ: أعوذُ بعزةِ الله وقُدْرته، من شر ما أَجدُ وأحاذرُ » (مسلم:٢٢٠٢)

Place your hand on the affected area in your body and say, `In the Name of Allah,' thrice. Then say, 'I seek refuge with Allah's Might and Power from the evil of what I am suffering from, and because of which I have become wary',seven times."

The remedy mentioned here entails reciting Allah's Name, relating all matters to Him and seeking refuge with His Might and Power from the pain, and will surely eradicate the pain. Also, repeating the supplication contained in the remedy frequently will make it even more effective and successful just as the case when the medication is frequently administered until the disease is fully eradicated.

In the *Sahihain* it is narrated that the Prophet used to visit some of his family members (who were ill) and would touch them with his right hand, saying:

« اللهم ربَّ النَّاسِ، أَذْهبِ البأس واشفِ أنتَ الشَّافِي، لا شِفاءَ إلاَّ شفاؤك، شفاءً لا يُغادِر سَقَمًا » (البخاري:٥٧٤٣)

``O Allah, the Lord of mankind! Do away with the complaint and bring about the cure. You Alone bring the cure, and there is no cure except Your cure, a cure that does not leave illnesses."

The last Islamic prayer formula includes begging Allah by His Perfect Lordship and Mercy to bring about the cure. The Islamic prayer formula also affirms that Allah is the only One Who brings the cure and that there is no cure except the cure that He brings about. The Islamic prayer formula includes begging Allah by His Oneness, Kindness and Lordship.

The Prophetís guidance on treating shock from disasters and calamities

Allah said:

﴿ وَبَشِّرِ ٱلصَّٰبِرِينَ ﴿١٥٥﴾ ٱلَّذِينَ إِذَآ أَصَٰبَتۡهُم مُّصِيبَةٞ قَالُوٓاْ إِنَّا لِلَّهِ وَإِنَّآ إِلَيۡهِ رَٰجِعُونَ ﴿١٥٦﴾ أُوْلَٰٓئِكَ عَلَيۡهِمۡ صَلَوَٰتٞ مِّن رَّبِّهِمۡ وَرَحۡمَةٞۖ وَأُوْلَٰٓئِكَ هُمُ ٱلۡمُهۡتَدُونَ ﴾

"... but give glad tidings to As-Sabiroon (the patient). Who, when afflicted with calamity, say: `Truly, to Allah we belong and truly, to Him we shall return. They are those on whom are the Salawaat (i.e. who are blessed and will be forgiven) from their Lord, and (they are those who) receive His Mercy, and it is they who are the guided ones." (2:155 -157)

In the *Musnad* (by Imam Ahmad) it is narrated that the Prophet said:

« ما مِن أحد تُصِيبه مُصِيبةٌ فَيقُول: إنا لله وإنّا إليه راجِعُون، اللّهمَّ! أْجُرني في مُصِيبَتي، وأخلِفْ لي خَيْرًا منها - إلاّ آجَره اللهُ في مصِيبته، وأخلف له خيرًا منها » (مسلم: ٩١٨)

``No person suffers a calamity and then says, `Truly! To Alla we belong and truly, to Him we shall return. O Allah! Reward m for the calamity that has befallen me and replace it with what i better.' Except that Allah will reward him for his calamity and wi replace it with what is better than whatever he lost."

The words that are contained in the *Hadith* are a truly effective an beneficial cure for those afflicted by disasters or calamities. These word contain two major aspects that if the slaves of Allah acquire knowledg of them, they will relieve them from the shock of the disaster. Firs the slave of Allah, his family and wealth are Allah's exclusive propert that Allah has loaned to the slave. When Allah takes back some c what he has loaned the slave, He is the Owner who takes back wha belongs to Him. Further, whatever Allah gives the slave is precede and followed by periods of non-existence, and the slave only take temporary possession of them when they come into existence. Alsc the slaves of Allah neither create whatever they own, and they are nc its true owners, nor are they capable of protecting such possession and property. Therefore, the slaves are only hired agents who do wha they are commanded, since they are not the real owners.

The slaves' return is to Allah, the True Lord, and consequently, the will have to sooner or later depart this life and leave it behind. The slave will return to Allah just as He created them the first time: dispossessed without a wife or a family or wealth or tribe. Only the good and ba deeds will the slaves have then. If this is the case with whatever Allal gives the slaves, its beginning and end, then why should the slaves b proud of whatever they have or get sad if they loose them? When th slaves remember their beginning and end, this thought will help then discard sadness and depression for their loss.

Also, sadness and depression will be relieved when the slaves realize that they have neither the power to avoid whatever has befallen them, nor to bring about what was not destined for them. Allah said:

﴿ مَآ أَصَابَ مِن مُّصِيبَةٍ فِي ٱلْأَرْضِ وَلَا فِيٓ أَنفُسِكُمْ إِلَّا فِي كِتَٰبٍ مِّن قَبْلِ أَن نَّبْرَأَهَآ ۚ إِنَّ ذَٰلِكَ عَلَى ٱللَّهِ يَسِيرٌ ﴿٢٢﴾ لِّكَيْلَا تَأْسَوْا۟ عَلَىٰ مَا فَاتَكُمْ وَلَا تَفْرَحُوا۟ بِمَآ ءَاتَىٰكُمْ ۗ وَٱللَّهُ لَا يُحِبُّ كُلَّ مُخْتَالٍ فَخُورٍ ﴾

``No calamity befalls on the earth or in yourselves but it is inscribed in the Book of Decrees (Al-Lauh Al-Mahfuz) before We bring it into existence. Verily, that is easy for Allah. In order that you may not grieve at the things over that you fail to get, nor rejoice over that which has been given to you. And Allah likes not prideful boasters." (57:22,23)

Also, the anguish caused by the calamity will be relieved when the slaves think deeply about what Allah has bestowed on them as compared to what they have lost. They will find that whatever they still have of Allah's bounty is much larger, especially since Allah has promised them what is even better than whatever they have lost, providing that they are patient with the calamity. If Allah wills, He could make the calamity even larger and more severe.

The shock of calamities could also be soothed by observing other people around him and realizing that wherever one looks he sees a disaster to his right and to his left. If someone searches the entire world, he will see that all of mankind is suffering some type of calamity: either losing a loved one, or from a disaster. He will also realize that the joys of this world are just daydreams or passing shadows, and that even if this earthly life brings a little joy, it also brings many tears, and if it brings a comfort for one day, it can bring about a long term disaster. Further, if this life brings some joy, it can prevent further joy from coming for a long time. In addition, no place of residence will be filled with any type of good, but could soon be filled with lessons and losses. Finally, if this life brings happiness for a day, it can be hiding the evil of the days to come.

Ibn Mas`ud رَضِيَ الله عَنْهُ said, ``Every joy will be followed by sadness, and no house is filled with joy but will soon be filled with anguish."

Also,Ibn Sirin said, ``There is not a laugh but a cry to succeed it.``

Further, Hind bint An-Nu`man said, ``One time, we were some of the most mighty people enjoying the most respected authority. Soon after, when the sun went down, we became the fewest people. It is Allah's promise that He will not fill a house with joy but it will soon be filled with lessons (or sadness)."

Once, a man asked Hind to tell him her story and she said, ``One morning, we woke up while none among the Arabs but seeks us in eagerness. When the night fell, all the Arabs felt pity for us."

Further, her sister Hurqah once cried, at a time when they were mighty. When she was asked about why she cried and if someone had bothered her, she said, ``No. I saw that my family was enjoying comforts and remembered that no house is filled with joy but would one day be filled with grief."

Furthermore, Ishaq bin Tallhah said, ``I came by her (Hurqah) one day and said to her, `What do you know about the lessons from the stories of the kings?' She said, ``What we enjoy today is better than what we enjoyed yesterday. We read in the books that no people of a house would enjoy a bounty, but would later on be tested with a trial. Also, time would never show a people a joyous day but would be hiding another day that they would hate."

Curing the shock of disasters and calamities also comes through knowing that sadness and grief will not avert the calamity but will intensify it.

Also, curing grief and anguish comes through knowing that missing the rewards for being patient and content, such as mercy and correct guidance that Allah has promised in return for being patient, is much larger than the calamity itself.

A part of the cure also comes through knowing that grief brings comfort to the heart of the enemy, grief to the friends, anger to the Lord, joy to the devil, destruction to the reward and weakness to the heart. On the other hand, when one observes patience and satisfaction, he will expel the devil and defeat his plots, will please the Lord, bring joy to the friends and sadness to the enemy. In this case, the person would say words of condolence to his friends instead they say to him. This, indeed, is the sought after perfection and firmness, unlike striking the cheeks, uttering foul words and being dissatisfied with what Allah has decided.

Curing grief after disaster strikes also comes through knowing that being patient and content would lead to a type of joy, tranquility and comfort that is much greater than what had been lost because of the disaster. In this case, it will be enough of a reward for the patient slave that he will acquire a house of praise that will be built for him in Paradise as a reward for praising his Lord and referring all matters to Him. Let one think about the bigger disaster the one that he had suffered or to lose the rewards that he would have gained in the Residence of Eternity [for being patient].

At-Tirmidhi related from the Prophet ﷺ that he said, ``On the Day of Resurrection some people would wish that their skins were sliced with scissors in the life of this world because of the reward that they witness the people who endured disasters would receive for being patient."

Some of the followers of the people of Al-Madinah once said, ``If it was not for the calamities of this life, we would be bankrupt of rewards on the Day of Resurrection."

Also, curing anguish and grief entails feeling content in the heart seeking Allah's rewards, for everything can be replaced, except for Allah's Pleasure. The cure also entails knowing that the calamity's effect on one is all what he will gain of it. Those who are content with the calamity will gain contentment, while those who are enraged, will only gain rage. The calamity will affect one as much as he allows it. One should then choose between the best of rewards or the most evil consequences. If one feels rage and disbelief, he will be written in the record of the destroyed ones. If one feels grief and abandons an obligation or commits a prohibition, he will be written in the record of those who neglect their duty. If the calamity caused one to complain and be impatient, he will be written with those who commit injustices against themselves. If one rejects Allah's decision and questions His wisdom, he will have knocked on the door that leads to hypocrisy or will have entered through it. If one is patient and firm for Allah's sake, he will be written among the patient ones. If one feels content, he will be written among the contented believers. If one praises and thanks Allah he will be written with the thankful slaves and will be gathered under the flag of those who praise Allah. If the calamity directed one to feel eager to meet his Lord, he will be written among the sincere persons in their love for Allah.

Ahmad and At-Tirmidhi related that the Prophet ﷺ said:

« إنّ اللهَ إذا أَحَبَّ قومًا ابتلاَهم؛ فمن رَضِي فله الرِّضَا، ومن سخِط فله السَّخَطُ » (الترمذي: ٢٣٩٦ وحسنه الألباني)

``When Allah loves a people, He tests them with trials. If they are content, then they will achieve contentment. Those who get enraged, will only reap rage."

Curing grief also entails knowing that no matter how much grief one feels he will sooner or later be forced to forego the matter. And then, he will not be rewarded for this forced patience.

A wise man once said, ``In the first day when a calamity strikes, the wise person behaves just like the ignorant person behaves days later. Those who do not observe an honorable patience, will soon be forced to forget just as the animals do."

Also in the *Sahih* it is related that the Prophet ﷺ said:

« الصَّبْرُ عِندَ الصَّدْمَةِ الأُولَى »

"Verily, patience is at the stroke of the calamity."

Further, Al-Ash'ath bin Qays said, "Observe patience with Faith and await the reward from Allah Alone. Otherwise, you will be forced to forget just as the animals do."

Among the cures of grief is that the person should know that the most useful remedies for his case are his agreeing with his Lord and God in what He has chosen for him, for the secret that love contains is that those who love agree with the loved one. Those who claim to love then disagree with what the loved one likes and seek what he dislikes will anger the loved one and will be testifying to the untruthfulness of their claimed love.

Abu Ad-Darda' once said, "When Allah decides a matter, He likes that His decision is accepted." Also, `Imran bin Al-Husain used to say when he was ill, "The most beloved to Him is also the most beloved to me." Abu Al-Aliyah also said similar words. This remedy only works for those who have sincere love for Allah and is not suitable for just any one.

Also, curing grief includes comparing what is more joyous, beloved and enduring: being content with the calamity or the joy of receiving Allah's reward. When one realizes and acquires the superior option, he should thank Allah for His guidance. If one chooses the lesser of the two, let him know that the affliction that his mind, heart and religion have suffered is more than the affliction he suffered through the disaster.

Curing grief also requires knowing that He Who has tested the slave with the affliction is the Most Wise, the Most Merciful, and that He did not test him with the affliction to destroy, punish or overwhelm him. Rather, the affliction is merely a test of his patience, contentment with Allah and faith. Also Allah wants to hear the slave's pleas, supplications, and humiiity before Him, seeking refuge with Him, his heart's humbleness before Him and his explaining his grievances to Him.

Shaikh Abdul Qadir said, ``My son! The affliction was not meant to destroy you. Rather, it was meant as a test of your patience and faith. My son! Fate is a lion, and lions do not eat carrion." The affliction is just like the bellows for the believer that rids him of impurities. The believer will either end up being pure gold or pure evil! When the bellows do not benefit the slave in this life, he will be faced with the mightiest bellows hell. The slave should thus know that his being tested with the bellows of this life is better for him than being tested with the bellows of the next life! Also, the slave has no other choice but to be tested with one of the two bellows, so let him appreciate Allah's bounty on him by testing him with the bellows of this world.

Curing grief also entails knowing that if it were not for the afflictions of this life, the slave would become arrogant, proud and hard-hearted, which would ultimately cause his destruction. It is the mercy of the Most Merciful that He tests the slave with afflictions sometimes so that these afflictions act as a prevention against evil manners, thus preserving the health of one's slavery to Allah. Also they extract spoiled substances from his system. All praise is due to Him Who sends down mercy with afflictions, and Who tests the slaves with the bounties He grants.

If it was not for the fact that Allah treats His slaves with the remedies of afflictions and trials, they would be arrogant and would commit injustices and aggression. When Allah decides to do good for a certain slave, He tests him with pain and affliction, according to the degree of his faith. This is how Allah rids the slaves of destructive ailments (sins and lusts), until the slave is purified and correctly guided, and Allah qualifies him to the highest degree in this world: being His slave. He will also qualify him for the best rewards in the Life Hereafter: Gazing at Allah and residing close to Him .

Curing grief also entails knowing that the bitterness of this life is itself the sweetness of the Life Hereafter, as Allah will turn it to sweetness later on. Also the sweetness of this life is itself the bitterness of the Life Hereafter. Moving away from a short-lived bitterness to acquire an eternal sweetness is surely better than vise versa.

If one does not comprehend these facts, let them remember the words of the truthful one,

« حُفَّتِ الجَنَّةُ بالمَكَارِهِ، وحُفَّتِ النَّارُ بالشَّهَواتِ » (مسلم: ٢٨٢٢)

``Paradise is surrounded with joys while the Fire is surrounded with lusts."

Therefore, bring yourself to what Allah has prepared for His loyal supporters – those who obey Him – of eternal joy, everlasting happiness and ultimate success. Also consider and remember the torment, everlasting sadness and the humiliation that Allah has prepared for the evil and wasteful slaves. Then choose which of the two destinations you deserve and seek,

﴿ كُلٌّ يَعْمَلُ عَلَىٰ شَاكِلَتِهِۦ ﴾

``Each one does according to Shakilatihi (i.e., his way or his religion or his intentions)." (17:84)

Every person seeks what is suitable for him and what he deserves. Do not think that the cures mentioned herewith are over-explained, for the utter need of them by both the doctor and the sick required explaining them in detail. Allah knows best.

The Prophetís guidance on treating sadness, grief and depression

In the *Sahihain* it is narrated that the Messenger of Allah ﷺ said:

« لا إله إلاّ الله العظيمُ الحَليم، لا إله إلاّ الله ربُّ العَرْشِ العظيم، لا إله إلا الله رَبُّ السَّموات السبع وربُّ الأرْض، ربُّ العَرْش الكَرِيم» (البخاري:٦٣٤٦)

``There is no deity worthy of worship except Allah, the Most Great, the Most Forbearing. There is no deity worthy of worship except Allah, the Lord of the Mighty Throne. There is no deity worthy of worship except Allah, the Lord of the seven heavens, the Lord of the earth and the Lord of the Honorable Throne."

Also, Abu Dawud narrated in his *Sunan* that Abu Bakrah ﷺ related from the Prophet ﷺ that he said:

« دَعَواتُ المَكْروب: اللّهم رَحْمَتَكَ أرجُو؛ فلا تَكِلْني إلى نَفْسي طَرْفة عَيْن، وأَصْلِح لي شأْنِي كُلَّه؛ لا إله إلا أنتَ » (أبو داود:٥٠٩٠ وحسنه الألباني)

``This is the supplication of those afflicted by distress, 'O Allah! I seek Your Mercy. Do not make me reliant on my own self for an instant, and lead all my affairs to success, there is no deity except You."

Also, Abu Dawud narrated that Asmaa bint `Umays رَضِيَ الله عَنْها said that Allah's Messenger said to her:

«ألا أعلِّمُكِ كَلِمات (تَقُولينَهُنَّ) عند الكَرْب – أو في الكرب – : الله اللهُ ربي لا أُشْرِكُ به شيئاً » (أبوداود:١٥٢٥ وصححه الألباني)

``Should I teach you some words that you should recite when in distress, `Allah, is my Lord with Whom I associate nothing and no one."

Imam Ahmad narrated that Ibn Mas`ud said that the Prophet ﷺ said:

« ما أصاب عَبْدًا هَمٌّ ولا حُزْنٌ - فقال: اللهم إني عبدُكَ ابنُ عبدكَ ابنُ أمتِكَ، ناصِيَتي بيدكَ، مَاضٍ فيَّ حُكمُك، عَدْلٌ فيَّ قضاؤُك؛ أسألك بكل اسم هولك، سمّيت به نَفْسَك، أو أَنْزَلْتَه في كتابِكَ، أو عَلَّمْتَه أَحَدًا مِن خَلْقِك، أوِ استَأْثَرْتَ به في عِلْم الغَيْبِ عِنْدَك؛ أَنْ تَجْعَلَ القُرْآن العَظِيمَ ربيعَ قَلْبِي، ونُورَ صَدْرِي، وجَلاءَ حُزْني، وذَهاب همِّي. إلا أذهبَ اللهُ حُزْنه وهَمَّه، وأبدله مكَانهَ فَرَحًا»

(احمد: ٣٩١،٢، ٤٠٢ وصححه الألباني في الصحيحة: ١٩٨)

``Whenever a sadness or grief strikes a slave and the slave then says, 'O Allah! I am Your slave, the son of Your slave, the son of Your female slave. My forelock is in Your grasp. Your decision about me will certainly come to pass. Your judgment on me is certainly just. I ask You by every Name that is Yours and which You call Yourself by, whether You revealed it in Your Book, taught it to some of Your creation or kept in the Knowledge of the Unseen that You have. Make the Noble Qur'an the spring of my heart, the light of my chest, the eliminator of may sadness and the end of my grief. Then, Allah will remove his sadness and depression and will replace them with joy."

Also, At-Tirmidhi narrated that Sa`d bin Abu Waqqas related from the Messenger of Allah that he said:

« دعوةُ ذِي النُّون إذ دعَا ربَّه وَهُو في بَطْن الحُوت »

``The supplication of Thu An-Nun (Jonah) which he supplicated to the Lord while in the belly of the whale."

﴿لَّآ إِلَٰهَ إِلَّآ أَنتَ سُبۡحَٰنَكَ إِنِّي كُنتُ مِنَ ٱلظَّٰلِمِينَ﴾

" La ilaha illa Anta [none has the right to be worshipped but You (O Allah)], Glorified (and Exalted) be You [above all that (evil) they associate with You]! Truly, I have been of the wrongdoers." (21:87)

« لم يَدْعُ بها رجلٌ مسلِمٌ في شيءٍ قطُّ، إلا استُجِيبَ له» (الترمزي: ٣٥٠٥١ وصححه الألباني)

``No Muslim man would supplicate with it concerning a matter but would be positively answered by Allah."

Imam Ahmad also narrated in the Musnad,

« أنّ النّبي صلى الله عليه وسلم، كان إذا حزَبه أَمْر فَزِع إِلَى الصَّلاة »

(أبو داود ١٣١٩ وحسنه الألباني)

``Whenever the Prophet would be concerned about a matter he would turn to prayer."

Furthermore, Allah said:

﴿وَٱسْتَعِينُوا۟ بِٱلصَّبْرِ وَٱلصَّلَوٰةِ﴾

``And seek help in patience and As-Salat (the prayer). (2:45)

In the *Sunan* it is also narrated, ``Revert to Jihad, because it is among the doors of Paradise with which Allah drives away sadness and depression from the hearts."

Ibn `Abbas رَضِيَ الله عَنْهما was also reported to have related from the Prophet that he said:

« مَن كَثُرت هُمومُه وغُمومُه: فلْيُكْثِرْ من قَوْل لا حَوْلَ ولا قوةَ إلاّ بالله »

(لم نجده وعند الحاكم والطبراني (المجمع ١٠/ ٩٨) هي دواء من تسعة وتسعين داءً أيسرها الهم لكنه ضعيف)

``Whenever sadness and grief intensify on someone, let him often repeat, `There is neither power nor strength except from Allah.' "

In the *Sahihain* it is also narrated that this supplication is a treasure of Paradise, while At-Tirmidhi narrated that it is a door of Paradise.

These cures that we mentioned are of fifteen types. If they are not sufficient to remove sadness, depression and grief, then the sickness has become chronic and needs to be completely removed and dissipated.

The first cure, affirming Allah's Oneness in His Lordship. The second, affirming Allah's Oneness in the worship. The third cure, the belief in the creed of *Tawhid* (There is no true god but Allah and Muhammad is His Messenger). The fourth, praising Allah for not dealing with His slave with injustice and for not punishing him without a reason. The fifth, the slave's affirming that it is he who has committed the injustice. The sixth, pleading to Allah by the most beloved methods to Him, by His Names,

attributes, such as *Al-`Hay* (The Ever Living), *Al-Qayyum* (Who Sustains everything and everyone). The seventh, depending and relying on Allah Alone for everything. The eighth, the slave affirms that his hope is only in Allah. The ninth, acquiring true dependence on Allah and relating all matters to Him, while admitting that the slave's forelock is in His Hands Alone and that He does with it whatever He wills. Also, admitting that Allah's decision on the slave will certainly come to pass and that His judgment is certainly just.

The tenth, the slave's heart should enjoy the gardens of the Qur'an and should make the Qur'an just like the spring of pure water to the animals. Also, the slave should use the light of the Qur'an to shatter the darkness of desires and lusts. The Qur'an should be one's companion when no one else is present; the comfort that relieves every type of calamity and the cure that discards every illness that attacks the slave's heart. In short, the Qur'an should be the remover of sadness and the end of depression and grief. The eleventh, turning to *Istighfar,* seeking forgiveness from Allah. Twelfth, repenting to Allah. Thirteenth, performing Jihad in Allah's cause. Fourteenth, performing prayer. Fifteenth, relating all power and strength to He Who grasps them in His Hands.

How divine remedies affect diseases

Allah has created the son of Adam and his body's organs and designated a state of perfection that each organ could attain and achieve. Consequently, when the organ looses its perfection, it feels pain. Allah has also designated a state of perfection for the heart, the leader of the organs. When the heart looses its perfection, it will fall down with various ills and sicknesses, such as sadness, grief and anguish.

Furthermore, when the eye looses what it was created for, sight; when the ear looses what it was created for, hearing; and when the tongue looses what it was created for, speech; then these organs will have lost their perfection.

The heart was created to acquire knowledge of its Creator and to love Him, worship Him Alone, be content with Him, to be joyous loving Him and to feel satisfied with Him. The heart was also created to rely on Allah, to love for His Sake, hate for His Sake, to be loyal for His Sake, to be enemy of His enemies for His Sake and to remember Him always. The heart was created to love Him more than anyone or anything else, to have Hope in Him rather than anyone or anything else and to revere Him more than anything or anyone else. There is no joy, happiness, delight or sweetness except by acquiring such qualities, which are just like food, good health and life for the heart. When the heart looses its food, health and life, then sadness, grief and affliction will attack it from all sides and will remain with it.

The worst diseases that attack the heart are *Shirk* (polytheism, making partners with Allah), sins, and forgetfulness, ignoring what Allah likes and is pleased with, abandoning relating all matters to Him and not depending on Him for everything. Diseases of the heart also include relying on other than Allah, rejecting His decisions and doubting and ignoring His warnings and promises.

When one thinks about the diseases of the heart, he will find that the reasons that we mentioned are the only ones behind these ills. Consequently, the only effective remedies for these ills are their opposites and antidotes that the Prophetic remedies contain. We stated before that the disease is removed by its opposite and that health is preserved by using what it is accustomed to which is included in the Prophetic remedies.

Tawhid opens the door to all types of good, happiness, joy, elation and enjoyment for the slave. Also, repenting to Allah extracts all types of harmful, sinful causes of the heart's ailment. Further, *Tawhid* is the diet of the heart against bad substances, for it closes the doors of evil. The doors of happiness and all types of good will be opened with *Tawhid*, while repentance and seeking forgiveness will close the doors of evil.

Doctors of old said, ``Whoever seeks to acquire good health for the body should consume less amounts of food and drink. Whoever seeks the well being of his heart, let him abandon sin." Also, Thabit bin Qurrath said, ``The body's well being requires consuming less food, the soul's comfort is in committing less sins and the consolation of the tongue is in uttering less speech."

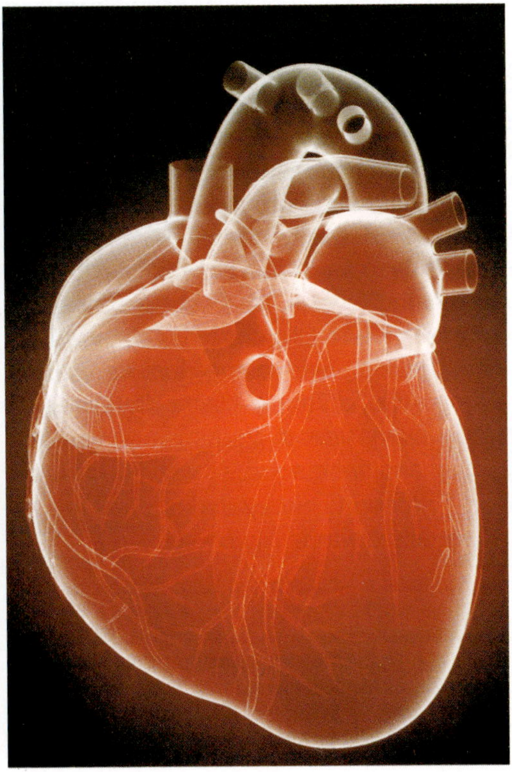

Sins are just like poison to the heart – if they do not destroy it, they will weaken it. Then when the heart is weaker, it will become less efficient in fighting disease.

The biggest of the heart's ills occur by satisfying its lusts and desires, while ignoring them constitutes its biggest cure. We should also mention that originally, ignorance and injustice were created in the self. Because the self is ignorant, it thinks that its cure is in following its desire, although this path leads it to its destruction and demise. And because the self is unjust, it does not accept the prescription of the sincere doctor. Consequently, when the self is prescribed the ailment instead of the cure, it accepts it while refusing to take the cure when it is prescribed. And because the self prefers the illness rather than the cure, which it tries to avoid, many other illnesses and diseases will break out and by then the doctor will not be able to diagnose them and consequently, the cure will not be available. The biggest calamity of all this is that the self absolves itself of guilt and blames Fate and its Lord, inwardly in the beginning and then explicitly later on![1]

When the ailing person reaches this stage, there is no hope of curing him, unless the Mercy of the Lord rushes to his aid and Allah allows him to start a new life while providing him with the required sustenance. This is why the *Hadith* that Ibn `Abbas رَضِيَ الله عَنْهما has narrated about the supplication during the time of distress contained Unity *(Tawhid)* of Allah in Lordship and worship, glorifying Him and mentioning His being Most Forbearing. These two Attributes (Glory and Forbearing) are necessary to add perfection to the Attributes of Ability, Mercy, Kindness and Forgiveness. Also, the same *Hadith* described Allah's Lordship above the upper and lower worlds and above the Throne, which is the ceiling and the mightiest of all creation. Affirming Perfect Lordship to Allah requires worshiping Him alone in Unity *(Tawhid)*, and loving, fearing, hoping, glorifying and obeying Him Alone. Also, affirming Allah's Perfect Glory requires affirming and attributing every type of perfection to Him and denying every type of shortcoming and being equated with the creation. In addition, Allah's being Most-Forbearing necessitates affirming the perfection of His Mercy and Kindness towards His creation.

(1) Editor's note: In Arabic the word *Ruh* means soul and the word *Nafs* means self. There is sometimes confusion about these words. Generally it is understood the *Ruh*, soul, is created pure without sin and becomes affected by how we live our individual lives and we will be judged by the condition it is in on the Day of Judgement. The *Nafs* on the other hand it is considered to be our instinctual animal qualities (self) that must be trained or at least restrained by the laws of Islam. Satan (the force of evil) appeals to our *Nafs* (self) and tries to encourage it to commit sins. This in turn causes negative damage to the soul, which we are responsible for.

When the heart has access to these facts, it will seek to acquire the qualities of loving Allah and glorifying Him in *Tawhid*. Then, the heart will acquire and enjoy such elation and delight that will allow it to overcome the feelings of affliction, sadness and grief. It is a fact that whenever the sick person hears of what brings happiness and joy to his heart, the body will be more effective in resisting the ailment.

Furthermore, when one compares the depressing feelings while in anguish to the wonderful meanings contained in the supplication while distressed, he will find that these words are perfectly suitable to deliver the heart from its depression and substitute it with the elation that accompanies happiness and joy. Only those who have had access to such feelings and whose hearts are filled with the light of the truth that comes with these feelings will give this subject matter its due consideration.

The Prophet's statement:

« يا حيُّ يا قيُّومُ برحمتِك أسْتغِيثُ » (الترمذي:٣٥٢٤ وحسنه الألباني)

``O the Ever-Living, the Self Subsisting! I urgently seek Your Mercy."

It has a special kind of effect in removing the grief.

Allah's Living is an attribute that includes every type of perfect quality, while the attribute ``The Self Subsisting" entails Allah's perfect Actions. That is why *Al-Hayy* (The Ever Living), *Al- Qayyum* (The Self Subsisting) are included in Allah's Mightiest Name, which if He is called by it, He will answer and if He is begged by it, He will give.

Furthermore, Perfect Life is the opposite of sickness and shortcomings since the residents of Paradise do not die, they do not feel any sadness, depression or any type of ailment. When life has an end, it indicates the existence of shortcomings in actions and inability to sustain. Being ever-living is thus suited to being ever-sustaining. The Ever-Living does not have any shortcoming in His being. The Self Subsisting *Al-Qayyum*, is Able to do everything He wills. This is why asking Allah by His Names *Al-Hayy*, The Ever-Living, *Al-Qayyum*, the Self Subsisting has profound effects on removing what is the opposite of life and Ability.

Related to this, the Prophet ﷺ used to ask Allah by His Lordship of Jibril, Michael and Israfil عليهم السلام to guide him to that which the people had differed in concerning the truth, by His Will, for the heart lives by correct guidance. The three angels mentioned in the supplication are responsible for the elements and necessities of life. For instance, Jibril عليه السلام is responsible for delivering the revelation with which the heart lives. Michael is responsible for the sustenance, which is the life of the body. Israfil عليهم السلام is responsible for blowing the Horn, which signals the resurrection of the souls and their being returned to their bodies Asking Allah by His Lordship of these three angels, who are responsible for all types of life, has a special effect in acquiring what one seeks and longs for.

Therefore, invoking Allah's Name *Al-Qayyum* has a special effect in answering supplications and ending afflictions. The *Sunan* and Abu Hatim in his *Sahih* narrated that the Prophet ﷺ said: ``Allah's Greatest Name is in these two Verses."

﴿ وَإِلَٰهُكُمْ إِلَٰهٌ وَاحِدٌ لَّا إِلَٰهَ إِلَّا هُوَ الرَّحْمَٰنُ الرَّحِيمُ ﴾

``And your Ilah (God) is One Ilah (God - Allah), La ilaha illa Huwa (there is none who has the right to be worshipped but He), the Most Gracious, the Most Merciful." (2:163)

And:

﴿ الم ۝١ اللَّهُ لَا إِلَٰهَ إِلَّا هُوَ الْحَيُّ الْقَيُّومُ ﴾

``Alif Laam Meem. Allah! La ilaha illa Huwa (none has the right to be worshipped but He), Al-Hayyul-Qayyum (the Ever Living, the One Who sustains and protects all that exists)." (3:1-2)

At-Tirmidhi commented that this is an authentic *Hadith*.

In the *Sunan* and the *Sahih* of Ibn Hibban it is also narrated that Anas رَضِيَ الله عَنْهُ said, ``A man once supplicated, 'O Allah! I ask You by Your owning the praise, there is no deity worthy of worship except You, the *Mannan* (Munificent), Who created the heaven and the earth. O Owner of the praise and Honor. '*O Hayy, Qayyum.*' "

The Prophet ﷺ said:

« لقَد دعا اللهَ باسمِه الأَعْظم الذي إذا دُعِيَ به أجابَ، وإذا سُئِل به أعطى »

(أبوداود:١٤٩٥ وصححه الألباني)

``He has asked Allah by His Greatest Name, which if He is called by it He answers, and if He is asked He gives."

This is why the Prophet ﷺ used to say when making *Du`a'* ,

« يا حيُّ يا قَيُّوم » (الترمذي:٣٤٣٦ وقال الألباني: ضعيف جدًا)

" O Hayy, O Qayyum."

The Prophet's statement:

« اللهم رَحْمَتَك أَرْجُو؛ فلا تكِلْني إلى نَفْسِي طرْفةَ عينٍ، وأصلِح لي شَأْنِي كلَّه؛ لا إلهَ إلاّ أنت » (أبوداود:٥٠٩٠ وحسنه الألباني)

``O Allah, I seek Your Mercy. Do not make me rely on my own self for an instant, and lead all my affairs to success. There is no deity worthy of worship except You."

This supplication entails invoking Allah, Who grasps all good in His Hands. It also includes depending on Allah Alone, relating all matters to Him Alone and pleading to Him to lead the slave's matters to success. It also includes asking Him not to allow the slave to rely on his own self, and invoking Him by mentioning His Oneness. All these have a special effect in removing grief. Such is the case with the Prophet's statement:

« اللهُ ربِّي لا أُشرِكُ به شيئًا »

``Allah is my Lord, I associate none with Him."

As for the *Hadith* that Ibn Mas'ood narrated:

« اللهم إني عَبدُك [و] ابنُ عَبْدِك »

``O Allah, I am Your slave, the son of Your slave..."

It contains what no one book can explain of divine knowledge and the secrets of the slavery to Allah. The *Hadith* includes attesting to the slavery of the person and the slavery of his father and mother to Allah, that the forelock of the slave is in the Hands of Allah and that He does what He will with the slave. The slave cannot bring about benefit, harm, life, death or resurrection without Allah. When the slave's forelock is in someone else's hand, the slave does not own anything regarding himself. Rather, he is a prisoner in the grasp, power and authority of his owner.

The Prophet ﷺ also stated that:

« ماضٍ فيَّ حُكْمُكَ، عَدْلٌ فيَّ قضاؤُكَ »

``Your decision on me will certainly come to pass, and Your judgment on me is certainly just."

This portion of the *Hadith* contains two major aspects of Unity (*Tawhid*). First, the *Hadith* affirms Predestination and that Allah's decisions will certainly come to pass on His slaves and that the slave can neither escape them nor fend them off.

Allah's decisions are certainly just and thus do not contain any injustice in them for His slave. Rather, Allah's decisions always conform to justice and kindness. Also, injustice is a shortcoming that constitutes a need of some sort, an ignorance or abuse. Such behavior can never occur by He Who has encompassing knowledge of everything, Who does not need anything or anyone, while everything and everyone stand in need of Him, and Who is the Most Just Disposer of affairs. No part of Allah's decisions can ever be empty of Wisdom and Perfection, just as none of it can ever escape His Power and Will. Allah's Wisdom is encompassing, just as His Power and Will are, and this is the reason why the Prophet Hud عليه السلام said when his people wanted to scare him with their idols:

﴿ إِنِّيٓ أُشْهِدُ ٱللَّهَ وَٱشْهَدُوٓا۟ أَنِّى بَرِىٓءٌ مِّمَّا تُشْرِكُونَ ﴿٥٤﴾ مِن دُونِهِۦ ۖ فَكِيدُونِى جَمِيعًا ثُمَّ لَا تُنظِرُونِ ﴿٥٥﴾ إِنِّى تَوَكَّلْتُ عَلَى ٱللَّهِ رَبِّى وَرَبِّكُم ۚ مَّا مِن دَآبَّةٍ إِلَّا هُوَ ءَاخِذٌۢ بِنَاصِيَتِهَآ ۚ إِنَّ رَبِّى عَلَىٰ صِرَٰطٍ مُّسْتَقِيمٍ ﴾

``I call Allah to witness and bear you witness that I am free from that which you ascribe as partners in worship, With Him (Allah). So plot against me, all of you, and give me no respite I put my trust in Allah, my Lord and your Lord! There is not a moving

(living) creature but He has the grasp of its forelock. Verily, my Lord is on the Straight Path (the truth)." (11:54-56)

This *Ayah* indicates that although Allah owns the forelock of His slaves and does what He wills regarding their affairs, He is on the Straight Path, meaning He never decides anything regarding them that is not full of wisdom, justice, kindness and mercy. The Prophet's statement:

« ماضٍ فيَّ حُكْمُكَ »

``Your Decision regarding me will certainly come to pass,"

It is similar to what Allah said:

﴿مَّا مِن دَآبَّةٍ إِلَّا هُوَ ءَاخِذُۢ بِنَاصِيَتِهَآ﴾

``There is not a moving (living) creature but He has the grasp of its forelock." (11:55)

Also, the Prophet's statement:

« عَدْلٌ فيَّ قضاؤُكَ »

``Your judgment on me is certainly just,"

It is also similar to what Allah said:

﴿إِنَّ رَبِّى عَلَىٰ صِرَٰطٍ مُّسْتَقِيمٍ﴾

``Verily, my Lord is on the Straight Path (the truth)." (11:56)

Then, the Prophet begged Allah by the Names that He has called Himself with, those which the slaves know and those which they do not know, such as the Names that He has kept with Him and did not allow any angel or Messenger to have access to. This type of supplication is one of the best and dearest to Allah, along with being the most beneficial in achieving what one seeks and longs for.

The Prophet ﷺ then asked Allah to make the Qur'an in his heart just like a spring is to the animals. He also asked Allah to make the Qur'an a remedy for his sadness and grief, so that it works just as medicine works when it removes an ailment, allowing the body to regain its health and youth. He also asked Allah to make the Qur'an the remover that clears rust and impurities from the heart. This remedy, when the ailing person uses it with a sincere heart, will certainly remove the ailment and will replace it with complete recovery, health and energy.

As for the supplication that Zhin An-Nun (Jonah) has made, it contains an affirmation of *Tawhid* (Unity) and praises Allah's perfection. Also, it contains the slave's affirming his own injustice and the sins that he has committed, making the supplication an especially effective remedy for sadness, grief and anguish. It is also a very effective means of approach to Allah that ensures deliverance of what one seeks. *Tawhid* (Unity) and praising Allah include affirming all types of perfection for Allah and denying every type of shortcoming from approaching Him. One's affirming his injustices indicates the slave's faith in the religion and belief in reward and punishment. It also leads the slave to being humble and to repent to Allah, asking Him to forgive his faults and affirming his slavery and meekness to Allah. There are four matters that the slave would be begging Allah with in this supplication: *Tawhid* (Unity), praising Allah, affirming one's slavery to him and admitting one's mistakes.

As for the *Hadith* narrated by Abu Umamah,

« اللَهُمّ؛ إني أعُوذُبكَ من الهمِّ والحزَنِ » (أبو داود:١٥٥٥ وضعفه الألباني)

``O Allah! I seek refuge with You from sadness and anguish,"

It contains seeking refuge with Allah from eight matters. There are four pairs of things that are related: grief and anguish, inability and laziness, cowardice and miserliness, and preponderance of debts and dominance of men. When a hated matter reaches the heart, it will be either a current concern, which will cause sadness, or it will be an anticipated matter of concern and anguish, which might affect the slave's important interests.

When one does not attain his vital interests, it will be because he is unable or unwilling to seek such interests. When one does not bring about benefit to others and to himself, it will be because he is either a coward or miserly and unwilling to spend from his money. When one falls under domination, it will be because of his being indebted, or because he is overwhelmed by other people unjustly. The *Hadith* includes seeking refuge from all types of evil.

Seeking forgiveness has a profound effect on repelling grief, anguish, sadness and depression.This is a fact agreed upon by those of wisdom of every nation. This is because sins and errors bring about grief, anguish, fear, sadness, distress, and ailments of the heart. After a while, those who are used to committing evil and sins will get bored with them. Then, they will commit these errors to drive away the depression and loneliness that they feel. Since these are the effects of sins and errors on the hearts, then the only remedy for this condition includes seeking forgiveness and repenting (to Allah).

As for the prayer, it has a profound effect on bringing relief and comfort to the heart, along with strengthening it and bringing about joy and elation to it. The prayer is the connection of the heart and soul with Allah and brings about feelings of joy by drawing closer to Him, remembering Him, feeling happy by speaking to Him, standing before Him, and using one's entire body and strength in implementing one's slavery to Him. The prayer also entails giving each organ and limb its due right of its slavery, while freeing the heart from remembering the creation, dealing with it or talking of it. The attention of the heart and limbs will thus be concentrated on the Lord and Creator, along with being free from the irritation caused by his enemy (Satan) while in prayer. This is why the prayer is one of the best types of medicines, remedies, and nutrition and is only suitable for healthy hearts. As for ailing hearts, they are just like ailing bodies, not fit for normal good foods.

The prayer is one of the best methods to acquire the good of this life and the life hereafter while fending off the harm of this and the next life. It also discourages people from falling into sin, cures diseases of the heart, fends off the ailments of the body, brings light to the heart and the face and elevates the energy of the limbs and the soul. It also brings about sustenance, fends off injustice, helps the oppressed, dissipates the lusts of the hearts, preserves one's bounty, fends off torment, brings about mercy, relieves calamity and helps against many ailments that attack the internal organs.

Ibn Majah narrated in his *Sunan* that Abu Hurairah رَضِيَ الله عَنْهُ said, ``The Messenger of Allah ﷺ saw me while I was asleep suffering from a pain in the stomach. He said to me:

يَا أبا هُرَيرةَ؛ أشِكَمِتُ دَرْدْ؟ قال: قُلتُ: نعم. يا رسولَ الله، قال: قم فصل؛ فإن في الصلاة شفاءً (ابن ماجه ٣٤٥٨ وضعفه الألباني)

" 'O Abu Hurairah! Does your stomach bother you (he said it in Persian)?' I said, `Yes, O Messenger of Allah ( ﷺ )!' He said, `Stand up and pray, because the prayer is a cure.'"

It was also reported that these words are not the Prophet's words but Abu Hurairah رَضِيَ الله عَنْهُ said them to Mujahid.

When the hypocrite doctor's heart is not pleased with all these facts, we talk to him in medical terms. We say to him that the prayer is an exercise for the body and soul, as it entails various movements and positions, such as standing up, bowing down, prostrating, sitting on the ground, moving between these positions during which most of one's joints are used. Also, most of the internal organs are exercised in the prayer, such as the stomach, the intestines and the rest of the body organs that are responsible for food and digestion. Who can deny that these acts and movements do not strengthen the body, especially when the soul is strengthened and relieved during the prayer? In this case the body will be strengthened and the pain will subside.

The disease of hypocrisy and rejecting what the Messengers were sent with and preferring atheism has no cure except for Fire.

Allah said:

﴿ نَارًا تَلَظَّىٰ ﴿١٤﴾ لَا يَصْلَاهَا إِلَّا الْأَشْقَى ﴿١٥﴾ الَّذِي كَذَّبَ وَتَوَلَّىٰ ﴾

``Blazing Fire (Hell). None shall enter it save the most wretched. Who denies and turns away." (92:14-16)

As for the effect of *Jihad* on repelling sadness and grief, it is well established, when the heart is forced to tolerate evil succeeding and becoming dominant and apparent, its sadness, depression, fear and distress increases. But when the soul performs *Jihad* for Allah's sake, Allah will turn that sadness and grief into happiness and strength. Allah said:

﴿ قَٰتِلُوهُمْ يُعَذِّبْهُمُ ٱللَّهُ بِأَيْدِيكُمْ وَيُخْزِهِمْ وَيَنصُرْكُمْ عَلَيْهِمْ وَيَشْفِ صُدُورَ قَوْمٍ مُّؤْمِنِينَ ﴿١٤﴾ وَيُذْهِبْ غَيْظَ قُلُوبِهِمْ ﴾

``Fight against them so that Allah will punish them by your hands and disgrace them and give you victory over them and heal the breasts of a believing people, and remove the anger of their (believers') hearts." (9:14,15)

No act is more capable of removing the heart's grief, sadness and anguish more than *Jihad*.

As for the effect of saying ``there is no deity worthy of worship except Allah" in removing depression, it is a fact because these words include referring all matters, power and strength to Allah Alone. They also include submitting all matters to Allah, not denying Him any supremacy over any matter and referring the Ability to make any changes in this and the higher worlds to Allah Alone. Nothing can supercede these words in this regard.

It was said that there is no angel who descends from or ascends to the heaven without uttering the words, ``there is no power or strength except from Allah". Finally, these words have an especially profound effect in repelling the devil.

The Prophetís guidance on curing fear and insomnia

At-Tirmidhi narrated in his Sunan that Khalid once complained to the Prophet ﷺ that he does not sleep well at night. The Prophet ﷺ said:

إذا أوَيْتَ إلى فِراشِك، فقل: اللّهم ربَّ السمواتِ السَّبْع وما أظَلّتْ، ورَبَّ الأرَضِينَ وما أقَلَّتْ، وربَّ الشياطينِ وما أضلّتْ؛ كن لي جارًا من شرِّ خلقِكَ كلهم جميعًا: أن يفرُطَ عليَّ أحدٌ منهم، أو يَبغى عليَّ؛ عزَّ جارُك وجلَّ ثناؤُكَ، ولا إله غيرُك.

(الترمذي:٣٥٢٣ وضعفه الألباني)

``When you go to bed say, 'O Allah! The Lord of the seven heavens and what is under them, the Lord of the earths and what they carry, and the Lord of the devils and whoever they misguide! Be my supporter against the evil of all of Your creation, preventing any of them to cause me any harm or injustice. Mighty indeed are those whom You support, honorable indeed is Your praise, and there is no deity worthy of worship except You.'''

Also, At-Tirmidhi narrated that the Messenger of Allah ﷺ used to teach his companions these words when they face any fear,

« أعوذُ بكَلِماتِ اللهِ التامَّةِ من غَضَبه وعِقابه وشرِّ عباده، ومن هَمَزاتِ الشَّياطينِ؛ وأعوذُ بك رَبِّ أن يَحضُرُونِ » (أبوداود:٣٨٩٣ وحسنه الألباني)

``I seek refuge with Allah's perfect Words from His anger and torment, and from the evil of His slaves and the whisperings of the devils. I seek refuge with You, my Lord from their presence.'''

Ibn Umar رَضِيَ الله عَنْهما used to teach these words to his children and would even write them for those who were not able to memorize them. There is no doubt that such words are suitable and effective in removing and repelling all types of harm.

The Prophetís guidance on treating burns

Burns are usually caused by fire, which is the substance from which the devil was created, and this is why the devil finds it befitting his nature and the evil that he seeks to achieve. Therefore, the devil helps the fire cause harm. The fire usually seeks domination and devastation. These two matters, domination and devastation, are the guidance of the devil that he calls to and with which he leads mankind to destruction. The fire and the devil both seek domination and affliction, while Allah's Pride always intervenes by extinguishing these evils and the acts of the devil.

This is why praising Allah that He is the Great has a profound effect on extinguishing the fire, for Allah's Greatness overwhelms anything and everything. When the Muslim praises Allah's Greatness, this supplication will cause the fire and the efforts of the devil to fade away and thus the fire will be extinguished, Allah willing. We have used this method before and found it to be true.

The Prophetís guidance on staying healthy

Preserving one's good health requires the help of wetness that resists heat. The wetness resists heat while the heat helps mature various substances and rids the body of its wastes. Otherwise, without wetness, the excessive heat would harm the body and would not allow its organs to function normally, while excessive dryness allows the heat to burn the body and make it dry. Each one of the two conditions, wetness and heat, thus needs the other to sustain and allow the body to function. Further, since the heat feeds on wetness, it preserves the moisture from rotting and decomposing. When one of these two conditions is more dominant than the other, the constitution of the body will be altered and changed.

As we have stated, heat decomposes wetness, compelling the body to seek to replace the lost moisture with food and drink, which also provides the body with sustenance. When moisture is present in excessive amounts, the heat is not able to decompose the excess wetness and thus the moisture decomposes and rots, causing harm to the body. In this case, various ailments attack the body, as much as the body and the various organs are susceptible to accept these ailments. All these facts are taken from what Allah said:

﴿ وَكُلُوا۟ وَٱشْرَبُوا۟ وَلَا تُسْرِفُوٓا۟ ﴾

``And eat and drink but waste not by extravagance..." (7:31)

Allah directs the slaves to consume what helps the body of food and drink and to replace lost energy. The amount [of food and drink] that should be consumed should not exceed what the body has lost plus what the body needs to function properly. Otherwise, the excess food will be an extravagance that brings about ailments and will not preserve the health, and such is the case when one eats excessively or does not consume sufficient amounts.

Therefore, the few words that Allah stated hold the key to staying healthy. There is no doubt that the body is always going through the process of decomposing and producing waste. The more the decomposition occurs, the less the heat will be effective, since decomposition feeds on moistures (which in turn feeds the inner heat). When the heat is weak, the digestion efficiency decreases until the moisture dissipates. Thus, the heat will be extinguished and consequently, the term (life span) that the slave was allowed in this life will come to an end.

The goal behind the person seeking a cure for himself and for others is to preserve the body until everyone reaches their final destination (death), not because preserving the necessary moistures and heat will keep the youth and health forever, for this goal is not attainable in this life. The goal that the doctor seeks to achieve entails preserving the existent wetness from what might spoil it and to preserve body-heat from what might weaken its power. The doctor thus preserves the balance between the two powers or conditions in the body, just as Allah has created the heaven and earth with justice and perfect balance. In fact, the entire creation thrives on and by justice and balance.

Those who study the guidance of the Prophet will find it the best guidance with which the health of the body can and will be preserved. Preserving good health depends on eating and drinking sensibly and on utilizing one's clothes, place of residence, the air, sleep, being awake, mobility, idleness, sex, extracting the excess material of the body and keeping whatever is necessary and important in the best form and shape. When these aspects are satisfied in the manner that is suitable for the body, the area, age and custom, the person is more likely to have good health and well being until it is his time to die.

Good health is one of the best bounties that Allah bestows on mankind and also one of His best rewards. In fact, good heath is the best earthly bounty of all, and those who have been bestowed with sound comprehension should strive to preserve their health and protect it against what might oppose or alter it.

Al-Bukhari narrated in his *Sahih* that the Messenger of Allah ﷺ said:

« نِعمَتانِ مغبُونٌ فيهما كَثِير من النَّاس: الصِّحَّةُ والفَرَاغُ » (البخاري:٦٤١٢)

``Two bounties regarding which many people cheat themselves, health and free time."

Further, At-Tirmidhi narrated that `Abdullh bin Mihsan Al-Ansari رَضِيَ الله عَنْه said, The Messenger of Allah ﷺ said:

« من أصبَحَ مُعَافًى في جَسَدِه، آمِنًا في سِرْبِهِ، عندَه قُوتُ يَوْمه، فكأنما حِيزَتْ له الدُّنيا »

(الترمذي: ٢٣٤٦ وحسنه الألباني)

" `He who reaches the morning while health in his body, safe in his residence and having his day's sustenance, will be as if the entire life of this world was granted to him."

Also, At-Tirmidhi related from Abu Hurairah رَضِيَ الله عَنْه that the Prophet said:

« أول ما يُسْأَلُ عنه العبدُ يوم القِيامةِ من النعيم؛ أن يُقالَ له: ألم نُصِحَّ لكَ جِسْمَكَ، ونُرَوِّكَ من الماءِ البارِدِ » (الترمذي:٣٥٥٨ قال الحسن: حسن صحيح)

``The first blessing that the slave will be asked about on the Day of Resurrection will be the saying to him, `Have We not made your body healthy and drove away your thirst with cold water?' "

This is why some of the *Salaf* (righteous predecessors) stated that the Verse:

﴿ ثُمَّ لَتُسْـَٔلُنَّ يَوْمَئِذٍ عَنِ ٱلنَّعِيمِ ﴾

``Then on that Day you shall be asked about the delights (you indulged in this world)." (102:8)

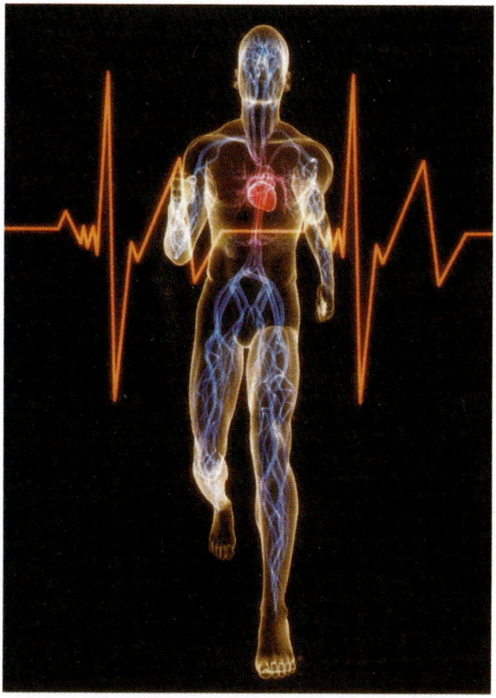

It is referring to health.

In addition, Imam Ahmad narrated that Abu Bakr As-Siddiq said, I heard the Messenger of Allah ﷺ saying:

«سَلُوا اللهَ الْيقِينَ والمُعَافاةَ، فما أُوتِيَ أحَد - بَعْدَ اليقين - خَيْرًا من العَافية»

(الترمذي:٣٣٥٨ وصححه الألباني)

``Ask Allah for certainty and good health, for indeed, no one will have a better possession after certainty of Faith than good health."

The Prophet ﷺ joined the well being of this life and the Next Life. Further, the slave's success cannot be complete in both lives except by joining certainty of faith and well being. Certainty of faith fends off the torments of the Next Life while well being fends off the ailments of this life that might attack the body or the heart.

An-Nasai' narrated that Abu Hurairah رَضِيَ الله عَنْه related from the Prophet ﷺ that he said:

« سَلُوا اللهَ العَفْوَ والعافية والمُعَافاةَ، فَمَا أُوتيَ أحد - بعد يقينٍ - خيرًا من مُعَافاة»

``Ask Allah for forgiveness, well being and health. Indeed, no one acquires a better possession after certainty of faith than good health."

The three matters mentioned in the *Hadith* entail removing the ills of the past with forgiveness, of the present with well being and of the future with immunity (from error and thus from the Torment). Indeed, these words entail the continuity of well being always.

Abdur-Rahman bin Abu Laila said that Abu Ad-Dardaa said, ``O Messenger of Allah ﷺ, it is more beloved to me to acquire good health so that I am thankful for it rather than being tested and I then observe patience. The Messenger of Allah ﷺ said:

« وَرَسُولُ الله يُحِبُّ معكَ العَافية » (مجمع الزوائد ٢/ ٢٩٠ وضعفه الهيثمي)

``The Messenger of Allah likes good health just like you."

Further, Ibn Abbas رَضِيَ الله عَنْهما is reported to have narrated:

``A Bedouin man came to the Messenger of Allah ﷺ and said to him, `What should I ask for after I finish the five prayers?' The Prophet ﷺ said, `Ask Allah for good health.' The man repeated the question, and the Prophet ﷺ said to him after the third time, 'Ask Allah for well being in this and the Next Life.'"

If this is how significant health is, we should then mention and study the Prophet's guidance on preserving health and well being, for we will come to realize that his guidance is the most perfect in this regard. With the Prophet's guidance, one attains health of his body and heart and also their very existence, both in this world and in the Next Life. Allah is sought for all types of help, and our dependence is on Him, and there is neither power nor strength except from Him.

The Prophet ﷺ did not restrict himself to eating one type of food

This would be harmful to one's nature. Also, the body could face weakness and even death if one consumed only one type of food. In addition, when someone is used to only one type of food his body does not accept any other type. Restricting the diet to only one type of food, even if it is the best type, is harmful and dangerous.

The Prophet ﷺ used to eat what his people used to eat in their regular diet, such as meat, fruits, bread, dates, and other types of food that we mentioned.

When one type of food needed to be made milder the Prophet ﷺ would use its opposite, such as neutralizing the hotness of ripe dates with watermelon. If he did not find what neutralized the effect of a type of food, he would eat of it the necessary amount without excessiveness.

When the Prophet ﷺ would not like a food, he would simply refrain from eating it and would not force himself to have it. This is a great aspect of preserving the health. When one eats what he does not have an appetite for, the food's harm will overweigh its benefit.

Abu Hurairah رَضِيَ الله عَنْهُ said, ``The Messenger of Allah ﷺ never criticized a food. If he had an appetite for it, he ate it. Otherwise, he did not eat from it." When the Prophet ﷺ was presented with lizard meat (Dhabb) he did not eat from it. He was asked, ``Is it disallowed?" He said:

« لا؛ ولكنْ: لم يكن بأرضِ قومي؛ فأجِدُني أَعَافُه » (البخاري:٥٣٩١)

``No; but, this food is not among the foods that my people used to eat, and I do not have an appetite for it."

The Prophet ﷺ used to eat a regular diet when he was offered a type of food that he was not used to eating and which he had no appetite for, he refrained from eating it. Yet, he did not prevent those who were used to that kind of food and who had an appetite for it from eating it.

The Prophet ﷺ used to like eating meat, especially the arm and the upper parts of the sheep. This is the part that was poisoned and offered to the Prophet ﷺ .

In the *Sahihain* it is narrated that the Prophet ﷺ was once brought some meat and that he was given the arm, which he liked. Furthermore, Abu `Ubaid narrated that Dhiba`ah bint Az-Zubair said that she slaughtered a sheep in her house. The Messenger of Allah ﷺ sent to her.

« أنْ أطعِمِينا من شاتِكم. فقالت للرَّسول: ما بقيَ عندَنا إلاَّ الرَّقَبةُ؛ وإني لأَسْتحِي أنْ أُرسلَ بها إلى رسولِ الله صلى اللهُ عليه وسلم. فرجَع الرسولُ فأخبَره، فَقَالَ: ارجِعْ إليها،فقلْ لها: أرسِلي بها؛ فإنها هاديةُ الشاةِ وأقربُ إلى الخير، وأبعدُها من الْأذى »

(أحمد ٦/ ٣٦١،٣٦٠ وضعف في تحقيقه)

``Feed us from your sheep." She said to the messenger, `Only the neck is left, and I feel shy to send it to the Messenger of Allah ﷺ .' The Prophet's emissary went back to the Prophet ﷺ to tell him what happened. The Messenger said, `Go back to her and tell her to send it, because the neck is the part that guides the sheep and is closer to the good things and far away from the septic things.' "

There is no doubt that the lightest part of the sheep's meat is the neck, arm and thigh. These parts are also the easiest to digest and the softest on the stomach. The method the Prophet ﷺ observed in this regard satisfies the three basic rules regarding food, which are, the food being beneficial and helpful to the nature, being light on the stomach and not heavy, and being quickly digested. This is the best type of food to consume and consequently, eating a small part of this food is better than consuming a large amount of the other types of food.

The Prophet ﷺ used to like eating sweets and honey. Meat, honey and sweets are the best foods and the most beneficial for the body, liver and various organs. Also, eating these types of food has a profound effect on preserving the health and strength, and that is why only those who are already suffering from an ailment would be harmed by consuming them.

The Prophet ﷺ used to eat bread with whatever condiment happened to be available. Sometimes he would eat bread with meat, sometimes with watermelon and sometimes with dates. One time, the Prophet ﷺ placed a dried date on a piece of bread and said that this, the date, is the condiment of that, the bread. Barley bread is cold and dry while dates are hot and wet, so eating both foods together is one of the wisest decisions, especially for those used to this type of food, such as the people of Al-Madinah. Sometimes, the Prophet ﷺ would eat bread with vinegar, saying, `What a good condiment vinegar is.' This praise for the vinegar came because it was the only available food in the house then, not because vinegar is better than the other types of foods, as some ignorant people think. The *Hadith* states that the Prophet ﷺ once came to one of his wives and asked if she had any condiment when they offered him some bread. When she said that they only had vinegar, he said, ``What a good condiment vinegar is."

Eating bread with a condiment preserves the health unlike eating only one type of food. Condiments are called as such because when they are added to the bread, the bread tastes better and the food helps preserve the health.

In addition, the Prophet ﷺ used to eat from the fruits that were in season in his land, as this also is one of the best methods of preserving health. Allah's wisdom decided that every land has its own fruits that are suitable and beneficial to that land when in season. When the people consume these fruits they will help preserve their health and well being and it serves as several medicines. On

the other hand, those who refrain from eating the fruits of their area will be among the most ailing persons and the farthest from good health and well being.

The wetness that the various fruits contain represents the favorable heat of the season and the land. The stomach would then be able to bring the fruits to maturity and would fend off their harm, if one does not eat them excessively causing his nature to bear what it cannot bear. Also, one should not spoil the food that his stomach is digesting by eating fruits, nor drink water with it. Fruits should be eaten only after the food in the stomach is digested to prevent constipation. Those who consume fruits in the proper manner, in the proper time and in the proper conditions the fruits act as a cure and a remedy for them.

The Prophetís guidance on the proper way to sit while eating

The Prophet ﷺ said:

«لا آكل متكئا وقال: إنما اجلِسُ كما يجلِس العبدُ، وآكلُ كما يأكل الْعبدُ»

(أبو يعلي:٤٩٢ وقال وفيه أبو معشر الهيثمي إسناده حسن ٩/ ١٩)

``I do not eat while leaning on my side." He also said, ``I only sit like the slave sits and eat like the slave eats."

Leaning on the side harms the stomach because it prevents the food from going down the proper channel and reaching the stomach quickly, as it pressures the stomach and does not allow it to be open properly for the food to pass through.

Eating while leaning on something is the practice of the arrogant people and this is why the Prophet ﷺ said that:

« آكُلُ كما يأكُلُ العَبْد »

``I only eat like the slave eats."

The Prophet ﷺ used to sit on his feet while eating. He used to place his knees on the ground and would place the bottom of his left foot on the upper part of his right foot in humility for the Lord and in respect for the food and for those present. This is the best way to sit for eating because the organs of the body will all be in their proper position, along with observing good manners.

As we have stated, the best way to eat is sitting up with the organs of the body in their natural position. The worst way of eating is leaning on one's side because the windpipe and the chewing organs will be pressured in this position and squeeze the stomach.

Also, the Prophet ﷺ could have meant that he does not sit while leaning on pillows as the arrogant do and those who want to eat more food. Rather, the Prophet ﷺ used to eat what is barely sufficient just as the slave does.

The Prophet ﷺ used three fingers while eating

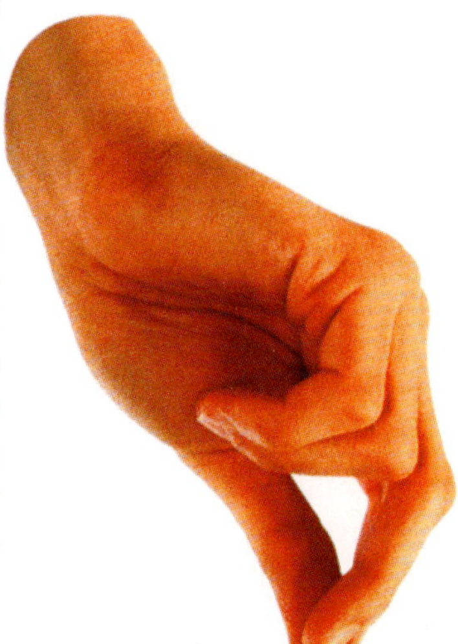

This is one of the best methods of eating. Eating with one or two fingers does not help the appetite or provide sufficient amount of food in each bite, and consequently, one would only be able to finish eating after a long time. Also, the organs responsible for handling the food would not be comfortable with the fact that they are getting so little food with each bite, in this case the organs will pass through periods of inactivity while one is still eating! If one eats one or two grains at a time, he will neither enjoy eating or feel comfortable. Eating with five fingers sends to the stomach more food than it can handle in each bite. Death might even occur if one of the organs becomes clogged with excessive food. Also, the organs of the body will be forced to handle large amounts of food and thus the person would neither enjoy eating it nor would thèir body be comfortable digesting it. Therefore, the best way of eating is by using three fingers as the Prophet ﷺ and those who imitate him do.

The Prophetís guidance on certain combinations of food

The Prophet ﷺ never mixed fish and milk, milk and sour foods or two hot dishes, or two cold dishes, two sticky dishes, two constipating dishes, two laxative dishes, two heavy dishes, two liquid foods or two types of foods that produced the same condition. Also, he did not join between two types of food that caused opposite effects, such as constipating and diarrhea, or easily digested with heavy foods broiled with cooked foods, dry with fresh foods, eggs and milk or meat and milk. Also, he neither ate a food when it is rather hot, nor old food that was heated for him the next day. Further, he did not eat any salty or rotten foods, such as pickles. All these types of foods are harmful and cause the health to change for the worst.

The Prophet ﷺ also used to neutralize the harm of some foods by their opposites, as much as he could. When the food is hot, he neutralizes its effect with a cold food, and when it is dry, he neutralizes it with wet foods, such as eating ripe dates with cucumbers and dried dates with butter. He also used to drink the water of soaked dates to neutralize the effect of heavy foods. Further, the Prophet used to eat dinner even if it only consisted of a few dates.

Abu Nu'aym mentions that the Prophet ﷺ used to discourage sleeping just after eating food because it will harden the heart. The doctors also advise the people to walk even a few steps after dinner, because sleeping just after dinner is very harmful. Muslim doctors add that one could also pray after eating his dinner, so that the food resides in the bottom of the stomach where it will be easily digested.

The Prophet ﷺ did not drink [water or milk] with his food, because the drink would spoil the food, especially when the water is hot or cold.

It is not preferred that one drinks water after sports activity, when tired, after sexual intercourse, before and after eating food and after eating fruit. Also, it is not preferred that one drinks water after taking a bath and after sleeping. All these activities will harm the health and one should not think about the benefits he might gain from drinking with the food.

The Prophetís guidance on beverages

The Prophet's guidance regarding beverages was also the most beneficial for preserving the health. The Prophet ﷺ used to drink honey with cold water, and this is an especially effective method to preserve the heath that only the best doctors could have knowledge of. Drinking honey on an empty stomach will dissolve phlegm, purify the stomach's protective layers and dissipate its viscidity and excrements while heating it mildly. Honey also helps against the clogs in the stomach, kidney, liver and prostate. Honey is much more profitable to the stomach than any other sweet.

We should state that honey might harm those suffering from bile, because it aggravates it. In this case, the harmful side effect of honey is neutralized when taking it with vinegar, as this method makes the honey very beneficial. In addition, honey is much more beneficial than any other sugar based drink, especially for those who are not used to these types of sweet drinks.

When one takes sweet drinks that he is not used to, he will not benefit as much as he will benefit from honey, as this is the role that one's customs play. The customs remove foundations and establish foundations.

When the drink is both sweet and cold, it will be most beneficial for the body and one of the best methods to preserve its health and the well being of the soul, strength, liver, and heart. Also, when the drink is both sweet and cold, the body will be eager for it, will benefit from it, nutrition wise, and will quickly digest and transfer it to the other organs of the body.

Cold water is wet, quenches the thirst, preserves the moistures in the body, regenerate the moistures that the body has lost, softens the food and helps transfer it through the veins quickly.

The doctors differed on if water is also nutritional, as some of them said that it is nutritious since the body grows and becomes milder and stronger, especially when it is in need of water. They also said that there are several similarities between man and animals, such as growing and becoming fairer and stronger. The plants also grow and have their own special kind of senses and movements. Since plants feed on water, how can anyone deny that water is nutritious, they asked?

They also say that they do not deny that food provides most of the nutritional intake of the body. They only deny that water is not considered of any nutritional value at all. They also say that the food only provides nourishment because of the watery parts it contains.

They also say that water is the resource of life for animals and plants. There is no doubt, they say, that the substance that is closer to the resource of life will provide more nourishment. How about if the substance is the resource of life itself?

Allah said:

﴿وَجَعَلْنَا مِنَ ٱلْمَآءِ كُلَّ شَىْءٍ حَىٍّ﴾

"And We have made from water every living thing."
(21:30)

They ask, how is it that the resource of life does not provide nutrition to the body?

They also add that the thirsty person would regain his strength and activity when he satisfies his thirst. He will also be able to restrict his food intake and rely on water. However, the thirsty person would not quench his thirst if he eats a large amount of food. They add, ``We do not deny that water helps transfer the food to the various parts and organs of the body. We only deny the statement that water does not have any nutritional value at all."

Another group denied that water is nutritional saying that water alone does not sustain life, or help the body grow, or restore the moisture that the body has lost through heat. However, their opponents do not deny these facts. They only say every substance provides nutrition in a different way compatible to its nature. For instance, good aroma provides a type of nutrition, and this fact makes the nutritional value of the water even more apparent.

In short, when the water is cold and mixed with a sweet substance, such as honey, raisins, dates or sugar, it will be one of the most beneficial substances that enters the body and will indeed preserve health. This is why the best drink to the Prophet ﷺ was cold and sweet. Warm water begets flatulence and is not favorable for the body or the health.

Since water that is kept overnight is more favorable than recently drawn water, the Prophet ﷺ said when he entered a garden of Abu At-Taihan:

« هل من ماءٍ باتَ في شَنَّةٍ ؟ »

``Do you have any water that was kept in its skin overnight?"

He was brought some of that water and he drank from it. [Abu Dawud, Ibn Majah and Ahmad]. This Hadith was collected by Al-Bukhari, who narrated that the Prophet ﷺ said:

« إن كان عندَكَ ماءٌ باتَ هَذِهِ اللَّيْلَةَ في شَنَّةٍ، وإلاَّ كَرَعْنا » (البخاري:٥٦١٣)

``If you have some water still in its skin (then bring me some). Otherwise we will sip (from the well).."

Water that is not freshly drawn is similar to yeasty dough, while freshly drawn water is similar to the dough that does not contain yeast. When water is soaked overnight, its earthly and sandy pollutants will rest on the bottom. It was mentioned the Prophet ﷺ liked kept water, as ' Aishah رَضِيَ الله عَنْه said:

« كان رسول الله صلى اللهُ عليه وسلم يُستَقَى له المَاءُ العَذْبُ من بئرِ السُّقْيا »

(أبو داود: ٣٧٣٥ وصححه الألباني)

``Fresh water was being brought to the Messenger of Allah drawn from the well designated for drinking."

The water that is kept in skins, especially leather skins, has a better taste than water kept in clay containers. This is why the Prophet ﷺ asked for the water that was kept in skin containers rather than the other types of containers. When the water is kept in skin containers, it will filter through the pores in the skin [thus making its taste better]. Similarly, the water that is kept in clay containers that allow the water to filter is better than that in the clay containers that do not allow the water to filter. The Prophet ﷺ had the best methods, the most honorable soul and the best guidance in every matter. He has showed his nation the most beneficial methods and means concerning the benefit of their hearts and bodies in this life and the Next Life.

'Aishah رَضِيَ الله عَنْها said that the best type of drink to the Prophet was cold and sweet. This statement might indicate that the Prophet's drink contained fresh, sweet water drawn from wells and springs. Her statement might also indicate that he used to drink water that is mixed with honey or soaked dates and raisins. Or, her statement could carry both meanings, which is the correct opinion.

The Prophet's statement:

« إن كان عندكَ ماءٌ باتَ في شَنٍّ، وإلاَّ كَرَعْنا »

``If you have some water in its skin. Otherwise we will drink from the pool (with the mouth)"

It indicates that it is allowed to drink the water directly from the pool or container with the mouth. Many doctors advise against this method and say that it is harmful for the stomach. It appears that the Prophet ﷺ did so only to demonstrate that it is allowed. Further, drinking with the mouth from the pool is harmful when one lays on his stomach and face, such as drinking from a river or a spring. Drinking with the mouth from an elevated pool of water while sitting up is not different from drinking using the hands.

The Prophet ﷺ guided his nation to drink while sitting down

He specifically commanded his nation not to drink while standing up. He also commanded those who drink while standing to vomit. Yet, he did drink while standing as is correctly reported of him.

Some people said that the Prophet's drinking while standing overrules his command not to drink while standing. Another group said that his drinking while standing only demonstrates that this practice is only disliked not prohibited. Another group said that there is no contradiction between the two *Ahadith*. The Prophet ﷺ drank while standing when he needed to do so, as he came to the well of Zamzam and was given a bucket of water that he drank from while standing.

Drinking while standing begets many ailments and does not quench the thirst, nor will the water settle in the stomach so that the liver transfers it to the rest of the body. In this case, the water will descend quickly to the stomach and will aggravate it, and the water will not be digested properly. However, if one does this occasionally, it will not harm him.

Drinking water in three separate breaths

Muslim narrated that Anas رَضِيَ الله عَنْهُ said that the Messenger of Allah ﷺ used to sip the water in three separate breaths and would say:

«إنه أَرْوَى وأَمْرَأُ وأَبْرَأُ» (مسلم:٨٠٢٨)

``This method quenches the thirst better and is more palatable and sanitary."

This *Hadith* indicates that the Prophet ﷺ used to remove the cup away from his mouth, take a breath and then drink some more. In another *Hadith* , the Prophet ﷺ commanded that one should not breathe in the cup, but should move the cup away from his mouth and breath away from it. This method of drinking is very beneficial for quenching the thirst and more sanitary as the Prophet ﷺ has stated. When the water enters the hot thirsty stomach in intervals, the second sip of water will quench the thirst left by the first, and the third will quench the thirst left by the first two. Also, this method is better suited for the temperature of the stomach, so as not to suddenly invade it with cold substances. Also, when one drinks the water in one breath, it will only partially quench the thirst unlike when he drinks it in separate sips.

This method [that the Prophet ﷺ taught us] gives better results than drinking the water or liquid in one breath, since water might dissipate the instinctive heat or weaken it, thus spoiling the temperament of the stomach and the liver. Water might also beget many other ailments, especially for those who live in warm areas, such as Yemen and Hijaz, and especially during summer. Drinking in one breath is dangerous for such people because their instinctive heat is weak especially during hot weather, as we have stated.

The Prophet's statement, ``It quenches the thirst better and is more palatable and sanitary," is similar to what Allah said:

﴿ فَكُلُوهُ هَنِيٓـًٔا مَّرِيٓـًٔا ﴾

``And enjoy it without fear of any harm." (4:4)

Also, when one takes the drink in one breath, he might choke on it because of the large amount of the liquid. However, there is no fear from choking when one takes a breath while drinking. Further, when one takes a drink, the hot gases accumulating in his body will ascend from around the liver and the heart because of the cold water or liquid that is descending on the stomach. In this case, the water will come rushing down while the gases are ascending, causing flatulence and sometimes choking the person. One will not enjoy the drink in this case.

Also, when cold water descends suddenly on the liver it will weaken it and cause a decrease in its temperature. However, when one takes the drink in separate sips, the liver will not lose its warmth and thus will not weaken. Similarly, when one pours water on a boiling pot, it will not decrease its temperature significantly.

At-Tirmidhi narrated that the Prophet ﷺ said:

« لا تَشْرَبوا نَفَسًا واحدًا: كشُرْب البَعير؛ ولكن: اشرَبُوا مَثْنَى وثُلاثَ؛ وسَمُّوا إِذا أنتم شَرِبْتم، واحمَدُوا إِذا أَنْتم فرَغْتُم »

(الترمذي:١٨٨٥ وضعفه الألباني)

``Do not drink in one breath just as the camel does. Rather, drink twice and thrice, and mention (Allah's) Name before drinking and thank (Him) upon finishing."

Mentioning Allah's Name before drinking and thanking Him upon finishing has a significant effect in benefiting from the drink, enjoying it while fending off its harm. Imam Ahmad said, ``When the food has four qualities, it will have become perfect: when Allah's Name is mentioned before having it, when Allah is thanked after finishing with it, when there are many hands to eat from it, and when it is from legal, pure sources."

Covering pots and closing water skins

Muslim narrated in his *Sahih* that Jabir bin `Abdullah رَضِيَ الله عَنْهُ said, I heard the Messenger of Allah ﷺ say:

«غَطُّوا الإِنْاءَ وأَوكُو السِّقاءَ؛ فإن في السَّنة ليلةً ينزل فيها وَباءٌ: ل يمُرُّ بإناءٍ ليس عليه غِطاءٌ - أوسقاءٍ ليس عليه وِكاءٌ - إلا وقع فيه من ذلك الداء» (البخاري:٥٦٢٣)

``Cover the pot and tie the knot of the water skin, for there is a day during the year in which a disease descends and falls in whatever pot that is not covered, or water skin, which is not tied, that it passes by."

This *Hadith* contains a type of divine knowledge that the doctors could never reach on their own. Laith bin Sa'd, one of the narrators of this *Hadith*, said,``Non-Muslims know which day it is, in January, and they try to avoid its harm."

The Prophet ﷺ commanded that the pots be covered, even with a branch, so that one makes covering it a habit. Also, when one covers the pot with a branch, crawling insects will not fall in the food but will pass over it on the branch.

Furthermore, the Prophet ﷺ commanded that we mention Allah's Name when covering the pot to repel Satan and insects and animals.

Drinking from the mouth of the water skin is not allowed

Al-Bukhari narrated that Ibn``Abbas رَضِيَ الله عَنْهما said:

«أن رسولَ الله صلى اللهُ عليه وسلم نَهى عن الشُّرْب مِن فِي السِّقاءِ» (البخاري:٥٦٢٩)

``The Messenger of Allah ﷺ disallowed drinking from the mouth of the water skin."

There are many benefits in this *Hadith*. For instance, when one drinks from the tip or the mouth of the water skin, he will breathe in it and will give it an offensive odor. Also, water may descend strongly and harm the stomach. In addition, there might be an insect in the water that one is unaware of, and that might harm him if he swallows it. Also, water might be polluted with harmful substances that will enter the person's stomach while he is unaware. Also, drinking from the mouth of the skin fills the stomach with air and thus the water will not have sufficient space.

Drinking from a chipped cup is not allowed

Abu Dawud narrated in his *Sunan* that Abu Sa'eed Al-Khudri رَضِيَ الله عَنْهُ said:

« نهى رسولُ الله صلى اللهُ عليه وسلم عن الشُّرْب مِنْ ثُلْمةِ القَدَح، وأن يُنْفَخَ في الشَّراب » (أبو داود:٣٧٢٨ وصححه الألباني)

"The Messenger of Allah ﷺ disallowed drinking from the chipped side of the cup and from breathing in the drink."

This *Hadith* also teaches the Muslim many types of good behavior. For instance, drinking from the chipped side of the cup might cause one to swallow the substances that have accumulated near the chipped side. Also, one might not be able to enjoy his drink when he is drinking from the cup's chipped side. In addition, dirt and fat concentrate near the chipped side and are usually not fully cleaned when rinsed.

Also, the chipped side of the cup is the worst and is not beneficial. One of our *Salaf* saw a man once buying inferior goods and said to him, ``Do not buy it, do you not know that Allah has not blessed inferior things?" Also, the chipped side of the cup might cause injury to the mouth.

As for breathing in the cup, it will transfer the foul odor from the person to the drink. This is why the Prophet ﷺ has disallowed breathing or blowing in it. In the *Hadith* that At-Tirmidhi narrated, Ibn `Abbas رَضِيَ الله عَنْهما said:

« نهى رسولُ اللهِ صلى اللهُ عليه وسلم: أن يُتنفَّسَ في الإِناء، أو يُنفخَ فيه »
(أبو داود:٣٧٢٨ وصححه الألباني)

``The Messenger of Allah ﷺ prohibited breathing in the pot (or cup) or blowing on it."

If some asks, ``What about the *Hadith* in the *Sahihain* in which Anas رَضِيَ الله عَنْهُ narrated:

«إن رسولَ اللهِ صلى اللهُ عليه وسلم كان يتَنَفَّسُ في الإِنْاءِ ثلاثاً » (مسلم:٢٠٢٨)

``The Messenger of Allah ﷺ used to take three breaths while drinking ?"

We say that we believe in this Hadith and that it does not contradict the Ahadith that we mentioned, because it only means that the Prophet ﷺ did not sip the drink in one breath.

The Prophet ﷺ drank milk undiluted or mixed with water

Drinking sweet milk in hot areas is very beneficial in preserving the health and providing moisture for the body and the liver. This is especially the case when the animals that produce the milk have grazed on wormwood, lavender, lavender cotton, and so forth, because their milk is both a food and a medicine.

At-Tirmidhi narrated that the Prophet ﷺ said:

« إذا أكَلَ أحدكم طَعامًا، فليقلْ: اللهم، باركْ لنا فِيه، وأَطْعِمنا خيرًا منه. وإذا سُقِيَ لبنًا، فلْيقل: اللهم، بارِكْ لنا فِيه، وزدنا منه. فإنه لَيْس شيْءٌ يُجزِىءُ منَ الطَّعامِ والشرابِ، إلاّ اللّبَنُ » (أبو داود: ٣٧٣٠ وحسنه الألباني)

``When any of you eats food, let him say, 'O Allah! Bless it for us and give us what is better than it.' When someone is given milk, let him say, 'O Allah! Bless it for us and give us more of it.' Certainly, milk is the only food or drink that is sufficient."

Further, Muslim narrated:

« إنَّه صلى اللهُ عليه وسلم كَانَ يُنْتَبذُ له أولَ الليل، ويشرَبُه- إذا أصبح - يَوْمَه ذلك، والليلة الَّتي تجِيءُ، والغَدَ والليلةَ الأُخْرى، والغدَ إلى العَصْر. فإنْ بقِيَ منه شَيْءٌ: سقاهُ الخادِمَ، أو أمرَ به فَصُبَّ » (مسلم: ٢٠٠٤)

``The Messenger of Allah ﷺ used to be made Nabith (some dates soaked in water) in the beginning of the night and would drink it in the morning of the next day, the next night and the next day, and another night, and the next day until `Asr. If any of it remained, he would then give it to a servant or would order that it be poured out."

The *Nabith* mentioned in this *Hadith* is some dates that are soaked in water to sweeten the water and it is used both in drinks and foods. The *Nabith* has a great benefit in strengthening the body and preserving the health. The Prophet ﷺ did not drink the *Nabith* that is more than three days old fearing that it might have started to decompose and become intoxicating.

The Prophetís guidance regarding clothes

The Prophet's guidance regarding clothes was the best guidance, the most beneficial for the body and the easiest to wear and take off.

The Prophet ﷺ used to wear an outer garment and *Izar* (which covered the body), as these types of clothes are the softest on the body. The Prophet ﷺ also liked to wear shirts, which was preferred by him.

What the Prophet ﷺ used to wear was the most beneficial for the body, as his clothes did not have excessively long or wide sleeves. Rather, the sleeves were to the wrists and would not be longer than the hand, as this would make them harder to wear and to move about easily. Further, the sleeves were not shorter than what we have described, so as not to expose the hands to the cold and heat.

In addition, the Prophet's shirts and garments did not reach the ankles and would usually reach the middle of his legs. Otherwise, if the clothes were longer, they will restrict the movement and make one feel restrained. They were not shorter than what we have described, so as not to expose the thighs to the heat and cold.

The Prophet's turban was not excessively big so that it did not harm the head. It was not very small either, otherwise it would not be sufficient to protect the head from the heat and cold. It was medium in size, and he used to pass a part of it under his chin to protect the neck from the heat and cold and to keep the turban firmly on the head when riding his horse or camel and when in battle.

Many people use some type of braces instead of passing the turban under the chin, although the two methods cannot be compared in terms of benefit or even beauty.

When one thinks about the types of clothes that the Prophet used, he will find that they are indeed among the best for the body and health and the farthest from extravagance and difficulty to wear.

Most of the time, the Prophet ﷺ used to wear *Khuffs* (socks) while traveling, because the feet would need such types of foot covering to fend off the effects of the heat and cold. Sometimes, he would use the *Khuffs* when he was not traveling.

The best colors that the Prophet ﷺ used to wear were white and striped garments. He did not wear all red, black or dyed garments.

As for the red garment the Prophet ﷺ was reported to have worn, it was a Yemeni garment that had black, red, and white stripes. We have mentioned this before and stated that some people erred when they thought that the Prophet ﷺ wore red garments.

The Prophetís guidance concerning oneís place of residence

The Prophet ﷺ had knowledge that this life-term was just a transit station in which one resides for the remainder of his earthly life and then moves on to the Next Life. It was not a part of his guidance or the guidance of his companions, and all those who followed and imitated him, to establish and be concerned with building houses, raising them, beautifying them and extending them. Rather, their places of residence were among the best transit stations that could benefit the traveler, fending off the cold, heat, people's eyes, the beasts and even the fear that it might fall down on them because of its considerable weight! Also, their residences were neither shared by wild animals, due to their size, nor did the air and wind buffet them due to their excessive height. They were neither built underground, because this would harm the inhabitants, nor were they very high above the ground. They were on the level of the ground. These are the best types of houses, most beneficial and least cold or hot. They were not so small that the inhabitants would be irritated by their smallness, nor very spacious, for the residents would not be able to benefit from the excess space. Their homes did not contain bathrooms so that they did not bother the people with a stinking odor. The scent in their homes was fresh, as the Prophet ﷺ used to like good smells and always had a good scent in his house. In fact, the Prophet's sweat was one of the best scents ever smelled, and such was the scent of his body. There is no doubt that this is the description of the best type of home, most suitable for the body and for staying healthy.

The Prophetís guidance concerning sleep

Those who read about the Prophet's guidance concerning being awake and concerning sleep will find that his sleep was the best and most beneficial for the body, the organs and one's strength. He used to sleep in the early part of the night and would wake up in the beginning of the latter part, use *siwak* (natural toothbrush), perform ablution and pray as much as Allah permitted him. Consequently, the body, the organs and one's strength will acquire their fair share of sleep, rest and physical activity, along with acquiring the complete rewards (from Allah). This method ensures righteousness of the heart and body in this life and the Next Life.

The Prophet ﷺ did not oversleep or deprive his body of necessary sleep, making his method in this regard the most perfect. He used to sleep when sleep is warranted and would lay on his right side and remember Allah in supplication until sleep overwhelmed his eyes. Also his body would not be burdened with overeating or overdrinking. He neither slept on the bare floor, or on high beds. Rather, he had mats made of leaves, used to lean on a pillow and would sometimes place his hand under his cheek.

We will now elaborate on the beneficial and harmful methods of sleep.

Sleep is a condition during which the body's instinctive heat becomes idle, so that the body gets some rest. There are two types of sleep: normal and abnormal. Normal sleep entails resting the inner powers and the senses. When these powers are idle, the body refrains from its usual activity and thus the vapors and wetness that were moving and decomposing while awake would ascend to the brain which is the residence of these powers. The brain then becomes idle, and this is the normal type of sleep.

Abnormal (i.e. heavy) sleep occurs because of an accident or a disease. In this case, the excess wetness will take over the brain in a manner that prevents the person from waking up easily. Or, excessive amounts of vapor and moisture ascend to the brain, just as what happens in the aftermath of overeating and overdrinking, and cause the brain to relax and thus the person goes to sleep.

There are two benefits in sleep: the senses get to rest from the fatigue that overtakes them. In this case, the senses will rest from the tiresome activity that occurs when one is awake. The second benefit is digesting food and leading the various mixtures, conditions or temperaments to maturity (processing bodily wastes). While one is asleep, his instinctive energy or heat concentrates on the digestion process and this is why the bodv gets cold and needs a cover while one is asleep.

The best type of sleep is for one to sleep on his right side so that the food sits in the stomach comfortably, for the stomach leans to left side as we have stated. One could also lay on his left side a little so that the digestion is made faster because the stomach leans on the liver. One should then turn again on his right side to help the stomach push the food down the stomach and this way one starts and ends his sleep while laying on his right side. Sleeping on the left side regularly harms the heart because the organs of the body will pressure the heart with their weight.

One of the worst types of sleep is on the

Siwak

back, although resting while laying on the back without going to sleep is not harmful.

Sleeping on the stomach is the worst way to sleep. Ahmad and Ibn Majah narrated that Abu Umamah رَضِيَ الله عَنْهُ said: ``The Prophetﷺ passed by a sleeping man in the mosque who was laying on his face (stomach) and he touched him with his foot, saying.

« قُمْ – أوِ اقعُدْ – فإنَّها نَوْمةٌ جهنَّميَّة »

(ابن ماجه:٣٧٢٥ وضعفه الألباني، وانظر أبوداود: ٥٠٤٠ والترمذي: ٢٧٦٨)

`Sit up, for it is a Hellish sleep."

Hippocrates said in his book, ``If an ailing person sleeps on his stomach whereas this was not his usual habit when he is not sick, then he will be either testifying to the weakness in his mind or that he is suffering from a pain in the stomach." Those who explained Hippocrates' book said that he meant to indicate that such a person sleeps on his stomach, which is a bad habit, instead of the good habit, without any apparent reasonable explanation for this act.

Good habits of sleeping help the natural powers of the body to fulfill their tasks and also strengthens the psychological health of the person.

Sleeping during the day is bad for health and causes humid ailments, makes the color pale, ails the spleen, softens the nerves, causes laziness and weakens desire, except during the summer time around noon. The worst type of sleep occurs in the early hours of the day and in the afternoon. Ibn `Abbas رَضِيَ الله عَنْهما once saw his son sleeping in the early morning and said to him, ``Wake up! Do you sleep at the hour during which sustenance is being divided."

It was said that sleeping during the day is of three types: good habit, which entails sleeping around noon; careless habit, which occurs in the early morning and keeps one busy from matters of this and the Next Life; and madness, which occurs after `*Asr* (afternoon). This is why some of our *Salaf* said, ``Those who sleep after `*Asr* and lose their minds should only blame their own selves."

Sleeping during the early morning prevents sustenance from coming, in that the early morning is the time when the creation goes out to seek their sustenance. Being asleep during this time in which sustenance is being divided causes one to miss out on this chance of gaining sustenance, except when one sleeps for a necessity or a need. This type of sleep is also very harmful for the body because it causes numbness in the senses and spoils the stomach's contents that should be being decomposed through physical activity. Further, sleeping in the early morning hours causes numbness and a general weakness in the body, especially if one goes to sleep before relieving himself (using the toilet), moving about, performing physical activity and before having the stomach busy (by eating some food). This itself is a difficult ailment that even leads to more ailments.

Sleeping under the sun excites otherwise dormant ailments, and such is the case with sleeping while a part of the body is under the sun and a part of the body is under the shade. Abu Dawud narrated that Abu Hurairah رَضِيَ الله عَنْهُ said that the Messenger of Allah ﷺ said:

« إذا كانَ أحدُكم في الشَّمْس، فقَلَصَ عنه الظِّلُّ - فصار بعضُه في الشمس، وبعضُه في الظِّلِّ - فليَقم » (أبو دواد: ٤٨٢١ وصححه الألباني)

``If one of you was in the shade and then the shade recedes and exposes a part of the body to the sun while the other part is still under the shade, let him move from that place." [Al-Hakim].

Ibn Majah and Abu Dawud also narrated:

«أن رسولَ الله صلى اللهُ عليه وسلم نهى أنْ يقعدَ الرَّجلُ بين الظِّلِّ والشَّمْس»

(ابن ماجه: ٣٧٢٢ وصححه الألباني)

``The Messenger of Allah ﷺ disallowed sitting between the shade and the sun."

This *Hadith* indicates that it is not allowed for one to sleep while partially in the shade and partially in the sun.

Further, in the *Sahihain* it is narrated that Al-Bara' bin `Azib said that the Messenger of Allah ﷺ said:

«إذا أتيت مَضْجَعَكَ: فتوضأْ وُضوءَكَ للصلاة، ثم اضطجعْ على شِقِّكَ الأيمَنِ؛ ثم قل: اللهم، إني أسْلَمتُ نفسي إليكَ، ووجَّهتُ وجْهي إليكَ، وفوَّضتُ أمري إليكَ وألجأْتُ ظهري إليكَ: رَغْبةً ورَهْبةً إليكَ؛ لاملْجأَ ولا مَنْجا منك إلاَّ إليكَ؛ آمَنتُ بِكِتابِكَ الذي أنْزلْتَ، ونبيِّك الذي أرْسلتَ، واجعلْهنَّ آخِرَ كلامِكَ. فإن مِتَّ مِن ليلتِكَ: مِتَّ على الفِطْرة » (البخاري:٦٣١٥)

``Whenever you go to bed perform ablution like that for the prayer, lie on your right side and say, 'O Allah! I surrender myself to You, turn my face towards You, entrust all my affairs to You and depend upon You for Your Blessings both with hope (in You) and fear of You. There is no fleeing from You, and there is no place of protection and safety except with You O Allah! I believe in Your Book (the Qur'an) which You have revealed and in Your Prophet (Muhammad) whom You have sent.' Make these words the last of your speech, because if you die on that very night, you will die on the Fitrah (i.e. on the religion of Islam)."

Also, Al-Bukhari narrated that ' Aishah رَضِيَ الله عَنْها said:

« أن رسول الله صلى اللهُ عليه وسلم كان إذا صلى ركعتي الفجر - يعني: سُنَّتها - اضطجَعَ علَى شِقِّه الأيمنِ » (البخاري:١٦٦٠)

``When the Messenger of Allah ﷺ would pray the two (voluntary) Rak`ah of Dawn, he would lay on his right side."

It was said that the wisdom behind sleeping on the right side of the body is that the person does not oversleep. Since the heart leans towards the left side, then sleeping on the right side prevents the heart from residing in its normal place thus causing the sleeping person to wake up when he feels restless. Sleeping on the left side makes the heart comfortable and thus the person oversleeps and misses out on the affairs of his life and religion.

Since sleeping is similar to death, it is not possible or suitable for the Ever-Living Who does not die. Further, sleeping is not suitable for the residents of Paradise. In addition, while asleep, people need to be protected from every type of harm or affliction, and since only Allah is Able to fulfill this need, the Prophet ﷺ has taught us to supplicate to Allah with words of reliance, fear and eagerness before going to sleep. With these words, one invokes Allah's prefect protection for himself and for his body. The Prophet ﷺ also directed us to remember our faith in Allah and making such words the last of our speech at night. Since one might die in his sleep, he then will enter Paradise if these words of faith were the last words he uttered in this world.

The Prophet's guidance in this regard has included the benefits of the heart, body and soul while awake and asleep and for this life and the Next Life. Allah's peace and blessings be on him whose nation has acquired all types of good through him.

The Prophet's statement:

« أسلَمتُ نفسي إليكَ »

``I submit myself to You."

This means I surrender myself to You just as the owned slave surrenders his freedom to his master.

Further; turning the face towards Allah means directing one's full attention to the Lord with sincerity with the intention and while affirming being a slave, humble and obedient to Him. Allah said:

﴿ فَإِنْ حَآجُّوكَ فَقُلْ أَسْلَمْتُ وَجْهِىَ لِلَّهِ وَمَنِ ٱتَّبَعَنِ ﴾

``So if they dispute with you (Muhammad ) say: ``I have submitted myself to Allah (in Islam), and (so have) those who follow me." (3:20)

The face is the most honorable part of the body and the residence of the senses and awareness.

Referring matters to Allah means submission and contentment in

the heart, while being pleased with what Allah decides and chooses o what He wills and with what He is pleased with. Referring all affairs to Allah is one of the most honorable parts of slavery to Allah.

Leaning one's back to Allah indicates the strength of one's depending on and trust in Him. He who leans his back to a firm foundation will no have fear of falling down.

The heart has two types of strength, seeking, which is also eagerness and running away, which is also fear. The slave seeks his interest and runs away from whatever might harm him. Therefore, the Prophet ﷺ has joined both powers in this *Hadith* by saying, ``With eagerness and fear.''

The Prophet ﷺ then praised the Lord by stating that the slave has no refuge or resort from Allah except Allah. Allah is the One Whom the slave seeks refuge with so that He saves him from Himself. In another *Hadith* , the Prophet ﷺ said:

« أعوذ برِضَاك من سَخَطِكَ، وَبِمُعَافَاتِكَ من عُقوبتِكَ؛ وأعوذُ بك منك »

(مسلم:٤٨٦)

``I seek refuge with Your Pleasure from Your Anger, and with Your Pardon from Your Torment, and I seek refuge from You with You."

Therefore, Allah Alone grants refuge to His slave and saves him from His torment, which also occurs by His will. Torment and Favor are both from Allah Alone. Further, the slave asks Allah for support against what He has (of Torment and trials) and seeks Him Alone for his safety. He Alone is the Lord of everything and nothing occurs except by His will.

﴿ وَإِن يَمْسَسْكَ ٱللَّهُ بِضُرٍّ فَلَا كَاشِفَ لَهُۥٓ إِلَّا هُوَ ﴾

``And if Allah touches you with hurt, there is none who can remove it but He..." (6:17)

And:

﴿ قُلْ مَن ذَا ٱلَّذِى يَعْصِمُكُم مِّنَ ٱللَّهِ إِنْ أَرَادَ بِكُمْ سُوٓءًا أَوْ أَرَادَ بِكُمْ رَحْمَةً ﴾

``Say: `Who is he who can protect you from Allah if He intends to harm you, or intends mercy on you?' " (33:17)

The Prophet then ended the supplication by affirming faith in Allah's Book and Messenger, which holds the key to the ultimate safety and success in this life and the Next Life. This is the Prophet's guidance concerning sleep.

The Prophetís guidance on waking

The Prophet ﷺ used to wake up when the rooster crowed and would then praise Allah, affirm His Greatness and Oneness, supplicate to Him, and he would use *siwak*. He would then perform ablution and stand before his Lord reciting His Speech (the Qur'an), praising Him and hoping in Him with eagerness and fear. What actions can be more preserving for the health of the heart, body, soul and general strength and that acquires the favors of this life and the Next Life than these actions?

The Prophetís guidance on physical activity

As for the Prophet's guidance while busy and while free, we will mention a part of the Prophet's guidance that will satisfy us that his guidance in this regard was the most perfect.

It is a fact that the body relies on food and drink for its survival. It is also a fact that not all of the food and nourishment is digested when consumed. Rather, a part of it remains, and as time goes by, these substances accumulate in various qualities and quantities in the body. These accumulations harm the body because they cause clogs in different vessels and make the body feel heavy. If one gets rid of these substances by extracting them with medication, the body is harmed because most of these medications are toxic to varying degrees. In fact, the medication extracts the beneficial substances along with the harmful ones. As for the quality of these substances, the body is harmed when they heat up, spoil, become cold or weaken the natural heat and energy from fully maturating the excess substances.

The clogs caused by the residual substances are harmful whether they remain in the body or get extracted. Moving about is one of the best methods to deny these substances the chance to accumulate. Moving heats the organs and dissipates the leftover substances disallowing them from accumulating by the passage of time. The body will also get used to being energetic and light through physical activity and would optimize the intake of food, firm up the joints and strengthen the muscles and the ligaments. Moderate physical activity immunizes the body against most ailments and mood changes, providing the activity is done at the right time and under the proper circumstances.

Physical activity should be practiced after one has digested his food. In addition, moderate physical activity is that which gives the cheeks color and which nourishes the body. As for the activity that causes sweat it is too excessive.

Any organ that is used regularly in a type of physical activity will get stronger, especially during enjoyable sports in which the organ is used. Those who practice sports regularly will strengthen their bodies and those who nourish their memory their memory will get stronger. Every organ has its own suitable sport or physical activity. For instance, the chest needs recitation, where one should start speaking with a low tone and then increases the volume of his tone. Hearing needs to hear various sounds and voices, gradually from the softer to the louder voices. The tongue needs to speak, and the eye needs to see while the legs need to walk while increasing the pace of walking gradually.

Horse riding, archery, wrestling and running are sports for the whole

body. These types of sports dissipate chronic ailments, such as leprosy, dropsy and constipation.

Furthermore, the heart needs a type of sport that entails learning, behaving, and feeling happiness, joy, patience, firmness, courage, forbearing, performing righteous good deeds, and so forth. Patience, love, courage and kindness are among the best types of sports or physical activity for the inner-self. When the heart learns these types of physical activities little by little, these attributes will firmly reside in the heart and will be characteristic of that person.

In short, when you learn the Prophet's guidance in this regard you will realize that it is the most perfect and beneficial and that it preserves good heath and the power of the body. It is also beneficial for the worldly affairs and the Next Life.

In addition, there is no doubt that prayer preserves the health of the body and helps dissolve its excess and residual substances. It also preserves faith and brings happiness for this and the Next Life. Standing up in prayer at night also preserves health. Prayer also helps against acute ailments and energizes the body, heart and soul profoundly. In the *Sahihain* it is narrated that the Prophet ﷺ said:

« يَعقِدُ الشيطانُ على قافِيةِ رأسِ أحدكم - إذا هو نام - ثلاثَ عُقدٍ، يَضربُ على كل عقْدةٍ: عليكَ ليلٌ طويلٌ فارقُدْ. فإنْ هو استيقَظَ، فذكرَ اللهَ انحلَّتْ عقدةٌ. فإنْ توضأ: انحلَّتْ عُقْدةٌ ثانيةٌ. فإنْ صلَّى: انحَلَّتْ عُقَدُهُ كلُّها، فأصبَحَ نشيطًا طيِّبَ النفْسِ. وإلّا أصبح خَبيثَ النفسِ كَسْلانَ » (البخاري:١١٤٢)

``Satan ties three knots at the back of the head of any of you if he is asleep. On every knot he reads and exhales the following words, `The night is long, so stay asleep.' When one wakes up and remembers Allah, one knot is undone. When one performs ablution, the second knot is undone. When one prays, the third knot is undone and one gets up energetic with a good heart in the morning. Otherwise one gets up lazy and with a mischievous heart."

The Islamic commandment of Fasting also preserves the health and is a type of physical activity for body and soul. No one whose character is not spoiled could ever deny these facts.

As for *Jihad* and what it entails of various movements and activities, it is one of the best preservers of strength, good health, firmness of the heart and body and extracting unwanted residual substances that accumulate in the body. *Jihad* also helps remove sadness, grief, anguish and depression. Only those who have tasted this cure know these facts. *Hajj* and performing the rest of its obligations, horseracing, helping other people achieve their needs and rights, visiting the sick, following funerals, walking to the mosque to perform *Jumu`ah* and congregational prayers, performing ablution and taking a bath all have similar effects and benefits.

All the acts that we mentioned will help preserve the health and aid the body towards the healthy passing of liquid and solid wastes. There is an added benefit in these acts as they help acquire the good of this life and the Next Life and fend off harm.

Now, we should realize that the Prophet's guidance in all of this is the best guidance. His guidance is superior regarding the treatment of the heart and the body, preserving their well being and fending off harm from them. There is no more proof for those who have been given the correct guidance than what we have already mentioned. Indeed, all success comes from Allah Alone.

The Prophetís guidance concerning sexual activity

His is the most effective guidance, as it preserves the health completes satisfaction, and acquires the goals that this activity was meant to achieve.

Sexual intercourse is meant to achieve three essential goals reproduction and the preservation of mankind until the number of souls that Allah has ordered to come to this world is fulfilled and completed Second, expelling the water (semen), which would cause harm if i remains inside the body. Third, satisfying sexual desire and enjoying sex and the bounty that it represents. The last essential goal is the only one that will be satisfied in Paradise, because there will be no reproduction in Paradise nor accumulation of sperm that needs to be discarded.

If this is how significant sperm is, one should realize that it should not be used or spent except to achieve reproduction or to legally rid the body of it when it gets old. When the sperm is congested in the body, i will cause certain ailments, such as obsession, madness, and epilepsy Discarding it, on the other hand, helps cure many of these ailments When the sperm is kept in the body for a long time, it becomes spoiled and turns into a toxic material that can cause certain ailments. This is why sometimes sperm is expelled from the body naturally.

Some of our *Salaf* said, ``Man should take care of three things: he should not ignore walking, so that when he needs it one day he is able to do it; he should not refrain from eating, because the intestines wi shrink; he should not refrain from sexual activity, because if the well's water is not drawn out, it will drain.''

Also, Muhammad bin Zakariyya said, ``Whoever ignores sex for a long time, his nerves will weaken, and their flowing will be blocked, and his penis will shrink. I have seen some people who did not have se claiming to observe some kind of abstinence and their bodies became

colder, their movements restricted and unexplainable depression touched them. Further, their appetite and digestive powers also decreased."

Sexual activity helps lower the gaze, repulse lust, allows one the ability to refrain from illegal sexual activity and also achieves these goals for the wife. When one uses his sperm in a legal manner, he will benefit himself and his wife in this life and the Next Life.

This is why the Prophet ﷺ used to fulfill his legal sexual desire, as he used to say:

« حُبِّبَ إليَّ من دنياكم النساءُ والطيبُ »(النسائي: ٣٩٤٠ وصححه الألباني)

"I was made to like women and perfume from your world."

Further, the Prophet ﷺ encouraged his nation to marry:

« تزوَّجُوا، فإني مُكاثرٌ بكم الأممَ » (أبوداود: ٢٠٥٠ وقال الألباني: حسن صحيح)

``Get married, because I will compete by your numbers with the other nations."

Also, Ibn `Abbas رَضِيَ الله عَنْهما said: ``The best of this nation are those who have the largest number of wives (up to four)." [1]Also, the Prophet ﷺ said:

« إني أتزوَّجُ النِّساءَ، وآكلُ اللحمَ، وأنامُ وأقوم وأَصومُ وأُفْطرُ. فمن رغِبَ عَنْ سُنَّتي فليس منِّي » (البخاري: ٥٠٦٣)

``I marry women, eat meat, sleep, stand in Qiyam, fast and break my fast. Whoever ignores my Sunnah is not from my people."

Furthermore, he said:

« يا معشرَ الشَّبابِ، من استطاعَ منكم الباءة فَلْيتزوَّجْ، فإنه أغضُّ للبَصَرِ، وأحفظُ للفَرْجِ. ومن لم يَستطِعْ، فعليه بالصَّوم؛ فإنه له وِجاءٌ » (البخاري: ١٩٠٥)

``O young men! Get married whoever can afford it, because it helps lower the gaze (from looking at what is prohibited) and protects the sexual organ (from illegal sexual activity). Those who cannot afford it should fast because fasting will cure them."

Also, when Jabir ﷺ married a matron woman, the Prophet ﷺ said:

« هَلاَّ بِكرًا تُلاعِبها وتُلاعبُكَ » (البخاري: ٢٠٩٧)

``Why not have a virgin who fondles you and you fondle her."

Also, Ibn Majah narrated in his *Sunan* that Ibn `Abbas رَضِيَ الله عَنْهما related from the Prophet ﷺ that he said:

« لم نَرَ للمُتَحابَّيْنِ مثلَ النِّكاحِ » (ابن ماجه: ١٨٤٧ صححه الألباني)

(1) Editor's note : This narration of Ibn Abbas could also be translated to mean: ``Get married, for the best of this (Muslim) nation (i.e. Muhammad) had the largest number of wives." (See Sahih Al- Bukhari, The Book of An-Nikah, 5069.) A.W.

``We do not see a better resort for those who love each other than marriage."[(1)]

Muslim also narrated in his *Sahih* that Abdullah bin 'Umar related from the Prophet ﷺ that he said:

« الدُّنيا متاعٌ؛ وخيْرُ متاع الدنيا: المَرْأةُ الصالحَةُ » (مسلم:١٤٦٩)

``The life of this world is enjoyment, and the best enjoyment in the life of this world is a righteous wife."

The Prophet ﷺ used to encourage his nation to marry beautiful virgin women who are also religious. An-Nasai' narrated that Abu Hurairah ؓ said, The Messenger of Allah ﷺ was asked, `Who among women is the best?' He said:

« التي تَسُرُّه إذا نَظرَ، وتُطيعه إذأَمَر، ولا تُخالِفُه فيما يَكرهُ في نَفْسِها ومالِه »

(النسائي:٣٢٣١ وقال الألباني حسن صحيح)

``The one who would please him (her husband) if he looks at her, obeys him if he commands her and avoids disobeying him in what he hates concerning herself and his money."

In the *Sahihain* it is also narrated that the Prophet ﷺ said:

«تُنكَحُ المرأةُ: لمالها، ولِحَسَبِها، ولِجَمالِها، ولدِينِها.فَاظفَرْ بذاتِ الدِّين؛ تَرِبَتْ يدَاك » (البخاري:٥٠٩٠)

``The woman is married for four reasons: her wealth, position, beauty and religion. So marry the religious woman, may your hand be filled with sand (a good expression)."

The Prophet ﷺ also used to encourage marrying women who bare children and did not like marrying women who cannot bare children. Abu Dawud narrated that Ma'qil bin Yasar said, ``A man came to the Prophet ﷺ and said, 'I know of a beautiful, rich woman whom I want to marry, but she does not bare children. Should I marry her?' He said,

(1) * Editor's note : The translator has chosen to translate the word *Nikah* as marriage. However the word *Nikah* also means sexual intercourse and could be understood as such in this narration (within the legal limitations of Islam). A.W. *

`No.' The man came a second time, and the Prophet ﷺ did not allow him. On the third time, the Prophet ﷺ said:

« تزوجوا الودود والولود؛ فإني مكاثر بكم » (أبو داود: ٢٠٥٠ وقال الألباني: حسن صحيح)

``Marry the kind woman who bares children, for I will compete concerning your large numbers with to the other nations."

At-Tirmidhi related from the Prophet ﷺ that he said:

« أَرْبَعٌ من سُنَنِ المُرْسَلين: النكاحُ، والسِّواكُ و التَّعطُّرُ، والحِنَّاءُ »

(الترمذي وعنده: الحياء برقم ١٠٨٠ وضعفه الألباني)

``Four are among the tradition of the Prophets: marriage, using siwak (natural toothbrush), wearing perfume and dyeing with Henna."

The husband should first fondle his wife before having sex with her, by kissing her and sucking her tongue sometimes. The Messenger of Allah ﷺ used to do the same with his wives. Abu Dawud narrated in his *Sunan* :

« إنه صلى اللهُ عليه وسلم كان يقبِّلُ عائشة ويمُصُّ لسَانَها » (أبو داود:٢٣٨٦ وضعفه الألباني)

``The Prophet ﷺ used to kiss 'Aishah رَضِيَ الله عَنْها and suck her tongue."

Also, Jabir bin `Abdullah narrated:

«نَهَي رسولُ اللهِ صلى اللهُ عليه وسلم عن المواقَعةِ قبلَ المُلاعَبةِ »

(الخطيب في تاريخ بغداد ١٣/ ٢٢١ وقال في الضعيفة :٤٣٢ موضوع)

``The Messenger of Allah ﷺ did not allow sexual intercourse before fondling (the wife)." .

Sometimes, the Prophet ﷺ would sleep with all of his wives in one night and would only take one bath afterwards. Sometimes, the Prophet ﷺ would take a bath after sleeping with each of his wives. Muslim narrated in his *Sahih* that Anas رَضِيَ الله عَنْهُ said, ``The Prophet ﷺ would sometimes sleep with all of his wives and take one bath afterwards.'

Also, Abu Dawud narrated in his *Sunan* that Abu Rafi' the Prophet's servant, said, ``The Messenger of Allah once slept with all of his wives and took a bath after each time. I said, 'O Messenger of Allah , why not take only one bath afterwards?' He said,

« هذا أزكى و أطْهرُ وأطيبُ » (أبو داود:٢١٩ وحسنه الألباني)

``This is more pure, cleaner, and better."

It is allowed for those having sexual intercourse to have sex for a second time after they perform ablution. Muslim narrated in his *Sahih* that Abu Sa'eed Al-Khudri said that the Messenger of Allah ﷺ said:

«إذا أتى احدُكم أهلَه، ثم أراد أن يعُود فلْيتَوَضّأْ » (مسلم:٣٠٨)

``When one of you sleeps with his wife and then wants to repeat, let him perform ablution."

Taking a bath or ablution after sex refreshes the energy and the strength and cleans whatever has remained during sex (semen, for example). It is also an act of purity and cleanness. The inner heat will also get back to its normal level of activity after it had been excited during sex. Also, taking a bath satisfies what Allah prefers of cleanliness and discards its opposite (impurity), which Allah hates. Thus, taking a bath after sex is one of the best acts that preserves one's health and strength.

Sex is best after your food has been digested

At that time the bodies' inner coldness, hotness, dryness and wetness are moderate. Sex is harmful when the stomach is full more than it is empty. Such is the case when the body feels excessive wetness, as compared to dryness, and heat as compared to coldness. Also, one should have sex when the desire is ignited and thus the body is naturally ready to have sex, not because one just thought about it.

One should not ignite his sexual appetite when it is not naturally excited and should not force himself to have sex. Also, when one feels that his sexual appetite is ignited, he should have sex to satisfy it. One should avoid having sex with an old woman, the very young who are not ready yet for sex or do not desire it, an ailing woman, a woman who isn't comely or a hated woman. Having sex in such cases will weaken the strength and the sexual drive.

Some doctors made an error when they stated that having sex with a matron woman is better for the health than with a virgin. This statement defies what the best minds have stated and goes against the nature of mankind in general. When one marries a virgin, his heart will be fully dedicated to her and will be filled with her love. Also, he will not divide the type of love he reserves for her with any other women (who he marries later on). This is why the Prophet ﷺ said to Jabir رَضِيَ الله عَنْهُ:

« هلَّا تَزَوَّجْتَ بِكرًا ! »

``Why didn't you marry a virgin?"

The women of Paradise, the Houris , have not been touched by any person before their future, believing husbands in Paradise, a bounty from Allah that makes them more appealing. In addition, 'Aishah رَضِيَ الله عَنْها once said to the Prophet ﷺ.

« أرأيت لو مررتَ بشَجَرة قد أُرْتِعَ فيها؛ وشجرةٍ لم يُرْتَعْ فيها؛ ففي أيِّها كنت تُرتِع بعيرك ؟ قال: في التي لم يُرْتَعْ فيها » (البخاري:٥٠٧٧)

``If you pass by a tree that has been grazed on and a tree that is still untouched, which one would you allow your camel to graze on?" He said, ``The tree that is still untouched by grazing."

She meant that he did not marry a virgin woman except her.

Having sex with a woman that one loves will not weaken the body and will expel the semen more effectively. Having sex with a woman that one does not like will weaken his strength and will not expel sufficient amounts of the semen congested in the body.

Having sex with a woman who is having her period is not allowed in the religion and by the nature of things, as it is very harmful and all doctors warn against it.

Furthermore, we should state that the best sexual position is for the man to get on top of his wife after having fondled and kissed her. This is why the woman is sometimes called "*Firash* (mat, or bed)". The Prophet ﷺ once said,

« الولَد للفراش »(البخاري:٦٨١٨)

``The son belongs to the Firash."

This (a sexual position that we mentioned above) is a part of man's being responsible for the woman, as Allah said:

﴿ٱلرِّجَالُ قَوَّٰمُونَ عَلَى ٱلنِّسَآءِ﴾

``Men are the protectors and maintainers of women." (*4:34*)

Also, Allah said:

﴿هُنَّ لِبَاسٌ لَّكُمْ وَأَنتُمْ لِبَاسٌ لَّهُنَّ﴾

``They (women) are Libas [i.e. body cover, or screen, or Sakan, (i.e., you enjoy the pleasure of living with them) for you, and you (men) are Libas for them." (2:187)

The favored sexual position that we mentioned is taken from the beautiful description the *Ayah* gave for the wife and her husband of being the garment or the cover for each other.

The worst sexual position is for the woman to get on top of the man during sex, because it is against the natural way that Allah has created men and women and males and females. In this case, the man will not be able to ejaculate all of the semen and whatever remains will get soiled and harm his body. Also, this position might allow some harmful moisture to descend from the woman's sexual organ to the penis. Also, the womb would not be able to hold on to the semen in this position and thus conception will be more difficult. Further, the woman is and should be the receiving party and when this position is turned around and she becomes the giver, the act will go against the natural way.

It was reported that the People of the Scripture used to have sex with their wives while leaning on their sides, saying that this position is the most comfortable for the women.

As for Quraish and the Ansar, they used to have sexual intercourse with their women from behind (in the vagina), and the Jews criticized them for this practice. Afterwards, Allah revealed:

﴿نِسَآؤُكُمْ حَرْثٌ لَّكُمْ فَأْتُوا۟ حَرْثَكُمْ أَنَّىٰ شِئْتُمْ﴾

``Your wives are a tilth for you, so go to your tilth, when or how you will..." (2:223)

In the *Sahihain* it is also narrated that Jabir رَضِيَ الله عَنْهُ said, ``The Jews used to say that if a man had sex with his wife from behind in the womb the offspring would be cross-eyed. Then Allah revealed:

﴿نِسَآؤُكُمْ حَرْثٌ لَّكُمْ فَأْتُوا۟ حَرْثَكُمْ أَنَّىٰ شِئْتُمْ﴾

``Your wives are a tilth for you, so go to your tilth, when or how you will..." (2:223)

In another narration of this *Hadith* by Muslim, the Prophet ﷺ commented (on the *Ayah*),

« إن شاء مُجَبِّيَةً وإن شاء غير مجبّيةٍ؛ غير أن ذلك في صِمَامٍ واحدٍ » (مسلم:١٤٣٥)

``If you wish from behind and if you wish from the front, but only in one valve (i.e. the vagina)."

Anal sex with the wife was never allowed by any Prophet, and it is a grave error that some people relate that some of the *Salaf* allowed men to have anal sex with their wives.

Abu Dawud narrated in his *Sunan* that Abu Hurairah رَضِيَ الله عَنْهُ related from the Prophet ﷺ that he said:

« مَلْعُونٌ مَن أَتَى المَرْأة في دُبُرِها » (أبو داود ٢١٦٢ وأحمد وقال في التحقيق حديث حسن برقم ٢/ ٤٤٤)

``Cursed be the person who has sex with a woman in her anal canal."

Also, Ahmad and Ibn Majah narrated that the Prophet ﷺ said:

« لاينظُرُ اللهُ إلى رَجُل جامَعَ امْرأته في دُبُرها» (الترمذي:١١٦٥ حسنه الألباني)

``Allah does not look at the person who has sex with his wife in her anal canal."

At-Tirmidhi and Ahmad mentioned another narration of this *Hadith* in which the Prophe ﷺ t said:

«مَن أتى حَائضا، أو امْرأة في دُبُرها، أو كاهنًا فصدَّقه: فقد كَفَر بما أنزِل على مُحمَّد صلى اللهُ عليه وسلم » (الترمذي :١٣٥ أحمد ٢/ ٤٧٦ وقال المحقق محتمل للتحسين)

``Whoever has sex with a woman during her period or in her anal canal, and whoever goes to a soothsayer and believes in him will have committed disbelief in what Allah has sent down to Muhammad."

In another narration of Al-Bayhaqi, the Prophet ﷺ said:

« مَن أتى شيئًا – من الرِّجال والنِّساء – في الأَدْبار: فقد كَفَر »

(لم نجده بهذا اللفظ "من الرجال" وانظر البيهقي ١/ ١٩٨ وسيأتي مكرر)

``Whoever has sex with a man or a woman in the anal canal will have committed Kufr (disbelief)."

Furthermore, Waki' narrated that the Messenger of Allah ﷺ said:

« إن اللهَ لا [يَسْتَحْيِي] من الحقِّ؛ لا تأْتُوا النِّساءَ في أعجازِهنَّ »

(ابن حبان: ٤١٩٨ ابن ماجه ١٩٢٤ وصحيحه المحقق)

``Allah is not shy to say the truth: Do not have sex with women in their anal canals."

Also, At-Tirmidhi narrated that Talq bin Ali said that the Messenger of Allah ﷺ said:

« لا تَأْتُوا النِّساءَ في أعجازهنَّ؛ فإن الله لا يستحي من الحقِّ » (الترمذي:١١٦٤)

``Do not have sex with women in their anal canals. Allah does not shy away from saying the truth."

Further, Ibn'Adi narrated in his book, *Al-Kamil*, that `Abdullah bin Mas'ud related from the Prophet ﷺ that he said:

« لا تأتوا النِّساءَ في أعجازهن » (البيهقي ٧/ ١٩٧)

``Do not have sexual intercourse with women in the anal canals."

Abu Tharr also related from the Prophet ﷺ that he said:

« مَن أَتَى الرجال والنساءَ في أَدبارهنَّ، فقد كفر »

(لم نهثر عليه وعند الترمذي: لاينظر الله إلأى رجل أتي رجلاً أو امرأة في الدبر ١١٦٥ وحسنه الألباني)

``Whoever has sexual intercourse with men or women in their anal canals, will have committed disbelief."

In addition, Isma'il bin 'Aiyash narrated that Jabir رَضِيَ الله عَنْهُ said that the Prophet ﷺ said:

« اسْتَحْيُوا من اللهِ – فإن الله لا يستَحِي من الحقِّ – لا تأْتُو النساءَ في حُشُوشِهِن »

(البيهقي ٧/ ١٩٧ انظر المطالب ١٦١٧)

``Be shy with Allah, but Allah is not shy to say the truth: Do not have sex with women in their anal canals."

Also, Ad-Darqutni narrated this *Hadith* using another chain of narrators and it reads:

« إن اللهَ لا يستحِي من الحق؛ ولا يَحلُّ إتيانُ النساءِ في حُشُوشِهِنَّ »

(نفس الحديث المذكور بأعلاه ابن ماجه ١٩٢٤ وصححه الألباني)

``Allah is not shy to say the truth: anal sex with women is not allowed."

Al-Baghawi also narrated that once Qatadah was asked about the person who had sex with his wife in her anal canal, and Qatadah related from the Prophet ﷺ that he said:

« تلك اللُّوطِيَّة الصُّغرى» (أحمد ٢/ ١٨٢ وحسنه في تحقيق المسند)

``That is the small sodomy (or homosexuality)."

Imam Ahmad also narrated that Ibn `Abbas رَضِيَ الله عَنْهما said:

﴿ نِسَآؤُكُمْ حَرْثٌ لَّكُمْ ﴾

``Your wives are a tilth for you ..." (2:223)

``The *Ayah* , was revealed regarding some people from the Ansar . They came to the Prophet ﷺ and asked him and he said, `Have sex with your wife however you like, but avoid anal sex.'''

Also in the *Musnad Imam Ahmad* it is narrated that Ibn 'Abbas رَضِيَ الله عَنْهما said that 'Umar bin Al-Khattab رَضِيَ الله عَنْه came to the Prophet ﷺ and said: ``O Messenger of Allah ! I am destroyed.'' The Prophet ﷺ said, ``What has destroyed you?'' 'Umar رَضِيَ الله عَنْهُ said, ``I turned over my *Firash* (mount, woman) last night (had sexual intercourse from the back in the vagina).'' The Prophet ﷺ did not answer him. Soon after, Allah revealed:

﴿ نِسَآؤُكُمْ حَرْثٌ لَّكُمْ فَأْتُواْ حَرْثَكُمْ أَنَّىٰ شِئْتُمْ ﴾

``Your wives are a tilth for you, so go to your tilth, when or how you will...`` (2:223)

The Prophet ﷺ said:

« أَقْبِل وأَدبِرْ، واتَّقِ الحَيْضَةَ والدُّبُرَ » (أحمد ١/ ٢٩٧ والترمذي ٢٩٨٠ وحسنه في تحقيق ابن حبان(٤٢٠٢))

``Do it from the front and from behind if you wish, but avoid menstruation and the anal canal.''

Furthermore, At-Tirmidhi narrated that Ibn `Abbas رَضِيَ الله عَنْهُ related from the Prophet ﷺ that he said:

« لا ينظُرُ اللهُ إلى رجل أتى رجلًا أو امرأة في الدُّبر » (الترمذي:(١١٦٥) وحسنه الألباني)

``Allah does not look at a man who had anal sex with another man or with a woman.''

'Uqbah bin 'Amir رَضِيَ الله عَنْهُ also narrated that the Messenger of Allah ﷺ said:

«مَلْعونٌ من يأتي النساء في محاشِّهِنَّ » (أبو داود:٢١٦٢ وحسنه الألباني)

``Cursed be whoever has sex with women in their anal canals.''

Furthermore, Musnad Al-Harith bin Abi Usamah narrated that Abu Hurairah ﷺ and Ibn `Abbas رَضِيَ الله عَنْهما said, ``The Messenger of Allah ﷺ gave us a speech just before he died and it was the last speech the

Prophet ﷺ gave in Al-Madinah until he went to Allah. He said:

« مَن نكَح امرأَةً في دُبُرِها، أو رجلاً أو صبياً حُشِرَ يومَ القيامة ورِيحُه أنتَنُ من الجِيفةِ، يتأذّى به الناس حتى يدخُلَ النارَ؛ وأحبطَ اللهُ أجره، ولا يَقْبل منه صَرفاً ولا عَدْلاً، ويُدخلُ في تابوتٍ مِن نارٍ، ويُسدُّ عليه بمَساميرَ مِن نارٍ»

(مسند الحارث كره من المطالب؟ وقال المحقق: موضوع:١٦٠٤)

``Whoever had sex with a woman in her anal canal, or with a man, or with a male child, will be gathered on the Day of Resurrection with an odor emitting from him that is more foul than rotted carrion. The people will be bothered by his smell until he enters Hellfire. Also Allah will destroy his rewards and will not accept from him a prayer or a fast. He will also be entered into a coffin of fire and the coffin will be shut closed on him using nails of fire."

Abu Hurairah رَضِيَ الله عَنْهُ commented, ``This is for whomever did not repent (from sodomy)."

Ash-Shafi' narrated that Khuzaymah bin Thabit رَضِيَ الله عَنْهُ said:

« إن رجلا سأل النبي صلى الله عليه وسلم عن إتيان النساءِ في أَدْبارهنَّ، فقال: حَلالٌ. فلمّا ولَّى دعاه، فقال: كيف قلتَ ؟ في أيِّ الخُربتَيْنِ؟ أو في أي الخُرْزَتين؟ أو في أي الخُصْفَتين؟ أمِن دبرِها في قُبُلِها: فنعَمْ، أمّا من دُبرها في دبرها: فلا. فإن الله لا يستحي من الحق، لاَ تأتوا النِّساءَ في أدبارهنَّ »

(الأم للشافعي ٥/ ١٣٧ وأخرجه البيهقي من طريق الشافعي في الصغرى (٢٤٩٠) والكبرى (٧/ ١٩٦) وفيه جهالة راوٍ ومعنا بت صحيح جهالة الراوي والاختلاف في سنده)

``A man came to the Messenger of Allah ﷺ and asked him about having sex with women from the rear. The Prophet ﷺ said, `It is allowed.' When the man left, the Prophet ﷺ summoned him and asked him, `What was your question? In which of the two holes?If it is from the rear in the vagina, then it is allowed. As for having sex in the anal canal from the rear, no. Allah is not shy to say the truth. Do not have sex with women in the anal canal."

Furthermore, Allah said:

﴿فَأْتُوهُنَّ مِنْ حَيْثُ أَمَرَكُمُ ٱللَّهُ﴾

``Then go in unto them as Allah has odained for you.''

Mujahid said, ``I asked Ibn `Abbas رَضِيَ الله عَنْهما about the meaning of what Allah said:

﴿فَأْتُوهُنَّ مِنْ حَيْثُ أَمَرَكُمُ ٱللَّهُ﴾

``Then go in unto them as Allah has ordained for you.''

He said, `Have sex with her in the same place where you were not allowed when she is menstruating.''

`Ali bin Abi Talhah commented, ``Meaning in the vagina.''

The *Ayah* has indicated that it is not allowed to have sexual intercourse in the anal canal in two different ways.

First, Allah has only allowed having sex in the place where the offspring is created not the anus, which is a harmful place. The place of offspring is mentioned in what Allah said:

﴿مِنْ حَيْثُ أَمَرَكُمُ ٱللَّهُ﴾

``As Allah has ordained for you (go in unto them in any manner as long as it is in their vagina).'' (2:222)

Having sex with the wife from the rear in the vagina is also entailed in the *Ayah*, because Allah said:

﴿فَأْتُوا حَرْثَكُمْ أَنَّىٰ شِئْتُمْ﴾

``So go to your tilth, when or how you will.'' (2:223)

It means that from wherever you wish, from the front or the rear. Also, Ibn `Abbas رَضِيَ الله عَنْهما said: meaning the vagina.

Allah has disallowed vaginal sex with the woman when there is a temporary harmful condition (menstruation). So what about anal sex in the place of harm which will also harm the cause of reproduction. Also, anal sex with the woman will surely encourage the man to have anal sex with young boys.

Also, the wife has a right on her husband to have natural sexual activity and anal sex does not satisfy this right nor fulfill her desire.

Further, the anal canal was not created for this act nor is it suitable for it, unlike the vagina. Those who refrain from sex in the vagina and perform anal sex will have deviated from Allah's Wisdom and Commandments.

Also, anal sex is very harmful for the man and this is why the wisest doctors advise against it. The vagina has a special quality in extracting the semen and relieving the man from it. The anal canal, on the other hand, does not help extract all of the semen because it is not in its nature.

Anal sex is also harmful to the man because it requires tiresome movements and because it goes against his nature.

The anus is also the place of dirt and filth. Yet, the man faces it with his face and embraces it [during anal sex]!

Anal sex is also very harmful for the woman because it is unnatural, abnormal and not suitable for what she was created for.

Anal sex also causes depression and distress, along with the people feeling hateful and estranged with both parties to the anal sex.

Anal sex also blackens the face, causes distress in the chest, extinguishes the light of the heart and gives the face a darkness that will become a trademark for those who do anal sex.

Anal sex also causes hatred (between the participants to the act) and will soon lead both participants to part from each other.

Anal sex also causes the nature of both participants to be terminally spoiled, unless they repent to Allah with a sincere heart.

Anal sex also erases all the good qualities and replaces them with their opposites. It also dissipates the affection and good relations between the two parties, who will soon curse and hate each other.

Anal sex is also one of the major reasons behind the destruction of the bounties and the coming of torment and disaster. It also leads to being cursed and hated by Allah, as He will ignore those who indulge in this act and would not look at them. What good can such people ever gain later on and what evil could they wish to avert? What kind of life can they live after Allah's curse falls on them, along with His hatred towards them, His ignoring them and His shunning them?

Anal sex also dissipates shyness, and shyness is the life of the heart. When the heart looses shyness, it will like the disliked and dislike the liked. Thus, the heart will have fallen into utter ruin and destruction.

Anal sex also alters human nature from the path that Allah has created it for, to a type of lower animal behavior. Rather, it is even lower. When the nature is altered and changed, the heart, the deeds and the guidance will also be altered. One will then like the evil things and deeds, leading him to fall into total disarray regarding his condition, deeds, and speech.

More than any other act, anal sex also causes one to have rude behavior and makes him dare to commit evil.

Anal sex also brings one humiliation, degradation and disgrace more than any other act.

Finally, anal sex causes the slave hatred and dislike, and the people will feel despise and disgust with him, as is evident all around us.

May Allah's peace and blessings be on he whose guidance gives those who follow it the happiness of this and the Next Life. On the other hand, destruction and demise of this and the Next Life are the result of deviating from his guidance and what he was sent with.

There are two types of harmful sexual activity

One type that the religion declares harmful and another type that defies nature.

The harmful sexual intercourse that the religion prohibits is in grades, some are worse than others. Temporarily prohibited sexual activity is less dangerous than those totally prohibited. For instance, sex is disallowed during the Fast, *Ihram, I`tikaf* , menstruation, and so froth. There is no punishment prescribed when one violates this type of limited prohibition. The second type, which is totally prohibited, falls under two categories, prohibited for eternity, such as marrying whom one is not allowed to marry, which is one of the worst types of illegal sexual activity. This category requires capital punishment according to a segment of the scholars, such as Ahmad bin Hanbal. There is an authentic *Hadith* that upholds this ruling too. The second category is totally prohibited but not for eternity, such as committing adultery or fornication with whom one is theoretically eligible

for marriage. In the case of adultery, it will be violating two rights: Allah's right and the husband's right. If the woman was forced to this act, it will be a violation of three rights (Allah's, her husband's and her own). If she had a family and relatives, they will be ashamed by the rape, and thus a fourth right would be violated. If the woman was not allowed for the man even theoretically, a fifth right will be violated. The harm of this type of act varies according to the grade of prohibition it violates.

There is a type of sexual activity that is harmful for one's nature, whether due to the form or the manner it takes. For instance, having excessive sexual intercourse will weaken the strength and harm the nerves. It will also cause convulsive shaking, facial paralysis and spasms. It also weakens the eyesight and the rest of the powers of the body, along with weakening the instinctive heat and energy, widening the body vessels and exposing them to accumulating harmful substances.

The best time to have sex is after the food has been digested in the stomach, but not when the stomach is empty for it weakens the instinctive heat. Also, one should not have sex when he is full, because in this case sexual intercourse causes clogs, nor when one is tired, after taking a bath, after vomiting or when one is nervous, sad, depressed distressed or very happy.

The best time to have sex is after the night falls, especially when the food had been digested. One then takes a bath or ablution and sleeps afterwards so that he regains his strength. One should not indulge in sports activity after sex because it is very harmful in this case.

The Prophetís guidance on treating passion

This is a disease that attacks the heart. Yet, it is a different type of disease concerning its symptoms, causes, and cure. When this ailment becomes acute, the doctors will not be able to cure it nor will the one afflicted be able to bear its effects.

Allah has mentioned the subject of passion concerning two types of people: women and lovers of beardless boys. For instance, Allah mentioned the story of the wife of Al-`Aziz (Ruler of Egypt) and the Prophet Yusef عليه السلام . He also mentioned the second type about the people of the Prophet Lut عليه السلام as He said about them when the angels came to visit the Prophet Lut عليه السلام .

﴿ قَالَ إِنَّ هَٰٓؤُلَآءِ ضَيۡفِي فَلَا تَفۡضَحُونِ ﴿٦٨﴾ وَٱتَّقُواْ ٱللَّهَ وَلَا تُخۡزُونِ ﴿٦٩﴾ قَالُوٓاْ أَوَلَمۡ نَنۡهَكَ عَنِ ٱلۡعَٰلَمِينَ ﴿٧٠﴾ قَالَ هَٰٓؤُلَآءِ بَنَاتِيٓ إِن كُنتُمۡ فَٰعِلِينَ ﴿٧١﴾ لَعَمۡرُكَ إِنَّهُمۡ لَفِي سَكۡرَتِهِمۡ يَعۡمَهُونَ ﴾

`` [Lut (Lot)] said: `Verily, these are my guests, so shame me not. And fear Allah and disgrace me not.' They (people of the city) said: `Did we not forbid you from entertaining (or protecting) any of the `Alameen (people, foreigners and strangers from us)?' [Lut (Lot)] said: `These (the girls of the nation) are my daughters (to marry lawfully), if you must act (so).' Verily, by your life (O Muhammad), in their wild intoxication, they were wandering blindly." (15:68-72)

There is a false claim that was started by those who do not give the Prophet ﷺ his due respect and appreciation, stating that the Prophet ﷺ once saw Zainab bint Jahsh(1) and said, ``All praise be to He Who changes the hearts as He wills!" They also claim that the Prophet ﷺ was inflicted with this disease, passion, and that his heart liked her. Yet, they claimed, he commanded Zaid to keep her and not divorce her, until Allah revealed:

﴿ وَإِذۡ تَقُولُ لِلَّذِيٓ أَنۡعَمَ ٱللَّهُ عَلَيۡهِ وَأَنۡعَمۡتَ عَلَيۡهِ أَمۡسِكۡ عَلَيۡكَ زَوۡجَكَ وَٱتَّقِ ٱللَّهَ وَتُخۡفِي فِي نَفۡسِكَ مَا ٱللَّهُ مُبۡدِيهِ وَتَخۡشَى ٱلنَّاسَ وَٱللَّهُ أَحَقُّ أَن تَخۡشَىٰهُ ﴾

``And (remember) when you said to him (Zaid bin Harithah رَضِيَ الله عَنْهُ --- the freed-slave of the Prophet) on whom Allah has bestowed grace (by guiding him to Islam) and you (O Muhammad too) have done favour (by manumitting him): `Keep your wife to yourself, and fear Allah.' But you did hide in yourself (i.e., what Allah has already made known to you that He will give her to you in marriage) that which Allah will make manifest, you did fear the people (i.e., their saying that Muhammad (married the divorced wife of his manumitted slave) whereas Allah had a better right that you should fear Him." (33:37)

(1) Editor's note : This is referring to before the prophet was married to Zaynab. She was at the time still married to Zaid bin Harithah. Therefore it is unimaginable , and impossible that the prophet of Allah would lust for the wife of another man! A.W.

Those who uttered this false claim also claimed that the *Ayah* is talking about passion. Consequently, some of them collected a book about passion in which they mentioned several Prophets who were afflicted with this disease, including the Prophet ! This is an utter ignorance of such people of the Qur'an and the Messengers and a misunderstanding that alters the true meaning of Allah's Words. Further, this false claim accuses the Prophet ﷺ with what he is truly innocent of.

Zaid bin Harithah رَضِيَ الله عَنْهُ , whom the Prophet had adopted before Islam until he was called Zaid bin Muhammad, married Zainab bint Jahsh. Zainab was not humble with her husband and he asked the Prophet's advice if he should divorce her. The Messenger of Allah ﷺ said, to him:

« أمسِكْ عَلَيْك زَوجَك واتَّق الله » (نحبط المصحف من الأحزاب ٣٣-٣٧)

``Keep your wife to yourself, and fear Allah."

The Prophet ﷺ thought that if Zaid would otherwise divorce her, he would marry her after him. But, the Prophet ﷺ hid this thought in his heart because he feared what the people might say if he married the ex-wife of his adopted son. This is why Allah mentioned in this *Ayah* His favors on the Prophet and commanded him not to fear what the people might say in doing what Allah has allowed for him. Allah also reminded him that it is He whom the Prophet ﷺ should fear, so he should not be hesitant in doing what Allah has allowed for him because of fear of what the people might say.

Further, Allah informed the Prophet ﷺ that He has given Zainab to him in marriage after Zaid رَضِيَ الله عَنْهُ had divorced her so that his nation imitates him when they know that the man is allowed to marry the ex-wife of his adopted son. This is why Allah said:

﴿ وَحَلَٰٓئِلُ أَبۡنَآئِكُمُ ٱلَّذِينَ مِنۡ أَصۡلَٰبِكُمۡ ﴾

`` and the wives of your sons who (spring) from your own loins (are forbidden for you to marry)...." (4:23)

And in this chapter (4:40), Allah said:

﴿ مَّا كَانَ مُحَمَّدٌ أَبَآ أَحَدٍ مِّن رِّجَالِكُمْ ﴾

``Muhammad (ﷺ) is not the father of any of your men." (33:40)

While in the beginning of the chapter Allah said:

﴿ وَمَا جَعَلَ أَدْعِيَآءَكُمْ أَبْنَآءَكُمْ ذَٰلِكُمْ قَوْلُكُم بِأَفْوَٰهِكُمْ ﴾

``...nor has He made your adopted sons your real sons. That is but your saying with your mouths." (33:4)

Therefore, think deeply about Allah's defense of the Prophet ﷺ that refuted the false accusation directed at him. All success comes from Allah.

Yes, the Prophet of Allah ﷺ used to love his wives, especially 'Aishah رَضِيَ الله عَنْها was the most beloved to him among them. Yet, his love for them did not reach the level of perfect love, which he reserved for his Lord. The Prophet ﷺ once said:

« لو كنتُ متَّخِذًا من أهل الأرض خليلاً، لاتَّخذْتُ أبا بكرٍ خليلاً» (البخاري:٤٦٦)

``If I was going to take an intimate friend from the people of the earth, I would have taken Abu Bakr."

And in another narration, he said:

« وإن صاحِبَكم خليلُ الرَّحْمن » (مسلم:٢٣٨٣)

``Your friend (himself, Muhammad) is the intimate friend of the Most Beneficent."

Having passion towards images only afflicts empty hearts

This affects hearts that are deprived of the love of Allah, ignoring Him and preferring someone else. When the heart is full of the love of Allah and eagerness to meet Him, this love will fend off the disease of love and passion for images. This is why Allah said about Prophet Yusef ﷺ.

﴿ كَذَٰلِكَ لِنَصْرِفَ عَنْهُ ٱلسُّوٓءَ وَٱلْفَحْشَآءَ ۚ إِنَّهُۥ مِنْ عِبَادِنَا ٱلْمُخْلَصِينَ ﴾

``Thus it was, that We might turn away from him evil and illegal sexual intercourse. Surely, he was one of Our chosen, (guided) slaves." (12:24)

This *Ayah* indicated that sincerity is a cause and a remedy that drives away passion which might lead to sin and fornication, which is the culmination of passion. When the cause behind the disease is repelled, the effects of the disease will also be repelled.

Some of our *Salaf* once described passion that it is the act of a heart that is empty of everything except what it has a passion for. Allah said:

﴿ وَأَصْبَحَ فُؤَادُ أُمِّ مُوسَىٰ فَٰرِغًا ۖ إِن كَادَتْ لَتُبْدِى بِهِۦ ﴾

``And the heart of the mother of Musa (Moses) became empty [from every thought, except the thought of Musa (Moses)]. She was very near to disclosing his case." (28:10)

This *Ayah* indicated that the heart of Moses's mother was empty of every concern except for Moses, because of her great love for him and her heart's affection for him. Passion has two parts, loving an object and an eagerness to possess the loved object. When one of these two parts does not exist, then passion does not exist either.

The ailment of passion has caused bafflement to many wise people and some of them issued some statements in this regard that should not be taken seriously.

We say that Allah's Wisdom has decided regarding His creation that there are similarities that occur between things and people, and that things and people are driven to their likes and to avoid what is not similar to them. The secret to the harmony that occurs in the world is due to the similarities between various creations. Various things [and people] thus lean towards similar objects, while dissimilar objects ignore each other. Allah said:

﴿ هُوَ ٱلَّذِى خَلَقَكُم مِّن نَّفْسٍ وَٰحِدَةٍ وَجَعَلَ مِنْهَا زَوْجَهَا لِيَسْكُنَ إِلَيْهَا ﴾

``It is He Who has created you from a single person (Adam), and (then) He has created from him his wife [Hawwa' (Eve)], in order that he might enjoy the pleasure of living with her." (7:189)

Allah has made this the reason why man feels attracted and consequently passionate, for woman. She is similar to him in essence. The reason for the attraction [between men and women] is not only the beauty of the image,but the similarity in the habits, goals, guidance and mannerism, all of which help ignite passion.

In the *Sahih* it is narrated that the Prophet ﷺ said:

« الأرواحُ جنودٌ مُجَنَّدةٌ فما تَعارفَ منها ائْتلَفَ، وماتَناكرَ منها اختلَفَ »

(مسلم:٢٦٣٨ والبخاري تعليقاً ٣٣٣٦)

``The souls are similar to recruited soldiers. Those who recognize each other will be intimate and those who do not recognize each other will be apart."

Also, Imam Ahmad narrated in his *Musnad* the reason behind this *Hadith,* ``A woman in Makkah used to be able to make people laugh and when she came to Al-Madinah she resided with a woman who also used to be able to make people in Al-Madinah laugh. The Prophet ﷺ said:

« الأرواحُ جُنودٌ مُجَنَّدةٌ »

``The souls are just like recruited soldiers."

The religion of Allah gives the same rulings to similar matters and thus does not differentiate between similar matters nor join between dissimilar matters. Those who think to the contrary are mistaken due to their lack of knowledge of the religion, or lack of effort on their part to acquire knowledge on the subject of similarities and dissimilarities. Or, their error comes from relating to the religion what is not a part of it without the authority that can justify it. With Allah's Wisdom and justice, His creation and command have been established by equating similar things and differentiating between dissimilar things. This fact is true both in this life and on the Day of Resurrection. Allah said:

﴿ ٱحْشُرُوا۟ ٱلَّذِينَ ظَلَمُوا۟ وَأَزْوَٰجَهُمْ وَمَا كَانُوا۟ يَعْبُدُونَ ﴿٢٢﴾ مِن دُونِ ٱللَّهِ فَٱهْدُوهُمْ إِلَىٰ صِرَٰطِ ٱلْجَحِيمِ ﴾

(It will be said to the angels): ``Assemble those who did wrong, together with their companions (from the devils) and what they used to worship, instead of Allah, and lead them on to the way of flaming Fire (Hell); ..." (37:22,23)

Also, Allah said:

﴿ وَإِذَا ٱلنُّفُوسُ زُوِّجَتْ ﴾

``And when the souls shall be joined with their partners (the good with the good and the bad with the bad)." (81:7)

This *Ayah* indicates that each person will be tied to his likes. Those who have love for each other for Allah's sake will be together in Paradise, while those who love each other for the devil's sake will be together in Hell. One is with those whom he likes, whether he likes it or not. Al-Hakim narrated that the Prophet ﷺ said:

« لا يُحِبُّ المرءُ قومًا إلاّ حُشِر مَعَهم » (أحمد وانظر المجمع ١/ ٣٧ وهو في الصحيحة:١٣٨٧)

``If a man loves a people, he will be gathered with them (on the Day of Resurrection)." .

There are several types of love. The best and most honorable of them is love for the sake of Allah, which requires loving what He loves and also loving Him and His Messenger.

Another type of love is that which occurs when the parties to it have a similar religion or way, or theology, or sect, or relation, or craft, or a goal that they both seek. Another type of love is what occurs when one loves to acquire a matter that the loved object has, whether a position, money, knowledge, or any other purpose that he seeks. This is material love that dissipates when the goal is reached. Indeed, he who likes you for a material purpose goes away when his goal is accomplished.

The love that results because of the similarities between the two parties does not fade away unless there is a reason that makes it fade away. This type of love includes passion because it is a love that the soul and the heart share. No other ailment can cause more profound effects on those afflicted, of obsession, weakness, concern and even destruction, like passion.

If one says that since the reason behind affection is what you have stated, the souls being connected and compatible, why is it not always exchanged between the two parties? Sometimes, love is one sided, although you stated that the reason for it is the similarity and the compatibility between the souls.

The answer is that there are reasons that arise and prevent the love from being exchanged by both sides. One-sided love is the result of one of three reasons: a deficiency in the love because it is accidental and not real. In this case, the loved person might even feel dislike for the other party. Second, sometimes the loved person might be the cause for the love to be one-sided, such as a deficiency in his mannerism, shape, path, actions, appearance, and so forth. Third, due to a specific reason that prevents the loved person from sharing the same feelings with the other party.

When these reasons are not present, and the love is thus real, love will be shared by both parties.

Arrogance, envy, loving various positions and enmity by the disbelievers were the main reasons the Messengers were not more beloved by them than their own selves, families and offspring. When these barriers were removed from the hearts of the Messengers' followers, their love for the Messengers was indeed more than the love they had for their own selves, wives, children and wealth.

Attainment of oneís love object is its cure and other cures for love

The subject is that since love is one of the ailments in general, it does have a cure or several cures. If the lover has a legal path to take to attain his loved object, it will be his cure.In the *Sahihain* it is narrated that Ibn Mas'ood said that the Prophet said:

« يا معشرَ الشَّباب؛ من استطاع منكمُ الباءةَ فلْيتزوَّج؛ ومن لم يستطِعْ فعليه بالصوم، فإنه له وِجَاءٌ » (البخاري:١٩٠٥)

``O young people! Whoever amongst you can afford marriage, let him marry. Those who cannot afford it should resort to fasting, for it will be a cure for them."

The Prophet ﷺ has directed the people to the best methods to obtain what they love, a major and a minor method. He ordered the men to resort to the first choice, marriage, which is the perfect cure for this disease. Thus, people should not prefer other solutions to the solution that the Prophet recommended.

Ibn Majah narrated that the Prophet ﷺ said:

« لم نَرَ للمُتحابَّيْن مثلَ النِّكاح » (ابن ماجه:١٨٤٧ صححه الألباني)

``We never saw anything like marriage for lovers."

This is the meaning that Allah indicated when He allowed in marriage both free and slave women when needed: Allah said:

﴿ يُرِيدُ ٱللَّهُ أَن يُخَفِّفَ عَنكُمْ وَخُلِقَ ٱلْإِنسَٰنُ ضَعِيفًا ﴾

``Allah wishes to lighten (the burden) for you; and man was created weak (cannot be patient to leave sexual intercourse with woman)." (4:28)

Therefore, Allah mentioned man's weakness in this *Ayah* and stated that He has made matters easy for him by allowing him to marry as many as he wishes, two, three or four. He also allowed him slave women in marriage if he wishes, so as to treat this ailment, passion, to cure the weakness in mankind and as an act of mercy [from Him] to His slaves.

When no legal method exists for the lover to attain his love object

If there is no legal method that the lover can attain his loved object or because of his inability to do so, or both, then passion will become a difficult disease in this case and the afflicted person needs to feel that he cannot satisfy it. It is a fact that when the heart feels hopelessness in something, it will no longer seek to acquire it.

If the disease, passion, still exists even under these hopeless conditions, then the nature of the person would have deviated and the person needs to try another solution, that is, attending to his state of mind. The person afflicted by passion should convince himself that his heart's affection with what it cannot attain constitutes madness, and that this case is similar to whoever loves the sun, the only way to acquire it is to ascend to it! Everyone understands this is madness.

If one cannot attain his loved object because of a legal barrier that the religion erected, he should convince himself that acquiring his passion is not feasible because Allah did not allow it to happen. He should know that for his safety he should abandon such a matter and be certain that it is virtually impossible that he will ever attain it.

If one's whose heart orders him to do evil does not comply with these cures, let the slave abandon the matter for fear of losing whoever is more beloved to him, more beneficial and who offers a longer period of contentment and joy. In this case, the afflicted person will come to realize the difference between the two objects. Therefore, one should not prefer the joy of an hour that would soon turn to pain compared to eternal joy that is incomparable. The reality of the short-lived joy is that it is a daydream or a mirage that will soon end and fade away, but the responsibility would remain.

Also, one should realize that this might lead to a hateful loss that is worse for him than losing the coveted object, and thus his loss would multiply, losing the coveted object and acquiring a hateful outcome. When one realizes these facts, then losing the coveted object becomes less serious in his heart and being patient becomes more worthwhile. The mind, religion, honor and human nature then require the afflicted person to be patient in the face of losing a lesser loved object, for in this case, patience would soon earn him joy, contentment and happiness. On the other hand, one's ignorance, transience, injustice and immaturity orders him to prefer the lesser coveted object whatever the cost. Those whom Allah gives immunity will be saved from this end.

When one's heart does not accept this solution and dislikes using the remedy that we mentioned, let him think about what evil repercussions satisfying his lusts would bring about and what gains it would cause him to lose. He should realize that satisfying his lust is the major cause of an evil outcome in this life, as it prevents the slave from using his mind that is the controller of his actions and which should be used to lead him to benefit instead.

If one's heart still does not accept the remedy we mentioned, let him remember the shortcomings and unlikable characteristics of the coveted object, so that he might dislike the object, as well. When one thinks about this subject, he will realize that such shortcomings supercede the good qualities that made him like that object. Let him also ask the neighbors of his loved one about what he does not know of their attributes and behavior. It is a fact that as much as the good qualities drive loved ones closer, the shortcomings drive them apart. Then, one should weigh the two sides and choose the best and most beloved path to take. He should not be among those who are deceived by the color of an otherwise leprous skin. Let one think beyond the beautiful exterior to the true reality of things. Let one look beyond the beautiful shape to the inner evil of the heart.

If all of these remedies do not work, there will be no resort except seeking Allah Who answers the calls of those in distress when they invoke Him. Let him throw himself before His Door seeking His help with humbleness, humility and meekness.

Those who are led to this type of success should act honorably and keep their affair a secret, so as not to expose the loved one to the people and cause them harm, or else he will be committing a transgression and an injustice.

The Prophetís guidance on preserving the health with perfume

Good scents and perfumes are nutrition for the soul, and the soul is the dynamo of the rest of the body's powers. Perfume helps the brain, the heart and the internal organs and brings comfort to the heart and the soul. Perfumes are also the most suitable and favorable remedy and substance for the soul. Also, there is a close connection between the good soul and scented perfumes. This is why perfumes were among the dearest substances in this world to the heart of the most pure of all people, the Prophet ﷺ.

Al-Bukhari narrated that the Prophet ﷺ used to always accept perfume when presented to him. Also, Muslim narrated that the Messenger of Allah ﷺ said:

« من عُرِض عليه رَيْحانٌ فلا يَرُدَّه: فإنه طيِّبُ الريح، خفيفُ المَحْمِلِ »

(مسلم:٢٢٥٣)

``He who is offered Raihan (basil) should not refuse it, because it is easy to wear and has a good scent."

Further, Abu Dawud and An-Nasai' narrated that the Prophet ﷺ said:

«من عُـرِض عليهِ طِيبٌ فلا يَـرُدَّه: فإنه خفيفُ المحمِلِ، طيِّبُ الرائحة » (أبو داود:٤١٧٢)

``Whoever is offered some perfume should not refuse it because it is light to wear and has a good scent."

Ibn Abi Shaibah also narrated that the Messenger of Allah ﷺ had a container that had some perfume and he used to perfume himself with it. The Prophet ﷺ also said:

« إن لله حقًّا على كل مسلم: أَن يغتسلَ في كل سبعةِ أيام؛ وإن كان له طِيبٌ: أن يمَسَّ منه »(البخاري:٨٨٠ ومسلم:٨٤٩)

``Allah has a right on every Muslim that he takes a bath (at least once) in every seven days and if he has perfume to wear some of it."

Furthermore, the angels like perfume while the devils dislike it, because the dearest scent to the devils are foul odors, while good souls like good scents. Every soul leans towards and deserves what it likes. Evil men are suitable for evil women and vise versa, while good men are suitable for good women and vise versa. Although this statement applies to men and women in general, it also applies to every type of deed, speech, food, drink, clothing and scent.

The Prophetís guidance on preserving the health of the eyes

Ibn `Abbas رَضِيَ الله عَنْهُ narrated:

« كان رسولُ الله صلى اللهَ عليه وسلم إذا اكْتَحَلَ: يجعلُ في اليُمنَى ثلاثًا، يبتدِىءُ بها ويختم بها، وفَي اليُسْرى ثِنتين ». أما (هذه الرواية عن أنس ذكرها الألباني في الصحيحة: كان يكتحل في عينه اليمنى ثلاث مرات واليسرى مرتين (٦٣٣)

``Whenever the Messenger of Allah ﷺ used to wear kohl, he would use it thrice in the right eye - beginning with it and finishing with it - and twice in the left eye."

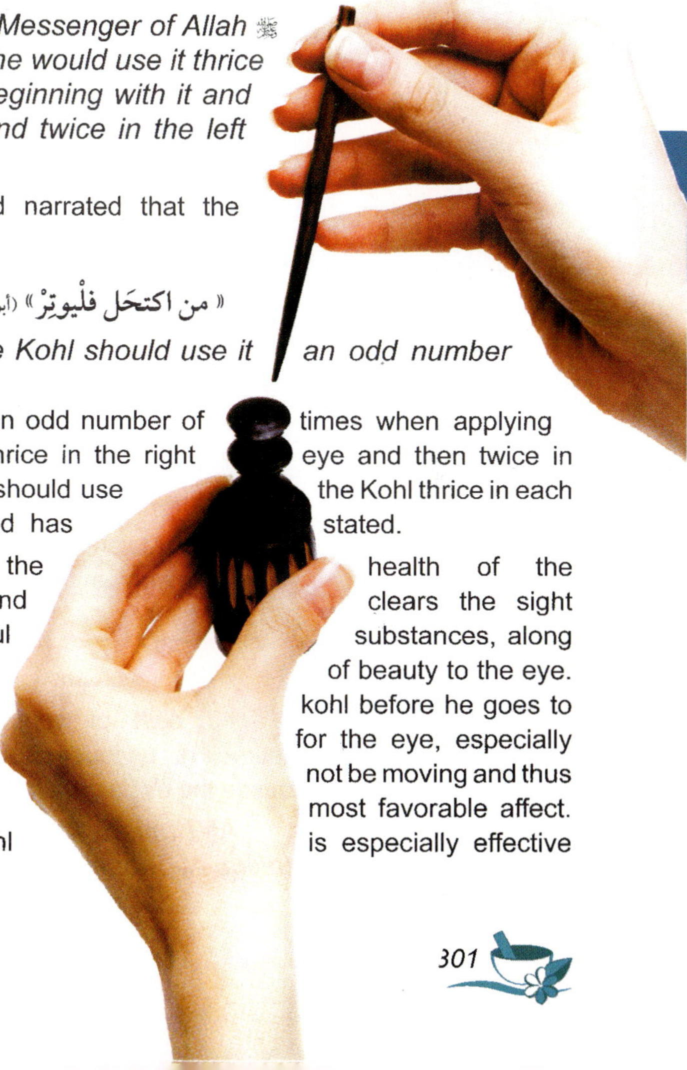

Also, Abu Dawud narrated that the Prophet ﷺ said:

« من اكتحَل فلْيوتِرْ» (أبو داود :٣٥ وضعفه الألباني)*

``Those who use Kohl should use it an odd number of times."

One should use an odd number of times when applying Kohl in both eyes, thrice in the right eye and then twice in the left eye. Or, one should use the Kohl thrice in each eye, as Imam Ahmad has stated.

Kohl preserves the health of the eye, strengthens and clears the sight and removes harmful substances, along with adding a touch of beauty to the eye. When one uses kohl before he goes to sleep, it is beneficial for the eye, especially since the eyes will not be moving and thus the kohl will have its most favorable affect. The Ithmid type of kohl is especially effective in this regard.

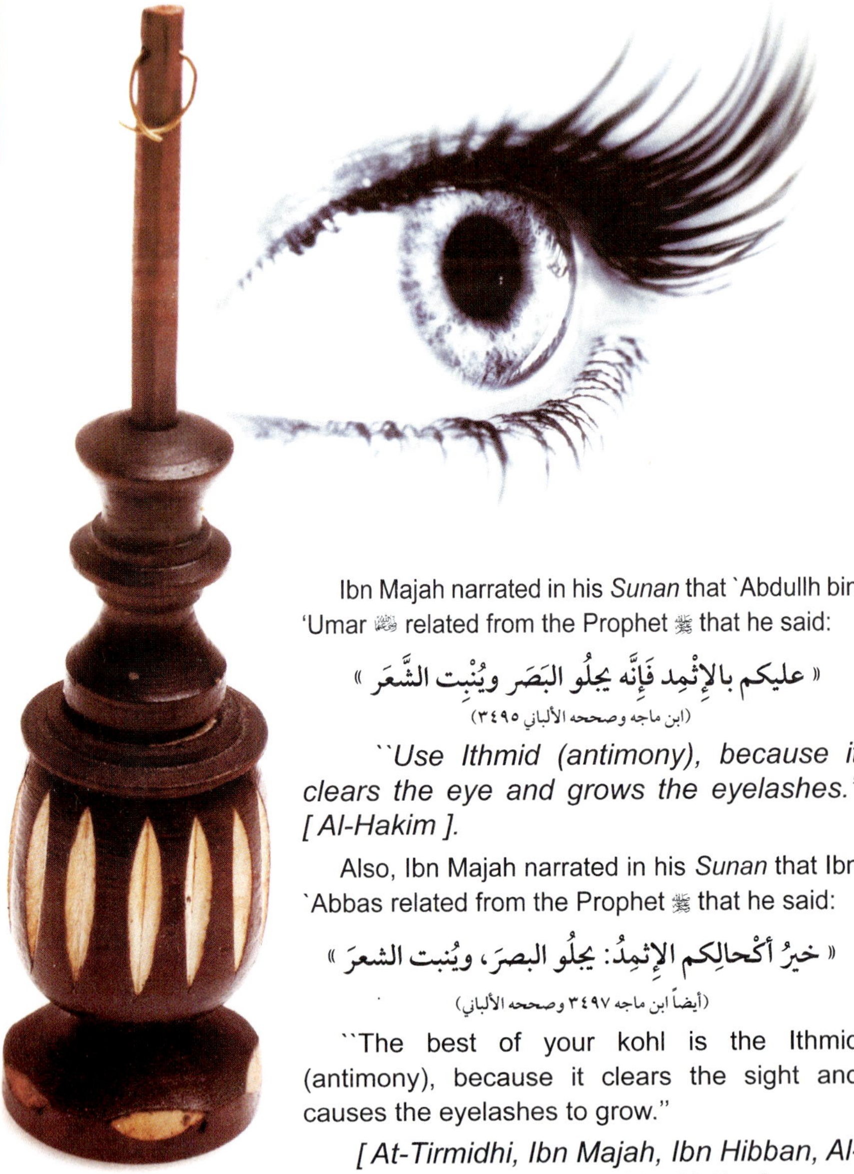

Ibn Majah narrated in his *Sunan* that `Abdullh bin 'Umar ﵄ related from the Prophet ﷺ that he said:

« عليكم بالإِثْمِد فَإِنَّه يجلُو البَصَر ويُنْبِت الشَّعَر »

(ابن ماجه وصححه الألباني ٣٤٩٥)

``Use Ithmid (antimony), because it clears the eye and grows the eyelashes.' [Al-Hakim].

Also, Ibn Majah narrated in his *Sunan* that Ibn `Abbas related from the Prophet ﷺ that he said:

« خيرُ أكْحالِكم الإِثمِدُ: يجلُو البصرَ، ويُنبت الشعرَ »

(أيضاً ابن ماجه ٣٤٩٧ وصححه الألباني)

``The best of your kohl is the Ithmid (antimony), because it clears the sight and causes the eyelashes to grow.''

[At-Tirmidhi, Ibn Majah, Ibn Hibban, Al-Hakim, At-Tabarani and Abu Na'im].

Part IV

Alphabetical Listing

4

Alphabetical Listing[1]

The Letter *Hamzah*

1. *Ithmid* (Antimony)

The *Ithmid* is the black Kohl stone. The best type of *Ithmid* is found in Asfahan (Iran), but it is also found in western areas. The best type of *Ithmid* is that which fragmentizes quickly and which has shiny morsels. Also, the interior of the *Ithmid* is polished and does not contain any impurities.

The Kohl tends to be cold and dry and it is beneficial to the eye in that it strengthens it and also strengthens the eye nerve. *Ithmid* dissolves excess flesh around ulcers and closes the wound while cleansing the area around them. *Ithmid* also relieves headaches when it is blended with pure watery (not thick) honey. When *Ithmid* is ground and mixed with tender fat and then used as a bandage over fire burns, it prevents blisters from appearing and also helps cure the skin damage that occurs in cases of burns by fire. *Ithmid* is the best type of Kohl used for the eye, especially for old people whose eyesight has weakened. In this case, it is better that Kohl is mixed with some Musk.

2. *Utrujj* (Citron)

In the *Sahih* it is narrated that the Prophet ﷺ said:

« مَثَل المُؤْمن الذي يَقْرَأُ القُرآن، كَمَثَل الأُتْرُجَّةِ: طَعْمُها طيِّبٌ، وريحُها طَيِّب »

(البخاري: ٥٠٢٠)

(1) * Editor's note : The following is a list in Arabic alphabetical order of different things that were mentioned by the Prophet ﷺ or Qur'an or were mistakenly attributed to the Prophet, in which case the false attribution is cleared up for the reader.

"The example of the believer who reads the Qur'an is the example of the Utrujj: its taste is delicious and its scent is pleasant."

The *Utrujj* has many benefits. There are four elements in the Utrujj, the peel, heart (or pulp), the pith and the seed. Each of these four elements has its own tendency: the peels, for instance, are hot and dry, while the pulp is hot and wet. The *Utrujj* pith is cold and dry, while its seed is hot and dry.

The peel of the *Utrujj* has many benefits. For instance, when its is placed within the clothes it prevents molding. The peel's scent refreshes decaying and polluted air. The peels of the *Utrujj* also improve the flavor of the foods and dissipate foul scents. Also, when the peels are mixed with the food they help the digestive process. The author of the Qanoon said, 'The pith of the (*Utrujj*) peels benefit in cases of snake bite, while the peels are used in bandages for snakebite. The ashes of the peels are used as an effective ointment against leprosy.'

The pulp of the citron (*Utrujj*) soothes the heat of the stomach, helps those who suffer from bile and subdues hot vapors. Further, Al-Ghafiqi said, "Eating the (citron) pulp relieves hemorrhoids."

The extract of the pith contained in the citron constipates, relieves bile, soothes hot pulsation, controls bilious vomiting, and when taken as a drink or a Kohl, relieves jaundice. The extract of the pith is also a good appetite stimulant, constipates and helps in cases of bilious diarrhea. The citron pith extract also soothes the lust of the woman and relieves and combats skin spots when used as a lubricant. It also cures herpes. The proof of the pith's effectiveness against ink is that when it touches the ink on the clothes, it effectively removes the stain. The pith contained in the *Utrujj* also soothes and has a chilling effect, cools the hotness of the liver, strengthens the stomach, eliminates bile and the accompanying depression and also quenches the thirst.

The seeds of the *Utrujj* have a decomposing and drying effect. Ibn Masawaih said that *Utrujj*, "When the skin of the seed is removed and cooked and taken as a drink with warm water, helps against deadly poisons when one drinks as much as two measures, each around twenty-five grams. When the seeds are ground and placed on a sting, they also help. The seeds also constipate and add good scent to the taste. Most of these benefits are also present in its pulp."

It was also said that, ``The seeds help against scorpion stings when two measures of it are taken with warm water, and also when it is ground and placed on the affected area." It was also said, ``Its seeds help against all types of poisons and all types of venomous stings."

It was also reported that one of the Persian rulers was angry with his doctors and that he ordered them be jailed. He gave them the choice to have only one type of food and they chose the *Utrujj*. They were asked, ``Why did you choose it in particular?`` They said, ``Because it turns into a type of perfume shortly, its sight is pleasant, its peel smells good, its pulp is a fruit, its pith is a food, its seeds an antidote and it contains fat."

Truly, such a beneficial substance deserves to be compared with the best of creation, meaning the believer who recites the Qur'an. We should mention that some of the *Salaf* used to like looking at the *Utrujj* because its sight is pleasant and comforting.

3. *Aruzz* (Rice)

There are two fake *Ahadith* regarding rice. The first, ``If it was a man it would be forbearing." The second *Hadith*, ``Everything that the earth produces has a disease and a cure, except the rice, for it is a cure and has no disease (or side effects)." We mentioned these incorrect *Hadiths* so that the people do not relate them from the Prophet ﷺ by mistake.

Rice is hot and dry and it is the most nutritious cereal after wheat. Rice is a beneficial substance as it tightens the intestinal cavity and coats and strengthens the stomach. The doctors of India claim that it is the most beneficial food when it is cooked with cows' milk. Rice is nutritious, enriches the body, increases semen production and purifies the color.

4. *Arz* (Pine)

Arz is also called *Sanawbar*. The Messenger of Allah ﷺ mentioned the pine, when he said:

«مَثلُ المؤمنِ مَثلُ الخامةِ مِن الزَّرع تُفَيِّؤُها الرِّياح: تُقيمُها مرَّةً، وتُميلُها أُخرى، ومَثلُ المنافقِ مَثلُ الأَرْزة: لا تزالُ قائمةً على أصلِها، حتى يكُونَ انْجِعافُها مرةً واحدةً»

(البخاري:٥٦٤٣)

``The example of the believer is the example of the green plant that the wind twists, sometimes leaving it straight and sometimes bending it. The example of the hypocrite is the example of the Arz, it will be standing on its roots then all of a sudden it is completely dry!"

The seed of the *Arz* is hot and wet. It is a relaxing and maturating substance, and has a sting that can be prevented if the *Arz* seeds are soaked in water. Further, the *Arz* seeds are difficult to digest but are nutritious, help relieve coughing and dries the moisture or vapor that accumulates in the lungs. They also energize semen production but constipate, unless one also eats bitter pomegranate seeds with them.

5. The *Ith-khir* (Lemon Grass)

In the *Sahih* it is narrated that the Prophet said in Makkah about its plants:

«لا يُختَلَى خَلاَها» (البخاري:١٣٤٩)

``Do not cut its plants."

Al-`Abbas رَضِيَ الله عَنْهُ said, ``Except for *Al-Ith-khir*, O Messenger of Allah , for their (the people of Makkah) servants use it and it is also used for their houses." The Prophet said: ``Except *Al-Ith-khir*."

Lemon grass is hot in the second degree and dry in the first degree. It is a light substance that opens clogs and the veins' orifices. It also increases urine and menstruation-flow, dissolves the stones and the hard tumors in the stomach, liver and kidneys, either as a drink or as a bandage. The stems of the lemon grass will strengthen the column of the teeth and the stomach, calm nausea and constipate the stomach.

The Letter *Baa*

1. *Bittikh* (Watermelon)

Abu Dawud and At-Tirmidhi narrated that the Prophet ﷺ used to eat watermelon with ripe dates, saying:

« يَدفعُ حَرُّ هذا بَرْدَ هذا » (الترمذي:١٨٤٣ و أبو داود:٣٨٣٦ وحسنه الألباني)

``The hotness of this substance (dates) neutralizes the coolness of that (watermelon)."

There are several *Ahadith* regarding watermelon none of them are authentic, except the *Hadith* that we mentioned above.

Green watermelon is cold and wet and is sweet. It also works as a cleanser (for the stomach and the intestines). Watermelon departs the stomach more quickly than cucumber and quickly blends with whatever substances are present in the stomach. It is beneficial to eat watermelon when it is warm, but when it is cold it is better to have it with some ginger to offset its harm.

Watermelon should be eaten before the meals. Otherwise, it will cause nausea. Some doctors said that when watermelon is, ``Eaten before the meal, it cleanses the stomach and removes ailments."

2. *Balah* (Dates)

An-Nasai' and Ibn Majah narrated in their *Sunan* that `Aishah رَضِيَ الله عَنْها said that the Messenger of Allah ﷺ said:

« كلُو البلَحَ بالتَّمْر . فإِن الشيطانَ إذا نَظَرَ إلَى ابن آدمَ يأكلُ البلَحَ بالتَّمر، يقولُ: بَقِيَ ابنُ آدمَ حتى أكل الحَديثَ بالعَتِيق » (ابن ماجه ٣٣٣٠ وأعده الألباني موضوعاً كما في الضعيفة :٢٣)

``Eat fresh dates with dried dates, for when Satan sees the son of Adam eating fresh and dried dates he comments, 'The

son of Adam remained until he started eating the new and the old together."

In another narration, the Prophet ﷺ said:

« كُلُو الْبَلَحَ بالتمر، فَإِن الشَّيْطَانَ يحزَنُ إِذَا رَأَى ابْنَ آدمَ يأكُلُه؛ يقول: عَاشَ ابنُ آدمَ حَتَى أَكَلَ الجَديدَ بِالخَلِق » (قوله "يحزن" وفي حرف: يغضب كما في المستدرك ٤/ ١٢٠ وهو موضوع كما في الضعيفة :٢٣)

``Eat fresh and dried dates, because Satan gets sad when he sees the son of Adam eating them, so he says: `The son of Adam has lived until (now) he eats the fresh and the old together."

Some of the Muslim doctors commented, ``The Prophet ﷺ ordered the Muslims to eat fresh and dried dates together rather than green dates with dried dates. Fresh dates are cold and dry while dried dates are hot and humid, thus neutralizing the effect of each other. On the other hand, green dates and dried dates are both hot, although the dried dates are more hot." Medically, it is better to avoid eating two types of foods that incline towards either hotness or coolness.

The *Hadith* indicates that the medical profession is generally correct when it inclines towards neutralizing the effects of medications and foods with other ingredients or foods to preserve good health.

Fresh dates are cold and dry and they benefit the mouth, the gums (gingiva) and the stomach. Yet, dates are not beneficial for the chest and lungs because of their coarseness. Also, the dates are difficult to digest and are not very nutritious. The example of fresh dates is the example of unripe grapes, as both cause flatulence and bloating, especially when one drinks water after eating fresh dates. To neutralize these side effects, one should eat them with dried dates, or honey and butter.

3. *Busr* (Green Dates)

In the *Sahih* it is narrated that when the Prophet , Abu Bakr and 'Umar رَضِيَ الله عَنْهما were guests of Abu Al-Haitham bin At-Taihan رَضِيَ الله عَنْهُ, he brought them a cluster of dates, which is similar to a cluster of grapes. The Prophet ﷺ said:

« هَلاَّ انتقَيْتَ لنا من رُطَبه » (الترمذي:٢٣٦٩ وصححه الألباني أخرجه مسلم مختصراً (٢٠٣٨))

``Why do you not choose some ripe dates for us?"

Abu Al-Haitham رَضِيَ الله عَنْهُ replied, ``I wanted you to choose whatever you like of its green and ripe dates."

Busr is hot and dry, and its dryness is more than its hotness. Also, the *Busr* dries out excess moisture, coats the stomach, relaxes the bowels and helps the gums and the mouth. The most beneficial type of *Busr* is the tender and sweet *Busr* . Yet, eating excessive amounts of *Busr* (green dates) regularly causes obstructions or clogs in the intestines.

4. *Baydh* (Eggs)

Fresh eggs are better than old eggs, and the best kind of eggs is chicken eggs. The eggs are mild but incline slightly towards being cold.

The author of the *Qanoon* said, ``The yolk is hot and wet and makes the blood sanitary, but is not nutritious. It is also digested quickly when it is still soft." Another person said, ``Egg yolk relieves the pain, polishes the throat and the trachea, helps the throat and relieves coughing and the ulcers of the lungs, liver and prostate. It also eliminates coarseness, especially when blended with the grease of sweet almonds. It also maturates and softens whatever is in the chest and softens the roughness of the throat."

When the albumen is used as an eye drop, it cools the hot tumors in the eye and relieves the pain. When it is used as an ointment and placed on the face, it prevents sunburn. Also, when the albumen is used as an ointment and placed on the forehead, it helps in cases of dysentery.

The author of the *Qanoon* mentioned eggs in the medicines and remedies of the heart. He also said, ``Its yolk has a strong effect in strengthening the heart. Egg yolk has three beneficial uses: it turns into blood quickly, it does not produce extensive wastes, and the blood that it produces is light and similar to the blood that feeds the heart. Further, the egg yolk is the most adequate substance against the diseases that affect the essence of the soul."

5. *Basal* (Onions)

Abu Dawud narrated in his *Sunan* that `Aishah رَضِيَ الله عَنْها was asked about *Basal* and she said, ``The last meal that the Prophet ﷺ had included onions in it."

In the *Sahihain* it is also narrated that the Prophet ﷺ disallowed those who eat onions from entering the mosque.

The *Basal* is hot in the third degree and has an excess wetness, helps against pollution and prevents hot wind (meaning in the stomach). It also excites the sexual drive, strengthens the stomach, helps semen production, makes the color lighter, dissolves the phlegm and cleanses the stomach.

Onion grains help against vitiate (lack of pigment in certain areas of the skin) and are used as an ointment around the area affected by alopecia (A skin disease characterized by loss of hair, partial or total). Further, warts will dissipate effectively when onions are blended with salt (and used as an ointment on the warts). When someone feels nauseous after taking a laxative, smelling onions will help against vomiting. Also, the onion will dissipate the smell of laxatives, and when onion water (extract) is administered through the nose, it will clear the head. Used as ear drops, onion extract also helps against weak hearing, innitus, pus and water that accumulates in the ear. Also, onion grains are used as an eyeliner, to dry out the water that attacks the eye, i.e. cataracts, when the grains are blended with honey and used on the white part of the eye.

Cooked onions are nutritious and help against icterus, jaundice, coughing and roughness in the chest. It is also diuretic and relaxes the bowels. It also heals dog bites when its water (extract) is blended with salt and rue and squeezed on the affected area. Finally, it will open the orifices of the hemorrhoids when used as suppository.

Onions cause migraines, headaches, flatulence and bring darkness to the sight

Eating onions in excessive amounts or regularly causes forgetfulness, affects the mind and changes the odor of the mouth and the taste of food. It also bothers those in your presence and the angels. Cooking onions dissipates these side effects of the onion. The *Sunan* narrated:

« أنه صلى الله عليه وسلم أمر آكِلَه وآكِلَ الثُّوم: أن يُمِيتَهما طَبْخًا » (مسلم:٥٦٧)

``The Prophet ﷺ ordered those who eat onion and garlic to kill them (make them milder) by cooking."

Also, chewing rue leaves dissipates the odor of the onions.

6. *Bathinjan* (Eggplant)

There is a fake *Hadith* that states that eggplant materializes the goals anticipated from eating it. This statement is not suitable to be related from a sane person let alone the Prophet ﷺ .

There are two types of eggplants: white and black. There is a difference of opinion whether it is hot or cold, although we think it is hot. Eggplants cause black bile, piles, clogs, cancer and leprosy. Eggplants also spoil ones color, make it black and cause bad breath. White eggplants do not have these side effects.

The Letter *Taa*

1. *Tamr* (Dried Dates)

In the *Sahih* it is narrated that the Prophet ﷺ said:

«من تَصَبَّح بسَبْع تَمَراتٍ – وفي لفظ: من تمْر العالية – لم يضرَّه ذلك اليومَ سُمٌّ ولا سِحْرٌ » (البخاري:٥٤٤٥ ولفظ "العالية" عند مسلم:٢٠٤٧)

``Whoever ate seven dates in the morning from the area of 'Aaliyah will not be harmed by poison or magic the rest of that day."

He also said:

« بيتٌ لا تمرَ فيه جِياعٌ أهلُه » (مسلم:٢٠٤٦)

"The people of a house where there are no dates are hungry."

Also, the Prophet ﷺ ate dried dates with butter, with bread and alone.

Tamr is hot in the second degree and either wet or dry in the second degree.

Dried dates strengthen the liver, relax the bowels, increase semen production, especially when taken with pine, and relieve soar throat. As for those who are not used to eating dried dates, such as the residents of cold areas, dried dates cause them clogs, harm the teeth and cause headaches, unless they are eaten with almonds and poppy.

Dried dates are among the most nutritious fruits, their essence is hot and wet. Also, when one eats dates in the beginning of the day, they help kill worms. Although dried dates are hot, yet they have the strength of an antidote against worms, killing or at least decreasing their numbers, especially when dried dates are taken frequently on an empty stomach. Dried dates are a fruit, a type of food, a cure, a drink and a sweet.

2. *Tin* (Figs)

The *Sunnah* does not mention figs because they did not grow in that area of the Hijaz or Al-Madinah. Figs require an environment that is different from that in the areas where dates grow. Allah has sworn by the *Tin* in His Book because of its tremendous benefits and uses.

Tin is hot and either dry or wet. The best type of figs are the white kind when they are ripe, as they cleanse the sand that accumulates in the liver and prostate and serve as a preventive substance against poisons. Figs are more nutritious than all other type of fruit, and help relieve the roughness in the chest, throat and trachea. It also cleanses the liver and the spleen, purifies the phlegm that accumulates in the stomach and provides good nourishment for the body. Yet, it makes one more susceptible to lice if eaten excessively.

3. *Tharid* (Meat & Bread Dish)

In the *Sahihain* it states that the Messenger of Allah ﷺ said:

« فضلُ عائشةَ على النّساء: كفَضْل الثّريدِ على سائِر الطّعام » (البخاري:٣٧٧٠)

``The virtue of `Aishah رَضِيَ الله عَنْها as compared to other women, is like the virtue of *Tharid* as compared to the rest of the foods."

Tharid is composed of some bread, which is the best food, and meat, which is the best flavoring. When these two are combined together, no other food can surpass them.

There are conflicting opinions regarding which is better, the bread or the meat. The correct opinion is that bread is used more while meat is better and superior to bread. Also, the meat resembles the true essence of the human body more than any other food. It is also the food of the people of Paradise. Allah said about those who sought to eat herbs, cucumbers, *Fum* (wheat or garlic), lentils and onions,

﴿أَتَسْتَبْدِلُونَ ٱلَّذِى هُوَ أَدْنَىٰ بِٱلَّذِى هُوَ خَيْرٌ﴾

``Would you exchange that which is better for that which is lower? (2: 61)

Many among the *Salaf* said that *Fum* is wheat. Hence this *Ayah* states that meat (quails) is better than wheat. Allah has the best knowledge.

The Letter *Jeem*

1. *Jummar* (Palm Pith)

In the *Sahihain* it is narrated that `Abdullh bin 'Umar رَضِيَ الله عَنْهما said.``While we were sitting with the Messenger of Allah ﷺ, he was brought a *Jummar* of a date tree. The Prophet ﷺ said:

« إنَّ من الشَّجرِ شَجَرةً مِثلَ الرّجلِ المُسْلم لا يسقُط ورقُها » (البخاري:٦١)

`There is a tree that resembles the Muslim as its leaves never fall."

Jummar is cold and dry in the first degree, and it seals the ulcers and relieves hemorrhage, diarrhea, yellow bile and blood pressure. Also, the *Jummar* is not harmful, but is not nutritious and is difficult to digest. The *Jummar* is all benefit and this is why the Prophet ﷺ said it resembled the Muslim, because of his tremendous usefulness and goodness.

2. *Jubn* (Cheese)

In the *Sunan* of Abu Dawud it is narrated that `Abdullh bin `Umar said that the Prophet ﷺ was brought some cheese while in the area of Tabuk and that he asked for a knife, mentioned Allah's Name and then cut it. Also, the Companions used to eat cheese in Iraq and Sham (Greater Syria) areas.

Unsalted cheese is good for the stomach, easy on the body organs, produces flesh and relaxes the stomach. Salted cheese, on other hand, is less nutritious and is bad for the stomach and the intestines. Old and grilled cheese heats the stomach and is beneficial in cases of ulcers and diarrhea.

Cheese is cold and wet and is better when it is grilled because the fire makes it milder, softer and better tasting and scented. The old salted cheese is hot and dry, and boiling also makes it softer and less sour because the fire extracts the hot residue from the cheese. Salted cheese makes the body weak and causes stones in the liver and prostate. It is also bad for the stomach, and mixing it with what people think will make it milder is even worse because these substances allow the cheese an easy access to the stomach.

The Letter *Haa*

1. *Hennaí*

We mentioned the benefits of henna' before and mentioned the *Ahadith* on this subject.

2. *Habbah Sawdaa* (The Black Seed)

In the *Sahihain* it is narrated that Abu Hurairah رَضِيَ الله عَنْه related from the Prophet ﷺ that he said:

« عليكم بهذه الحَبَّةِ السَّوْداء. فإن فيها شفاءً من كُل داءٍ، إلا السامَ » (البخاري:٥٦٨٨)

``Use the Black Seed, because it contains a cure for every type of ailment, except for death." [At-Tirmidhi, Ahmad and Ibn Hibban].

The Black Seed (or Habbat Al-Barakah) is called *Shuneiz* in Persian black cumin and Indian cumin. Al-Harbi narrated that Al-Hasan said, ``It is the mustard seed" while Al-Harawi said that it is the green seed which is the seed of the terebinth. These are not correct opinions, because the Prophet ﷺ stated that it is the Black Seed, which is the *Shuneiz* as we stated.

The Black Seed has many benefits, as indicated by the Prophet's statement:

``It is a cure for every type of disease." This statement is just like what Allah said:

﴿ تُدَمِّرُ كُلَّ شَيْءٍ بِأَمْرِ رَبِّهَا ﴾

``Destroying everything by the Command of its Lord!" (46:25)

Its means destroys everything that is prone to destruction.

The Black Seed helps against all types of cold ailments. Also, the Black Seed helps introduce the effective ingredients of cold medications to the areas affected by hot and dry ailments, as it helps the body absorb the medicine quickly when taken in small dosages.

The author of the *`Qanoon'* and other people stated that saffron blended with camphor has similar effects, because saffron helps the camphor reach the affected area quickly. There are several types of plants that have similar effects as saffron. It is possible that the hot substance benefits in cases of hot diseases. For instance, the *Anzarut,* which is a type of eyeliner, is mixed with other remedies for Ophthalmia, conjunctivitis, and so forth. Ophthalmia is a hot tumor as the doctors agree. Also, sulfur is a remedy for hot mange.

Shuneiz is hot and dry in the third degree, eliminates flatulence, extracts the helminthes (worms), relieves leprosy, and phlegmy fevers, opens clogs, decomposes accumulating gas and excess moisture in the stomach. When the *Shuneiz* is ground, blended with honey and drunk with some warm water, it will dissolve the stones that appear in the kidney and the prostate, and it is also diuretic. It increases the flow during menstruation and the production of milk if it is drunk for several days. When it is heated with vinegar and placed on the stomach, it will eliminate helminthes (worms). When it is blended with wet or cooked colorynth water, it is more effective in removing helminthes (worms). It also clears up, decomposes and relieves cold symptoms when it is ground in a rag and inhaled through the nose on a regular basis until the ailment is cured.

Black seed oil helps against snakebites, hemorrhoids and spots. When around twenty-five grams of it is drunk with water it will help against gasping and hard breathing.

When the black seeds are cooked in vinegar and then one rinses his mouth with it, it will relieve toothache resulting from sensitivity to cold. When one inhales powdered black seed, it will help against water that accumulates in the eye. When it is used in a bandage while blended with vinegar, it heals spots and exposed skin ulcers and decomposes the acute mucus tumors and also hard tumors.

The oil of the Black Seed also helps against facial paralysis when administered by the nose. When one drinks around twenty-five grams of its oil, it helps against spider bite. When it is ground finely and blended with the oil of the green Seed and used as ear drops, only up to three drops, it helps against cold symptoms, flatulence and various clogs.

When the Black Seed is fried and finely ground, soaked in oil and then drops are administered in the nose, it will help against col conditions accompanied by intensive sneezing.

When the Black Seed is burned and mixed with melted wax alon with henna' or iris oil, it helps remove the ulcers that appear on the ski of the legs, after washing the skin with vinegar.

When the Black Seeds are crushed in vinegar and laid on leprou skin, the skin affected by black pigmentation and on the head that i affected by dandruff, it helps relieve these ailments.

When the Black Seeds are ground finely and one swallows aroun twenty-five grams of it each day with cold water, it instantly help against the bite of rabid dogs, and might prevent death as a result c hydrophobia. When one administers the oil of the black seed in th nose, it will help against facial paralysis and tetanus by eliminating the causes. Finally, when the black seeds are burned, they help repulse th venomous beasts.

When Persian kohl is dissolved in water and then placed on th interior of the throat and then the black seeds are sprinkled on it, it act like an effective remover of hemorrhoids. There are many other benefit for the *Shuneiz*. We should state that the dose should be around twenty five grams, as some people claim that using excessive dosages of might cause death.

3. *Harir* (Silk)

We mentioned that the Prophet ﷺ allowed Az-Zubayr and Abdur Rahman bin `Awf to wear silk because of a rash that they suffered from We mentioned the benefits of the silk in that chapter.

4. *Hurf* (Cress)

Abu Hanifah Ad-Daynoori said, ``Cress seeds are used in remedie and are also called Ath-Thuffaa, which the Prophet ﷺ mentioned. It plant is called *Al-Hurf* while *Rashad* seeds is its popular name." Also Abu Ubayd said that *Ath-Thuffaa* is the *Hurf*.

The *Hadith* that Abu Hanifah referred to is what Abu Ubay and other scholars have related from Ibn `Abbas that the Prophet ﷺ was reported to have said:

« ماذا في الأَمَرَّين من الشِّفاء !: الثُّفَّاءِ والصَّبِرِ » (وأيضاً البيهقي ٩/ ٣٤٦ وهو في ضعيف الجامع ٥٠٦٧)

``What a cure do the two bitter remedies carry: the Thuffaa and aloe."

Cress is hot and dry in the third degree, and it heats and relaxes the stomach, removes different types of worms, decomposes the spleen tumors, excites the sexual drive and heals the ulcers of mange and herpes.

When the cress is used as a bandage along with honey, it will decompose spleen tumors. When it is cooked with henna, it will extract harmful accumulations in the chest, while taking it as a drink helps against venomous bites and stings.

When it is burned, its smoke repulses venomous beasts and also prevents the hair from falling. Also, when it is mixed with barley flour and vinegar and used as a bandage it helps against sciatic nerve and decomposes hot tumors.

Further, when it is used as a bandage with water, it brings the pustules to maturity and helps against flabbiness in various organs, strengthens the sexual drive and works as an appetite stimulant. It also helps against asthma, hard breathing, relieves the thickness in the spleen, purifies the chest and increases the menstrual flow. It also helps against sciatic nerve and the cavity of the hip, due to the extraction power of the cress when one drinks it or is injected with it. It also purifies the chest and the lungs from phlegm.

When cress is crushed and taken in a drink with warm water, it will work as a laxative, decomposes flatulence and helps against the pain caused by constipation. Further, cress also helps against leprosy when it is crushed and used in a drink.

Also, when the cress is blended with vinegar and used as an ointment on leprous skin and on white pigmentation disorder, it helps relieve these conditions. It also relieves headaches that are caused by colds and by phlegm accumulation. When it is fried and drunk (with water), it constipates, especially when it is not crushed, as its consistency will be softened when it is fried.

Galinus said that the strength of the cress, ``Is similar to the effectiveness of mustard grains. Hence it could be used to heat the pain in the hip, which is known as *Nasa* and headaches, as each of these symptoms requires heat, similar to mustard seed. Sometimes, cress is mixed with other remedies and used to treat asthma, as it is known that it dissolves thick mixtures, again just as mustard seed does. It is similar to mustard seed in every respect."

5. `*Hulbah* (Fenugreek)

The Prophet ﷺ was reported to have visited Sa`d bin Abi Waqqas رَضِيَ الله عَنْه once when he was ill while in Makkah and he asked that a doctor be brought to examine him. They brought Al-Harith bin Kaladah who examined him and said, ``There is no harm with him, just cook some fenugreek with dates and let him eat them." Sa'd was reported to have done that and was then healed.

Hulbah is hot in the second degree and dry in the first degree.

When the fenugreek is cooked in water, it will soften the throat, chest and the stomach. It also relieves coughing, dryness, asthma, hard breathing and increases the sexual drive. It also relieves flatulence, phlegm, piles and the various accumulations in the intestines. It also dissolves the phlegm from the chest and helps against gastric ulcer and lung diseases. `*Hulbah* is used to heal the intestines, mixed with some ghee and *fanith*.

When five measures of fenugreek is taken in a drink, it will increase the flow of menstruation, and when it is cooked and the hair is washed with it, it will make it curly and will combat dandruff.

When the flour of the fenugreek is blended with some vinegar and natron and used as a bandage on the tumor of the spleen, it will dissolve it. Also, the woman who suffers from pain in the vagina due to a tumor will benefit if she sits in the water in which the fenugreek was cooked. When it is used as a bandage and placed on hard, cold tumors, it will help dissolve these tumors. Also, when its water is drunk, it will help against the pain in the stomach that results from accumulating gaseous materials and will cleanse the intestines.

When one eats the *Hulbah* cooked in honey, dates or figs on an empty stomach, it will dissolve the phlegm that accumulates in the chest and stomach, and will also help against coughing that accompanies such ailments.

Hulbah also relieves urine retention and works as a laxative. When it is placed on the erratic nail, it will heal it, while its oil helps against cracked skin due to extreme cold, when it is mixed with wax. There are many other benefits for the *Hulbah* (fenugreek).

Some doctors stated, ``If the people had knowledge of its benefits, they would buy it with its weight worth of gold."

The Letter *Khaa*

1. *Khubz* (Bread)

In the *Sahih* it is narrated that the Prophet said:

«تكونُ الأرضُ يوم القيامةِ خُبْزةً واحدةً، يَتكفَّؤُها الجبَّارُ بيده أَحَدُكُمْ خُبْزَتَهُ فِي السَّفَرِ نُزُلاً لأهل الجنة» (البخاري: ٦٥٢٠)

``On the Day of Resurrection, the earth will look like one piece of bread which the Most Mighty would prepare with His Hand as a residence for the people of Paradise."

There is a fake *Hadith* that disallows cutting bread with a knife. There is also another fake *Hadith* that disallows cutting meat with a knife.

Muhanna said that he asked Imam Ahmad about the *Hadith* related from 'Aishah رَضِيَ الله عَنْها which narrates that the Prophet ﷺ disallowed using a knife to cut meat, because it is an act of non-Arabs. Imam Ahmad said that it is not correct and that it contradicts the *Hadith* narrated by `Amr bin Umayyah and Al-Mughirah. The *Hadith* that he referred to is what `Amr bin Umayyah related that the Prophet used to cut some pieces of ewe meat with a blade. Also, Al-Mughirah narrated that when he asked the Prophet ﷺ to be his guest, he ordered that a piece of meat be broiled and he then started cutting the meat with a blade.

The best type of bread is yeasty and kneaded

The next best is furnace bread, then oven baked bread, then bread cooked under hot ashes, using fresh flour.

The most nutritious kind of bread is semolina bread, because it digests slowly and because it does not have excessive amounts of bran, then chalky bread and lastly black bread.

The best time to eat the bread is in the last part of the day when it is baked. Also, unlike dry bread, soft bread is lighter, more nutritious, humidifying and digests faster.

Wheat bread is hot in the second degree and is mild concerning wetness and dryness, unless dried by fire.

Wheat bread also fattens the body rapidly. The *Qatayif* (similar to pancakes) cause a thick condition, while breadcrumbs provoke swelling in the stomach and digests with difficulty. Further, bread made with milk causes clogs and is difficult to digest, although it is nutritious.

Barley bread is cold and dry in the first degree and is not as nutritious as wheat bread.

2. *Khall* (Vinegar)

Muslim narrated in his *Sahih* that Jabir bin `Abdullah رَضِيَ الله عَنْهما said, ``The Messenger of Allah asked his wife for food and she said that I have vinegar. He asked for some of it and started eating from it while saying:

« نِعْمَ الإِدامُ الخَلُّ » (مسلم:٢٠٥٢)

``What an excellent food is vinegar." (He ate it with bread.)

Khall is a substance that is both hot and cold, although coldness is usually more apparent. It is also dry in the third degree and a strong drying agent. Vinegar also soothes the body and softens the nature.

Wine vinegar helps against gastric inflammation and bile and prevents the harm of toxic medications. It also decomposes milk and the blood when coagulated, and helps the spleen, coats the stomach, constipates, quenches the thirst and prevents tumors from occurring. It also helps the digestion process, works against phlegm, softens thick foods and softens the consistency of the blood.

When vinegar is drunk with salt, it will help against poisonous mushrooms. When vinegar is sipped, it will dissolve the clogs that occur in the blood in the lower jaw. When one rinses his mouth with warm vinegar, it relieves toothache and strengthens the gingival.

Vinegar also helps against a septic finger when it is anointed with it, and also relieves pustules, hot tumors and fire burns. Vinegar is an appetite stimulant, softens the stomach, and favorable for young people and for those who live in warm areas.

3. *Khilal* (Toothpick)

Toothpicks are helpful for the gingival and teeth and preserve their health, and help keep the breath fresh. One of the best types of toothpicks are those made from olive wood. It is not advised to use reed, myrtle, or basil to pick the teeth.

The Letter *Dal*

1. *Duhn* (Fat or Grease)

Fat closes the pores of the body and prevents the skin from decomposing. When it is used after one takes a bath with hot water, it will humidify the body and polish it. When the hair is anointed with grease, it will beautify it and make it longer. It also helps against measles and most other ailments that could affect the hair.

At-Tirmidhi narrated that Abu Hurairah رَضِيَ الله عَنْه related from the Prophet ﷺ that he said:

« كلو الزَّيت، وادَّهِنوا به » (ابن ماجه: ٣٣٢٠ وهو حسن لغيره (الصحيحه: ٣٧٩)

"Use grease in your food and as an ointment."

In the warm areas, such as Hijaz, grease works as one of the best preservers of health and as a remedy, making it necessary for the residents of such areas. As for those who live in cold areas, it is not as necessary for them. We should mention that using grease on the head on a regular basis causes harm to the sight.

The most beneficial simple kinds of grease are regular oil, then fat and then sesame oil.

As for the compound greases, some kinds are wet and cold, such as the essence of violet, which helps against hot headaches and brings sleep to the eye. It also moisturizes the brain, helps against cracks (or fractures) and excessive dryness of the skin. It is also a beneficial ointment against mange and dry rashes, along with helping the joints be flexible. It is also suitable for those who tend to be hot during the summer.

Some types of compound greases are hot and wet, such as ben-tree grease, which is the extract of white seeds that look like dusty pistachio and which is greasy and fatty. This type of grease relaxes the nerves and helps against spots and lack of pigment in certain areas of the skin. It also draws thick phlegm, softens dry ligaments and heats the nerves. It also cleans the teeth, makes them shiny and helps them against corrosion. Also whoever anoints his head and face with ben-tree grease will not come down with measles or cracks. Anointing the sexual organs and groins with it also helps against the coldness of the kidneys and dripping urine.

The Letter *Thal*

1. *Tharirah* (Hemarthria/Arum)

In the *Sahihain* it is narrated that `Aishah رَضِيَ الله عَنْها said that during the Farewell *Hajj*, she perfumed the Messenger of Allah ﷺ with Tharirah for his *Ihram* and otherwise.

We mentioned the *Tharirah* and its benefits before.

2. *Thubab* (Flies)

We mentioned the *Hadith* by Abu Hurairah رَضِيَ الله عَنْه in the *Sahihain* about the Prophet's command to dip the housefly in the food or drink when it falls in it to get the antidote that its wing carries. This antidote works as the antidote of the poison that the fly carries on the other wing. We also mentioned the benefits of the flies before.

3. *Thahab* (Gold)

Abu Dawud and At-Tirmidhi narrated that the Prophet ﷺ allowed Arfajah bin As`ad, who lost his nose during the battle of Kulab and had to use a nose made of silver that later rotted, to wear a nose made of gold. `Arfajah is only mentioned in this one *Hadith*.

Gold is the joy of the life of this world and the precious material possession of this existence that brings joy to the hearts and strength to the back. It is also Allah's secret on His earth. Gold's condition is suitable in all types of environments and has a soft hotness that is used in various light and soothing remedies. It is also the most mild of all minerals.

When gold is buried in the ground, sand does not affect it adversely. When gold is used in certain remedies, it helps cure weak hearts and the fibrillation that accompanies black bile. It also helps against obsession, sadness, depression, fear and love. It brings fatness to the body, dissipates pallor and lightens the color. It also helps against leprosy and the various other ailments including black bile. Drunk or used as an ointment, gold is an effective ingredient in the remedies for treating alopecia (a skin disease characterized by loss of hair, partial or total), and viper stings. It also clears the eye and strengthens it, and helps against several ailments while brining strength to the various organs of the body.

Foul breath would dissipate if one holds some gold in his mouth. Also, those who have a disease that requires cauterization and use gold for this purpose it will heal quickly and the wound would not be covered with blisters. Also, when gold is used as kohl, it purifies and strengthens the eyes. Further, when a golden ring is heated and applied on pigeon wings, the pigeons will be accustomed to their homes and will not abandon them.

Gold is especially effective in strengthening the hearts and this is why it was allowed in times of war and in times of peace, except when there is proof to the contrary. At-Tirmidhi narrated that Buraydah Al-`Asri said, ``The Messenger of Allah ﷺ entered (Makkah) the Day of *Al-Fath* (conquering of Makkah) with gold and silver on his sword."

Gold is such a beloved object to the hearts that when they acquire it, it will be sufficient for the people to forget the other beloved objects of this earthly life.

Allah said:

﴿ زُيِّنَ لِلنَّاسِ حُبُّ ٱلشَّهَوَٰتِ مِنَ ٱلنِّسَآءِ وَٱلْبَنِينَ وَٱلْقَنَٰطِيرِ ٱلْمُقَنطَرَةِ مِنَ ٱلذَّهَبِ
وَٱلْفِضَّةِ وَٱلْخَيْلِ ٱلْمُسَوَّمَةِ وَٱلْأَنْعَٰمِ وَٱلْحَرْثِ ﴾

``Beautified for men is the love of things they covet; women, children, much of gold and silver (wealth), branded beautiful horses, cattle and well-tilled land." (3:14)

Also, in the *Sahihain* it is narrated that the Prophet ﷺ said:

« لو كان لابنِ آدمَ وادٍ من ذهب: لابْتَغَى إليه ثانيًا. ولو كان له ثانٍ: لابتَغى ثالثًا. ولا يَمْلأُ جَوفَ ابنِ آدمَ إلاَّ التُّرَابُ؛ ويَتوبُ الله على مَن تابَ » (البخاري:٦٤٣٩)

``If the son of Adam had a valley of gold, he would seek a second. If he had two, he would seek a third. Nothing fills the stomach of the son of Adam except dirt, and Allah forgives those who repent."

Gold is the biggest barrier that stands between mankind and acquiring the ultimate success on the Day of Resurrection. It is also the biggest object with which Allah has been disobeyed. Because of gold, relations of the womb were severed, blood was shed, prohibitions were violated, rights were unjustly taken and slaves committed injustice against each other. Gold is the reason behind liking the life of this world and its shortness, and the cause behind disliking the Next Life and what Allah has prepared in it for His loyal supporters. With gold, so many truths were and are buried, so much falsehood was and is brought to life, so many unjust people were and are given support and so many innocent people were and are being dealt with unjustly.

The Letter *Raa*

1. *Rutab* (Ripe Dates)

Allah said to Mary:

﴿وَهُزِّىٓ إِلَيْكِ بِجِذْعِ ٱلنَّخْلَةِ تُسَٰقِطْ عَلَيْكِ رُطَبًا جَنِيًّا ﴿٢٥﴾ فَكُلِى وَٱشْرَبِى وَقَرِّى عَيْنًا﴾

``And shake the trunk of date palm towards you, it will let fall fresh ripe dates upon you. So eat and drink and be glad" (19: 25, 26)

Also, in the *Sahihain* it is narrated that `Abdullah bin Ja'far رَضِيَ الله عَنْهما said:

"I saw the Messenger of Allah ﷺ eating cucumbers with ripe dates."

Abu Dawud also narrated in his *Sunan* that Anas رَضِيَ الله عَنْهُ said:

"The Messenger of Allah ﷺ used to break his fast on some ripe dates, and if he did not have any, on dry dates. Otherwise, if he did not have dry dates, he would have several sips of water."

Ripe dates are just like water, hot and wet, and they are favorable for and strengthen the cold stomach, increase the production of semen and fertility, are suitable for cold temperaments and are very nutritious.

Ripe dates are the best types of fruit for the people of Al-Madinah specifically and for all others in general where ripe dates grow. It is also a very beneficial fruit for the body, although ripe dates spoil quickly in the stomach of those who are not used to eating them and thus produce putrid blood. Also, eating excessive amounts of ripe dates cause headaches and black bile and also harms the teeth. Oxymel *(Sakanjabin)* helps neutralize the irritants that accompany eating ripe dates.

When the Prophet ﷺ used to break his fast, he used to first eat ripe or dry dates, or would drink some water. This is a wise decision, because fasting empties the stomach of food. Thus the liver would not find any sufficient energy that it could transfer to the various organs. Sweets are the fastest food to reach the liver and are also favored by the liver, especially when one eats ripe dates, in which case the liver accepts it even more favorably, benefits from it and then transfers the benefit to the rest of the organs of the body. If there are no ripe dates available, one should eat dried dates because they are sweet and nutritious. Otherwise, some sips of water would extinguish the heat of the stomach and the Fast. The stomach's appetite would then increase and become ready to accept (and digest) food.

2. *Raihan* (Myrtle / Basil)

Allah said:

﴿ فَأَمَّآ إِن كَانَ مِنَ ٱلْمُقَرَّبِينَ ﴿٨٨﴾ فَرَوْحٌ وَرَيْحَانٌ وَجَنَّتُ نَعِيمٍ ﴾

``Then, if he (the dying person) be of the Muqarrabun (those brought near to Allah), (There is for him) rest and provision, and a Garden of Delights (Paradise)." (56:88,89)

And He said:

﴿ وَٱلْحَبُّ ذُو ٱلْعَصْفِ وَٱلرَّيْحَانُ ﴾

``And also corn, with (its) leaves and stalk for fodder, and sweet-scented plants." (55:12)

Muslim narrated that the Prophet ﷺ said:

«من عُرِض عليه رَيْحانٌ فلا يرده: فإنه خفيفُ المَحْمِلِ،طيِّب الرائحةِ » (مسلم:٢٢٥٣)

``Whoever was presented with Rayhan should not refuse it, because it is easy to wear and has a good scent."

Ibn Majah narrated in his Sunan that Usamah رَضِيَ اللهُ عَنْهُ *related from the Prophet* ﷺ *that he said:*

« ألا مُشَمِّرٌ لِلْجنَّة؛ فإن الجَنَّة لا خطرَ لها، هي - وربِّ الكعبة نورٌ يتلألأ وريحانةٌ تهتزُّ ، وقصرٌ مَشِيدٌ، ونهرٌ مطَّرِدٌ، وثمرةٌ نَضِيجَةٌ، وَزَوْجةٌ حَسْناءُ جملةٌ، وحُلَلٌ كثيرةٌ، في مَقامٍ أبدًا، فِي حَبْرَةٍ ونَضْرَةٍ ، في دُورٍ عاليةٍ سَلِيمَةٍ بَهِيَّة ». (ابن ماجه: ٤٣٣٢ وضعفه الألباني)

``Is there anyone who is ready to enter Paradise, for Paradise is all good (and pure). It is, by the Lord of the Ka`bah, a shining light, a twinkling Raihan , a luxurious palace, a running river, a ripe date, and a beautiful, pretty wife. It has many suits, eternal residence in a good place of dwelling, fruits, vegetables, comfort and bounty in an exalted, comfortable dwelling."

They said, " `Yes, O Messenger of Allah ﷺ! We are ready for it!' He said, `Say, by Allah's Leave.' They said, By Allah's Leave.' "

Every plant that has good scent is called `*Raihan*'. Therefore, every area gives a certain plant that name. For instance, the people of the west, as well as, the Arabs call the aromatic plants *Raihan*. The people in Iraq and Sham call the *Hibk* (a type of mint) a *Raihan*.

Raihan or myrtle is cold in the first degree and dry in the second degree. Yet, it is a compound of several qualities, most of which consist of earthly cold essence. Myrtle also consists of a soft hot substance. Myrtle dries the head nicely and is effective as a constipating agent.

Myrtle prevents bile diarrhea and dissipates hot and wet vapor when one smells its scent. Its scent also brings relief to the heart and prevents various ailments, especially when the plant is spread around the house.

Also, myrtle heals the tumors that occur in the two ureters when it is coated on them. When fresh myrtle leaves are ground and blended with vinegar and then placed on the head, they will stop nose bleeding. When dried myrtle leaves are crushed and the powder is sprinkled on wet ulcers it will heal them and will help weak organs when used as a bandage, relieve septic finger and heal spots and the ulcers on the hands and feet.

When myrtle is used to rub the body it eliminates sweat, dries the excess wetness and dissipates underarm odor. When one sits in the water that myrtle was cooked in, it will help against infections on the buttocks and vagina and will heal weak joints and also broken bones, when it is poured on the wound.

Also, myrtle helps eliminate dandruff and the wet ulcers and the spots that appear on the head. It also helps the hair against falling and gives it a black color. When myrtle leaves are ground with a little water and then blended with some oil or rose grease and then used as a bandage, it will be suitable against fresh (or humid) ulcers, canker sores, erysipelas (skin infection), acute tumors, urticaria (hives) and hemorrhoids.

Myrtle seeds also help against hemoptysis (spiting up blood) of the chest and lungs. It also coats the stomach and does not harm the chest or the stomach and cleanses them. It also helps against diarrhea and coughing, and this is a special quality for myrtle that is rarely found in other medications. Myrtle seeds also help urine production and heal vesica (bladder) infections, spider bites and scorpion stings. Using myrtle roots to clean between the teeth is harmful, though.

Persian *Raihan*, which is also called *Hibq*, is hot, and when its scent is smelled, it helps against hot headaches when water is sprinkled on the Hibq and then is allowed to cool down. It is also said that this kind of myrtle is cold, but it looks like it has some of the four types of temperament. It also helps bring sleep to the eye.

The seeds of Persian myrtle relieve diarrhea of the bile, stomach, strengthen the heart and help against black bile ailments.

3. *Rumman* (Pomegranate)

Allah said:

﴿ فِيهِمَا فَٰكِهَةٌ وَنَخۡلٌ وَرُمَّانٌ ﴾

``In them (both) will be fruits, and date palms and pomegranates.'' (55:68)

Also, `Ali رَضِيَ الله عَنْهُ was reported to have said: ``Eat *Rumman* with its pulp, because it coats the stomach.''

Sweet pomegranate is hot and wet, good for the stomach, and strengthens it because of its being a mild constipating agent. It is also good for the throat, chest and lungs, along with relieving coughing. The water (or juice) in the pomegranate softens the stomach and is a nutrient for the body. It also digests quickly because it is light and produces heat along with some air in the stomach. It helps increase the semen production and is not favorable for those who have fever. Pomegranate has a special quality, that is, when one eats bread with it, it prevents it from being spoiled.

Bitter pomegranate is cold and dry and constipates mildly. It is also good for overheated stomach and helps produce more urine than the other types of pomegranate. It also softens bile symptoms, relieves diarrhea, prevents vomiting and is slightly tarry. It also stops the heat in the liver, strengthens the organs, helps against bilious shaking, heartaches and the ache of the tip of the stomach. It also helps the stomach and rids it of excrements and extinguishes the bile and benefits the blood.

When pomegranate's juice is extracted and is cooked with some honey until it becomes like an ointment and used as eye drops, it will clear the yellow color from the eye and will dissipate the thick wetness. When it is placed on the gingival (gums), it will help against the rashes that appear on the gingival. Also, pomegranate juice extracted with the rind will work as a laxative and will rid the body from septic bilious moistures, along with helping against short-term fever.

As for sour pomegranate, its qualities are in the middle between the two other kinds we mentioned, although this kind leans more towards being sour. Pomegranate seeds that are mixed with honey will alleviate septic finger and malignant ulcers. Pomegranate flowers also help heal wounds. It is said that if one swallows three pomegranate flowers each year, he will be immune from ophthalmia (conjunctivitis) for an entire year.

The Letter *Zay*

1. *Zait*[1] (Olive Oil)

Allah said:

﴿ يُوقَدُ مِن شَجَرَةٍ مُّبَٰرَكَةٍ زَيْتُونَةٍ لَّا شَرْقِيَّةٍ وَلَا غَرْبِيَّةٍ يَكَادُ زَيْتُهَا يُضِىٓءُ وَلَوْ لَمْ تَمْسَسْهُ نَارٌ ﴾

``Lit from a blessed tree, an olive, neither of the east (i.e. neither it gets sun-rays only in the morning) nor of the west (i.e. nor it gets sun-rays only in the afternoon, but it is exposed to the

(1) * Editor's note : Oil was understood to mean olive oil.

sun all day long), whose oil would almost glow forth (of itself), though no fire touched it." (24:35)

At-Tirmidhi and Ibn Majah narrated that Abu Hurairah رَضِيَ الله عَنْهُ related from the Prophet ﷺ that he said:

« كلو الزَّيْت وادَّهِنُوا به؛ فإنه من شَجَرةٍ مباركةٍ » (ابن ماجه : ٣٣٢٠ وانظر الصحيحه:٣٧٩)

``Eat the Zait and use it as an ointment, because it is produced by a blessed tree."

Al-Bayhaqi and Ibn Majah also narrated that `Abdullh bin `Umar رَضِيَ الله عَنْهما said that the Messenger of Allah ﷺ said:

« ائْتَدِموا بالزيتِ وادَّهِنوا به، فإنه من شَجَرة مبارَكةٍ » (أيضاً ابن ماجه : ٣٣١٩)

``Eat oil and use it as an ointment because it is from a blessed tree (olive tree)."

Zait is hot and wet in the first degree. Also, the quality of the oil depends on the tree that produces it. For instance, the best type of olive oil is that squeezed from ripe olives, while oil from unripe olives is cold and dry. Red olives produce oil that is between these while black olives produce hot and wet oil. Olive oil helps against poisons, works as a laxative and rids the body of worms. Old olive oil leans more towards being hot and decomposing. When the oil is blended with water, it becomes less hot and milder and thus more beneficial. All kinds of olive oil soften the skin and slow the aging process. The salty water blended with oil helps burned skin against blistering. It also strengthens the gingiva (gums), while olive leaves help against erysipelas (skin infections), sores, septic ulcers and urticaria (hives). There are many other benefits for olive oil.

2. *Zubd* (Butter)

Abu Dawud narrated in his *Sunan* that the two children of Busr said, ``The Messenger of Allah ﷺ came by us and we offered him some butter and dried dates, as he used to like eating butter and dried dates."

Butter is hot and wet and has many benefits, such as maturing the mixtures (bodily wastes) and decomposing them, along with relieving the tumors that appear next to the ears and ureters (tubes leading from the kidney to the bladder). When butter is used alone it also heals mouth cankers and the various other types of tumors that attack children and women. When one licks butter, it will help against lung hemoptysis (spitting up blood) and will mature the tumors of the lungs.

Butter softens the nature, the nerves and the hard tumors that result from black bile and phlegm and relieves the dryness in the body. When butter is laid on the place where children's teeth emerge, it will help the teeth grow. Butter also soothes the coughing that accompanies colds and dryness. It also heals herpes and the roughness in the body and works as a laxative. Yet, butter reduces the appetite and the sweetness of honey and dates.

The wisdom behind the Prophet ﷺ eating dried dates with butter is that they would neutralize the effect of each other.

3. *Zabib* (Raisins)

The best type of *Zabib* is the largest in size, the fattest and that has thin skin and small seeds, especially when the seeds are removed before eating them. Raisins are hot and wet in the first degree, while their seeds are cold and dry.

Raisins are similar to the type of grape they are made of, as sweet raisins are hot, sour raisins are cold and constipating and white raisins are more effective constipating agents. Raisin pulp is suitable for the windpipe and relieves coughing and liver and prostate pain. It also strengthens the stomach and soothes the intestinal cavity.

Sweet raisin pulps are more nutritious than grapes, but less nutritious than dried figs. Also, sweet raisin pulps possess maturing qualities and mildly constipate. In general, raisins strengthen the stomach, the spleen and the liver and benefit the throat, chest, lung, liver and prostate.

The best way to have raisins is to eat them without the seeds. Raisins provide good nutrition and do not cause clogs like dates do. Eating raisins with their seeds will increase the nutritious intake and will benefit the stomach, liver and spleen. When one is suffering from loose nails and places raisin pulps on them, they will remove the nails quickly. Sweet, seedless raisins benefit those who suffer from excessive wetness and phlegm and help the liver.

Raisins also help memory power, as Az-Zuhri said, ``Those who seek to memorize the *Hadith* should eat raisins.'' Also, it was reported that Abdullah Ibn 'Abbas described the raisins that, ``Their seeds are an ailment while their pulp is a cure.''

4. *Zanjabil* (Ginger)

Allah said:

﴿وَيُسْقَوْنَ فِيهَا كَأْسًا كَانَ مِزَاجُهَا زَنجَبِيلًا﴾

``And they will be given to drink there of a cup (of wine) mixed with Zanjabil (ginger).'' (76:17)

Abu Nu'aym also narrated in his book on the Prophetic medicine that Abu Sa'eed Al-Khudri رَضِيَ الله عَنْهُ said:

« أهدى ملك الرُّوم إلى رسولِ الله صلى اللهَ عليه وسلم جَرَّةَ زَنْجَبيلٍ، فأطعم كلَّ إنسان قِطعةً، وأَطْعَمَني قِطْعَةً » (لم نجده لعدم الكتاب المذكور)

``The Byzantine king gave the Messenger of Allah ﷺ a barrel of ginger as a gift and he gave each person a part of it. I too got a piece.''

Ginger is hot in the second degree and wet in the first degree. It heats the body, helps the digestion process, softens the stomach mildly, helps open the clogs of the liver that are caused by coldness and wetness and helps against the wetness that causes sight impairment, when it is eaten or used as kohl. Ginger also strengthens the sexual power and decomposes the thick gases accumulating in the intestines and the stomach.

In general, ginger is good for the cold temperament of the liver and the stomach. When one takes some ginger along with two measures of sugar and some hot water, it will work as a laxative and will rid the body of harmful excrements. Ginger is an effective ingredient in the ointments that dissolve the phlegm.

Sour ginger is hot and dry and it excites the sexual drive, increases semen production, heats the stomach and the liver, helps the digestion process, dries the phlegm that prevails in the body and increases the memory power. It is also suitable for the coldness in the liver and stomach and washes the harmful effect of eating fruit. It also makes the scent better and fends off the harm of thick, cold foods.

The Letter *Seen*

1. *Senna*

We mentioned *Senna* before and stated that it is also called *Sanut*. There are seven opinions regarding what the word *Senna* means.

Senna is said to mean honey, the thick juice that appears on the surface of the butter and which looks like black stripes, cumin like seeds, Persian cumin, dill, dried dates or fennel.

2. *Safarjal* (Quince)

Quince is cold and dry, constipates and benefits the stomach. Sweet quince is cold and dry and is somewhat mild. Sour quince constipates more than sweet quince and is colder and drier. All types of Safarjal quench the thirst, stop vomiting, help produce urine and constipate. Safarjal also helps against stomach ulcers, hemoptysis (spitting up blood), diarrhea and nausea. Safarjal also prevents the ascending of gaseous material when one eats it after the meal. Also, the ashes of washed Safarjal leaves and stems are similar to zinc in benefit.

Consuming *Safarjal* before the meal constipates, while consuming it after the meals softens the stool and helps the digestion process. Eating excessive amounts of *Safarjal* harms the nerves and causes painful constipation. *Safarjal* helps extinguish the yellow bile of the stomach.

When the quince is broiled, it will become softer and milder. When one removes the pips of the quince, stuffs them with honey, dips them in a paste and then broil them under hot ashes, they will become very beneficial.

The best way to eat the quince is broiled or cooked in honey. The seeds of *Safarjal* also help against dryness in the throat, the windpipe and several other ailments. Its oil stops sweating and strengthens the stomach. *Safarjal* jam also strengthens the stomach and the liver and relieves the heart and the soul.

3. Siwak

In the *Sahihain* it is narrated that the Prophet ﷺ said:

«لَوْ لاَ أن أَشُقَّ على أمَّتي: لأمرتُهم بالسِّواك عند كل صَلاَة » (البخاري:٨٨٧)

``If it was not for the fact that my nation would not be able to bear it, I would have ordered them to use Siwak before every prayer."

Also, in the *Sahihain* it is narrated that:

« أنه صلى اللهُ عليه وسلم كان إذا قامَ من اللَّيل: يَشُوصُ فاهُ بالسِّواك » (البخاري:٢٤٥)

``Whenever the Prophet would wake up at night, he would clean his mouth with Siwak."

Al-Bukhari also narrated that the Prophet ﷺ said:

« السِّوَاك مَطْهَرَةٌ لِلْفَم، مرضَاة للربِّ »(النسائي:٥ صححه الألباني)

" Siwak cleans the mouth and pleases the Lord."

Further, Muslim narrated that:

« أنه صلى اللهُ عليه وسلم كان إذا دخل بيتَه: بدأَ بالسِّواك » (مسلم:٢٥٣)

"Whenever the Prophet would enter his house, he would first use the Siwak ."

There are many other *Ahadith* on this subject.

An authentic *Hadith* also stated that just before he died, the Prophet used the *Siwak*. The Prophet ﷺ also said:

« أكثرتُ عليكم في السِّواك » (البخاري:٨٨٨)

"I have troubled you by frequently stressing using the Siwak ."

The best type of *Siwak* is made from Arak trees. Further, one should not use an unknown tree for *Siwak* for it might be poisonous. Also, *Siwak* should be used moderately, because it might cause the coating of the teeth to wear away and thus the teeth will be susceptible to the hot vapors or gasses that ascend from the stomach and to all kinds of dirt. When the *Siwak* is used moderately, it will polish the teeth, strengthen the roots of the teeth, help the tongue, prevent plaque, perfume the breath, clear the mind and strengthen the appetite.

The best way to use the *Siwak* is by soaking it in rose water. Also, the best type of *Siwak* is made from walnut stems. The author of *At-Taysir* said, "It was said that when one uses the *Siwak* once every five days, it will clear the head, sharpen the senses and alert the mind."

Siwak is beneficial for many reasons, such as perfuming the breath, strengthening the gingiva, clearing the phlegm and the sight and preventing cavities. It also preserves the health of the stomach, clears the voice, helps the digestion process, helps make the speech clear and encourages one to recite the Qur'an, remember Allah and pray. *Siwak* also fights sleepiness, pleases the Lord, delights the angels and increases the number of the good deeds.

Siwak is preferred at any time, especially before the prayer, ablution, when waking up and when the mouth emits foul odor. It is also preferred for those who are fasting and all other people at all times. There are

Ahadith that allow this practice for those who are fasting, because it is beneficial for them and pleases the Lord. Pleasing the Lord when one is fasting is even more desired than at other times. Also the *Siwak* cleans the mouth, and cleanliness for the fasting person is one of his best deeds.

In the *Sunan* it is narrated that `Amir bin Rab'ah رَضِيَ الله عَنْهُ said: ``I saw the Messenger of Allah ﷺ on numerous occasion using the *Siwak* when he was fasting."

Al-Bukhari also said that Ibn `Umar رَضِيَ الله عَنْهما said that the Prophet used the *Siwak* at the two ends of the day.

There is a consensus that the fasting person rinses his mouth while performing ablution, and rinsing the mouth is an obligation or a more preferred act than using the *Siwak*. Also, Allah does not have a use for the people to worship him while their mouths are emitting foul odor, nor is it an act of worship. When the Prophet ﷺ mentioned that the odor that the mouth of the fasting person emits is better in His Sight than the scent of Musk , he meant to encourage the practice of fasting, not the practice of allowing the mouth to emit foul odor. Hence the fasting person needs the *Siwak* more than anyone else. Also, Allah's Pleasure is much better than His preferring the odor that the mouth of the fasting person emits.

Further, Allah prefers using the *Siwak* more than for the odor that comes out of the mouth of the fasting person to remain.

Also, using *Siwak* does not prevent the good scent that Allah creates in the fasting person's mouth on the Day of Resurrection. Rather, the mouth of the fasting person will smell better than Musk on the Day of Resurrection as a sign of his observing the Fast, even if the odor that used to come from his mouth was removed by the *Siwak*. Similarly, whoever suffers a wound [for the sake of Allah] in this life is commanded to remove the blood from his body in this life, but his wound would still have the color of blood on the Day of Resurrection.

Furthermore, the *Siwak* does not completely remove the odor of the mouth for the fasting person because its reason still remains, that is, the stomach being empty of food. Only the effect of this fact will be lessened from the teeth and gums.

The Prophet ﷺ taught his nation the preferred and the disliked acts of the Fast. He did not mention the Siwak among the disliked acts although he knew they were using it. Rather, he encouraged them in general to use the *Siwak* and they saw him using it himself at innumerable times, knowing that they would imitate him. Never did he discourage them from using the *Siwak* in the afternoon (when they are fasting). It is a fact that the Prophet ﷺ is required to offer the religious ruling when it is needed.

4. *Samn* (Shortening)

There is a weak *Hadith* that narrates that the Prophet ﷺ encouraged the Muslim to drink cow milk, because it is a remedy and because the butter of that milk is a cure, while stating that cow meat is an ailment. The chain of narrators for this *Hadith* is not authentic.

Samn is hot and wet in the first degree and it is mild and helps eliminate the various tumors that attack the soft parts of the body. *Samn* is stronger than butter as a maturing agent. Galinus said that he used shortening to cure the tumors that occur in the ear and the tip of the nose. Also, when the base of the teeth is anointed with shortening, the teeth will emerge faster.

When shortening is blended with honey and bitter almonds, it will clear the chest and the lungs and will dissipate various ailments. Shortening is harmful for the stomach, especially if the person has a mucus condition.

When the shortening made of cow and goat milk is mixed with honey, it helps against toxic materials and snake and scorpion stings. Ibn As-Sunni mentioned that `Ali رَضِيَ الله عَنْهُ said that the people never use a better remedy than shortening.

5. *Samak* (Fish)

Imam Ahmad and Ibn Majah narrated that 'Abdullh Ibn 'Umar ﵄ said that the Prophet ﷺ said:

«أُحِلَّتْ لنا مَيتَتان ودَمَان: السَّمَكُ والجَرَاد، والكَبِد والطِّحال»

(ابن ماجه: ٣٣١٤ وصححه الألباني)

``We were allowed two dead animals and two bloods: fish and locust, and liver and spleen."

There are many kinds of fish, the best of which is the most delicious, the best scented, moderate in size, which has fine scales, the softest meat, which live in fresh water that flows on pebbles and which eat plants and not organic waste. The best areas for the fish to live are those with the freshest water that runs through rocks, then the areas that have sandy ground void of filth or wastes and which are mildly calm and exposed to the sun and wind.

Sea fish are also soft and delicious. The meat of sea fish that has soft skin is cold and wet, difficult to digest and produces excessive amounts of phlegm, but also produce acceptable temperament, increase semen production and fertility and suit hot conditions.

The best kind of salted fish is the most recently salted. Salted fish is hot and dry, and the older they get the hotter and drier they become. Silurid (similar to catfish) is very viscous, and the Jews do not eat this type of fish. Yet, soft silurid meat softens the stomach, and when it is salted, kept and then eaten, it will clear the windpipe and make the voice finer. When it is ground and used as an external ointment, it will extract the wastes that accumulate inside the body, as it has the quality of extracting such substances.

Sitting in the salty water of silurid relives the effects of newly formed ulcers and extracts the harmful substances to the surface. Salty water of silurid also relieves sciatic nerve ailment when one is injected with it.

The best part of fish meat is closer to the tail, and the soft and fatty fish meat produces fatness and flesh.

In the *Sahihain* it is also narrated that Jabir bin 'Abdullh رَضِيَ الله عَنْهُ said, ``The Prophet ﷺ sent us with three hundred riders under the leadership of Abu 'Ubaidah bin Al-Jarrah. We went by the seashore and were soon very hungry until we ate tree leaves. The sea then threw out a whale that is called `Anbar. We ate from it for a half a month and also used its fat in our food. Abu 'Ubaidah then took a rib of the fish and asked a man to ride on his camel and then pass under the rib, which he easily did."

6. *Silqh* (Chard)

At-Tirmidhi and Abu Dawud narrated that Umm Al-Munthir said, ``The Messenger of Allah ﷺ came by along with 'Ali رَضِيَ الله عَنْهُ , when he was still recovering from an illness. Then, we had some hanging clusters of dates. The Messenger of Allah ﷺ started eating from it, and he (Ali) joined him. The Messenger of Allah ﷺ then said to him:

« مَهْ يا عليُّ ! فإنك ناقِهٌ »..... « يا عِلِيُّ، فأَصِبْ من هَذا: فإنه أوفَقُ لك»

(أبو داود:٣٨٥٦ وحسنه الألباني)

``You are still recuperating, until `Ali stopped eating.' I then made some barley with chard and brought it to them. The Prophet ﷺ said, to `Ali رَضِيَ الله عَنْهُ `Eat from this; this is more beneficial for you.' "

Silqh is hot and dry in the first degree and has a soothing coolness in it. Chard also decomposes and opens the clogs. The black chard constipates and helps against alopecia (A skin disease characterized by loss of hair, partial or total), spots, dandruff and warts if its water is used as ointment. It also kills lice and is used as ointment when blended with honey to cure herpes. Silqh also opens the clogs in the liver and spleen.

The black chard constipates as we have stated, especially when taken with lentils, both of which are not suitable for the stomach. However, white chard with lentils softens the stomach and is used as a laxative and is used to treat hemiplegia (Paralysis affecting only one side of the body), when blended with food aliments and condiments.

Yet, it is not nutritious, produces harmful mixtures and burns the blood. Eating it with vinegar and mustard helps neutralize these side effects. Finally, eating it excessively causes constipation and flatulence.

The Letter *Shine*

1. *Shuneiz* (The Black Seed)

We talked about the Black Seed before under the letter `*Haa.*

2. *Shubrum* (Euphorb)

At-Tirmidhi and Ibn Mjah narrated that the Messenger of Allah asked Asma' bint `Umais رَضِيَ الله عَنْها

«بماذا كنتِ تَسْتَمْشِينَ؟ قَالَت: بالشُّبْرُم. قال: حارٌ جارٌ» (ابن ماجه: ٣٤٦١ وضعفه الألباني)

``How do you treat constipation? She said, `with Shubrum '. The Prophet ﷺ said, `Hot and too strong of a laxative."

Shubrum is a small tree that sometimes grows to be as tall as a man. The *Shubrum* has red branches with some whiteness, while the tips of its branches end with a cluster of leaves. *Shubrum* flowers are small and yellowish with some whiteness. When its flowers they fall they are replaced by small stems that have small grains and which look like terebinth. The color of these stems is reddish and has red peels that cover its ribs. The parts of the Shubrum that are used are its peels, ribs and stem extract.

Shubrum is hot and dry in the fourth degree and drives away the black bile, yellow water and phlegm. It also causes nausea and distress. Using it in excessive amounts might even case death. When intending to use the Shubrum , it should first be soaked in milk for a day and a night, and the milk should be changed twice or thrice during the day. Then, the Shubrum should be dried in the shadow and blended with roses, tragacanth (also known as goats' horn) and then consumed with honey water or grape juice.

Two to four small measures of the *Shubrum* constitute one dose. We should state that Hunain said, ``As for *Shubrum* milk, I do not see any goodness in it and thus do not recommend it. Common doctors have killed many people with it."

3. *Shaiir* (Barley)

Ibn Majah narrated that 'Aishah رَضِيَ الله عَنْها said: ``When a member of the family of the Messenger of Allah ﷺ would fall sick, he would order that barley soup is made and then the ill person would be commanded to have some of it. He used to say, `It strengthens the heart of the sad person and relieves the heart of the ill person, just as one of you would wash the dirt off of her face with water.' "

We mentioned that the remedy mentioned in this *Hadith* entails boiled barley water which is more nutritious than its flour. Barley water helps against coughing and throat roughness, relieves the irritant excess excrement, produces more urine, cleanses the stomach, quenches the thirst and extinguishes heat. It also provides comfort and has a decomposing quality.

This remedy entails preparing a portion of a good type of barley and five times as much water, placing them in a clean pot and cooking them under moderate temperature until only two fifths of the mixture remains in the pot. The resulting soup is then purified and used as much as needed.

4. *Shawii* (Roasted Meat)

Allah said that when Prophet Ibrahim عليه السلام had the honorable guests:

﴿فَمَا لَبِثَ أَن جَآءَ بِعِجْلٍ حَنِيذٍ﴾

``And he hastened to entertain them with a roasted calf." (11:69)

Ibrahim عليه السلام had roasted the calf on heated stones.

At-Tirmidhi narrated that Umm Salamah رَضِي الله عَنْهُ said that she once brought the Prophet ﷺ a roasted piece of meat and that he ate from it and then stood up to pray without repeating the ablution. At-Tirmidhi then commented that this *Hadith* is authentic. At-Tirmidhi also narrated that `Abdullh bin Al-Harith said, ``We ate some roasted meat with the Messenger of Allah ﷺ inside the mosque." Further, At-Tirmidhi narrated that Al-Mughirah bin Shu`bah رَضِي الله عَنْهُ said, ``I was a guest of the Messenger of Allah ﷺ one night and he ordered that a piece of meat be roasted and then took the blade and started to cut pieces of it for me. Then, Bilal came to make the call to prayer and the Prophet ﷺ dropped the blade and said, `What is the matter with him?"

The best type of roast is the meat of a one-year old sheep, then a fat sheep. This type of food is hot and wet, produces black bile, but is one of the most nutritious foods for healthy, ill and recovering persons alike. Cooked meat is better, lighter on the stomach and also has more wetness. Fried meat is less beneficial while meat dried in the sun is the worst kind. Also, roasting meat on burning stones is better than flame broiled meats.

5. *Shaíhm* (Fat or Grease)

In *Al-Musnad* it is narrated that Anas رَضِي الله عَنْهُ said that a Jewish man asked the Prophet ﷺ to be his guest and that he offered him some barley bread and melted grease.

In the *Sahih* it is also narrated that `Abdullah bin Mughaffal said, ``On the Day of Khaibar, a bag full of grease was lowered and I took possession of it and said, `By Allah! I will not give anyone any of it!' When I turned around I found that the Messenger of Allah ﷺ was laughing and did not comment.' "

The best type of grease is that taken from a grown animal. Grease is hot and wet but less wet than clarified butter. This is why when both grease and clarified butter are melted, grease hardens faster.

Grease helps against throat roughness, it represses and causes rotting. To neutralize the harmful effects of grease, one should use lemon, salt and ginger. Also, goat grease constipates more than any other type of grease, while billy goat grease is more decomposing and helps against stomach ulcers. Goat grease helps against stomach ulcers and is used as an injection to relieve excoriation (the rubbing away of skin from injury or disease), and tenesmus (spasms of the bladder or anus).

The Letter *Sad*

1. The *Salat* (The Formal Prayer)

Allah said:

﴿ وَٱسْتَعِينُوا۟ بِٱلصَّبْرِ وَٱلصَّلَوٰةِ ۚ وَإِنَّهَا لَكَبِيرَةٌ إِلَّا عَلَى ٱلْخَـٰشِعِينَ ﴾

``And seek help in patience and *As-Salat* (the prayer) and truly, it is extremely heavy and hard except for *Al-Khshi`n* [i.e. the true believers in Allah – those who obey Allah with full submission, fear much from His punishment, and believe in His Promise (Paradise) and in His Warnings (Hell)]." (2:45)

And:

﴿ يَـٰٓأَيُّهَا ٱلَّذِينَ ءَامَنُوا۟ ٱسْتَعِينُوا۟ بِٱلصَّبْرِ وَٱلصَّلَوٰةِ ۚ إِنَّ ٱللَّهَ مَعَ ٱلصَّـٰبِرِينَ ﴾

``O you who believe! Seek help in patience and As-Salat (the prayer). Truly, Allah is with As-Sabirun (the patient)." (2:153)

Also, Allah said,

﴿ وَأْمُرْ أَهْلَكَ بِٱلصَّلَوٰةِ وَٱصْطَبِرْ عَلَيْهَا ۖ لَا نَسْـَٔلُكَ رِزْقًا ۖ نَّحْنُ نَرْزُقُكَ ۗ وَٱلْعَـٰقِبَةُ لِلتَّقْوَىٰ ﴾

``And enjoin As-Salat (the prayer) on your family, and be patient in offering them [i.e. the Salat (prayers)]. We ask not of you a provision (i.e. to give Us something: money): We provide for you. And the good end (i.e. Paradise) is for the Muttaqun (the pious)." (20:132)

Furthermore, in the *Sunan* it is narrated:

«كان رسولُ الله صلى الله عليه وسلم إذا حزَبه أمرٌ فزِع إلى الصَّلاة»

(أبو داود: ١٣١٩ وحسنه الألباني)

``Whenever the Messenger of Allah ﷺ would be concerned about a matter, he would turn to prayer."

We also mentioned using the prayer as a cure for various types of illnesses before these illnesses progress.

The prayer brings about sustenance, preserves the health, discards harm, eradicates illness, strengthens the heart, radiates the face with light, brings joy to the soul and dissipates laziness. Also, the prayer energizes the limbs, sustains power, opens the chest, nourishes the soul, brings light to the heart, protects the bounty, shields from the anger (of Allah), brings about blessings, takes one away from Satan and draws him closer to the Most Beneficent.

In general, the prayer has a profound effect in preserving the health of the body and the heart. The prayer also discards harmful substances. No two persons would catch a type of disease or suffer an affliction, but whoever prays among them would suffer the minimal effects of the illness or the affliction.

The prayer has a profoundly wonderful effect in repelling the evils of this life, especially when the prayer is given its due right inwardly and outwardly. Certainly, the evils of this life and the Next Life would be most effectively repelled while their good would be most effectively brought forth through prayer. The secret in this is that the prayer is the connection with Allah. The closer the connection is between the slave and his Lord, the more open the doors of all types of good will be for him, while closing the ways to evil. In this case, the tools of success will descend on the slave from his Lord, along with good health, many bounties and riches, comfort, delight, joy, happiness and the good things of life.

2. *Sabr* (Patience)

Sabr , patience, is one half of Faith, which is half patience and half praise and thankfulness. Some of the *Salaf* said, ``Iman has two halves, one half patience and one half praise (and appreciation)." Allah said:

﴿إِنَّ فِي ذَٰلِكَ لَآيَاتٍ لِّكُلِّ صَبَّارٍ شَكُورٍ﴾

``Verily, in this are indeed signs for every steadfast, grateful (person)." (4:5)

To Faith, *Sabr* is just like the head to the body. There are three types of Sabr . First, there is the *Sabr* while performing Allah's Commands, so that one does not ignore [or get bored with] them. There is a Sabr with shunning the prohibitions, so that one does not violate them. There is also a *Sabr* with the appointed destiny and decisions of Allah, so that one is not enraged because of them. When one acquires all three types of *Sabr* , his *Sabr* will be complete and the delight of this and the Next Life will be whole, along with gaining and winning in both lives. No person shall achieve these great prizes except by passing on the bridge of *Sabr* , just as no person will reach Paradise except by passing over the *Sirat* (the bridge over hell). 'Umar رَضِيَ الله عَنْهُ said, ``We achieve the best living by *Sabr*."

When one thinks about the grades of perfection achieved in this life, he will realize that all of them are connected to *Sabr*. On the other hand, when one thinks about the blame worthy types of failure that one can and should avoid, he will realize that they are all connected to impatience. For instance, courage, honor, generosity and preferring others with good things are patience for a short time only (meaning this life is short).

Much of the illnesses and the sicknesses that attack the body and the heart are a result of impatience. Also, *Sabr* is the best preserver for the health of the heart, the body and the soul, as it is the great distinction and the biggest cure. If *Sabr* only carries the reward of Allah being with the patient slaves and His love for them, it would be sufficient. Allah loves *Sabr* and supports its people:

« إن النَّصْرَ مع الصبر » (الترمذي ٢٥١٦ وأحمد ١/ ٣٠٧ وصححه في التحقيق)

``Certainly, victory comes with patience"

Also, patience is good for its people.

﴿ وَلَئِن صَبَرْتُمْ لَهُوَ خَيْرٌ لِّلصَّـٰبِرِينَ ﴾

``But if you endure patiently, verily, it is better for As-Sabirun (the patient)." (16:126)

Further, patience is the tool to achieve success.

﴿ يَـٰٓأَيُّهَا ٱلَّذِينَ ءَامَنُوا۟ ٱصْبِرُوا۟ وَصَابِرُوا۟ وَرَابِطُوا۟ وَٱتَّقُوا۟ ٱللَّهَ لَعَلَّكُمْ تُفْلِحُونَ ﴾

``O you who believe! Endure and be more patient (than your enemy), and guard your territory by stationing army units permanently at the places from where the enemy can attack you, and fear Allah, so that you may be successful." (3:200)

3. *Sabir* (Aloe)

Sabir has many benefits, especially the Indian *Sabir*, as it rids the body of bilious excrements in the brain and the optic nerves. When the *Sabir* is used as an ointment on the forehead and the cheeks, after blending it with rose oil, it helps relieve headaches. It also helps relieve the sores and cankers that appear in the mouth and nose and helps against black bile and depression.

The Persian *Sabir* sharpens the mind and brings firmness to the heart, and also releases from the body bilious mixtures and the phlegm that accumulates in the stomach, when one takes two spoons of Sabir mixed with water.

Caution: drinking *Sabir* in cold weather might cause diarrhea with blood.

4. *Sawm* (Fasting)

Fasting is a shield from many illnesses of the soul, the heart and the body and has tremendous benefits. Fasting also preserves the health and rids the body of harmful substances while preventing it from consuming what might harm it, especially when one fasts in the best times that the religion states or when the body needs it. Fasting relieves the muscles and the rest of the body and ensures regenerating its strength. Fasting also has a characteristic that should make one eagerly prefer it, that is, bringing joy and relief to the heart sooner or later (i.e. on the Last Day). Fasting is the best resort for those suffering from excess bodily moistures and substances and also protects and preserves their health.

Fasting is a type of spiritual and physical remedy. When the fasting person observes various rulings and guidelines regarding the Fast, his heart and body will benefit from the Fast the most. Also, the body will get rid of the harmful foreign substances that his body is susceptible to receive, along with getting rid of the harmful substances that have already penetrated the body. The Fast also helps the fasting person to stay away from what he is supposed to avoid and to implement and seek the goals behind the Fast and what it is supposed to achieve for him. Fasting does not only entail abstaining from food and drink. There is another goal that fasting seeks to achieve which made it an act that Allah will specify its reward [only on the Day of Judgment]. The Fast is also a shield between the slave and what might harm his body and soul sooner or later, and this is why Allah said,

﴿ يَٰٓأَيُّهَا ٱلَّذِينَ ءَامَنُوا۟ كُتِبَ عَلَيْكُمُ ٱلصِّيَامُ كَمَا كُتِبَ عَلَى ٱلَّذِينَ مِن قَبْلِكُمْ
لَعَلَّكُمْ تَتَّقُونَ ﴾

``O you who believe! Observing As-Saum (the fasting) is prescribed for you as it was prescribed for those before you, that you may become Al-Muttaqun (the pious)." (2:183)

Fasting is a shield and a protection making it a type of tremendously beneficial diet. Another goal that the Fast seeks to achieve is the heart being busy with Allah, thus enlisting and recruiting the various powers of the body to implement what Allah loves and the requirements of worshiping Him. We mentioned some of the secrets of the Fast when we mentioned the Prophet's guidance on this subject.

The Letter *Dhad*

1. *Dhabb* (Lizards)

In the *Sahihain* it is narrated that Ibn 'Abbas رَضِيَ الله عَنْهما said that the Messenger of Allah ﷺ was asked if eating the *Dhabb* was disallowed, because he did not eat from it when it was presented to him. The Prophet ﷺ replied:

« لا؛ ولكنْ لم يكن بأَرْضِ قَوْمي، فأجِدُني أعافُه » (البخاري:٥٣٩١)

``No. But this food is not found in my people's land and I do not have the appetite to eat it."

The *Dhabb* was then eaten in the presence of the Prophet ﷺ. Also, in the *Sahihain* it is narrated that Ibn 'Umar رضي الله عنه related from the Prophet ﷺ that he said:

« لا أُحِلُّه، ولا أُحَرِّمُه » (البخاري:٥٥٩٦)

``I neither allow it nor disallow it."

The meat of the *Dhabb* is hot and dry and strengthens the sexual drive. When it is ground and placed on a thorn that pierced someone's skin, it will extract the thorn.

2. *Dhifdi`* (Frog)

Imam Ahmad said, ``(Killing) frogs is not allowed for medicinal purposes, because the Messenger of Allah ﷺ has disallowed killing them." Ahmad was referring to the *Hadith* that he narrated in his *Musnad* in which 'Uthman bin Abdur-Rahman said that a doctor mentioned using frogs for medicinal purposes, and the Messenger disallowed killing them.

The author of `*Al-Qanoon* said, ``Eating the meat or the blood of the frog might cause swellings in the body, pale color and [uncontrollable] ejaculation until death. This is why the doctors hesitate to use it for medicinal purpose because of its harm." There are two types of frogs, land and water frogs. Some of the land frogs are poisonous.

The Letter *Ta'*

1. *Teeb* (Perfume)

The Messenger of Allah ﷺ said:

« حُبِّبَ إِلَيَّ من دُنياكم النساءُ والطِّيبُ؛ وجُعِلَتْ قُرَّةُ عيني في الصَّلاة »

(النسائي: ٣٩٤٠، ٣٩٣٩ وصححه الألباني)

``From your world, women and Teeb (perfume) were made beloved to me and the comfort of my eye is the prayer."

The Messenger of Allah ﷺ used to frequently use *Teeb* and did not like foul odors.

Teeb (perfume) is the fuel of the soul, which is the engine of the powers of the body. Therefore, various strengths and powers in the body are nurtured in the presence of *Teeb*. Similarly, the powers of the body are nurtured by consuming food and drink, feeling comfort and elation, being close to loved ones, receiving good news and by the absence of hateful, disliked persons whose presence is heavy on the heart. Indeed, associating with disliked persons weakens the strength and causes sadness and depression, just as the effects that fever and foul odor have on the body. This is why the Companions of the Messenger were disallowed from acquiring the characteristics that would bother the Prophet and make them detested and disliked by him. Allah said:

﴿إِذَا دُعِيتُمْ فَادْخُلُوا فَإِذَا طَعِمْتُمْ فَانتَشِرُوا وَلَا مُسْتَـْٔنِسِينَ لِحَدِيثٍ إِنَّ ذَٰلِكُمْ كَانَ يُؤْذِى النَّبِىَّ فَيَسْتَحْىِۦ مِنكُمْ وَاللَّهُ لَا يَسْتَحْىِۦ مِنَ الْحَقِّ﴾

``But when you are invited, enter, and when you have taken your meal, disperse without sitting for a talk. Verily, such (behaviour) annoys the Prophet, and he is shy of (asking) you (to go); but Allah is not shy of (telling you) the truth." (33:53)

In short, the *Teeb*, perfume, was one of the dearest objects to the Prophet of Allah ﷺ. It also has a good effect on preserving good health and removing many ailments because it arouses the power of the body.

2. Teen (Clay or Argil)

Several invented *Ahadith* were mentioned regarding the benefits of clay. We should state that every *Hadith* that talks about the benefit of clay is untrue and must not be related from the Messenger of Allah. Clay is harmful and causes clogs in the veins, and it is cold, dry and a strong drying agent. Also, clay prevents diarrhea and causes hemorrhages and sours in the mouth.

3. *Talh* (Banana or Acacia)

Allah said:

﴿وَطَلْحٍ مَّنضُودٍ﴾

``And among Talh (banana-trees) with fruits piled one above another." (56:29)

The majority of the scholars said that *Talh* means bananas, as they grow in piles one over the other just as the comb's teeth. It was said that the *Talh* is the tree that has thorns and which get replaced by fruits, each in the place of a thorn, just like what occurs on banana trees. This is the best opinion about the meaning of *Talh*. Hence, the *Salaf* (righteous predecessors) who said that the *Talh* means banana trees are just using the banana tree as an example to explain the meaning of the word *Talh*, not that it only means banana trees. Allah has the best knowledge.

Bananas are hot and wet. The best type of bananas are ripe and sweet.

Bananas help against the roughness of the chest and lung, relieve coughing and help against the ulcers of the kidney and prostate. Bananas also produce urine (diuretic), stimulate semen production, soften the stomach and arouse the sexual drive; and they should be eaten before meals. Bananas harm the stomach and aggravate the bile and the phlegm, but eating them with sugar and honey reduces their harmful side effects.

4. *Tal'* (Shoots or Clusters of dates)

Allah said:

﴿ وَٱلنَّخْلَ بَاسِقَٰتٍ لَّهَا طَلْعٌ نَّضِيدٌ ﴾

"And tall date-palms, with ranged clusters." (50:10)

And He said:

﴿ وَنَخْلٍ طَلْعُهَا هَضِيمٌ ﴾

"And green crops (field) and date-palms with soft spadix." (26:148)

The *Tal'* of the date trees is the fruit when it is still young.

There are two types of *Tal'* (clusters): male and female. The reproduction process of date trees requires transferring pollen, which resembles the male organ and which looks like a fine powder, and placing it on the female organ. This process is called *Ta'bir.*

Muslim narrated in his *Sahih* that Talhah bin 'Ubaidullah said:

"I and the Messenger of Allah ﷺ passed by some date trees and found some people doing *Ta'bir*. The Prophet ﷺ asked about what they were doing and they said that they were removing the male sexual organ and placing it in the female sexual organ. The Prophet ﷺ said, 'I do not think that this process will be of much help.' When they heard what the Prophet ﷺ said, they abandoned what they were doing and the trees did not reproduce. The Prophet ﷺ then said, `It was only a guess on my part. If (the *Ta'bir*) does help, then do it. I am only human just like you and my guess is either correct or incorrect. But, whatever I inform you from Allah (is true), I will never utter a lie on Allah."

The *Tal'* stimulates semen production and strengthens the sexual drive. When a woman takes the powder of the *Tal'* before having sex, it will help her get pregnant. The clusters of date trees are cold and dry in the second degree, strengthen the stomach and dry it out, and calm irritated blood, but are hard to digest.

Only those who have hot temperament can tolerate eating the *Tal'* . In addition, those who eat the *Tal'* regularly should also eat hot sweets with it. The *Tal'* constipates and strengthens the intestines, just as the *Jummar*, fresh dates and *Busr* that we mentioned before. Eating the *Tal'* in excessive amounts harms the stomach and the chest and might cause painful constipation, while taking it with butter and sweets helps reduce these side effects.

The Letter *'Ayn*

1. *'Inab* (Grapes)

The Messenger of Allah ﷺ was reported to have liked eating grapes and watermelon. Also, Allah has mentioned grapes in six instances in the Qur'an while listing the various bounties that He has bestowed on His slaves in this and the Next Life. Grapes are among the best and most beneficial fruits, and they are eaten fresh, dried, green and ripe. Further, Grapes are a type of fruit and nutritious food, along with their benefits as a remedy and a drink. Wetness and hotness are among the characteristics of grapes just as other grains. The best type of grapes are the big grapes that are full of juice, while white grapes are better than the black grapes when both are equal in sweetness. Also, eating fresh grapes two or three days after harvest is better than eating them immediately otherwise they cause diarrhea and flatulence. The grapes are left on their hanging grapevines until their skin becomes thin. They are a source of good nutrition, just like raisins and figs, and also strengthen the body.

When the seeds of the grapes are removed, the grapes become a more effective laxative. Eating grapes excessively causes headache, unless one also eats sour pomegranate. Grapes in general are a good laxative and provide a good source of nutrition. The best types of fruits are three: grapes, dates and figs.

2. *'Asal* (Honey)

We mentioned the benefits of honey before.

Ibn Jurayj said that Az-Zuhri said, ``Eat honey because it is good for the memory.'' The best type of honey is the white, pure, light and sweet honey. Also, the honey that is collected from trees and mountains is better than the honey that is grown in cells. Further, the quality of the honey varies according to the area where the bees collected their food.

3. *`Ajwah* (Pressed, Dried Dates)

Sa`d bin Abu Waqqas رَضِيَ الله عَنْهُ narrated that the Prophet ﷺ said:

« مَن تصبَّح بسَبْع تَمَرَاتٍ عجوةٍ، لم يضُرَّه ذلك اليومَ سُمٌّ ولا سِحْرٌ »

(البخاري:٥٤٤٥)

``Whoever eats seven dates of `Ajwah in the morning will not be harmed by poison or magic the rest of that day.''

Also, An-Nasai' and Ibn Majah narrated that the Prophet ﷺ said:

« العَجْوةُ من الجنة، وهي شِفاء من السُّمِّ. والكَمْأةُ من المَنِّ، وماؤها شِفاءٌ للعين »

(الترمذي:٢٠٦٦ وقال الألباني: حسن صحيح)

``The `Ajwah is from Paradise, and it is an antidote against poison. The Kamah (truffles) is a type of Manna and its water (extract) cures the eye.''

There is an opinion that this *Hadith* is talking about the `*Ajwah* of Al-Madinah in particular, which is one of the best types of dates in the area of Hijaz. The `Ajwah , pressed dried dates, is a good type of dates, has firm skin and is one of the softest and most delicious types of dates.

We mentioned the various benefits of the dates and the Tamr when we talked about the letter *Taa*. We also mentioned the benefits of the `*Ajwah* in treating poison and fending off the harm of magic.

4. ` *Anbar* (Ambergris; Whale)

We mentioned the *Hadith* that is narrated in the Two *Sahihs* about Abu `Ubaydah and the Muslim army finding a huge fish, or whale, and that they ate from it for a half a month. They also took some of its meat with them to Al-Madinah and gave the Prophet ﷺ some of it. This *Hadith* indicates that it is allowed for Muslims to eat whatever comes from the sea even when it is dead.

Some people who [disagree with what we stated above] said that the whale was thrown on the shore while still alive and that when the water receded it died. So, they say, the whale died because of the lack of water not naturally.

This opinion is incorrect, because the Companions found the whale dead at the seashore. They did not see it alive and then the water receded causing its death as claimed. Further, if the whale was still alive, the sea would not have thrown it on the shore, since the sea usually throws dead animals and dead fish on the shore.

Furthermore, even if what they claimed had happened to the whale, it will not affect the ruling of permissibility [to eat dead marine creatures]. The Prophet ﷺ disallowed eating game if one finds it dead in the water because there is a doubt if it had died from drowning and not from his weapon. So, if what the opponents say were true, then the fact that there is a doubt concerning how the whale died would disallow eating it [i.e. if their suggestion that the whale died because of lack of air and that dead marine creatures are disallowed dead were both true].

As for *Al-`Anbar, amber*, which is a type of *Teeb* (perfume), it is one of the best types of perfume after *Musk*. Some people mistakenly preferred `Anbar to Misk . However, the Prophet described Musk:

« هو أطيبُ الطِّيب »

``It is the best Teeb (perfume)."

Soon afterwards, we will mention the benefits and characteristics of *Musk*, which is the *Teeb* of Paradise. In addition, the seats in Paradise that belong to the truthful believers are made of *Musk* not *`Anbar*.

Those who thought that *`Anbar* is better than *Musk* were deceived by the fact that the *`Anbar* does not spoil, just like gold. This fact alone does not indicate that the *`Anbar* is better than *Musk*.

There are several types of *`Anbar*: white, gray, red, yellow, green, blue, black and multicolored. The best type of the *`Anbar* is gray, then the blue and then the yellow in color, while the black *`Anbar* is the worst type.

People have conflicting opinions regarding the origin of *`Anbar*, where some people said that it is a plant that grows on the seabed and which sea reptiles eat and then discard to later be thrown on the seashore. Some people say that *` Anbar* is the waste of sea creatures that looks like cow manure. Some people even said that it is a type of foam that the sea discards on the shore. The author of the *`Qanoon'* discounted the last two opinions but said that the amber might originate from an undersea spring.

*` Anbar* is hot and dry and strengthens the heart, the mind and the senses. It also strengthens the body and helps relieve facial paralysis, hemiplegia (paralysis), phlegmy ailments, stomach and flatulence. `Anbar also helps open various clogs if it is used as an ointment or as a drink. When it is inhaled, *` Anbar* will relieve cold symptoms, headaches and migraines.

5. *` Ud* (Indian Aloe Tree)

The Indian *` Ud* comes in two types. One type is used for medicinal purposes, which is called *Al-Kust* and some people called it *Al-Qust*.

We will mention this type under the letter *Qaf*. The second type of ` *Ud* is called *Aluwwah*, aloe wood, which is used as perfume.

Imam Muslim narrated in his *Sahih* that Ibn `Umar ﷺ used to burn dry aloe wood along with some *Kafur* (camphor), and states that the Messenger of Allah ﷺ used to do the same. Also, the Messenger of Allah ﷺ has described the bounties that the people of Paradise will be enjoying, such as having the aloe wood.

The `*Ud* is hot and dry in the third degree, opens the clogs and does away with gas. Also,`*Ud* dries unnecessary moisture while strengthening the intestines and brings relief and comfort to the heart. `*Ud* also helps the mind, sharpens the senses, constipates and helps relieve the enuresis, bed wetting that results from coldness of the prostate.

Ibn Samjun said, ``There are several kinds of `*Ud* , and they all carry the general name of *Aluwwah*. `*Ud* is used in and out of the body and is burned alone or with other substances. There is a medicinal significance when the `*Ud* is mixed with *Kafur* (camphor), as each of them makes the other milder. Also, burning the `*Ud* helps cleanse the air, which is one of the six necessary elements for the body's well-being."

6. `*Adas* (Lentils)

It was reported that the `*Adas* (lentils) was described as the lust of the Jews that they preferred over Manna and quails.

The `*Adas* is the companion of garlic and onions. It is cold and dry and has two opposing effects, one that constipates and one that works as a laxative. The skin of the `*Adas* is hot and dry in the third degree and also works as a laxative. The benefit in the lentils is concentrated in the peelings, and this is why whole lentils are more beneficial than ground lentils, less heavy on the stomach and less harmful.

Lentils cause black bile and harm the melancholy profoundly, along with having a negative effect on the nerves and the eyesight.

` *Adas* produces thick blood; and those who suffer from black bile should avoid eating it, for when they eat lentils excessively, the lentils will beget obsession, leprosy, quartran fever (a fever that occurs on every fourth day), and other ailments. However, eating lentils with chard and large amounts of grease will lessen their negative side effects. Also, one should avoid eating lentils with sweets, because lentils could cause clogs in the liver in this case. Further, eating `*Adas* on a regular basis causes harm to the eyesight because they are very dry. Lentils also cause urine retention, cold swellings and excessive flatulence. The best type of ` Adas is the fat, white ` *Adas* that digests faster.

Some ignorant people claimed that Prophet Ibrahim عليه السلام used to cook lentils for his guests. However, the Qur'an mentioned that he hosted his guests with a fat roasted calf.

The Letter *Ghayn*

1. *Ghayth* (Rain)

The *Ghaith* is mentioned in the Qur'an in many instances. The word *Ghaith* is soft on the ear and delightful for the body and the soul. The ears like to hear the word *Ghaith*, while the hearts enjoy its falling.

Rainwater is the best type of water there is and the softest, most beneficial and most blessed. This is especially the case when the rainfall is accompanied by lightning and thunder and is then collected in mountainous areas.

Rainwater is lighter than the other types of water because it is fresh and did not remain on the ground for a long time, in which case it would acquire some of the earth's dryness and hard substances. This is why rainwater gets spoiled quickly because it is pure and light.

There are two opinions regarding which is softer and lighter: rainwater that falls in the spring or winter.

Those who prefer winter rainwater say that in winter, the sun's heat is less and it thus evaporates the softest parts of the seawater. Also, the air then would be clean and void of dust, and consequently, would not be polluted. Hence, rainwater will not dissolve any pollutants while falling, and this is why rainwater is the softest and the lightest.

Those who prefer spring rainwater say that the hot sun then evaporates heavy substances in the air and makes the air itself lighter and cleaner. In this case, rainwater will be the lightest and the softest, at a time when the plants, the trees and the air become ready to receive rainfall.

Ash-Shafi' narrated that Anas bin Malik رَضِيَ الله عَنْهُ said, ``Once, we were with the Prophet ﷺ when the rain fell. The Prophet ﷺ removed his outer garment (until the rain fell on him) saying:

« إنه حَديثُ عَهْدٍ بِرَبِّهِ » (مسلم:٨٩٨)

``It has just come from its Lord."

We mentioned the Prophet's guidance in invoking Allah for rain and stated that he used to seek the blessings [that Allah endows] in the rain when it falls.

The Letter *Faa*

1. *Fatihah Al-Kitab* (the First Chapter in the Qurían)

Fatihah is the mother of the Qur'an, the seven frequently recited Versus that the Prophet ﷺ was given and the ultimate cure and beneficial remedy that contains the prefect *Ruqyah* , Islamic prayer formula. The *Fatihah* is the key to acquiring the richness, success and strength. The *Fatihah* also removes sadness, depression, anguish and fear. Only those who appreciate the value of the *Fatihah* and give it its due consideration, reciting it as it should be recited and knowing the secret of its value as a medicine and as a cure, will acquire such bounties.

One of the Companions unveiled a few of the secrets of the *Fatihah* when he used it as a *Ruqyah* for scorpion stings. The affected person was instantly cured and the Prophet asked the Companion:

«وما أَدْراكَ أَنَّها رُقْيَةٌ؟» (البخاري:٢٢٧٩)

``How did you know it is a cure?"

They are successful ones who uncover some of the secrets of the *Fatihah* and what it contains of Tawhid, knowing Allah and His Names, Attributes, Actions and Decisions. Those who acquire knowledge of what the *Fatihah* contains of affirming the religion, Predestination, Resurrection, Allah's Oneness in worship and in Lordship and trusting and depending on He Who owns all affairs, the praise and all pure things and to Whom everything must return. Those who acquire the habit of showing meekness to Allah seeking correct guidance which is the basis of the ultimate happiness in this and the Next Life. Those who acquire knowledge in the connection between the meanings contained in the *Fatihah* and acquiring the good and fending off the harm of both lives. Those who understand that their ultimate well-being and receiving the perfect Favor of Allah are all linked to implementing these meanings. It is they who will be able to substitute the *Fatihah* in place of many medicines and use it as an Islamic prayer formula (*Ruqyah*), and will use it to open the doors of goodness and drive away the elements of evil.

Understanding this subject requires a new nature, a new heart and a new type of Faith. By Allah! You will not find any evil statement, nor misguiding innovation, but the *Fatihah* will contain what nullifies and refutes it with the best, most correct and most direct manner. Also, you will not find a door that leads to acquiring divine knowledge, correct guidance of the heart and the remedy of the soul against its ills, but that the *Fatihah* will possess its key and the method to best use it. Finally, you will not find a path on which those who seek the Lord of the Worlds are passing, but you will find the *Fatihah* in its beginning and end.

By Allah! The *Fatihah* is much more important than what we have emphasized. The slave who holds fast to the *Fatihah*, comprehends it in the proper manner, relies on it as a perfect remedy, a shield, an immunity, and as a light of guidance. He understands its implications as they should be understood. It is he who will not fall into an innovation, or Shirk, or catch an ailment in the heart except briefly!

The *Fatihah* is the ultimate key for the treasures of the earth and Paradise, as well. But not every person knows how to use this key so as to have access to these treasures. If those who seek these treasures were able to uncover the secrets of this chapter [in the Qur'an] and acquire knowledge of its implications, they would add teeth to the key and would have easy access to these treasures.

We are certain of the statements that we have asserted herein because they are true. Allah has Perfect Wisdom in hiding the secrets [of *Al-Fatihah*] from the hearts of the majority of mankind, just as He has a perfect Wisdom in hiding the treasures of the earth from them.

The hidden treasures of the earth are surrounded by the devils that stand between mankind and these treasures. Only the good souls will be able to defeat these devils with True Faith, which is the weapon that the devils cannot withstand. However, the majority of the souls of mankind are not of this type (are not truly faithful). Therefore, they cannot resist the evil or defeat them to acquire their possessions for, ``Whoever kills a combatant will have his possessions."

2. *Faghiyah* (Henna Blossom)

Faghiyah, henna blossom, is one of the best kinds of perfumes. *Faghiyah* is mild in its hotness and dryness and constipates mildly. When Faghiyah is placed between folded wool clothes it protects them from mold and mites. Also, *Faghiyah* is used in ointments against facial paralysis and aneurysm (dilatation of a portion of the wall of an artery), while its oil helps the organs and relaxes the nerves.

3. *Fiddah* (Silver)

There is an authentic narration that states:

« أن رسولَ الله صلى اللهُ عليه وسلم كان خاتَمُه من فضة، وفصُّه منه» (البخاري: ٥٨٧٠)

« وكانت قَبِيعةُ سيفه فضةً » (أبو داود مختصراً: ٢٥٨٣ وصححه الألباني)

"The Messenger of Allah ﷺ had a silver ring with a silver face. Also, the grip of his sword was made from silver."

Unlike disallowing drinking in silver containers, there are no authentic narrations that disallow wearing silver. The category of containers for food and drink is more specific than the category of clothes and adornments. For instance, women are allowed to wear all types of clothes and adornments, while there are specific containers for food and drink that are not allowed to be used (i.e., gold and silver containers). Therefore, the fact that Muslims are not allowed to use some types of containers does not necessarily apply to clothes and adornments [which are a wider category as we have stated]. In the *Sunan* it is narrated that the Prophet ﷺ said:

« وأما الفضة فالعَبُوا بها لَعْبًا » (أبو داود: ٤٢٣٦ وحسنه الألباني)

"As for silver, play with it as you like."

Furthermore, disallowing wearing silver adornments needs a specific Text (Qur'an or *Sunnah*) or a consensus (of the scholars) for the heart to accept it with certainty. Once, the Prophet ﷺ held some gold in one hand and some silk in the other hand and said:

« هذان حرامٌ على ذُكور أمتي، وحِلٌّ لإناثهم » (أبو داود: ٤٠٥٧ وصححه الألباني وابن ماجه: ٣٥٩٥)

"These two are not allowed for the males of my nation and allowed for the females among them."

Silver is one of the wonders that Allah has created on the earth. It is the key to acquiring ones needs and high positions among the people of the earth. Those who have silver are honorable in the eyes of the people and respected in their hearts, allowing them to sit at the head of various meetings and opening all doors in front of them. Also, the people do not feel bored by sitting next to owners of silver, nor will their presence be heavy. Fingers point at them, while eyes look at them [in admiration]. If they speak, people listen and if they intervene, their mediation will be accepted. If they present their witness, their testimony will be accepted and if they give a speech, they will not be blamed for being incompetent; and even the white hair that they have will be considered more youthful than youth itself!

Silver is one of the remedies that bring joy to the hearts and drive away sadness, depression, and weakness in the heart and its heartbeat. Also, silver is used in some of the best kinds of ointments and helps extract the harmful substances or conditions of the heart, especially when blended with pure honey and saffron.

Silver is originally cold and dry but also produces hotness and wetness.

There are four types of gardens that Allah has prepared for His loyal slaves when they meet Him: two made of gold and two made of silver, including all their containers, adornments and whatever is in them.

In the *Sahih* it is narrated that the Prophet ﷺ said:

« الذي يشْرَب في آنية الذَّهَب والفضة، إنما يُجَرْ جِرُ في بطْنه نارَ جهنم »

(البخاري:٥٦٣٤)

``Those who drink from golden or silver bowls are only pushing the Fire of Jahannam down into their stomachs."

He also said, as narrated in the *Sahih* :

لا تشرَبُوا في آنية الذَّهَب والفضة، ولا تأكلوا في صِحَافِها فإنها لهم في الدنيا، ولكم في الآخرة » (البخاري:٥٤٢٦)

``Neither drink from golden or silver bowls nor eat on golden on silver plates. It is for them (the disbelievers) in the life of this world and for you in the Next Life."

Some people said that the wisdom behind disallowing using golden and silver containers is to tighten the money supply. They say that if people use silver and gold as containers, then the interests of mankind will not be served well. In addition, some people said that they are disallowed so that whoever uses them does not become arrogant and proud, or so that the poor persons do not become humbled when they see such items, and so forth. These opinions are not sound.

For instance, tightening the money supply should also include disallowing wearing golden and silver adornments and canes [not only golden and silver containers]. Further, pride and arrogance are not allowed regarding anything. In addition, making the poor feel humbled is not a precise subject that we can define, for they could also feel humbled when they see luxurious homes, spacious gardens and lavish means of transportation, clothes and delicious foods. All these items are allowed for people.

What we think is the valid reason for this prohibition, and Allah has the best knowledge, is that using gold and silver in this manner affects the heart in such a way that contradicts true slavery to Allah. This is why the Prophet ﷺ said that it is for the disbelievers in this life, because the disbelievers do not have a share in the true slavery [to Allah] that will give them the rewards of the Next Life. The slaves of Allah should not use these items in this manner, because only those who do not implement the requirements of their slavery (to Allah) use them in this life, as they prefer the life of this world to the Next Life. Allah has the best knowledge.

The Letter *Qaf*

1. *Qur'an*

Allah said:

﴿ وَنُنَزِّلُ مِنَ ٱلْقُرْءَانِ مَا هُوَ شِفَآءٌ وَرَحْمَةٌ لِّلْمُؤْمِنِينَ ﴾

``And We send down of the Qur'an that which is a healing and a mercy to those who believe (in Islmic Monotheism and act on it)." (17:82)

And He also said:

﴿يَٰٓأَيُّهَا ٱلنَّاسُ قَدْ جَآءَتْكُم مَّوْعِظَةٌ مِّن رَّبِّكُمْ وَشِفَآءٌ لِّمَا فِى ٱلصُّدُورِ﴾

``O mankind! There has come to you a good advice from your Lord (i.e. the Qur'an, enjoining all that is good and forbidding all that is evil), and a healing for that which is in your breasts..." (10:57)

The Qur'an is the ultimate cure from all types of illnesses and sicknesses that attack the body and the heart and from all the calamities of life and death. Yet, not everyone is suitable or guided to successfully seek the Qur'an as a cure.

When the ill person successfully uses the cure contained in the Qur'an and applies it on his ailment with faith, sincerity, complete acceptance and trust, all the while observing the necessary guidelines in this regard, no illness can resist the cure.

How can any ailment resist [the Book that contains] the Words of the Lord of the earth and heaven, which if it were revealed to a mountain, it would cause it to humble itself and render it asunder. Further, if the Qur'an were revealed to the earth, it would tear it apart. No ailment that attacks the body or the heart, but the Qur'an contains its remedy and cure and would provide immunity against it, that is, for whomever Allah has endowed with the bounty of comprehending His Book.

We stated before that the Qur'an contains the major aspects and basis of the knowledge of medicine: preserving health, diet and extracting of harmful substances. As for the ills that attack the heart, the Qur'an mentions them in detail and directs the people to the cures and remedies to treat them. Allah said:

﴿أَوَلَمْ يَكْفِهِمْ أَنَّآ أَنزَلْنَا عَلَيْكَ ٱلْكِتَٰبَ يُتْلَىٰ عَلَيْهِمْ﴾

``Is it not sufficient for them that We have sent down to you the Book (the Qur'an) which is recited to them?" (29:51)

May Allah never cure those whom the Qur'an does not cure, nor suffice for those for whom Allah is not Sufficient as a Helper.

2. Qith-thaí (Wild Cucumber)

In the *Sunan* it is narrated that Abdullah bin Ja`far said:

« أن رسول الله صلى اللهُ عليه وسلم كان يأكلُ القِثَّاءَ بالرُّطَب » (البخاري: ٥٤٤٠)

``The Prophet ﷺ used to eat Qith-tha' with ripe dates." [At-Tirmidhi].

Qith-tha' is cool and wet in the second degree and it cools the hotness in the stomach. it does not spoil quickly and helps relieve prostate pain. Also, *Qith-tha'* helps relieve nausea while its seeds are a diuretic. When *Qith-tha'* leaves are used as a bandage, they help against dog bites.

Qith-tha' does not digest easily and its coolness sometimes hurts some parts of the stomach. Hence, one should eat *Qith-tha'* with what would make its coolness and wetness milder, just as the Prophet ﷺ did by eating ripe dates with it. Also, eating it with raisins or honey makes it milder on the stomach.

3. Qust , or Kust (Costus)

In the *Sahihain* it is narrated that Anas رَضِيَ الله عَنْهُ related from the Prophet ﷺ that he said:

« خيرُ ما تداوَيْتُم به: الحِجامةُ، والقُسْطُ البَحْريُّ » (البخاري: ٢١٠٢)

``Cupping and marine costus are the best of your remedies."

Also, Imam Ahmad narrated that the Prophet ﷺ said:

« عَلَيكم بهذا العُودِ الهنديِّ؛ فإن فيه سبعةَ أشْفِيةٍ، منها: ذاتُ الجَنْب »

(البخاري: ٥٦٩٢)

``Use this Indian wood, because it contains seven types of cures, among them a cure for pleurisy."

There are two kinds of *Qust*, the white kind that is called sea-*Qust* and the Indian *Qust*, which is the hottest among them while the white type is the mildest. Both kinds have many benefits.

Both kinds of *Qust* are hot and dry in the third degree, and they dry out the phlegm and colds. When they are taken as a drink, they help weak liver and stomach and the colds associated with such cases. Costus also helps against victular and quartan fever (fever that comes on every fourth day), the pain on the side of the body and poisons. When the face is anointed with *Qust* that is kneaded with water and honey, they heal the spots that appear on the face. Galinus said that the costus, ``Heals tetanus, the pain in the sides and kills spots (which he called the seeds of the pumpkin)."

Some ignorant doctors are unaware of and deny the *Qust* as an effective remedy against the pain in the sides of the body. If these ignorant doctors become aware of what Galinus has stated about the *Qust,* they will quickly embrace it as if it was a divine text. Moreover, many doctors have also stated that *Qust* helps against the pain in the flank that is accompanied by phlegm, as Al-Khattabi related from Muhammad bin Al-Jahm.

We stated before that the difference between the remedies contained in the Prophetic medicine and the remedies of regular doctors, is much larger than the difference between folk medicine as compared to regular medicine. We also stated that what is sent down of the divine revelation, as compared to what is proven by experimentation, compares to the difference between the noble master and the commoner.

In addition, if any of the ignorant doctors [who ignore the Prophetic medicine] were able to discover a remedy that the Jews, the Christians and the polytheist doctors have prescribed, they would embrace it and would certainly prescribe it.

We do not deny that habits have a role in making the cure work or fail. Those who are used to certain foods and medicines would benefit from such items more than those who are not used to them and who sometimes would not benefit at all from them.

The statements of the best doctors do not apply in all cases and places. Taking the statements of these doctors as being specific and not general does not lessen the degree of their knowledge. The same ruling applies even more to the statements of the Prophets. Yet, the hearts of mankind have a built-in degree of ignorance and injustice, except for those whom Allah has endowed with the light of correct Faith and enlightened their hearts with true guidance.

4. *Qasab As-Sukkar* (Sugarcane)

Sugar is a relatively new substance that the people of old did not mention or even have knowledge that it existed. This is why they did not describe its role in various types of drinks or cures. Honey, on the other hand, was extensively used as a drink and as a medicine.

Sugarcane is hot and wet, helps relieve coughing and dissipates the excess moistures in the body, prostate and chest. It is more effective as a laxative than sugar itself. Also, sugarcane induces vomit, is diuretic and stimulates semen production.

`Affan bin Muslim As-Saggar said, ``Those who suck on sugarcane after eating their meal, will find comfort for the rest of the day." When sugarcane is broiled, it relieves the roughness in the throat and chest. Yet, it causes the accumulation of gasses that would be pacified when sugarcane is peeled and washed in hot water.

Sugar is hot and wet. The best type of sugar is white crystalline, especially when it is old. When sugar is boiled and skimmed, it quenches the thirst and relieves coughing. Sugarcane is not good for the stomach that suffers from bile. The side effects of sugarcane could be pacified by mixing it with lemon water (juice), *Naranj* (bitter orange) and peeled pomegranate.

Some people prefer sugarcane to honey because it is not as hot as honey and because it is milder on the stomach. This is not fair for honey, which is much more profitable than sugarcane. Also, Allah has made honey both a cure and a type of sweet. So how can anyone compare the benefits of honey and the benefits of sugarcane? Honey strengthens the stomach, soothes the natural process, strengthens the eyesight and heals diphtheria when gargled, facial paralysis and hemiplegia (paralysis affecting only one side of the body). It also helps against all types of cold illnesses that occur in the body because of excess moistures. Honey extracts and pulls excess moistures from the body, preserves the health, increases semen production, cleanses and decomposes the contents of the stomach. Also, honey cleanses the intestines, fights worms and prevents septic repletion (over eating). Further, honey is a good type of food and favorable for those who suffer from phlegm and for old people. In short, no substance is more beneficial for the body as a food, as a remedy and as an ingredient and a preserver of medications, which also strengthens the stomach, than honey. There are many more benefits for honey. So how can anyone compare it to sugarcane, which does not have even a fraction of the benefits contained in honey?

The Letter *Kaf*

Kitab (Books or Writings)

This chapter contains books or writings of divine remedies, Islamic prayer formulas, as Islamic amulets (prayer formulas written down and worn for a specific purpose).(1)

(1) * Editor's Note : The issue of the permissability of writing *Tama'im* (prayer Formulas to be worn or hung) and *Ta`weedh* (amulets of protection) from Qur'anic verses and supplications is one of difference amongst the Muslim Scholars. Even the Companions of the Prophet are reported to have differed concerning its legality. The author was clearly of the view that such writings were permissable. Other scholars of the early predecessors (including Ibn Mas`ood, and Ibn `Abbas) held such amulets to be prohibited due to their understanding of various statements of the Prophet. Shaikh Muhammad bin Salih Al-Uthaymeen concludes in his book *Al-Majmoo' Ath-Thameen* that the correct view is that such Qur'anic amulets are not permissable to use. Allah knows best .AW.

1. An Amulet for Fever

Al-Mirwazi said, ``Abu `Abdullh (Imam Ahmad) was informed that I was suffering from fever and he wrote to me a supplication for fever that reads like this, `In the Name of Allah, the Most Gracious, the Most Beneficent. In the Name of Allah, and depending on Allah.

﴿ قُلْنَا يَٰنَارُ كُونِي بَرْدًا وَسَلَٰمًا عَلَىٰٓ إِبْرَٰهِيمَ ۝٦٩ وَأَرَادُواْ بِهِۦ كَيْدًا فَجَعَلْنَٰهُمُ ٱلْأَخْسَرِينَ ﴾

``We (Allah) said: 'O fire! Be you coolness and safety for Ibrahm (Abraham)! And they wanted to harm him, but We made them the worst losers. (21:69,70)

O Allah, the Lord of (angels) Gabriel, Michael and Israfil: cure this person with this supplication by Your Power, Strength and Might, O Lord of the creation. *Aameen*.'"

Also, Al-Mirwazi said that Abu Ja`far, Muhammad bin `Ali was asked about wearing [a written] *Ruqyah* (divine remedy, Islamic prayer formula or amulet). He said, ``If it was from the Book of Allah or a *Hadith* [correctly] related from the Prophet, then wear it and use it as a remedy as much as possible." Abu `Abdullh was listening to this narration and Al-Mirwazi commented, ``Should I write this *Ruqyah* for quartan fever, 'In the Name of Allah...?' " Imam Ahmad said, ``Yes."

Imam Ahmad said that `Aishah رَضِيَ الله عَنْها and other Companions have agreed to this practice. `Harb added that Imam Ahmad also agreed to this practice, although he narrated that Ibn Mas`ud used to strongly dislike it.

Also, Imam Ahmad did not object when he was asked about wearing a *Ruqyah* amulet after an illness or a calamity strikes. Al-Khallal also narrated that `Abdullh bin Ahmad told him that his father used to write some supplication in a *Ruqyah* amulet for those who have a certain fear and for fever after it strikes.

An Amulet for Difficult Pregnancies

Also, Al-Khallal narrated that Abdullah bin Ahmad said that his father wrote a *Ruqyah,* Islamic prayer formula, as an Islamic amulet, on a pure object for women who suffered from difficult pregnancies. In the, amulet, Ahmad wrote the *Hadith* narrated by Ibn Abbas, ``There is no deity worthy of worship except Allah, the Most Forbearing, the Most Generous. All praise is due to Allah, the Lord of the Mighty Throne.

﴿ٱلْحَمْدُ لِلَّهِ رَبِّ ٱلْعَٰلَمِينَ﴾

``All the praises and thanks are to Allah the Lord of the `Alameen (mankind, jinn and all that exists)"

﴿كَأَنَّهُمْ يَوْمَ يَرَوْنَهَا لَمْ يَلْبَثُوٓا۟ إِلَّا عَشِيَّةً أَوْ ضُحَىٰهَا﴾

``The Day they see it, (it will be) as if they had not tarried (in this world) except an afternoon or a morning." (79:46)

﴿كَأَنَّهُمْ يَوْمَ يَرَوْنَ مَا يُوعَدُونَ لَمْ يَلْبَثُوٓا۟ إِلَّا سَاعَةً مِّن نَّهَارٍۭ ۚ بَلَٰغٌ﴾

``On the Day when they will see that (torment) with which they are promised (i.e. threatened, it will be) as if they had not stayed more than an hour in a single day. (O mankind! this Qur'an is sufficient as) a clear Message (or proclamation to save yourself from destruction). (46:35)

Al-Khallal said that a man came to Abu Abdullah and asked him to write an Islamic prayer formula as an Islamic amulet for a woman who had gone into labor for two days. Imam Ahmad asked the man to bring a wide cup with some Saffron [and wrote the amulet for the man's wife]. He also narrated that Imam Ahmad wrote the same amulet for several other people.

It was reported that `Ikrimah narrated that Ibn `Abbas رَضِيَ الله عَنْهما

said, ``Jesus, the Messenger of Allah , once passed by a cow that was suffering from hard labor. The cow said [to Jesus], 'O, Word of Allah (be and he was)! Ask Allah to relieve me from what I am suffering from.' He said, 'O Creator of the soul from another soul, Who brings to life a soul from within another soul, relieve her.' The cow then gave birth and soon started to smell her newly born." Ibn `Abbas رَضِيَ الله عَنْهما then said, ``Therefore, when the woman is suffering from hard labor, write [and recite] this supplication for her."

The types of Islamic prayer formulas as Islamic amulets that we mentioned are beneficial, Allah willing. Further, several scholars among the *Salaf* have allowed writing the Qur'an and drinking its water as a cure.

Another Amulet for Pregnant Women

One should write the following *Ayah* in a pure pot:

﴿إِذَا ٱلسَّمَآءُ ٱنشَقَّتْ ۝١ وَأَذِنَتْ لِرَبِّهَا وَحُقَّتْ ۝٢ وَإِذَا ٱلْأَرْضُ مُدَّتْ ۝٣ وَأَلْقَتْ مَا فِيهَا وَتَخَلَّتْ﴾

``When the heaven is split asunder, and listens to and obeys its Lord and it must do so. And when the earth is stretched forth, and has cast out all that was in it and became empty." (84:1-4)

Then the pregnant woman should drink from this pot and pour some of it on her stomach.

An Amulet for Nose bleeds

Ibn Taymiyyah used to write the following *Ayah* on his forehead:

﴿وَقِيلَ يَٰٓأَرْضُ ٱبْلَعِى مَآءَكِ وَيَٰسَمَآءُ أَقْلِعِى وَغِيضَ ٱلْمَآءُ وَقُضِىَ ٱلْأَمْرُ﴾

``And it was said: 'O earth! Swallow up your water, and O sky! Withhold (your rain). And the water was made to subside and the Decree (of Allah) was fulfilled (i.e. the destruction of the people of Nuh (Noah)." (11:44)

I also heard him say, ``I wrote [this *Ayah* ] for several people and they were cured." He also said [about the *Ayah* ], ``It is not allowed to write it with the blood of the nosebleed as some ignorant people do, because blood is impure and one is not allowed to use it to write Allah's Speech."

Another Amulet for nose bleeds

It was reported that Prophet Musa عليه السلام once went out wearing an outer garment and then suffered from nosebleed and covered [his nose] with his garment while reciting:

﴿يَمْحُوا اللَّهُ مَا يَشَاءُ وَيُثْبِتُ وَعِندَهُ أُمُّ الْكِتَابِ﴾

``Allah blots out what He wills and confirms (what He wills). And with Him is the Mother of the Book (Al-Lauh Al-Mahfooz)" (13:39)

An Amulet for fungus

One should write [the following *Ayah*] for it:

﴿فَأَصَابَهَا إِعْصَارٌ فِيهِ نَارٌ فَاحْتَرَقَتْ﴾

``...then it is struck with a fiery whirlwind, so that it is burnt...?" (2:266)

By Allah's Will and Power.

Another Amulet for fungus

When the sun becomes yellow, one should write [the *Ayah*],

﴿يَا أَيُّهَا الَّذِينَ آمَنُوا اتَّقُوا اللَّهَ وَآمِنُوا بِرَسُولِهِ يُؤْتِكُمْ كِفْلَيْنِ مِن رَّحْمَتِهِ وَيَجْعَل لَّكُمْ
نُورًا تَمْشُونَ بِهِ وَيَغْفِرْ لَكُمْ وَاللَّهُ غَفُورٌ رَّحِيمٌ﴾

``O you who believe [in Musa (Moses) (i.e. Jews) and Musa (Jesus) (i.e., Christians)]! Fear Allah, and believe in His Messenger (Muhammad) He will give you a double portion of His Mercy, and He will give you a light by which you shall walk (straight). And He will forgive you. And Allah is Oft-Forgiving, Most Merciful." (57:28)

An Amulet for three-day Fever

One should write on three separate papers, ``In the Name of Allah it is running away. In the Name of Allah it has subsided. In the Name of Allah it has decreased."

Every day [that the fever lasts], one should swallow the paper with some water.

An Amulet for sciatica

One should write, ``In the Name of Allah. O Allah, Lord of everything, Owner of everything and Creator of everything! You have created me and the sciatic nerve. Do not give it power over me, nor allow me to cut it. Heal me completely and eradicate the illness. There is none who can heal except You."

An Amulet for bleeding veins

At-Tirmidhi narrated that Ibn `Abbas رَضِيَ الله عَنْهما said that the Messenger of Allah used to teach them to recite [the following *Ruqyah* ], against fever and various pains, `In the Name of Allah, the Most Great. I seek refuge with Allah, the All-Mighty, from the evil of bleeding veins and from the evil of the fire's heat."

An Amulet for Toothache

One should write on the cheek that is closer to the pain, ``In the Name of Allah, Most Gracious, Most Merciful.

﴿ وَهُوَ ٱلَّذِىٓ أَنشَأَ لَكُمُ ٱلسَّمْعَ وَٱلْأَبْصَٰرَ وَٱلْأَفْـِٔدَةَ ۚ قَلِيلًا مَّا تَشْكُرُونَ ﴾

``It is He Who has created for you (the sense of) hearing (ears), eyes (sight), and hearts (understanding). Little thanks you give." (23:78)

Or,

﴿ وَلَهُۥ مَا سَكَنَ فِى ٱلَّيْلِ وَٱلنَّهَارِ ۚ وَهُوَ ٱلسَّمِيعُ ٱلْعَلِيمُ ﴾

``And to Him belongs whatsoever exists in the night and the day, and He is the All-Hearing, the All-Knowing." (6:13)

An Amulet for abscess

One should write [this amulet and place it] on the abscess,

﴿وَيَسْـَٔلُونَكَ عَنِ ٱلْجِبَالِ فَقُلْ يَنسِفُهَا رَبِّى نَسْفًا ﴿١٠٥﴾ فَيَذَرُهَا قَاعًا صَفْصَفًا ﴿١٠٦﴾ لَّا تَرَىٰ فِيهَا
عِوَجًا وَلَآ أَمْتًا﴾

``And they ask you concerning the mountains: say, ``My Lord will blast them and scatter them as particles of dust. Then He shall leave them as a level smooth plain." (20:105,107)

2. *Kamah* (Truffles)

In the *Sahihain* it is narrated that the Prophet ﷺ said:

« الكَمْأَة من المَنِّ، وماؤُها شفاءٌ للعين » (البخاري:٥٧٠٨)

``The Kamah is among the Manna and its water (extract or juice) cures the eye."

The *Kamah* grows wild underground, and it is called *Kamah* because it grows hidden beneath the earth. The *Kamah* does not have leaves or stems.

The essence of the *Kamah* is partly earthly and partly steamy and remains concealed underground during winter and then starts to grow above the ground with spring rainfall. This is why it is called the smallpox of the land, for it is similar to smallpox, which is caused by moistures clogged with blood that get aggravated during the early childhood years when the body starts to gain strength.

Kamah (truffles) grow in the spring and are eaten raw or cooked. The Arabs used to call truffles `the plant of the thunder', because they grow in the aftermath of thunderstorms. The nomads in the desert use mushrooms in their regular diet. Further, the best type of truffles grow on sandy dry land. There are several types of *Kamah*, among which is a poisonous plant which is reddish in color and which causes asphyxiation.

The *Kamah* is cold and wet in the third degree, and it is not favorable for the stomach and not easily digested. Eating *Kamah* on a regular basis causes constipation, gastric pain, facial paralysis, stomachache and dysuria (painful urination). Humid kinds of mushrooms are less harmful than dry ones. Therefore, those who wish to eat *Kamah* should bury them in a muddy area and then boil them in water, add salt and mint, and then eat them with oil and spices. This is because the *Kamah* has a heavy earthly essence, although it contains a fair amount of water in its essence that makes it a little light. Also, using the *Kamah* as kohl helps in cases of bad eyesight and ophthalmia (conjunctivitis).

Some of the best doctors have agreed that truffle water or juice helps strengthen the eyesight.

There are two opinions regarding the meaning of what the Prophet ﷺ said:

« الكَمْأة من المَنِّ »(البخاري:٥٧٠٨)

``The Kamah is among the Manna."

Some people said, `the Manna that Allah has sent down to the Children of Israel was not only the sweetmeat that we know, but also several other plants that grow in the wild without effort or planting on the people's part to grow. The Manna, in their opinion, means the Favor, and thus, every type of plant or bounty that Allah grants to mankind without effort on their part is called Manna. All of Allah's bounties that He grants to mankind are a Favor from Him. Yet, Allah specifically mentioned the types of His Favors concerning which the slave does not make any effort, whether in growing or producing them, and called these Favors, Manna.

During the years of wandering in the earth with which Allah tested the Children of Israel, they used to sustain themselves on truffles that sufficed for bread. Also, Allah gave them quails that sufficed as meat, and made their sweet the Manna that descends from trees. Therefore, their diet was complete.

Further, the Prophet's statement:

« الكَمْأة من المنِّ الذي أنزله اللهُ على بني إسرائيل » (مسلم:٢٠٤٩)

``The Kamah is a type of the Manna that Allah has sent down on the Children of Israel."

Some considered that the *Kamah* is a type of Manna, although the word ` Manna ' is usually used to describe the dew that descends on trees, which is originally called Taranjabin.

The second opinion states that the *Kamah* was called Manna because it resembles the Manna that descends on trees, in that it is collected without effort to plant or water.

If one asks, this is the case with *Kamah*, then what about the harm that it contains?

Know that Allah created everything in a perfect shape and essence. What Allah created is free from defects and harm and is beneficial for mankind. The various types of ailments occur later on when what Allah creates becomes spoiled somehow by being mixed or polluted by other substances, and so forth. If what Allah creates is left in its original shape that Allah has created, it does not contain any harm.

Those who have knowledge of the world and of the creation realize that all types of evil or harm in the air, land, plants and various creations occur after they are created. Also, ever since mankind started disobeying their Prophets, all types of general and private evil occurred, that which causes them pain, illnesses, diseases, plagues, famines and loss of blessings in the land and in what it produces. The fruits and plants have thus lost their value and benefit gradually.

If one does not comprehend these facts, the following Ayah should be enough for him to understand.

﴿ ظَهَرَ ٱلْفَسَادُ فِى ٱلْبَرِّ وَٱلْبَحْرِ بِمَا كَسَبَتْ أَيْدِى ٱلنَّاسِ ﴾

``Evil (sins and disobedience to Allah) has appeared on land and sea because of what the hands of men have earned (by

oppression and evil deeds)." (30:41)

One should apply this *Ayah* to what occurs in this world and compare them together.

Further, the people notice how various illnesses and sicknesses occur in plants, animals and fruits. These illnesses only produce other types of illnesses and diseases. The more mankind starts a new type of evil and sin, the more illnesses and diseases Allah brings to their foods, fruits, air, water sources, bodies, shapes and outer appearance. Also, the people's behavior suffers a type of harm or alteration that is compatible with what their bodies commit of injustice and sin.

Before this time, the crops and grains used to be larger in size than at the present time, for the blessings in such items was bigger than at the present time. Imam Ahmad narrated, ``A bundle that contained some wheat seeds as big as date seeds was found in a safe that belonged to members of the Umayyad dynasty. On it, these words were written, `This used to grow during the times when justice prevailed.' ``Imam Ahmad mentioned this story after narrating one of the Prophet's *Ahadith*.

The majority of the diseases and illnesses are the remnant of the torments that were inflicted on the nations that lived before our time. These illnesses and diseases remained for those who followed their lead and imitated the previously tormented nations. This is a just judgment that the Prophet ﷺ mentioned when he stated that the Plague:

« إنه بَقِيَّةُ رِجْزٍ – أو عَذَابٍ – أُرْسِلَ على بَنِي إسْرَائِيلَ » (مسلم واللفظ وعنده: آية رجز ٢٢١٨)

``It is the remnant of an affliction that Allah has sent on the Children of Israel."

Also, Allah sent the wind on the people of `Ad for seven nights and eight days. Allah has left some of this strong wind for the people who came after them to serve as a reminder [of what happened to `Ad].

Allah made the works of the righteous and the sinning people as reasons behind much of what has happened in this world. For instance, when the people do not work righteousness or give in charity, the rain does not fall on them, and thus famine occurs. Also, when the meek and powerless people are dealt with unjustly, when the people cheat in weights, and when the strong transgress the rights of the weak, the injustice committed by the [tyrant] rulers intensifies as a consequence. Such unjust rulers do not grant mercy if they are asked for mercy, nor are they kind when they are called on to be kind. In reality, what the rulers do and commit is a mere reflection of what their subjects do and commit. Allah, with His Wisdom and Just Decisions, makes people's work appear to them in various forms that are compatible to their works. Sometimes Allah strikes mankind with famines, sometimes with an enemy, sometimes with unjust rulers, sometimes with diseases, and sometimes with depression and sadness that will remain with them. Sometimes Allah strikes mankind with preventing the blessings from descending on them and by allowing the devils to have power over them, and leading them to what is certain torment. In this case, mankind will revert to what they were created for [either Paradise or the Fire].

The wise person thinks about the world and seeks the areas where Allah exerts His Justice and Wisdom. Then he will realize that the Prophets and their followers are passing on the path of safety, while the rest of mankind are leading themselves to the path of destruction and the land of failure. Allah will certainly bring His judgement and command to a successful conclusion, none can avert His decisions or commands. All success comes from Allah.

There are three opinions regarding the meaning of the Prophet's statement:

« وماؤُها شِفاءٌ لِلْعَيْن »

``And its water cures the eye."

First: that the *Kamah* water is an ingredient in the remedies for eye ailments, not that it is used alone.

Second: that *Kamah* is used alone after broiling it and extracting its juice. The fire matures and softens the truffles, thus dissolving the harmful wetness and excrements that the *Kamah* contains and leaving the beneficial ingredients.

Third: that the meaning of `its water' entails the rain that makes the mushroom grow and which is the first patch of rain that falls. In this case, the *Hadith* will be talking about the rain not the mushrooms themselves. Ibn Al-Jawzi mentioned this opinion, which is the weakest among the three opinions mentioned herewith.

Other people said that this portion of the *Hadith* entails using *Kamah* water to cool the eye. Hence its water alone is a cure, while the other parts are used as ingredients in compound remedies.

Al-Ghafiqi said, ``The *Kamah* water (juice) is the best remedy for the eye when kneaded with the Ithmid (antimony type of Kohl) and then used as kohl (i.e. eyeliner). It also strengthens the eyelid and the eyesight and prevents many illnesses from attacking the eye."

3. *Kabath* (Arak Tree Fruit)

In the *Sahihain* it is narrated that Jabir bin `Abdullah رَضِيَ الله عَنْهما said, ``We were with the Messenger of Allah ﷺ collecting *Kabath* when he said, ``Collect the black type of *Kabath* because it is the best type."

The *Kabath* is the fruit that grows on the plant called Arak which grow in the area of Hijaz [and whose branches are used for *Siwak* as we have stated]. It is hot and dry and carries the same benefits as the Arak tree: strengthening the stomach, helping the digestion, dissolving phlegm and relieving back pain and several other illnesses. Ibn Juljul said, ``Drinking its soup produces urine as a diuretic, and cleanses the prostate." Also, Ibn Radhwan said, ``[The *Kabath*] strengthens the stomach and constipates (mildly)."

4. *Katam* (Plants Used to Dye the Hair Black)

Al-Bukhari narrated that Uthman bin `Abdullh bin Mawhab said, ``We came to Umm Salamah رَضِيَ الله عَنْها and she took out some of the Messenger's hair that was dyed with henna and *Katam* ." Also in the four books of *Sunan* (Abu Dawud, At-Tirmidhi, An-Nasai' and Ibn Majah) it is narrated that the Prophet ﷺ said:

« إن أَحْسنَ ما غَيَّرتُمْ به الشَّيْبَ، الحِنَّاءُ والْكتَمُ » (أبو داود:٤٢٠٥ وصححه الألباني)

" Henna and Katam are the best of what you use to change (the color of) white hair."

Also, in the *Sahihain* it is narrated that Anas رَضِيَ الله عَنْهُ said, ``Abu Bakr once dyed (his hair) with henna and *Katam* ." Further, Abu Dawud narrated that Ibn `Abbas said, ``A man who tinted (his hair) with henna passed by the Prophet ﷺ who said, `How good this is.' Then another man who tinted (his hair) with both henna and *Katam* passed by and the Prophet ﷺ said, 'This is even better.' Then another man who tinted with Sufrah (a black dye) passed by and the Prophet said, `This is the best of all.'"

Al-Ghafiqi said, ``*Katam* is a plant that grows in valleys and its leaves are similar to olive-leaves and grows higher than a (man's) shoulders. Its fruit grows to the size of peppers and have seeds in the middle. When the seeds are crushed, they turn black and when the leaves are squeezed and one drinks a small measure [of the extract], it causes vomiting. *Katam* also benefits against dog bites. When the stem is boiled in water, it is used as ink." Al-Kindi also stated that, ``If one uses the *Katam's* seed as Kohl (i.e., eyeliner), it will clear the eye from the water that accumulates in it."

Some people thought that *Katam* is the Wasmah or the Nile-Leaves. This is not true, because *Wasmah* is a different plant. The author of the *Sahih* said, ''*Katam*, which is used to dye the hair, is a plant that is mistakenly taken for Wasmah ." The *Wasmah* has long leaves that are bluish in color and which are larger than the *Khilaf* (Chalef) leaves and are similar to pea leaves but larger in size. Further, Wasmah is collected in Hijaz and Yemen.

If someone asks, ``In the *Sahih* it is narrated that the Prophet did not dye (his hair)." We answer that Imam Ahmad said that other Companions have narrated that the Prophet ﷺ dyed (his hair). Those who were witnesses to an act are not like those who did not witness it. Hence, Imam Ahmad affirmed that the Prophet had indeed used Khidhab (dyed the hair), although Imam Malik denied it.

If someone says that in *Sahih Muslim* it is narrated the Hadith that disallows dying the hair black, when Abu Bakr's father was brought to the Prophet with all his hair being white. The Prophet said at that time:

« غيِّروا هذا الشَّيْب، وجنِّبوه السَّواد » (مسلم:٢١٠٢)

``Change this white hair but avoid the black color."

Katam changes the color of the hair to black.

There are two ways to answer this argument.

First, the Prophet disallowed dying the hair black. But if the black color is mixed with henna and *Katam,* there is no harm in it. *Katam* and henna dye the hair between red and black colors, unlike *Wasmah* which turns the hair black. This is the most plausible answer to the argument.

The second answer is that dying the hair black sometimes occurs for the purpose of deceiving others, such as when an old woman dyes her hair black to deceive the husband or other people, or when an old man dyes his hair black to deceive a woman. This is a type of cheating that is disallowed. On the other hand, if dying the hair black does not entail deceit, it is allowed. There are authentic narrations that Al-Hasan and Al-Husayn used to dye their hair black, as Ibn Jarir has reported.

He also reported that this is the opinion of Uthman bin `Affan, `Abdullh bin Ja`far, Sa`d bin Abu Waqqas, `Uqbah bin `Amir, Al-Mughirah bin Shu`bah, Jarir bin `Abdullh and `Amr bin Al-`Aas رَضِيَ الله عَنْهُم . He also related this opinion to several of the Tabi`in, the second generation of Islam, such as `Amr bin Uthman, `Ali bin `Abdullh Ibn `Abbs, Abu Salamah bin Abdur-Rahman, Abdur-Rahman bin Al-Aswad, Musa bin Talhah, Az-Zuhri, Ayyub and Isma`il bin M`ad Yakrib. Ibn Al-Jawzi also related this opinion to Mu`harib bin Dithar, Yazid, Ibn Jurayj, Abu Yusuf, Abu Is`haq, Ibn Abu Layla, Ziyad bin `Alaqah, Ghaylan bin Jami', Nafi' bin Jubayr, `Amr bin `Ali Al-Muqaddami and Al-Qasim bin Sallam.

5. *Karm* , which is the grapevine

It is not preferred that one calls the grapevine *Karm,* as Muslim narrated that the Prophet ﷺ said:

« لا يقولَنَّ أحدكم للعِنَب الكَرْمُ؛ الكَرْمُ: الرجلُ المسلم » (مسلم:٢٢٤٧)

``None of you should call the grapevine Karm, for Al-Karm is the Muslim man."

In another narration the Prophet ﷺ said:

«إنما الكَرْم: قلبُ المؤمن »

``The Karm is the believer's heart."

Also another narration states:

«لاتقُولوا: الكَرْمُ وقولوا: العِنَب والحَبْلَة» (مسلم :٢٢٤٨)

``Do not say (for grapes) Al-Karm, rather say `Inab (grape), and Hablah (grapevine)."

This *Hadith* entails two meanings that the Arabs used to call the grapevine *Al-Karm* because of its tremendous benefits. This is why the Prophet ﷺ disliked calling it *Karm* because this exotic name drives the heart to like it and to later like what it is used to produce: alcohol, which is the mother of all impure things. The Prophet disliked calling what is used to produce alcohol with one of the best names.

The second, this *Hadith* is similar to the *Ahadith,*

« ليس الشديد بالصّرعة » (البخاري:٦١١٤)

``The strong person is not one who overpowers others physically."

And

« ليس المِسْكين بالطَّوَّاف » (البخاري:١٤٧٩)

``The Miskin (poor) is not one who keeps wandering in the land."

In this case, the *Hadith* (about *Al-Karm*) means, ``You call the grapevine *Karm* because of its many benefits, while the believing heart or the Muslim person deserves this good name even more, for indeed, the believer is all pure and beneficial." The *Hadith* then draws the attention to what the believer's heart has of goodness, generosity, faith, enlightenment, guidance, fear from Allah and the rest of the good characteristics because of which the believer deserves the name *Karm* more than the grapevine.

The grapevine is cool and dry, while its leaves are cool in the first degree. When the grape leaves are crushed and their powder is used as a bandage for headache, they relieve the pain and also relieve swelling and stomach infections.

When one drinks the juice of grapevine stems, it will get rid of nausea sensation and will constipate the stomach, and when its hearts are chewed wet, they also produce the same benefits. Also, the extract of grapevine leaves helps relieve stomach ulcers, hemoptysis (spitting up blood), vomit and stomach ache in general.

The sap contained in hanging grapevine stems acts just like gum extracts if one drinks it, as it dissipates stones. Further, when it is used as ointment, it will bring relief to the hearts and will heal the open sores caused by mange, but it is better to wash the affected wound beforehand with water and Natron. When one uses it as an ointment along with oil, it will remove the hair effectively.

The ashes of grapevine stems are also used as a bandage, blended with vinegar, rose oil and rue, to relieve spleen swellings. Also, just as rose oil (or essence), the oil of vine blossoms constipates the stomach and has many other benefits. In general, grapevines have as much benefit as the date tree.

6. *Karfas* (Celery)

Karfas has a good aroma and when it is hung under the neck, it relieves toothache.

Karfas is hot and dry, and it opens the clogs of the liver and the spleen. Wet celery leaves helps the stomach and the cold liver, causes urine as a diuretic, menstrual flow, and dissolves stones. Celery grains are more effective in this regard. *Karfas* also stimulates semen production and relieves offensive breath. Ar-Razi said, ``One should avoid eating it if he fears he might suffer a scorpion sting."

7. *Kurrath* (Leek)

There are two types of *Kurrath*, a Nabatean type and a Shami (Syrian) type. People eat the Nabatean type, which is a vegetable, while the Syrian type has many heads. *Kurrath* is hot and dry and causes headaches. When *Kurrath* is cooked, one could eat it or drink its water to help against cold hemorrhages. When its seeds are crushed and kneaded with some tar and then applied on decaying teeth, they will cleanse the rotted teeth and will relieve the pain. Further, the smoke of burnt *Kurrath* seeds helps dry out hemorrhages. All these benefits are for the Nabatean *Kurrath*.

Yet, the *Kurrath* is harmful for the teeth and the gums, causes headaches and nightmares and brings darkness to the sight. Also, it provokes offensive breath, is diuretic, stimulates menstruation flow and semen production, and is not easily digested.

The Letter *Lam*

1. Lahm (Meat)

Allah said:

﴿وَأَمْدَدْنَـٰهُم بِفَـٰكِهَةٍ وَلَحْمٍ مِّمَّا يَشْتَهُونَ﴾

``And We shall provide them with fruit and meat such as they desire." (52:22)

﴿وَلَحْمِ طَيْرٍ مِّمَّا يَشْتَهُونَ﴾

``And with the flesh of fowls that they desire." (56:21)

In the *Sahih* it is also narrated that the Prophet ﷺ said:

« فضلُ عائشةَ على النساء، كفضل الثَّريد على سائِر الطعام » (البخاري: ٣٧٧٠)

``The virtue of 'Aishah رَضِيَ اللهُ عَنْهَا as compared to the rest of the women is like the virtue of the Tharid as compared to the rest of the foods." (Tharid means bread and meat).

Az-Zuhri said, ``Eating meat brings about strength in seventy different ways." Also, Muhammad bin Wasi' said, ``Eating meat strengthens the sight." Also, `Ali رَضِيَ الله عَنْهُ was reported to have said, ``Eat meat, because it makes the skin's color lighter, the stomach firmer and the behavior better." Nafi said, ``Ibn `Umar رَضِيَ الله عَنْهما used to eat meat frequently when Ramadhn started and when traveling." Finally, `Ali رَضِيَ الله عَنْهُ was reported to have said, ``Whoever refrains from eating meat for forty days will acquire bad behavior."

There are different types of meat that we will mention, describe briefly and elaborate on their benefit or harm.

Sheep Meat (Mutton)

Mutton is warm in the second degree and wet in the first degree. The best type of mutton comes from the one-year old animal, which generates good blood if digested properly. This type of meat is suitable for those who have hot or cold temperaments and for those who practice sports activity in cold areas and cold weather. It is also beneficial for those who suffer from black bile, and it also strengthens the mind and the memory. However, the mutton of old, thin animals is not good, as is the ewe's meat.

The best type of mutton is the dark meat of the male animal, for it is lighter, tastier and more beneficial. The mutton of castrated sheep is even better and more beneficial. The red meat of fat sheep is lighter and more nutritious, while the chest of the goat is less nutritious and floats in the stomach.

The best parts of mutton meat are the meat that covers the bones, the right side, which is lighter and tastier than the left side, and the front parts rather than the back parts. The best part of sheep meat to the Prophet was the front part, which is closer to the head, but not the head itself. The front part is lighter and tastier. Once, Al-Farazdaq gave a man some money to buy meat for him, saying, ``Buy the front parts and avoid the head and the intestines, because that is where disease resides."

The meat on the neck is also tasty and easy to digest. The meat that covers the arm is the lightest meat, the tastiest, the healthiest and the easiest to digest. In the *Sahihain* it is narrated that the Messenger of Allah ﷺ used to like eating the meat of the sheep arm. Furthermore, the meat on the back of the sheep is nutritious and produces sanitary blood.

Goat Meat

It is cold and dry, and the mixtures that goat meat produces are harmful. Goat meat is not digested easily and is not significant nutrition-wise. The meat of billy goats is not beneficial, because it is rather dry, heavy on the stomach and produces black bile.

Al-Jahith once said, ``A skilled doctor once said to me, 'O Abu

'Uthman! Avoid goat meat because it causes depression, causes black bile, forgetfulness, and spoils the blood. By Allah! It also drives children wild.'"

Some doctors say that the goat meat that is not preferred is the meat of old goats, especially for old people. They also say that goat meat is not bad for whoever is used to eating it.

When the doctors state that goat meat is not beneficial, they specifically mean those who have weak stomachs and those who are not used to eating it, such as the people who live in luxury in cities and who are used to the better types of foods. But this is not the majority.

The meat of young – but not very young – goats is milder, especially when the goat is still nursing. This type of goat meat is digested faster, because it still possesses the strength of its mother's milk. The meat of young goats is also milder for most people and lighter than camel meat. Also, young goat's meat produces moderate blood.

Cow Meat

Cow meat is cold and dry, heavy on the stomach and produces black, bilious blood that is only suitable for hard workers. Eating cow meat excessively for those who are not used to it causes such black bilious illnesses as vitiligo (a skin condition of unknown cause, characterized by patchy loss of pigment), mange, herpes, leprosy, elephantiasis, cancer, obsession, quartran fever and various tumors. The harm that this meat causes will be neutralized when one eats it with spices, garlic, ginger and cinnamon. The meat of male cows is colder than female cows' meat, which is less dry.

The meat of fat calves is one of the best, mildest and tastiest types of food. It is warm and wet, and if fully digested, it provides good nutrition.

Horse meat

In the *Sahih* it is narrated that Asma' رَضِيَ الله عَنْها said, ``We slaughtered a horse during the time of the Messenger of Allah ﷺ and ate it." Also, the Prophet ﷺ :

« أنه أذِن في لُحوم الخَيْل »(البخاري:٥٥١٠) « و نَهى عن لحوم الحُمُر » (البخاري:٤٢١٩)

``Allowed eating horsemeat but disallowed eating (domesticated) donkey meat." [Al-Bukhari and Muslim].

The fact that Allah mentioned horses along with mules and donkeys [in the Qur'an] does not indicate that the ruling about their meat is identical. Sometimes Allah mentions several similar things together and sometimes mentions several different things together. What Allah said is:

﴿لِتَرْكَبُوهَا﴾

``For you to ride." (16:8)

This does not indicate that horsemeat is not allowed, just as it does not indicate that one is not allowed to benefit from horses except by riding. Rather, the *Ayah* only mentioned the best benefit and value that the horse represents, which is its being a means of transportation. Furthermore, the two *Ahadith* we mentioned unequivocally indicate that horsemeat is allowed.

Horsemeat is hot, dry, tough and dark. It is also harmful for soft stomachs and bodies.

Camel Meat

The difference between the Shiites and the Sunnis and between the Jews and Muslims is that the Muslims eat camel meat. In addition, the Shiites and the Jews neither praise nor eat camel meat. It is well established in the religion that Muslims are allowed to eat camel meat and that the Messenger of Allah ﷺ and his Companions used to eat it while traveling and otherwise.

Young camel meat is one of the tastiest and most nutritious types of foods, and those who are used to eating it find it as light and beneficial as sheep meat. Some doctors did not like eating camel meat for residents of the cities because they are not used to it. Camel meat is hot and dry, difficult to digest and begets black bile.

Camel meat has an especially strong effect on the body and this is why the Prophet ﷺ ordered the Muslims to perform ablution after eating it.[1] We should state here that it is an erroneous method to alter the meaning of the two correct *Ahadith* on this subject so that `ablution' only means washing the hands, thus altering the true meaning of the word. Also, the Prophet ﷺ made a distinction between eating camel meat and sheep meat, as he gave the choice to Muslims if they want to perform ablution after eating sheep meat. Meanwhile, the Prophet commanded the Muslims to perform ablution after eating camel meat. If ablution in these *Ahadith* was held to mean just washing the hands, it should also apply to what the Prophet ﷺ said:

« مَن مَسَّ فَرْجه فليتَوَضَّأْ » (أبو داود: ١٨١ وصححه الألباني)

``Whoever touched his sexual organ is obliged to perform ablution."

Furthermore, those who eat camel meat might not touch the meat with their hands. So if `ablution' in this case means just washing the hands, it would be a senseless act and would alter the true meanings desired by the *Ahadith*. Also, claiming that the *Hadith* which states,

``The last ruling that the Prophet ﷺ chose is that he abandoned performing ablution from eating what is cooked by fire," includes camel meat is not correct.

First, this Hadith carries a general meaning, while the Hadith about camel meat is specific.

Second, the two Ahadith are not talking about the same subject. For instance, one should perform ablution even if he eats dried, cooked or uncooked camel meat. Using fire does not have a bearing on the ruling about camel meat. As for abandoning performing ablution after eating

(1) Editor's note : This is the ritual washing before prayer. It is called, and wudhu in Arabic translated into English as ablution.

what is cooked by fire, it only indicates that using fire does not require ablution. Therefore, there is a difference between the two *Ahadith,* as one of them orders the Muslims to perform ablution after eating camel meat while the other indicates that performing ablution is not required after eating the food that was cooked by fire.

Third, the *Hadith* about the Prophet ﷺ abandoning performing ablution after eating the food that was cooked on fire came after the Prophet ﷺ had performed ablution from eating such meat earlier. The *Hadith* states that the Prophet ﷺ was once brought meat and that he ate from it and then performed ablution and prayed. Later on, he was brought meat and he ate from it and then prayed without performing ablution. The *Hadith* states, the last ruling on this matter is that it is not necessary to perform ablution after eating what was cooked by fire. So there are two rulings regarding the same subject [eating what was touched by fire], one came earlier than the second ruling. Some of the narrators of the *Hadith* only mentioned the latter incident to make the story short. Therefore, how can anyone use this *Hadith* to prove that it overrules performing ablution from eating camel meat (when the earlier *Hadith* that was overruled talks about another subject)? Even if the *Ahadith* in general allow not performing ablution after eating what was cooked on fire, the specific *Hadith* still stands because it entails a specific ruling [concerning camel meat].

Dhabb Meat

We stated before that eating *Dhabb* meat is allowed. This type of meat is hot and dry and excites the sexual drive.

Gazelle meat

Gazelle meat is the best among the meats of wild game. It is hot and dry and beneficial for the healthy body, especially the fawn's meat.

Antelope Meat

Antelope meat is hot and dry in the first degree, dehydrates the body and is beneficial for the humid bodied.

The author of the `*Qanoon*' said, ``The best type of game meat is the antelope's, although it tends to cause black bile."

Rabbit Meat

Rabbit meat was mentioned in the *Sahihain*, as Anas رَضِيَ الله عَنْهُ said, ``We hunted a rabbit after pursuing it for a while. Afterwards, Abu Talhah رَضِيَ الله عَنْهُ sent its hip to the Messenger of Allah who accepted it."

Rabbit meat is mildly hot and dry, and the best part of it is the hip. The best way to eat rabbit meat is by roasting it. Rabbit meat constipates, produces urine, as a diuretic, and dissolves stones. Eating the rabbit's head benefits against convulsive shaking.

Zebra meat

In the *Sahihain* it is narrated that Abu Qatadah رَضِيَ الله عَنْهُ said that the Companions were once with the Messenger of Allah ﷺ during an *Umrah* trip and that he hunted a zebra and the Prophet ﷺ told them to eat it. They were assuming the state of *Ihram* then, unlike Abu Qatadah.

Ibn Majah also narrated that Jabir رَضِيَ الله عَنْهُ said, ``During the battle of Khaibar, we ate horsemeat and zebra meat."

Zebra meat is hot and dry, nutritious and produces thick, bilious blood. Its fat is beneficial when mixed with *Qust* oil to treat toothache and flatulence that weakens the kidneys. Further, when its grease is applied on spots, it will heal them.

In general, all types of wild-game meat produce thick, bilious blood. In addition, the best type of wild-game meat is gazelle then rabbit meat.

The meat of animal fetuses is not preferred because the blood is still trapped in it. However, it is still allowed, for the Prophet ﷺ said:

« ذَكَاةُ الجنين: ذَكَاةُ أُمِّه » (أبو داود:٢٨٢٨ وصححه الألباني)

``*Slaughtering the fetus is included in slaughtering its mother.*"

The scholars of Iraq do not allow eating fetus's meat except if one kills it before it dies. They altered the meaning of the last *Hadith* saying that the fetus should be slaughtered as its mother was slaughtered according to the *Hadith*, as they claimed.

However, this claim is false. The *Hadith* states that the Prophet ﷺ was asked, ``O Messenger of Allah ! We slaughter a sheep and sometimes find a fetus still in its womb, should we eat it?" The Prophet ﷺ said, ``Eat it if you wish, because slaughtering it is included in slaughtering its mother."

Also, when one studies this matter further, his analysis will also demonstrate that it is allowed to eat animal fetuses. The fetus is still a part of the mother, and since slaughtering the mother allows us to eat all of its parts, then the fetus should be included, as well. This is the meaning that the Prophet ﷺ meant when he said:

« ذكاتُه ذكاةُ أمه » (ابن ماجه: وهو صحيح كما سبق آنفاً)

``Slaughtering it is included in slaughtering its mother."

If the authentic *Sunnah* had not specifically allowed eating the fetus, the correct mind would still guide us that it is allowed.

Eating Dried (Jerked) Meat

In the Sunan it is narrated that Thawban رَضِيَ اللهُ عَنْهُ *said, ``I slaughtered a sheep for the Messenger of Allah ﷺ while we were traveling, and he said to me:*

« أصلحْ لَحْمها » (مسلم:١٩٧٥)

``Dry its meat."

I kept feeding the Prophet ﷺ from its meat until we reached Al-Madinah."

Dried meat is better than old meat and strengthens the body, although it causes skin rashes sometimes, a side effect that could be neutralized with cold, humid spices. Also, jerked meat is favorable for hot conditions. Old meat is hot and dry, favorable for hot conditions and the best type of this meat is that which is fat and wet. Finally, old meat constipates unless cooked in milk and grease.

Fowl meat

Allah said:

﴿ وَلَحْمِ طَيْرٍ مِّمَّا يَشْتَهُونَ ﴾

``And with the flesh of fowls that they desire." (56:21)

Some types of fowl meats are allowed and some are prohibited. The prohibited types include the birds that have claws, such as the falcon, hawk and peregrine, and those that eat carrion, such as the eagle, vulture, stork, magpie, spotted and black crows. Also, this list includes the birds that we are not allowed to kill, such as the hoopoe and the shrike, and some of the birds that we are allowed to kill, such as kite and crow.

There are many types of fowl that are allowed, such as chicken meat. In the *Sahihain* it is narrated by Abu Musa رَضِيَ الله عَنْهُ that the Prophet ﷺ ate chicken meat.

Chicken Meat

Chicken meat is hot and dry in the first degree and it is easy on the stomach and digests quickly. Chicken meat strengthens the mind and increases the production of semen. It also makes the voice softer, the mind stronger and produces healthy blood. It was said that eating chicken meat on a regular basis causes gout, but this is not confirmed by fact.

The cock meat, on the other hand, is hotter and less wet. The meat of old cocks helps against constipation, asthma and thick flatulence when cooked with safflower, canella and chabt (Shibit). The castrated cock meat is nutritious and easy to digest. Pullet meat is easy to digest and mild on the stomach and produces mild blood.

Francolin Meat

Francolin meat is hot and dry in the second degree, soft and light, easy to digest and produces mild blood. Eating this type of meat also strengthens the sight.

Partridge meat

This type of meat produces good blood and is easily digested.

Goose Meat

Goose meat is hot and dry and is not healthy if eaten on a regular basis, and it does not produce extensive excrement.

Duck Meat

Duck meat is hot and wet, and it is not suitable for the stomach, difficult to digest and produces excessive excrements.

Bustard Meat

Bustard meat is hot and dry, heavy on the stomach but good for those who perform sports activities and for hard workers.

Crane Meat

This type of meat is dry and light. It produces bilious blood, and it is good for hard workers. It is better to eat the crane's meat one or two days after it is slaughtered.

Bird and Lark Meat

An-Nasai' narrated in his *Sunan* that `Abdullah bin 'Umar رَضِيَ الله عَنْهما said that the Prophet ﷺ said:

«ما من إنسان يَقتلُ عُصْفُورًا فما فوقَه - بغير حقه - إلا سأله اللهُ عزوجل. قيل: يا رسول الله؛ وما حقُّه؟ قال: تذبَحُه فتأكُلُه، ولا تقطَع رأسه وترمي به.»

(النسائي:٤٣٤٩ وضعفه الألباني)

``No person kills a bird and a larger animal without justification, but will be asked about it on the Day of Resurrection. He was asked, 'O Messenger of Allah! When is it justified?' He said, `You slaughter it and eat it, but do not cut its head and discard its body (i.e. for sport only).'"

Also, An-Nasai' narrated that the Messenger of Allah ﷺ said:

« من قَتلَ عُصْفورًا عَبَثًا، عَجَّ إلى الله يقول:يا رب؛ إن فلاناً قتلني عَبَثًا، ولم يقتلْني لِمَنْفَعة» (النسائي:٤٤٤٦ وضعفه الألباني)

"Whoever kills a bird for fun, the bird will complain to Allah, 'O my Lord, Such and such person killed me for fun, not for a useful purpose.'"

Bird meat is hot and dry, constipates and stimulates semen production. Bird meat soup constipates and helps the joints. If one eats birds' brain with ginger and onion, it excites the sexual desire. The mixtures that bird's produce is not favorable.

Pigeon Meat

Pigeon meat is hot and wet, although the meat of wild pigeons is less wet. The meat of pigeon chicks is more humid, especially the chicks of domesticated pigeons. Young pigeons are less meaty but a better food. The meat of male pigeons is a good cure for numbness, narcosis, apoplexy and convulsive shaking or trembles. Pigeon chick meat is favorable for the sexual drive and the kidneys and produces more blood.

Sand Grouse Meat

This type of meat is dry and causes black bile and constipation. It is not a good food, except that it helps cure dropsy.

Quail Meat

Quail meat is hot and dry and helps the joints. It harms the hot kidney unless it is taken with vinegar and coriander. Eating the meat of the quails that live in filthy areas should be avoided.

Fowl meats are all more easily digested than cattle meat. The parts of the birds that are the most easily digested are the necks and the wings. Also, the brains of the fowls are a better food than cattle brains.

Locust Meat

In the *Sahihain* it is narrated that `Abdullah bin Abi Awfa رَضِيَ الله عَنْهُ said, ``We went to seven battles with the Messenger of Allah ﷺ during which we used to eat locust." The *Musnad* also narrated that the Messenger of Allah ﷺ said:

« أُحِلَّتْ لنا مَيْتتانِ ودمَانِ: الحوتُ والجرادُ، والكبِدُ والطِّحالُ »

(ابن ماجه :٣٣١٤ وصححه الألباني)

``We were allowed two types of dead animals and two bloods: fish and locust; liver and spleen."

This *Hadith* is also related from Ibn 'Umar رضي الله عنهما .

Locust meat is hot and dry and not very nutritious. Also, eating locust meat regularly makes the body thin, emaciated. The smoke of burnt locust helps in cases of dysuria (impaired ability to pass urine), especially for women, and is favorable for hemorrhoids. Eating fat wingless locust roasted is a good cure for scorpion stings. Also, locust meat is not favorable for those suffering from epilepsy and produces septic mixtures in the stomach.

There is a difference on allowing eating locust when it is dead, where the majority of the scholars except Mlik allow it. Yet, there is no difference that it is allowed if the locust died because of a reason, such as being burnt or pressed.

It is not good for the health to eat meat on a regular basis because it causes bloody sanguineous illnesses and various types of allergies. Hippocrates once said, ``Do not turn your stomachs to a graveyard for animals."

2. *Laban* (Milk)

Allah said:

﴿ وَإِنَّ لَكُمْ فِي الْأَنْعَامِ لَعِبْرَةً نُّسْقِيكُم مِّمَّا فِي بُطُونِهِ مِن بَيْنِ فَرْثٍ وَدَمٍ لَّبَنًا خَالِصًا سَائِغًا لِّلشَّارِبِينَ ﴾

``And verily, in the cattle, there is a lesson for you. We give you to drink of that which is in their bellies, from between excretions

and blood, pure milk; palatable to the drinkers." (16:66)

Also Allah said, while describing Paradise:

﴿فِيهَآ أَنۡهَٰرٞ مِّن مَّآءٍ غَيۡرِ ءَاسِنٖ وَأَنۡهَٰرٞ مِّن لَّبَنٖ لَّمۡ يَتَغَيَّرۡ طَعۡمُهُۥ﴾

``In it are rivers of water the taste and smell of which are not changed, rivers of milk of which the taste never changes." (47:15)

In the *Sunan* it is also narrated:

« مَن أطعَمه الله طَعامًا، فليَقُلْ: اللّهم، باركْ لنا فيه، وارزُقْنا خيرًا منه. ومَن سقاه اللهُ لَبَنًا، فليقل: اللهم باركْ لنا فيه، وزِدْنا منه. فإني لا أعلم ما يُجزِىءُ من الطَّعام والشَّراب، إلا اللَّبَنَ » (أبو داود: ٣٧٣٠ وحسنه الألباني)

``Whoever Allah gives some type of food, let him supplicate, 'O Allah! Bless it for us and grant us what is better.' Whoever Allah grants some Laban, let him say, 'O Allah! Bless it for us and grant us more of it,' for I do not know of a more complete food or drink than milk.'"

Although milk is a simple type of food, it is very natural to the body as it contains three major substances: cheese, fat and water. Cheese is cold and wet and provides good nutrition. The fat contained in the milk is mild regarding warmth and wetness, and it is very beneficial for healthy bodies.

The water part contained in milk is hot and wet, and it softens the stomach and provides the body with beneficial moistures. *Laban* in general is mild regarding warmth and wetness, although there are other opinions in this regard.

Milk is best when it has just been milked, and its value decreases by the passage of time thereafter. When it is freshly milked, milk is less cold and more humid. Sour milk is the opposite. Also, milk is better forty days after the animal has given birth. The best type of milk is the most white in color, as it has a good scent, delicious taste, mildly sweet, less fat and light consistency. It is also best when young healthy animals are milked, especially those that have less meat and which graze in healthy grazing lands. Milk is good and produces red blood, brings wetness to the body and is also a nutritious food. Also, milk helps relieve depression, obsession and black bile ailments. When milk is drunk with honey, it will help cleanse the insides of septic materials. Drinking milk with sugar makes the color of the skin fairer. Milk helps the body regain its strength after sexual intercourse and is also favorable for the chest, the lungs and for those suffering from tuberculosis.

Further, milk is not favorable for the head, the stomach, the liver and the spleen. Also, drinking milk excessively is harmful for the teeth and the gums, and this is why it is better to rinse the mouth after one drinks it. In the *Sahihain* it is narrated that the Prophet ﷺ once drank some milk and then asked for some water and rinsed his mouth, saying: ``It has fat."

Milk is not good for those suffering from fever and headaches and not favorable for the weakness in the head and the brain. Excessive drinking of milk causes darkness in the sight, sight impairment, gout, kidney clogs and swelling in the stomach and the intestines. These side effects will be neutralized when mixing milk with honey, ginger, and so forth, for those who are not used to drinking it.

Sheep Milk

Sheep milk is the most watery, and it has more fat and bad odor than goat or cow milk. Sheep milk produces phlegm and causes white spots or stains on the skin if one drinks it on a regular basis. This is why it is better that sheep milk is mixed with water so that its concentration becomes less. Sheep milk quenches the thirst quicker and cools the body faster than other milks.

Goat Milk

Goat milk is mild and light, works as a mild laxative, is wet for dry bodies and helps cure mouth cankers, dry cough and epistaxis (nosebleeds).

Milk in general is the most beneficial drink for the body due to its nutritional value and closeness to the nature of the body and to the childhood of mankind. In the *Sahihain* it is narrated:

« أن رسولَ الله صلى اللهَ عليه وسلم أُتِيَ ليلةَ أُسرِيَ به، بقَدَحٍ من خَمْر، وقدحٍ من لَبَن. فنظر إليهما، ثم أخذ اللَّبن فقال جبريلُ عليه السلام: الحمد لله الَّذي هداك للفِطْرة؛ لو أخذتَ الخَمْر: غوتْ أمَّتُك » (البخاري:٥٥٧٦)

``The night of the Isra' (the Prophet's journey from Makkah to Jerusalem and then to heaven), the Messenger of Allah ﷺ was given two cups, one containing milk and the other wine. The Prophet ﷺ looked at them and then took the cup of milk. Gabriel said, `You have accepted what is natural, (True Religion i.e. Islam) and if you had taken the wine, your followers would have gone astray.'"

Sour goat milk is not digested quickly and produces unfavorable mixtures. The hot tempered stomach benefits from goat milk, though, and easily digests it.

Cow Milk

Cow milk provides nutrition for the body and is also a mild laxative. Cow milk is one of the best milks, between sheep milk and goat milk regarding thickness and fat.

`Abdullah bin Mas'ud narrated that the Prophet ﷺ once said:

« عليكم بألبانِ البَقَرِ؛ فإنها تَرُمُّ من كل الشَّجَرِ » ((المستدرك ٤/ ١٩٧ وهو حسن، كما في تحقيق الزاد)

``Drink cow milk because it grazes on all types of trees."

Camel Milk

We mentioned camel milk in the beginning of the chapter, so there is no need to repeat it.

3. *Luban* (Frankincense), which is the Kundur

It was reported that once a man complained to `Ali رَضِيَ الله عَنْهُ that he forgets and that `Ali رَضِيَ الله عَنْهُ said to him, ``Resort to the Luban, because it strengthens the heart and does away with forgetfulness."

Also, it was reported that Ibn `Abbas ﷺ said,``Drinking Luban with sugar on an empty stomach is favorable for the urine and helps against forgetfulness." Also, it was reported that Anas رَضِيَ الله عَنْهُ said to a man who complained to him of forgetfulness, ``Resort to Kundur! Soak it overnight and in the morning take a sip of it on an empty stomach, because it is good against forgetfulness."

There is an apparent reason for this benefit. Forgetfulness is the result of cold, humid, bad moods that affect the brain in a way that makes the brain not recall the memory easily. In this case, Luban helps. When forgetfulness is a result of other physical causes, refreshing drinks help in that case. The difference between the two cases is that dry substances help one stay up at night and recall old memories rather than current memories. The wet drinks have the opposite effect.

Sometimes forgetfulness occurs because of cupping on the back of the head and excessive eating of wet coriander and sour apples. Also, depression, sadness, looking at stagnant water for a long time and urinating in it might cause forgetfulness. Also, looking at crucified people, reading grave commemorations, walking between two tarred camels, eating mice wastes by mistake, all cause forgetfulness.

Luban is hot in the second degree and dry in the first degree. It is also a mild constipation agent. It is very beneficial and its side effects are minimal. Among the benefits of the Luban is that it stops and heals bleeding, stomach ache, diarrhea, helps digest the food, gets rid of flatulence, cures eye sores, helps the body grow flesh on most ulcers and strengthens the weak stomach. Luban also dries the phlegm and the moistures accumulating in the chest, cures eyesight impairment and prevents malignant sores from progressing.

When Luban is chewed alone or mixed with Persian thyme, it will provoke phlegm, release and relax the tongue muscles and help the mind become sharper. When the Luban is burnt, it helps cure some illnesses and makes the air smell fresh.

The Letter *Mim*

1. *Maai* (Water)

Maa' (Water), is the resource of life, the best drink there is, and one of the pillars of existence. Rather it is the most important pillar of life, as Allah has created every living thing from water.

There is a difference of opinion if water is a source of nutrition for the body, or if it only helps wash down and dissolve the food. Water is a wet, cold substance that removes heat, preserves the body's moisture, restores the moisture that the body has lost, makes the food softer and helps carry it through the blood vessels.

There are ten standards with which we test water's freshness. First, its color should be crystal clear. Second, water should not have any odor at all. Third, water should be sweet and fresh just as the water of the Nile and the Euphrates. Fourth, water should be light. Fifth, water sources should be pure and not stagnant. Sixth, water is fresher when its source is deeper or farther. Seventh, water should be exposed to the wind and the sun, not hidden under the earth. Eighth, water sources should not be stagnant and should be fast running. Ninth, water should be plentiful which helps purify whatever impurities it might carry. Tenth, water source should be running north to south or west to east.

When all these characteristics are sought together, they will all be found in four rivers, the Nile, the Euphrates, Say'han (or Sayhoun) and Jay'han (or Jayhoun). In the *Sahihain* it is narrated that Abu Hurairah related from the Prophet ﷺ that he said:

«سَيْحَانُ وجَيْحَانُ والنِّيلُ والفُرَات، كُلُّها من أنهارِ الجنة » (مسلم:٢٨٣٦)

``Sayhan, Jayhun, the Nile and the Euphrates are all among the rivers of Paradise."

As for the water being light, there are three methods to verify it. First, water should easily absorb the cold and the heat. Hippocrates said, ``The water that becomes hot or cold easily is the lightest water." Second; by weight. Third; when one wets two pieces of cotton, which are exactly the same weight, with water from two different sources, and then both pieces are dried and weighed. The one that has the lightest weight indicates the water it absorbed was the lightest.

The environment that the water passes through has a profound effect on the water. For instance, water sources that are located to the north are generally cooler and their water is generally thicker due to the northern wind. Also, the water that passes through mineral rich rocks is affected by this fact.

Fresh water is beneficial for both the ill and the healthy. Cool or chilled water is the most beneficial and has the best taste. Yet, one should not drink water soon after he wakes up, after sex, taking a bath or eating fruit. There is no harm if one drinks water while eating, but not excessively. Rather, having a few sips of water in this case is better and does not harm the stomach but strengthens it, excites the sexual drive and quenches the thirst.

Warm water, on the other hand, swells the stomach and causes the opposite effects that we mentioned regarding cold water. Old warm water is better than fresh warm water.

Cold water is better than warm water inside the body, as it cleanses the blood and clears the head. Also, cold water removes rot and is mild and favorable for the teeth, the mood and hot weather. Yet, cold water is not good for those suffering from colds or swelling, since such cases need heat to decompose. Very cold water harms the teeth and drinking it on a regular basis could cause bronchitis and chest pains.

Very hot and very cold waters are very harmful to the nerves and most of the limbs and body organs. One of them decomposes (hot water), while the other concentrates moistures. Warm water relieves hot mixtures, decomposes, matures and extracts excrement and brings wetness and hotness, but does not help the digestion as the food then floats up close to the upper side of the stomach. Warm water also does not quench the thirst quickly, weakens the body and causes many harmful illnesses. Yet, warm water is good for old people and those suffering from epilepsy, cold headaches and ophthalmia (inflammation of the eye).

There is no *Hadith* about sun heated water, nor did any of the renowned doctors of old discourage drinking it. Yet, very hot water dissolves the fat around the kidneys.

We talked about rainwater when we talked about the letter *Ghayn*.

Water contained in ice and hail

In the *Sahihain* it is narrated that the Prophet ﷺ used to say the following supplication after starting the prayer:

«اللهم، اغسلني مِن خَطَايايَ بِالمَاءِ والثَّلْجِ والبَرَدِ» (البخاري:٧٤٤)

``O Allah! Wash my sins with water (rain), snow and hail."

Snow is accumulated due to the moisture in the air. We mentioned the wisdom in asking Allah to wash the sins with snow, as the heart needs the coolness and its strength. We stated before the subject of curing the ills of the heart and treating them with their opposites and neutralizers.

Hail water is sweeter than snow water, while the quality of melted ice water depends on its source.

We should mention that the quality of the snow is affected by the area and the mountains that it falls on.

One should avoid drinking icy water after taking a bath, having sex, sports activity, eating hot foods, when coughing and having chest pains, weak liver and cool tempers.

Water from wells and ground water

Well water is not favorable, while underground water is heavy. This is because the first one (well water) rarely escapes rot, while underground water is not exposed to fresh air. Hence, one should not drink such types of water until exposing the water to air for at least a night. The worst type of well or underground water is that which runs through lead-rich stones and unused wells, especially if its soil is not good.

Zamzam Water

Zamzam water is the best, freshest, most beneficial, most beloved and most precious water there is. Further, Zamzam water was dug up by Jibril and the source that Prophet Isma'il عليه السلام drank from.

In the *Sahihain* it is narrated that the Prophet ﷺ said to Abu Tharr, who remained at the Ka'bah for forty days without food (or drink) living on Zamzam water: ``It is a nutritious food.'' Muslim added that the Prophet ﷺ said:

« وشِفاءُ سُقْمٍ » (البيهقي :٥/١٤٨ وسنده صحيح كما في تحقيق الزاد)

``And a cure from ailment.''

Furthermore, Ibn Majah narrated that Jabir bin 'Abdullah related from the Prophet ﷺ that he said:

« ماءُ زمزمَ لِما شُرِب له » (ابن ماجه :٣٠٦٢ وصححه الألباني)

``Zamzam water is for whatever was intended behind drinking it.''

We were told that `Abdullh bin Al-Mubarak once said, ``O Allah! Ibn Al-Mu'ammil told us that Muhammad bin Al-Munkadir related from Jabir رَضِيَ الله عَنْهُ that your Prophet ﷺ said:

« ((ماءُ زمزَم لما شرِب له)) وقال ابن المبارك: فإني أَشرَبُ لِظَمَإِ يومِ القيامة. »

(ورد الأثر عن طريق ابن أبي الموالي وهوحسن كما في تحقيق الزاد)

``The water of Zamzam is for the purpose it is drank for, and I drink it to relieve my thirst on the Day of Resurrection."

This *Hadith* is *Hasan*.

Many other people and I have tried drinking from Zamzam water for the purpose of being cured from various illnesses, and by the will of Allah, I was indeed cured from several illnesses. I also saw some people who lived on Zamzam water for a long time, fifteen days or a little longer without complaining from hunger. Such people would perform *Tawaf* with other people at a normal pace. Someone even told me that Zamzam water was his only food and drink for forty days and that he still had enough strength to have sex with his wife, fast and perform *Tawaf* many times.

The Nile

The Nile is one of the rivers of Paradise that flows from deep inside Ethiopia. It is collected from the rainfall and the floods that supply it with water. Then, Allah directs this river that flows with water to dry areas, causing the vegetation, on which people and animals live, to grow and flourish.

The land that the river flows to is dry and does not keep rainwater that falls on it, which is insufficient to grow vegetation anyway. On the other hand, when such a land receives more than the normal rainfall, the houses and life will be destroyed. Allah has caused the rain to fall on far lands and then directed this rain to flow in a huge river in sufficient amounts that would benefit the people and the animals. When the river provides enough water for farming and to grow vegetation, the water level then decreases so that the people are able to tend and harvest the vegetation. The water of the Nile has the ten characteristics that we mentioned before, and this is why it is among the lightest, sweetest and freshest waters.

Seawater

The Prophet ﷺ said about the sea:

« هُو الطَّهور ماؤُه الحِلُّ ميتَتُه » (أبو داود: ٨٣ وحسنه الألباني)

"Its water is pure and its dead is allowed (to eat)."

Allah has made the sea salty for the benefit of the people and the animals of the earth. Seawater is plentiful and has sufficient amounts of animals [and fish] that die but do not get buried in it. If the seawater is fresh and sweet, the animals that would die in it would make it rotten, adversely affecting the quality of the air on the earth. Allah's wisdom has decided that seawater is salty, that even if the entire dead corpses produced on the earth were thrown in it, it would still be fresh until Allah brings this world to its inevitable end. This is one of the reasons why seawater is salty, along with its soil and sand also being salty.

Taking a bath in seawater helps relieve many illnesses and infections that appear on the skin. Drinking seawater is harmful, it causes diarrhea, weakens the body and causes rashes, mange and thirst.

Those who have to drink seawater do so for certain medicinal purposes. In this case, seawater should be boiled in a pot that is covered by wool, which will absorb the water vapor. Then, the collected water should be squeezed out of the wool and consumed when there is sufficient amount of it. Meanwhile, the salt and the minerals will remain in the pot.

Also, one could dig a hole near the seashore to collect the water through several parallel tunnels that would make the water fresh at the end [when it passes through them repeatedly].

If one has to drink seawater, he should first mix it with apricot pips, burning coal, Armenian argil (type of earth), oak wood or fine wheat flour. This way, most of the minerals and mud will be collected in the bottom of the pot or the cup.

2. *Misk* (Musk)

Muslim narrated that Abu Sa'eed Al-Khudri said that the Prophet ﷺ said:

«أَطيبُ الطِّيب: المِسكُ» (مسلم:٢٢٥٢)

``The best type of perfume is Musk ."

In the *Sahihain* it is also narrated that `Aishah رَضِي الله عَنْها said, ``I used to anoint the Prophet ﷺ with perfumed Musk before assuming *Ihram*, on the Day of the Sacrifice and before performing *Tawaf* around the (Sacred) House."

Musk is the king of all perfumes, it has the best aroma. Other types of perfumes are usually compared to Musk , but *Misk* is never compared to them. Also, the hills and sands of Paradise are made of Musk.

Musk is a hot, dry substance of the second degree, and it brings comfort and joy to the hearts and strengthens the inner organs when it is drunk or smelled. Musk also brings strength and comfort to the external organs when anointed with it. Musk is profitable for old people and those who have excessive skin moistures, especially during winter, and also helps against fainting, shaking and the general weakness in the body as it excites the instinctive heat. Musk clears the white part in the eye and dries excess moisture in it, and also dissipates swelling in various organs. Musk also works as an antidote for some poisons, and helps against snakebite. It has many other benefits.

3. *Marzanjush* (Marjoram)

Marzanjush is hot in the third degree and dry in the second degree, and when its aroma is smelled, it relieves cold headache caused by phlegm, colds, black bile and thick flatulence pressure. It also relieves the congestion, and clogs in the nose and head and dissipates most cold, wet swellings.

When *Marzanjush* is used as suppository, it will increase the blood flow during menstruation and is favorable during pregnancies. When its dry leaves are crushed and used as a bandage, it will relieve blood traces that appear under the eye. It also helps relieve the pain of scorpion stings when it is mixed with vinegar [and then the affected area is bandaged with it].

Marzanjush ointment also helps relieve backache, knee pain and fatigue. Those who are used to smelling *Marzanjush* aroma will not suffer from water accumulation in the eye, cataract. When one administers its extract or water blended with the essence of bitter almonds in the nose, and helps against stuffiness that affects the nose and the head.

4. *Milh* (Salt)

Al-Bazzar narrated that the Prophet ﷺ said:

« سيُوشِكُ أن تكُونوا في الناس كالمِلْح في الطَّعام ولا يصلُح الطعام إلا بالمِلْح »

(الطبراني قال الهيثمي المجمع ١٠/ ١٨: وإسناد الطبراني حسن)

``You will soon be to the people just like what the salt represents to food, and the food's flavor doesn't become favorable unless there is salt in it."

Al-Baghawi said in his commentary on the Qur'an that `Abdullh bin `Umar ﷺ related from the Prophet ﷺ that he said, ``There are four blessings that Allah has sent down to the earth from the heavens: iron, fire, water and salt." This *Hadith* should only be related from Ibn 'Umar رَضِيَ الله عَنْهما .

Salt is favorable for people's bodies and food. Further, salt is favorable and beneficial when blended with any substance, including gold and silver, as it makes gold more yellowish and whitens silver. Salt decomposes, cleanses, dries the thick humidity, strengthens and purifies the body and helps against open mangy sores.

When used as eyeliner salt, especially gem- salt, will remove the excess fat or flesh and the yellowish color from the eye. Salt also prevents malignant infections from spreading, works as a laxative and helps against pleurisy when the stomach is anointed with it. Salt cleanses the teeth, prevents them from decaying, and strengthens the gums and makes them firm. There are many other benefits for the salt.

The Letter *Noon*

1. The *Nakhl* (Date Palm)

The date palm is mentioned in the Qur'an in several places. In the *Sahihain* it is narrated that Ibn `Umar رَضِيَ الله عَنْهما said, ``We were with the Prophet ﷺ and a spadix of date-palm was brought to him. On that he said, `Among the trees, there is a tree which resembles the Muslim.' I wanted to say that it was the date-palm tree but as I was the youngest of all (of them) I kept quiet. And then the Prophet ﷺ said, `It is the date-palm tree.' I mentioned what happened to `Umar رَضِيَ الله عَنْهُ , and he said, `Had you said it that would have been better to me than such and such."

This *Hadith* contains many benefits, such as the scholar training his students by asking them questions and testing their knowledge. It also contains parables and demonstrates the shyness of the Prophet's Companions, the leaders and the commoners among them, as they all kept quiet and were shy to answer the Prophet's question. The *Hadith* also demonstrates that the parent would be happy if his child does something right. The *Hadith* also demonstrates that it is allowed for the children to answer questions in the presence of their parents, even if the father did not know the answer, as this does not constitute misbehaving with the father. Also, this *Hadith* compares the Muslim with the *Nakhlah*, the date palm, because of its tremendous benefit, constant shade and sweet fruit that it produces throughout the year.

Dates are eaten fresh, dried, ripe and unripe and are both a type of food and a cure. Dates are nutritious, a type of sweet, a drink and a fruit. The date-tree's trunk is used for building purposes, in making pots, and so forth and its leaves are used to make woven mats, baskets, vases and funnels, and so forth. Its fibers are used to make ropes and mattresses. Also, its stones are used as fodder for camels and as ingredients in various medicinal remedies and in Ku'hl. Also, the fruit of the date-tree is known for its beauty, refreshing shape, and the handsome way the fruits are arranged on their branches, which also brings comfort to the eye.

Merely looking at the fruits of the date tree reminds one of its Creator, Whose creation is both excellent and perfect, just as is His Wisdom. Therefore the date tree resembles the righteous believer, for he is pure goodness who brings about benefit both inwardly and outwardly.

Also, the *Nakhlah* was the tree trunk that yearned and longed for the Messenger of Allah ﷺ when he no longer used it as a podium. The trunk yearned for the Prophet's closeness and for hearing his speech! Also, we should mention that the tree that Mary took refuge under when she gave birth to Jesus was the date palm.

There is a difference of opinion regarding which is better the date-tree or the *Habalah* (vine tree). Allah has mentioned both trees together in several *Ayat* (Verses) in His Book (the Qur'an). Also, both trees are truly similar to each other, although each is at its prime in its natural habitat and the land that accepts it the most.

2. *Narjis* (Narcissus)

The *Narjis* is hot and dry in the second degree and its stems are used to relieve deep cankers that reach the nerves. Also, *Narjis* cleanses and extracts septic substances. If the *Narjis* is cooked and one drinks its water, or boils it and eats it, it will cause vomiting and will extract the moistures that reside in the bottom of the stomach. When the *Narjis* is cooked with lentil plant and honey, it will cleanse the cankers from septic excretions and will cause the gastric ulcers to rupture.

Narjis blossoms are mild and beneficial against colds. They have a strong power of decomposition, open the nose and cerebral clogs, and help against headaches and black bile. Those who repeatedly smell *Narjis* during winter will have immunity form pleurisy during summer. Also, *Narjis* helps relieve headaches caused by phlegm and black bile. *Narjis* aroma sharpens the mind and the heart and helps relieve many of their ailments. The author of `*At-Taysir*' once said, ``Inhaling *Narjis* aroma heals against the epilepsy that attacks boys."

3. *Noorah* (Slaked Lime)

It is two parts lime and one part arsenic mixed with water and left to dry in the sun until it turns blue. Then one uses it as ointment and waits an hour until it starts its effect before touching water. Then one takes a bath and anoints himself with henna to remove the lime's hotness.

4. *Nabq* or *Nabiq*

It has several names: Nabq, Christ's thorn, lotus jujube, or rhamnus. Abu Nu'aym mentioned these in his book on Prophetic medicine, when he mentioned the *Hadith,*

« إن آدم لما هَبَط إِلى الأرض، كان أولَ شيء أَكَلَ من ثِمار » (لم نعثر عليه لعدم الكتاب)

``When Adam was sent down to earth, the first of its fruits he ate was Nabiq ."

Also, the Messenger of Allah ﷺ mentioned the *Nabq* in a *Hadith* narrated by the Two *Muhaddithain*,

« أنه رأى سِدْرَةَ المُنْتَهى ليلةَ أُسْرِيَ به: وإِذا نَبَقُها مِثلُ قِلالِ هَجَرَ » (البخاري:٣٢٠٧)

``On the night that I was taken on the Night Journey, I was shown Sidrat Al-Muntaha (a tree in the seventh heaven) and I saw its Nabq fruits which resembled the clay jugs of Hajr (a town in Arabia)"

Nabq is the fruit produced by the lote-tree. *Nabq* soothes the natural digestive process, helps against diarrhea, coats the stomach, relieves bile, provides nutrition for the body, taste to the food and causes phlegm. It also helps against inflammation caused by bile. *Nabq* is slowly digested while its flour strengthens the bowels and is favorable for bilious temperaments. The harm of the *Nabq* will be neutralized when eating honeycomb with it.

There is a conflict of opinion concerning if *Nabq* is wet or dry. The correct opinion is that wet *Nabq* is cold and wet while dry *Nabq* is cold and dry.

The Letter *Haa'*

Hindaba (Chicory)

Hindaba temperament changes according to the season. It is cold and wet in winter, hot and dry in summer and mild in spring and autumn. In general, *Hindaba* is cold and dry. *Hindaba* is beneficial and cools the stomach and causes constipation. When *Hindaba*, especially wild *Hindaba*, is cooked and eaten with vinegar, it constipates even more and is more favorable for the stomach and invigorating.

When *Hindaba* (chicory) is used as a bandage, it will relieve gastric inflammations, gout and hot ocular inflammations. In cases of scorpion stings, *Hindaba* helps when its leaves and stems are used as a bandage.

Hindaba also strengthens the stomach and opens the clogs in the kidneys, spleen, veins and intestines. It also clears and purifies the kidneys and helps them against the various hot and cold aches.

The sour *Hindaba* is best for the liver, while its extract helps against icter (jaundice), especially when mixed with wet fennel extract. When *Hindaba* leaves are bruised and placed on hot swellings, it will cool and dissipate them. *Hindaba* also cleanses and clears the chest and dissipates the heat of irritated blood and bile.

The best way to eat *Hindaba* is without washing it so as to preserve its effective ingredients. *Hindaba* works as an effective antidote against most poisons.

When *Hindaba* extract is used as eyeliner, it will clear and cleanse the eyes. *Hindaba* leaves are used in antidotes against scorpion stings, and against most poisons as we have stated. When the *Hindaba* is squeezed and its water is mixed with oil, it will help against all toxic substances in general. When *Hindaba* stems are squeezed and their water drunk, it will help against scorpion and hornet stings and against snakebite. Finally, the sap of its stems whitens the white area in the eye.

The Letter *Waw*

1. *Warss* (Ceylon Cornel tree)

Umm Salamah رَضِيَ الله عَنْها narrated, "The woman who has just delivered would remain for forty days afterwards [without praying or fasting]. One of us would then overlay *Warss* on her face to help against spots." Abu Hanifah, a linguist, said, " *Warss* does not grow in the wild. Rather, it is cultivated. I think that it is only grown in the Arab lands, especially in Yemen."

Warss is dry and hot in the second degree. The best type of *Warss* is the red *Warss*, which is soft in the hand and does not have much bran. *Warss* is used as an ointment to treat spots, rashes and pimples that appear on the surface of the skin. *Warss* constipates, has a dyeing quality and helps against leprosy when taken as a drink.

Warss has similar benefits to sea *Qust*, and if it is used as an ointment it relieves vitiligo (skin condition of unknown cause, characterized by patchy loss of pigment), rashes, pimples and ulcers. When the clothes are dyed with *Warss*, they strengthen the sexual drive.

2. *Wasmah* (Woad)

Wasmah is similar to the Nile's leaves and it is used to dye the hair black. We mentioned the subject of dying the hair black before.

The Letter *Yaa*

Yaqtin (Gourd)

Yaqtin means gourd or pumpkin, although the word *Yaqtin* entails more meanings than these two. *Yaqtin* in Arabic entails every tree that does not have a stem, such as watermelon and cucumbers. Allah said:

﴿ وَأَنۢبَتۡنَا عَلَيۡهِ شَجَرَةً مِّن يَقۡطِينٖ ﴾

``And We caused a plant of gourd to grow over him." (37:146)

If someone says that the word tree means every plant that has a stem or a trunk and that which does not have a stem or a trunk is called *Najm*, not a tree. Hence, why did Allah say,

﴿ شَجَرَةً مِّن يَقۡطِينٖ ﴾

``A plant of gourd to grow over him." (37:146)

We answer this question by stating that the word `tree' describes the plants that have stems in general. Yet sometimes, this word is meant to describe something specific [to describe *Yaqtin* for instance]. Understanding the areas where the texts speak in general terms and the areas where a specific meaning is meant is a great door to understanding the Arabic Language. The *Yaqtin* mentioned in the Qur'an is the pumpkin, which is also called *Dubbaa, Qar'* and *Yaqtin.*

In the *Sahihain* it is narrated by Anas bin Malik رَضِيَ الله عَنْهُ that a tailor once invited the Messenger of Allah ﷺ to eat from some food that he made. So I (Anas) went with the Messenger of Allah ﷺ, and the tailor brought forth some bread made from barley and some soup that had *Dubbaa* and dried meat. I saw the Messenger of Allah ﷺ follow the traces of the *Dubbaa* all around the edge of the pot, which made me love *Dubbaa* ever since that day."

Abu Talut also said, ``I entered upon Anas bin Malik رَضِيَ الله عَنْهُ while he was eating *Dubbaa* and saying [referring to the *Yaqtin* tree], `You are a tree that is so dear to me because the Messenger of Allah ﷺ used to like eating you.'"

Yaqtin is a type of cold and wet plant and a light food that is easily digested. If the gourd was not spoiled in the stomach before being completely digested, it produces a good mixture in the stomach, especially when one eats similar or compatible types of food with it. For example, mixing mustard and pumpkin produces bitter humor, while eating it with salt makes it salty and with constrictive substances makes it constipate. When it is cooked with *Safarjal* (quince), it will provide good nutrition for the body.

Gourd is light on the stomach, especially for those who do not suffer from phlegm or cold condition. The wetness contained in this plant helps ease the thirst and headaches if one drinks its extract or washes his head with it. Also, gourd soothes the stomach however one uses it, and is very beneficial for those who have hot temperaments.

Also, when the *Yaqtin* is kneaded with dough and baked in the oven and then its extract is mixed with some light drinks, it helps cool down fever, quenches the thirst and constitutes a good, nutritious food. If it is mixed with quince jam and Manna, it eliminates bile.

When pumpkin is cooked and its juice is mixed with some honey and Natron, it will cause phlegm and acid. If gourd was ground and then the head is bandaged with it, it will help ease the hot swellings in the cerebral.

When the gourd rinds are squeezed and the extract is mixed with rose oil and used as ear drops, it will help against hot tumors. Also, its rind helps ease the swelling of hot eye infections and against gout.

Also, gourd is very useful for those who have hot temperaments and those suffering from fever. When gourd finds some spoiled mixtures in the stomach it also gets spoiled causing harmful mixtures in the stomach. In this case, one should treat this condition with vinegar and sour substances.

In general, gourd is one of the lightest foods and the most easily digested. Anas رَضِيَ الله عَنْهُ narrated that the Messenger of Allah ﷺ used to like eating it.

Conclusion[1]

I thought that the best way to end this chapter is by mentioning a general advice concerning preventive measures so as to complete the book's benefit.

This is a chapter that Ibn Masawayh has collected in his book, *Al-Mahathir*. He said,

``Whoever eats onion for forty days and then his face becomes full of spots, has only himself to blame.

Those who want to economize and eat salted foods will have only themselves to blame if they catch mange or vitiligo.

Those who eat fish and eggs will have only themselves to blame if they catch hemiplegia (paralysis affecting only one side of the body) or facial paralysis."

Those who catch hemiplegia when they take a bath with their stomach full [of food], will have only themselves to blame.

Those who eat milk and fish will have only themselves to blame if they catch leprosy, gecko or gout.

* Whoever mixes milk and wine and then catches gecko or gout has only himself to blame. Whoever has a wet dream but does not take a bath until he has sex with his wife and then if his wife gives birth to a retarded child, will have only himself to blame.

* Whoever eats his full of cold, boiled eggs and then catches Asthma will have only himself to blame.

* Whoever has sexual intercourse but did not wait until he ejaculates

(1) Editor's note : Some of the advices contained in this chapter are not based upon evidence from Qur`an and *Ṣunnah*, but are merely wide spread notions about health that were popular in the author's time. Some of these will be clearly recognized by the reader as superstitions. Thus it is important for the reader to remember that only that which can be substantiated by sound proof from Qur'an and authentic *Hadeeths* should be depended upon religiously. A.W.

and then catches urinary calculus, (stone like mass that may form in the body under abnormal conditions), will have himself to blame. And whoever looks at himself in the mirror at night and then catches facial paralysis or another disease will have only himself to blame."

Also, Ibn Bukhtayshu' said, ``Beware of eating eggs and fish together because they cause constipation, hemorrhoids and toothache. Also, eating eggs excessively begets spots on the face. Further, eating salted foods and salted fish and having venesection (puncturing of a vein) after one takes a bath causes vitiligo and mange. Eating goat kidney on a regular basis will cause the prostate to be sterile, while taking a bath with cold water after eating soft-meat fish causes facial paralysis. Also, having sex with a menstruating woman causes leprosy, and sexual intercourse that is not followed by taking a bath causes stones. Finally, spending too much time while answering the call of nature causes serious ailments."

Hippocrates said, ``Less of a harmful substance is better than too much of a beneficial substance." He also said, ``Preserve good health by preferring tiresome activity to laziness and abandoning having your fill of foods and drinks."

Further, a wise man once said, ``Whoever wants to be healthy, let him eat good food, preserve cleanness and purity while eating, drink while thirsty, refrain from drinking excessive amounts of water and take a rest after lunch. Also, let him walk after dinner and avoid going to sleep before first answering the call of nature or taking a bath after eating his fill. Further taking a bath once during summer is better than ten times during winter. Eating dried jerky meat at night helps bring about death. Having sex with old women brings the person closer to old age and sickens the healthy body." These words were falsely attributed to Ali. However, some of these words are from Al-Harith bin Kaladah the renowned Arab doctor.

Al-Harith said, ``Whoever seeks longevity, although eternal living is not possible, should have lunch and dinner early, wear light clothes and refrain from excessive sexual activity."

He also said, ``Four things weaken the body: sexual intercourse when one is hungry, taking a bath when one is full, eating dried meat and having sexual intercourse with an old woman."

When Al-Harith was dying, some people visited him and said, ``Give us an advise that we could use after you." He said, ``Only marry young women, eat ripe fruits when in season and refrain from seeking medications when you can bear the illness. Clean your stomachs once a month (i.e. vomit intentionally), so as to dissipate the phlegm and the bile and to allow the flesh to grow. When one of you eats lunch, let him lay down for an hour and when he eats dinner, let him walk at least forty steps."

A king once said to his doctor, ``You might not remain with me for ever, so give me a prescription that I can use after you." He said, ``Only marry young women, eat fresh meat and take medication when you are ill. Eat the fruit when ripe and in season and chew the food well. If you eat during the day, there is no harm if you lay down. If you eat at night, do not sleep until you walk even fifty steps. Do not eat except when hungry and do not force yourself to have sex or refrain from urinating. Cool hotness because it causes you tiredness. Do not eat food when your stomach already has food, nor eat what your teeth cannot chew, because your stomach will not be able to digest that food. Try to vomit once a week to cleanse your body. What a good treasure the blood in your body is, so do not cup it without necessity. Finally, take a bath, because it rids you of what the medication cannot rid you of."

In addition, Imam Shafi' said,

-- ``Four matters bring strength to the body:

* eating meat, smelling perfume, taking baths without having sexual intercourse and wearing Kittan (linen).

-- Four matters weaken the body:

* excessive sexual intercourse, depression, drinking water repeatedly while the stomach is empty and consuming too much sour foods.

-- Four matters strengthen the sight:

* sitting next to the Ka`bah, using Kohl before going to sleep, looking at green things and cleaning up the sitting area [in the house].

-- Four maters weaken the sight:

* looking at dirt, crucified persons,' a woman's vagina and sitting while your back is to the *Qiblah* (direction of the prayer).

-- Four matters increase sexual power:

* eating fowl-meat, the large *Itreefal* (a non-Arabic medication for constipation), pistachio and carob.

-- Four matters sharpen mind power:

* avoiding unnecessary speech, using *Siwak*, and sitting with righteous people and with the scholars."

Plato said, ``Five matters dissipate the strength of the body and might lead to death:

* weakness, leaving loved ones behind, rage, rejecting good advice and the clever persons falling victim to deceit by ignorant people."

The doctor of Al-Ma`mun said, ``Hold fast to five characteristics that whoever preserves them would never catch a disease other than death:

* Do not eat food while there is still food in your stomach.

* Do not eat a type of food that your teeth cannot chew, because then your stomach would not be able to digest it. Refrain from excessive sexual activity because it shortens life.

* Do not have sex with an old woman because it leads to sudden death.

* Do not revert to cupping without necessity. Vomit during the summer."

Hippocrates also said,

* ``Everything that is excessive is unnatural."

Galinus was once told:

* ``Why do you not get sick that often?" He said, ``I do not mix two types of unfavorable foods together, nor eat food while not hungry, nor keep a food in my stomach which is bothering it."

* Excessiveness in four matters causes sickness:

* speech, sexual activity, sleep and eating habits.

* Excessive speech weakens the mind and hastens old age.

* Excessive sleep turns the face yellow, blinds the heart, irritates the eyes, makes one lazy to work and causes excess humidity in the body.

* Excessive eating habits spoil the orifice of the stomach, weaken the body, cause thick flatulence and difficult ailments.

* Having sexual intercourse excessively depletes the strength, weakens the body, dries the moistures in the body, adversely relaxes the nerves, causes various clogs and harms the entire body, especially the brain because of the psychological effects it will have on it. Weakness in the brain, which will also weaken the soul, is worse than weakness in any other organ.

* The best time to have sex is when one feels a strong desire for a lawful partner (wife) who is beautiful, especially when the spouse is young, ready and excited. Also, occasional legal sex makes it more desirable, especially when one does not have any concerns and does not use it excessively. Also, legal sex is best when one is not full or hungry, not after conducting serious physical activity and not during extremely hot or cold weather. When one takes care of these ten matters we mentioned, sex will be most beneficial. Otherwise, if some of these matters were ignored, harm might be caused according to the seriousness of the matters that were ignored. If one does not take care

of all these ten matters, he will be faced with a shorter life span.

* Excessive diet is as dangerous to the healthy person as excessive eating habits when one is ill.

* Galinus said to some of his companions, ``Beware of three matters and seek four matters, and you will not need a doctor.

* Avoid dust, smoke and foul odors. Seek nutritious foods, good scents (or aromas), sweets and take baths. Do not eat above your fill, nor pickle *Batharuj* (a plant) and basil, and do not eat walnuts at night. Whoever caught a cold should not sleep on his back nor should a depressed person eat sour foods.

* Whoever had venesection (puncturing of a vein), should not walk fast because this might cause death.

* Those who have an ache in the eye should not vomit.

* Do not eat too much meat during summer.

* Whoever is suffering from fever should not sleep in the sun. Do not eat old, seeded eggplant.

* Those who drink a cup of warm water every day during winter will save themselves from illness.

* Those who rub their bodies with pomegranate rind while taking a bath will not catch a rash or mange.

* Whoever eats five flowers of iris with Greek mastic, roe aloes and Musk, will persevere the strength and health of his stomach the rest of his life.

* Eating watermelon seeds with sugar will cleanse the stomach from stones and will prevent burning sensation while urinating."

Four matters bring demise to the body:

* depression, sadness, hunger and staying up late at night

Four matters bring joy:

* looking at greenery, running water, loved ones and fruits.

Four matters bring darkness to the sight:

* walking bare footed, seeing hated faces mornings and afternoons or seeing the enemy, excessive crying and looking at thin lines for extended periods of time.

Four matters bring strength to the body:

* wearing soft clothes, taking a bath moderately, eating sweet and nutritious food and smelling good scents.

Four matters harden the face and rid it of its youth and health:

* lying, rudeness, asking too many questions without knowledge [or useful purpose] and sinning.

Four matters increase the youth of the face:

* chivalry, faithfulness, generosity and fear of Allah.

Four matters bring about anger and hatred:

* arrogance, envy, lying and spreading calumnies.

Four matters bring sustenance:

* standing up in prayer at night, seeking forgiveness [of Allah] often at night, giving away in charity and remembering Allah morning and evening.

Four matters prevent sustenance:

* sleeping in the morning, not praying often, laziness and treachery.

Four matters harm the mind and the intellect:

* eating sour foods and fruits excessively, sleeping on the back, depression and sadness.

Four matters strengthen the intellect and the mind:

* when the heart is not busy [or concerned], consuming moderate amounts of food and drink, dieting on good combinations of sweets and nutritious foods and getting rid of the harmful substances in the body.

There are some matters that harm the mind:

* eating onions, beans, olives and eggplant excessively, having too much sexual intercourse, loneliness, worrying, intoxication, excessive laughing and depression.

Some wise men also said, ``I became tired three times and could not find a reason for that except for three matters:

* I ate too much eggplant one day, olives another day and beans a third day."

We have mentioned several beneficial basics of the medicinal sciences that one might not be able to find except in this book. We also affirmed that the religion and medicinal science are close to each other. We also stated that Prophetic medicine cannot and should not be compared to the medicine of the doctors just as the medicine of the doctors cannot be compared to folk medicine.

This matter is deeper and more serious than we explained, but we mentioned what is sufficient for the reader to recognize its importance. Those whom Allah did not endow with sound comprehension in such matters let them know the difference between the power that is supported by divine intervention and knowledge, strong mind and sound comprehension that Allah has endowed the Prophets with, and between what all others have in this regard.

Someone might ask, ``What does the guidance of the Prophet have to do with the subject of medicines and cures and preserving the health?"

This question exposes the lack of understanding of such people, because this subject and many others are among what the Prophet was sent with and what he has directed us to do. Sound understanding and knowledge of Allah and His Messenger are a bounty that Allah endows to whom He will among His creation.

We have explained the three principal basics of medicine in the Qur'an. How can anyone deny that the religion of he who was sent with the righteousness of this and the Next Life also contains what preserves the body? How can anyone deny that the religion also directs us to the best methods of staying healthy, just as it directs to the best methods of preserving the heart and preventing sicknesses that might attack them? These cures [that the religion contains] are mentioned in general terms and the specifics are left to those of correct minds and pure hearts to seek and implement, just as one does regarding matters of Fiqh . Do not be among those who reject something simply because they have no knowledge of it.(1)

When the slave is endowed with sufficient knowledge of Allah's Book and the *Sunnah* of His Messenger ﷺ , along with sound comprehension of the Texts [of the Qur'an and *Sunnah*], he will rely on these sources and would not need anything else. Also, he will be able to acquire all types of good knowledge from these sources.

All types of knowledge depends on knowing Allah, His Commands and creation. The Messengers of Allah are the only source that we can acquire such knowledge from, because they have the best knowledge of Allah, His Commandments and creation. The Messengers also have the best knowledge of the wisdom behind Allah's creation and Commandments.

This is why the remedies provided by the followers of the Prophets are better and more efficient than the remedies of all others. Also, the remedies provided by the followers of the best and the master of the Prophets, Muhammad bin `Abdullh, are the best, most sufficient and beneficial remedies.

Only those who have true knowledge of the science of medicine and doctors and the medicine offered by the Prophets, can know the difference between them. The Prophets are those with the best minds, purest ways and deepest knowledge. They are the nearest to the truth among the creation. They are the best of mankind that Allah has

(1) Editor's note : The author is telling the people that vision and subject are noted then the scholars or professionals who are most competent in those fields should follow these guidelines to further wisdom. This was the same method applied to jurisprudence and the wisdom that was realized from this method was well known and understood among the people. His basic message is follow the Prophet Muhammad, there is no better guide.

chosen, just as the Messenger, Muhammad ﷺ, is the best among all the Messengers. The knowledge that Allah has endowed the Prophets and Messengers with and the wisdom and forbearing puts them in a category that does not permit comparison. Imam Ahmad narrated that the Messenger of Allah ﷺ said:

« أنتم تُوَفُّون سبعين أمَّةً؛ أنتم خيرُها و أكرمُها علَى الله » (الترمذي:٣٠٠١ وحسنه الألباني)

``You (mankind) are seventy nations (or distinct communities); you (Muslims) are the best and most honored among them to Allah."

This honor that Allah has endowed the Muslims with has appeared in their knowledge, minds, intellects and natural ways. The Muslims are the ones who searched through the knowledge of all other nations before them and also their wisdom, progress and their works, then added this knowledge to their own knowledge, forbearing and wisdom that Allah has endowed them with.

This is why the Christians are set aback by their silliness, lack of intelligence and apathy, while the Jews are set aback by their sadness, grief and anguish. Muslims, on the other hand, are endowed with sound minds, courage, understanding, joy, happiness and the tendency to help those in distress.

These are some secrets and facts that can only be comprehended by those who have sound minds, sharp intellect, deep knowledge and acquaintance with what the people have [of wisdom, knowledge, and so forth]. All success comes from Allah.

END OF THE BOOK

Printed by :
M. Publication - New Delhi, India